Basil Kennett

Romae Antiquae Notitia

Or, the Antiquities of Rome

Basil Kennett

Romae Antiquae Notitia
Or, the Antiquities of Rome

ISBN/EAN: 9783337008673

Printed in Europe, USA, Canada, Australia, Japan

Cover: Foto ©ninafisch / pixelio.de

More available books at **www.hansebooks.com**

Ostendunt terris quem tantum fata Supremis
Hunc saltem accumulem donis, et fungar inani
Munere. ———

Romæ Antiquæ Notitia:

OR, THE
ANTIQUITI[ES]
OF
ROME

IN TWO PARTS.

I. A Short HISTORY of the *Rise*, *Prog[ress and]* Decay of the COMMONWEALTH.

II. A Description of the CITY; An Acc[ount of] the *Religion*, *Civil Government*, and *Art of War*; [with the] *Remarkable Customs* and *Ceremonies*, *Public* and *Pr[ivate]*.

With *Copper* CUTS of the *Principal Building[s]*.

To which are prefixed Two *ESSAYS*, conce[rning] *Roman* LEARNING, and the *Roman* EDUCAT[ION].

By BASIL KENNETT, of C. C. C.

——— *Ne desinat unquam*
Tecum Graia loqui, tecum Romana vetustas. Cla[ud.]

The SIXTEENTH EDITION, Corrected and I[mproved].

LONDON:

Printed for D. BATHURST, A. HORSEFIELD, E. OWEN, [Dil]LON, R. CROWDER, D. LONGMAN, T. LAW, S. RO[bin]N. JOHNSTON, B. FULLER, and C. BEECROFT.

M.DCC.LXXXIV.

To His Highness the

Duke of Gloucester.

S I R,

AMONG all the Noble Presages of *Wit* and *Honour*, there is not One by which Your Highness hath given greater Encouragement to the Hopes of these Kingdoms, than by a surprising Curiosity, and impatient Desire of Knowledge. For the Satisfying of so Generous Inclinations, Your High-

The Epistle Dedicatory.

HIGHNESS cannot but seek an early Acquaintance with the *Roman* State. It must needs please You, SIR, to understand the Constitution of that People, before you appear the Rival of their Glory: And the first Steps to both these Attainments will be alike uneasy. Many Fatigues are to be undergone ere You surpass them in Action and Conduct: And in the same Manner, before You are introduced into the more delightful Scenes of their Policy and Government, YOUR HIGHNESS should be *first* presented with the rougher Prospect of their Customs and Ceremonies.

FOR YOUR Direction in so noble (though intricate) a Path of Ancient Story, YOUR HIGHNESS is desired to accept this small Endeavour, no otherwise than You would a few Shadows, or a little Model, to give You, SIR, the first Notion of some admired Picture, or some magnificent Building.

THERE is one Custom which, I make myself

The Epistle Dedicatory.

self believe, YOUR HIGHNESS will read with some Pleasure; I mean, SIR, the TROJAN GAME, a Martial Exercise, performed by the Youth of the first Quality in *Rome*, under such a Captain as YOURSELF; and deriving its Original from young *Ascanius*; whom I need not fear to mention as YOUR Precedent, since YOU have already honoured him with YOUR Imitation.

IT may be expected, perhaps, that, out of the many illustrious *Romans*, I should here propose to YOUR HIGHNESS some of the most Celebrated Examples of *Virtue* and great *Atchievements*. But this would prove a needless Piece of Service; since YOU cannot miss YOUR Way in the Pursuit of the *First*, while YOUR HIGHNESS goes on like the *Trojan* Prince,

Matre Dea monstrante Viam.

And to the *Second*, the short Advice, which that

The Epistle Dedicatory.

that Hero gave his Son, will engage You as the Highest motive:

—*Te animo repetentem exempla tuorum,*
Et Pater Æneas & Avunculus excitet Hector.

I am, SIR,

Your Highness's

Most Humble and

Most Obedient Servant,

Basil Kennett.

THE
PREFACE.

THE usefulness of such a design as this not being like to be called in question, I am obliged no farther than to give a short history of what attempts have hitherto been made of the same nature, with some account of the present undertaking.

Not to make a catalogue of the many tracts on particular subjects of Roman antiquities, the two authors most in use for this knowledge are Rosinus and Godwin; the first as a full system, the other as an abridgement or compendium. We have nothing more complete than Rosinus taken all together: But he will appear very deficient in many points, if compared with other learned men, who have laboured in the adorning some one part of his general subject. Thus, I believe, his Book of War has scarce been looked into since the publishing of Lipsius's admirable Comment on Polybius. His accounts of the habits, Senate, laws, and funerals, will never be set in competition with the more accurate pieces of Ferrarius and Rubenius, of Paulus Manutius and Kirchman. Not to urge, that the names, the money, the private games, with several lesser topics, are entirely omitted; and many more substantial customs but lightly touched. The Paralipomena of Dempster, which are added in the best editions,

PREF[ACE]

editions, under the name of [...], for the moſt part, barely a [...]ces, gathered from the [...], with little connection; and [...] now and then, for a ſupple[ment...] impoſſible they ſhould be v[...]

Godwin's Anthologia ([...] with in our ſchools) beſides [...] the advantages which we have [...]ed within theſe threeſcore ye[ars...] un-ſatisfactory in ſubjects of the [...]; ſo crowded with phraſes, which [...] all our dictionaries; ſo ſtuffed w[ith...] La-tin, untranſlated; has ſo litt[le...] ſo dry and heavy in the read[ing...] a general wiſh, it were excha[nged...]lſe in the ſame kind, of greater [...]ble entertainment.

For Cantelius de Romano [...] the Jeſuit ſeems very unhappy, th[at...] his book in giving us a long rela[tion...]ars, battles, deaths, &c. which [...]-ther learn from the origin[al...] ſo ſtraitened himſelf in the rem[...] paſs for no extraordinary epitomi[zer...] he cannot ſpare room to ſet down [...]rity for what he ſays.

As for theſe papers; the t[wo...]man Learning and Education are [...] not been before attempted in any [...] at account will be the more eaſi[ly...] the better accepted in the world. [...]ory of the riſe, progreſs, and deca[y...] this
at

PREFACE.

at least to say for itself, that it carries its own credentials along with it, in constant references to the ancient writers. I will not here compose a table of contents for the second part, which has run out into such length, as to make the body of the work; only I may hint in a word or two, that the many omissions of Rosinus and Godwin are largely supplied, and scarce any thing material (that I know of) passed by: That the city, with the famous structures of all sorts, are described from the relations of eye-witnesses, and authors of credit: That the laws which occur in the best classics, and often prove a great hindrance to the reader, are disposed under proper heads in a very convenient manner; and the truest accounts of their import, and the time when they were made, collected from the most approved commentators, and from the admired treatise of Manutius de Legibus Romanis: That in some subjects it was thought proper to follow (for the most part) one particular author, who had managed his province with universal approbation; as Sigonius in the Comitia and the Judgments; Lipsius in the Art of War, in the Gladiators, and in the names; Kirchman in the Funerals, and Brerewood in the Account of the Money: That the curious remarks of Scaliger, Casaubon, Grævius, Monsieur and Madam Dacier, are inserted on many occasions. In short, that no pains or charges have been spared, which might render the attempt truly serviceable, to the good end for which it was designed, the pleasure and benefit of the reader.

The great incorrectness of the second edition was occasioned by the haste and the necessities of the then unfortunate proprietor; from whom no sight of the sheets

PREFACE.

sheets could be obtained, till the whole was so dishonourably finished. Yet the necessary alterations and additions, before given in, were inserted in their places. It was and is with all gratitude acknowledged, that the best part of this assistance hath been afforded by the late noble collections of the excellent Grævius, a catalogue of which is here subjoined. The compiler wishes it may be imputed not to idleness, but to design, that he hath borrowed only a mite *from that* treasury. *For intending an* abridgement, *not a full* body, *he thought it alike unreasonable, either to swell the bulk above the name and use, or to forbear such improvements as could scarce in honesty be denied; either to* burthen the reader for the *bookseller's advantage, or, under a pretence of* easing the former, to *injure both. This new impression has not only been amended by a careful supervisal, but adorned by the beauty of the letter, and of the additional sculptures. But the chief recommendation of the design is owing to the favourable acceptance and kind encouragement of private persons and of societies, especially of a royal and most flourishing seminary, to which our thanks can be returned in no better wishes, than that it may for ever continue in the same happy state, and under the like prudent government and direction.*

CONTENTS.

Two previous essays, *viz.*

ESSAY I. *Of the Roman Learning.*
ESSAY II. *Of the Roman Education.*

PART I.

The Original, Growth, *and* Decay *of the* ROMAN COMMONWEALTH.

CHAP. I. *Of the Building of the* CITY. Page 1
Chap. II. *Of the Roman Affairs under the Kings.* 4
Chap. III. *Of the Roman Affairs, from the beginning of the Consular Government, to the first Punic War.* 6
Chap. IV. *Of the Roman Affairs, from the Beginning of the first Punic War, to the first Triumvirate.* 10
Chap. V. *Of the Roman Affairs, from the Beginning of the first Triumvirate, to the End of the twelve Cæsars.* 14
Chap. VI. *Of the Roman Affairs, from Domitian, to the End of Constantine the Great.* 21
Chap. VII. *Of the Roman Affairs from Constantine the Great, to the Taking of Rome by Odoacer, and the Ruin of the Western Empire.* 26

CONTENTS.

PART II. BOOK I.

Of the CITY.

CHAP. I. *Of the Pomœrium, and of the Form and Bigness of the City, according to the seven Hills.* P. 29
Chap. II. *Of the Division of the City into Tribes and Regions, and of the Gates and Bridges.* 34
Chap. III. *Of the Places of Worship, particularly of the Temples and Luci.* 38
Chap. IV. *Of the Theatres, Amphitheatres, Circos, Naumachiæ, Odea, Stadia, and Xysti, and of the Campus Martius.* 43
Chap. V. *Of the Curiæ, Senacula, Basilicæ, Fora, and Comitium.* 47
Chap. VI. *Of the Porticos, Arches, Columns, and Trophies.* 51
Chap. VII. *Of the Bagnios, Nymphæa, Aquæducts, Cloacæ, and Public Ways.* 56

BOOK II.

Of the Religion *of the* ROMANS.

CHAP. I. *Of the Religion and Morality of the Romans in general.* P. 61
Chap. II. *Of the Luperci, Lupercalia, &c. Of the Potitii and Pinarii, and of the Arval Brothers.* 64
Chap. III. *Of the Augurs, Auguries, &c.* 67
Chap. IV. *Of the Aruspices and Pontifices.* 69
Chap. V. *Of the Flamines, Rex Sacrorum, Salii, Feciales, and Sodales.* 72
Chap. VI. *Of the Vestals.* 77

CONTENTS.

Chap. VII. *Of the Duumviri, Decemviri, and Quindecemviri, Keepers of the Sibylline Writings, and of the Corybantes, or Priests of Cybele, and the Epulones.* Page 79
Chap. VIII. *Of the Roman Sacrifices.* 84
Chap. IX. *Of the Roman Year.* 86
Chap. X. *Of the Distinction of the Roman Days.* 89
Chap. XI. *Of the Kalends, Nones, and Ides.* 91
Chap. XII. *The most remarkable Festivals of the Romans, as they stand in the Kalendar.* 92

BOOK III.

Of the Civil Government of the ROMANS.

Chap. I. *Of the general Divisions of the People.* P. 97
Chap. II. *The* SENATE. 101
Chap. III. *The general Divisions of the Magistrates, and the Candidates for offices.* 105
Chap. IV. *The Consuls.* 107
Chap. V. *The Dictator, and his Master of the Horse.* 109
Chap. VI. *The Prætors.* 111
Chap. VII. *The Censors.* 112
Chap. VIII. *The Quæstors.* 114
Chap. IX. *The Tribunes of the People.* 115
Chap. X. *The Ædiles.* 116
Chap. XI. *The Decemviri.* ib.
Chap. XII. *Tribuni Militum Consulare Potestate.* 117
Chap. XIII. *Civil Officers of less Note, or of less frequent occurrence in Authors, and of the public Servants.* 120
Chap. XIV. *The Provincial Magistrates, and first of the Proconsuls.* 124
Chap. XV. *The Provincial Prætors and Proprætors, the Legati, Quæstors, and Proquæstors.* 127

Chap.

CONTENTS.

Chap. XVI. *The Comitia.* Page 128
Chap. XVII. *The Roman Judgments, and first of Private Judgments.* 134
Chap. XVIII. *Public Judgments.* 137
Chap. XIX. *Judgments of the whole People.* 141
Chap. XX. *The Roman Punishments.* 143
Chap. XXI. *The Roman Laws in general.* 148
Chap. XXII. *The Laws in particular, and first of those relating to Religion.* 150
Chap. XXIII. *Laws relating to the Rights and Privileges of the Roman Citizens.* 152
Chap. XXIV. *Laws concerning Meetings, &c.* 154
Chap. XXV. *Laws relating to the* SENATE. 156
Chap. XXVI. *Laws relating to the Magistrates.* 157
Chap. XXVII. *Laws relating to Public Constitutions, Laws, and Privileges.* 160
Chap. XXVIII. *Laws relating to the Provinces and the Governors of them.* 161
Chap. XXIX. *Leges Agrariæ; or, Laws relating to Divisions of Lands among the People.* 163
Chap. XXX. *Laws relating to Corn.* 165
Chap. XXXI. *Laws for the regulating Expences.* 166
Chap. XXXII. *Laws relating to martial Affairs.* 168
Chap. XXXIII. *De Tutelis; or, Laws concerning Wardships.* 169
Chap. XXXIV. *Laws concerning Wills, Heirs, and Legacies.* 170
Chap. XXXV. *Laws concerning Money, Usury, &c.* ib.
Chap. XXXVI. *Laws concerning the Judges.* 171
Chap. XXXVII. *Laws relating to Judgments.* 173
Chap. XXXVIII. *Laws relating to Crimes.* ib.
Chap. XXXIX. *Miscellany Laws not spoken of under the General Heads.* 180

BOOK

BOOK IV.

The ROMAN *Art of War.*

CHAP. I. *The Levies of the Roman Foot.* Page 183
Chap. II. *Levy and Review of the Cavalry.* 185
Chap. III. *The Military Oath, and the Levies of the Confederates.* 188
Chap. IV. *Of the Evocati.* 189
Chap. V. *Of the several Kinds of the Roman Foot, and their Division into Manipuli, Cohorts and Legions.* 190
Chap. VI. *The Division of the Cavalry, and of the Allies.* 192
Chap. VII. *The Offices in the Roman Army: And, first, Of the Centurions and Tribunes; with the Commanders of the Horse, and of the Confederate Forces.* 193
Chap. VIII. *Of the Legati, and the Imperator, or General.* 196
Chap. IX. *Of the Roman Arms and Weapons.* 199
Chap. X. *The Order of the Roman Army drawn up in Battalia.* 203
Chap. XI. *The Ensigns and Colours; the Music; the Word in Engagements; the Harangues of the General.* 207
Chap. XII. *The Form and division of the Roman Camp.* 210
Chap. XIII. *Of the Duties, Works, and Exercises of the Soldiers.* 212
Chap XIV. *Of the Soldiers Pay.* 214
Chap. XV. *Of the Military Punishments.* 29
Chap. XVI. *Of the Military Rewards.* 220
Chap. XVII. *The Roman Way of declaring War, and of making Leagues.* 229

CONTENTS.

Chap. XVIII. *The Roman Method of treating the People they conquered; with the Constitution of the Coloniæ, Municipia, Præfecturæ, and Provinces.* P. 231
Chap. XIX. *The Roman way of taking towns, with the most remarkable Inventions and Engines made Use of in their Sieges.* 235
Chap. XX. *The Naval Affairs of the Romans.* 239

BOOK V.

Miscellany Customs of the ROMANS.

Chap. I. *Of the Private Sports and Games.* 247
Chap. II. *Of the Circensian Shows; and first of the Pentathlum, the Chariot Races, the Ludus-Trojæ, and the Pyrrhica Saltatio.* 252
Chap. III. *Of the Shows of wild Beasts, and of the Naumachiæ.* 265
Chap. IV. *Of the* GLADIATORS. 270
Chap. V. *Of the* LUDI-SCENICI, *or Stage-plays; and first, of the Satyres, and the Mimic-Pieces; with the Rise and Advances of such Entertainments among the Romans.* 282
Chap. VI. *Of the Roman Tragedy and Comedy.* 286
Chap. VII. *Of the sacred, votive, and funeral Games.* 296
Chap. VIII. *Of the Roman Habit.* 306
Chap. IX. *Of the Roman Marriages.* 326
Chap. X. *Of the Roman Funerals.* 334
Chap. XI. *Of the Roman Entertainments.* 365
Chap. XII. *Of the Roman Names.* 370
Chap. XIII. *Of the Roman Money.* 372
INDEX Rerum & Verborum.

ESSAY

ESSAY I.

Of the ROMAN Learning.

WHOEVER considers the strange beginning of the Roman state, the frame and constitution on which it was first settled, together with the quality of the original members, will think it no wonder that the people, in that early age, should have a kind of fierceness, or rather wildness in their temper, utterly averse to every thing that was polite and agreeable. This savage disposition by degrees turned into a rigid severity, which encouraged them to rely solely on the force of their native virtue and honour, without being beholden to the advantage of art, for the improvement of their reason, or for the assistance of their courage. Hence a grossness of invention passed current with them for wit, and study was looked on as an unmanly labour; especially while they found, that their exact discipline, and unconquered resolution, rendered them masters of nations much more knowing than themselves. All this is frankly acknowledged by their own authors: *Literæ in homine Romano* go for a wonder with Tully*. And Virgil, in a reign when all the civility and learning of the world were transplanted to Rome, chuseth to make the art of government and war the distinguishing excellencies of his countrymen:

Excudent alii spirantia mollius æra,
Credo equidem: vivos ducent de marmore vultus:
Orabunt causas melius; cœlique meatus
Describent radio, & surgentia sidera dicent:
Tu regere imperio populos, Romane, memento:
Hæ tibi erunt artes; pacifque imponere morem;
Parcere subjectis, & debellare superbos †.

Others

* *De Nat. Deor.* lib. 1. *De Senectute.* † *Aeneid.* 6.

Others shall best inspire the mimic brass,
Or out of marble carve a living face;
Plead with more force, and trace the heav'nly roads,
Describing the wide empire of the gods:
The wand'ring stars to steady rules confine,
And teach expecting mortals when they'd shine.
Thee heavens, brave Roman, form'd for high command,
Be these thy arts, from thy victorious hand,
To make glad nations own their peace bestow'd,
To spare the suppliant, and pull down the proud.

The reasons which Horace gives for the slow advances of poesy will hold in every other part of polite learning:

Serus enim Græcis admovit acumina chartis *,

Their little acquaintance with the fine wits of Greece, who had settled the staple of arts and learning in that country, deprived them of an opportunity to cultivate and beautify their genius, which was form'd by nature capable of the highest attainments. Some kind of poetry, indeed, they had in their rustic times, but then the verses were such rude, doggrel stuff, as old Ennius describes:

——— *Qualis Fauni vatesque canebant,*
Quum neque Musarum scopulos quisquam superárat,
Nec dicti studiosus erat.

Cicero is inclined to think, that the old Romans might probably have gained some little knowledge in philosophy from the instructions of Pythagoras, the famous author of the Italic Sect, who flourished in Italy about the same time as the Tarquins were expelled the city. But the ancient custom of singing to the flute the praises of famous men at great entertainments, is the only relic he can find of this doctrine which was delivered in poetical numbers †.

Their intercourse with Greece began upon their undertaking the defence of that country against Philip of Macedon, who had a design on its liberty about the year of Rome 555; when, according to their usual practice, under the name of deliverers, they

* Lib. 2. Epist. 1. † *Cicero Tusc. Quæst.* lib. 5.

they made themselves rather the masters of that people. And then,

> *Græcia capta ferum victorem cepit, & artes*
> *Intulit agresti Latio* *.

The greatest number of eminent poets, especially dramatic writers, flourished between the end of the first and the third Punic wars; or from the year of the city 512 to 607. The most considerable were, Livius Andronicus, Nævius, Ennius, Pacuvius, Accius, Cæcilius, Plautus, Afranius, Terence, and Lucilius. And therefore Horace means only the first Punic war, when he says,

> *Et post Punica bella quietus, quærere cæpit,*
> *Quid Sophocles, & Thespis & Æschylus utile ferrent:*
> *Tentavit quoque, rem si dignè vertere posset* †.

The studies of philosophy and rhetoric never made any tolerable progress before the arrival of the Achaians, who in the year of Rome 585 or 587, to the number of a thousand, or more, were sent for out of their own country, where they had shown themselves disaffected to the Romans, and were dispersed in several parts of Italy. Among these was the famous Polybius the Megalopolitan, whose great parts and learning not only gained him the entire friendship of Scipio Æmilianus and Lælius, two of the greatest Romans in that age, but procured too the release of all his countrymen that remained after some years exile.

Most of that company, though not equal to Polybius, yet being the principal members of the chief cities in Greece, brought away a great share of the politeness and refined arts of that country: And being now reduced to a state of life, which took from them all thoughts of public action, they applied themselves wholly to the pursuit of letters, as well to divert the sad reflections of their banishment, as to improve and cultivate their mind ‡.

In a few years their examples and instructions had wrought such a strange conversion in the Roman youth, that the senate, fearing lest the ancient discipline should by this means be corrupted, and the minds of the people softened and enervated by study, consulted how to put a stop to this vein of politeness, so contrary to the rough and warlike dispositions of their ancestors.

---

* Lib. 2. Epist. 1.   † Ibid.   ‡ *Casaubon. Chronol. ad Polyb. & Comment. ad Sueton. de Grammat.*

anceſtors. To this purpoſe, we meet with a decree bearing date in the conſulſhip of C. Fannius Strabo, and M. Valerius Meſſala, A. U. C. 392; by which it appears, "that whereas "Marcus Pomponius the prætor had made a report to the ſe- "nate about the philoſophers and rhetoricians, the fathers did "hereby order the ſaid prætor to take cognizance of the bu- "ſineſs, and to ſuffer no ſuch men in Rome *."

The eager paſſion for learning, which this prohibition had in ſome meaſure allayed, broke out with greater heat and force about ſixteen years after, upon this famous occaſion, as the ſtory may be made up out of ſeveral authors †.

The Athenians having plundered Oropus, a city of Bœtia, the inhabitants made their complaint at Rome; the Romans refer- ring the caſe to the judgment of the Sicyonians, a mulct of 500 talents was impoſed on the Athenian ſtate. Upon this account it was reſolved, that commiſſioners ſhould be ſent to the Roman ſenate to procure a mitigation of the fine. The perſons pitched on for this ſervice were Carneades the academic, Diogenes the ſtoick, and Critolaus the peripatetick. About the time of their coming authors are very little agreed; but Petavius and Ca- ſaubon fix it in the ſix hundred and third year after the building of Rome. Moſt of the ſtudious youths immediately waited on the old gentlemen at their arrival, and heard them diſcourſe frequently with admiration. It happened too, that they had each of them a different way in their harangues; for the eloquence of Carneades was violent and rapid, Critolaus's neat and ſmooth, that of Diogenes modeſt and ſober. Carneades one day held a full and accurate diſputation concerning juſtice; the next day he refuted all that he had ſaid before by a train of contrary arguments, and quite took away the virtue that he ſeemed ſo firmly to have eſtabliſhed. This he did to ſhew his faculty of confuting all manner of poſitive aſſertions; for he was the founder of the Second Academy, a ſect which denied that any thing was to be perceived or underſtood in the world, and ſo introduced an univerſal ſuſpenſion of aſſent. It ſoon flew about the city, that a certain Græcian, (by whom they meant Carneades) carrying all before him, had impreſſed ſo ſtrange a love upon the young men, that, quitting all their pleaſures and paſtimes, they run mad, as it were, after philoſophy. This to the genera- lity of people was a very pleaſant ſight, and they rejoiced extremely

---

* Sueton. de Clar. Grammet. cap. 1. A. Gell. lib. 15. cap. 11.
† Plut. Cat. major. A. Gel. l.b. 7. cap. 14. Macrob. Sat. 1. cap. 15.

tremely to find their sons welcome the Græcian literature in so kind a manner. But old Cato the censor took it much to heart, fearing lest the youth, being diverted by such entertainments, should prefer the glory of speaking to that of acting. So that, the fame of the philosophers increasing every day, he resolved to send them packing as soon as possible. With this design, coming into the senate, he accused the magistrates for not giving the Ambassadors a speedier dispatch; they being persons who could easily persuade the people to what they pleased. He advised, therefore, that in all haste something should be concluded on, that, being sent home to their own schools, they might declaim to the Græcian children, and the Roman youth might be obedient to their own laws and governors as formerly.

The same grave disciplinarian, to fright his son from any thing of the Græcians, used to pronounce, like the voice of an oracle, in a harsher and louder tone than ordinary, " That the " Romans would certainly be destroyed when they began once " to be infected with Greek." But it is very likely that he afterwards altered his mind; since his learning Greek in his old age is a known story, and depends on good authority *. The Lord Bacon says, " It was a judgment upon him for his " former blasphemies †."

The ambassadors, upon the motion of Cato, had a quick dismission, but left so happy an inclination in the young gentlemen to philosophy and good letters, that they grew every day more enamoured of study; and showed as much diligence in their pursuits of knowledge as they had ever done in their applications to war.

In the year of the city 608 or 609, Greece, which had hitherto retained some shadow of liberty, tho' it had been a long while at the Romans command, was, upon some slight occasion, entered with an army under L. Mummius, and reduced to the common state of the other conquered nations. This exploit happening in the very same year that Carthage was destroyed by P. Scipio Æmilianus, it will be very pleasing to observe the different genius of the two commanders, who had the honour of these atchievements; and to see how politeness and the ancient simplicity were now at strife in Rome. Mummius was so far unskilled in the curious inventions of art, that, after the taking of Corinth, when a great number of admirable pictures and statues, by the best masters, came into his hands, he told
the

---

* *Cicero* Academ. 1. *De Senect. Quinctilian. Inst.* lib. 12, cap. 11.
† Advancement of learning, *Book* 1.

the servants that were to carry them into Italy, "If they lost any by the way, they should certainly find him new ones in their room *."

Scipio, on the other hand, to the courage and virtue of ancient heroes, had joined a profound knowledge of the sciences, with all the graces and ornaments of wit. His patronage was courted by every one that made any figure in learning. Panætius, whom Tully calls the Prince of the Stoicks, and the incomparable historian Polybius, were his bosom friends, the assisters of his studies at home, and the constant companions of his expeditions †. To which may be added the remark of a very great man, "That he passed the soft hours of his life in the conversation of Terence, and was thought to have a part in the composition of his comedies ‡."

The highest pitch of the Roman grandeur, in the time of the commonwealth, is thought to have been concluded before the final reduction of Carthage and of Greece ‖; and the common reason assigned for its decay is, that Athens, being now become the mart of the world for wit and breeding, imported the arts of debauchery, among her more noble productions, to Rome; and maintained their luxury, as well as their studies and conversations, at her charge. But however their ancient prowess might decline, it is certain the conquest of the great empire of science was now carried on more vigorously than ever. The tide of learning and humanity ran every day with greater force, and, after the famous Cato, scarce met with any to oppose it. Between this period and the death of Sylla, (scarce seventy years) the most renowned orators, Crassus and Antony, ruled the forum, who were succeeded by Sulpicius, Cotta, Hortensius, and other great names recorded by Tully in his Brutus. At the same time, the two Scævolæ, the Augur, and the Pontiff, advanced civil law to its full perfection. And Lucretius, (who wrote about the time of the Jugurthine war) as he excelled even the Græcian disciples of Epicurus, in explaining and defending his doctrine, so he directs us where to begin, in fixing the height and purity of the Roman poesy and style §. Philosophers were now in universal honour and request, being invited from all parts for the education and instruction of young noblemen, and for advice and assistance of the greatest ministers of

---

* *Vell. Paterc.* lib. 1. cap. 13.   † Ib.   ‡ Sir *Will. Temple's Miscell.* P. 2. Essay 4.   ‖ *Casaubon. Chronolog. ad Polyb.*   § Sir *Will. Temple's Miscell.* P. 2. Essay 1.

of state. And what is most surprising, arts and civility were rather encouraged than frighted away by the wars, and the Muses, like their patroness Minerva, had very often their residence in the camp. Sylla himself wrote two and twenty books of memoirs *, and contributed in an extraordinary manner to the advancement of knowledge, by transporting to Rome the famous library of Apellicon the Peripatetick, in which were most of Aristotle's and Theophrastus's works, which had been long unknown to the greatest part of his followers †.

Sylla's rival, Marius, was the only man of note, in that age, who retained the old sourness and unpolished manner of the first Romans. He indeed would never study Greek, nor suffer that language to be used in any matters of consequence; as thinking it ridiculous to bestow time in that learning, the teachers whereof were little better than slaves ‡.

But then Lucullus, who succeeded Sylla in the military glory, as to matters of learning was much his superior. In his youth he had so absolute a command of the two only tongues then in request, that, upon a project of compiling an history, he fairly took his chance, whether he should write in Greek or Latin, in prose or verse. And after all his feats of arms in the Mithridatic war, when he was deprived of his command by the prevailing faction of Pompey, the great employment of his privacy and retreat was the promoting of knowledge. With this design he built a library, furnished it with a vast number of books fairly transcribed, and made it free to all comers. The walks and schools, which he raised near the library, were always full of Græcians, who, retiring thither from business, diverted one another with conferences and debates, in the same manner as was used in their own country; making advantage of friendly conversation toward the improvement of their understandings. Lucullus himself often studied there, sometimes disputing with the learned men, and sometimes giving his advice in matters of state, to those that desired it; though he meddled with no public business in person. He was very well versed in all the sects of philosophy, but adhered closely to the old academy, whereas his friend Cicero was a great stickler for the new. Hence it is that we find the latter book of the Academic Questions inscribed Lucullus, where that great man is brought in defending the opinions of his sect ‖

The

* *Plutarchus* in *Sylla*.   † Ibid. &. *Strabo*, lib. 13.   ‡ *Plutarch*, in *Mario*.
‖ *Plutarchus* in *Lucullo*.

The whole majesty of language, and height of eloquence, shone out, as it were, all at once, in Tully; so that Paterculus has well observed, *Delectari ante eum paucissimis, mirari vero neminem possis, nisi aut ab illo visum, aut qui illum viderit* [*].

Perhaps the same remark will hold good in his philosophy; or, at least, with respect to his predecessors, the latter study will yield him an equal praise with the former. For to handle this subject in Latin prose, was purely a new province reserved for his management, and left untouched till that time by the learned. Thus much he lets us know in several parts of his works, particularly in his poem to the Tusculan Questions; where at the same time he gives us a short account of the progress and advances of arts among the Romans, infinitely worth the transcribing: *Meum semper judicium fuit*, &c. "It was al-
"ways my opinion," says he, "that either our countrymen
"have been more happy in their inventions of every kind, than
"the Greeks; or, That they have made a vast improvement
"in whatever they borrowed from that nation, and thought
"worth their while to polish and refine. For as to the conduct
"of life, and the rules of breeding and behaviour, together with
"the management of family concerns, we are masters of more ex-
"actness, and have a much genteeler air. If we ascend to the
"governing and regulating of public spirits, our ancestors may
"justly claim the preference in this part of wisdom, on account
"of their admirable laws and institutions. In military affairs
"we have made a more considerable advance than any before
"us, which is owing no less to our discipline, than to our na-
"tive bravery.

"It is true, Greece has always had the renown beyond us for
"their attainments in every part of learning, and it was an
"easy matter to conquer, when they met with no opposition.
"Poetry, the most ancient sort of writing, had but a late re-
"ception among us: For Livius Andronicus presented his first
"dramatick piece 510 (it should be 514) years after the building
"of Rome, in the Consulship of C. Claudius, son to Appius
"Cæcus, and M. Tuditanus, a year before the birth of Ennius,
"who is senior to Plautus and Nævius."

As he goes on, he attributes the slow progress of poesy to the want of due reward and encouragement, and tells us, that in a public oration of Cato's, it was objected as a reproach to Marcus Nobilior, that he had carried the poet Ennius with him to Ætolia, when he went to reside there as governor: That there

[*] *Hist.* lib. 1. cap. 17.

there was no part of the mathematics (which the Græcians esteemed so honourable a study) of use in Rome, but the bare practice of measuring and casting accompts. For oratory, he observes, that the Romans embraced this very soon, but at first without the advantage of a learned institution; which were afterwards added with so much success, as to set them on equal terms with the most eloquent masters of Greece: But that philosophy had lain neglected till that time, and had met with no eminent author to adorn it in the Latin tongue. This therefore he professeth to undertake as his proper office; and how happily he succeeded in the attempt, his works on that subject will be a lasting argument.

If we compare Tully with his friend Atticus, we find them both together answering the two excellent ends of philosophy, the service of the public, and the private ease and tranquillity of an inoffensive life: The former directed all his studies to action, in the defence of the commonwealth, and the opposing all designs on its liberty: The latter, by never entering the scene of business, made himself equally honoured and courted by all parties, from Sylla to Augustus Cæsar. The one gained to himself more glory, the other more hearty love and esteem; and I believe most persons would be inclined to follow Atticus, and to commend Cicero.

Crassus, Pompey, Antony, Cæsar, Cato, and Brutus, who made such a noise in the world, almost all at the same time, were the most refined scholars of their age. The three first indeed confined themselves to the practice of eloquence, till they were wholly diverted by the profession of arms. But the three last, as they outshone the former in oratory, so they had made much greater advances in the other parts of human learning. Poetry and philosophy were the diversion of Cæsar's leisure hours; and his history will be the model of good language, as long as himself is the example of great achievements.

The whole conduct of Cato's life shows him a greater stoick than the most rigid professors of that sect; or, however they might equal him in knowledge, it is certain he shamed them in practice.

Brutus had been a hearer of all the sects of philosophers, and made some proficiency in every one. When a soldier under Pompey, in the civil wars, all the time that he was in the camp, except what he spent in the general's company, he employed in reading and study. And the very day before the decisive battle at Pharsalia, though it was then the middle of summer, and the camp under many inconveniencies, and he himself extremely harassed and out of order; yet while others were either laid down to sleep, or taken up with apprehensions about the issue of the fight, he spent all his time, till the evening, in writing the epitome of Polybius *.

It is universally known, that the Roman literature, as well as empire, was in its highest ascendant under Augustus. All the delicate fruits, transplanted from Greece, were now in their blossom, being cherished by the calmness of the season, and cultivated by the hand of an emperor.

I have often wondered that Mæcenas should all along carry away the sole honour of encouraging the wit and knowledge of this reign; when it seems probable that he acted only in imitation of his master; as the humours of princes commonly determine the inclinations of their favourites. The quite contrary happened to the other great minister Agrippa; the glory of his exploits was referred to the emperor, whilst the emperor's bounty advanced Mæcenas's esteem. And, indeed, the celebration of Augustus's triumphs, and the panegyrics on his piety, were sufficient to set him out in the most taking colours: But, had Mæcenas been denied the shining character of a patron, he might have rolled on in silence among Epicurus's herd, and we should scarce have seen him drawn by the poets hands, unless in the same posture as Silenus:

Inflatum hesterno venas, ut semper, Iaccho:
Serta procul capiti tantùm delapsa jacebant,
Et gravis attritâ pendebat cantharus ansâ †.

But which ever of the two was the nobler patron, Augustus must be acknowledged to have been the greater scholar. And for proof we need go no farther than Suetonius, who has spent no less than six chapters on the learning of this emperor. His prodigious industry in the study of eloquence and liberal arts; his labour in composing every thing that he spoke in public, though he had a very good faculty at extempore harangues; his polite and clean style; his accurate knowledge of the Grecian literature, by the assistance of their best masters of rhetoric and philosophy; the thirteenth book of the history of his
own

---

* *Plutarch.* in *Brut.* † *Virgil.* Eclog. 6.

own life; his exhortation to philosophy, with several other works in prose; his book of hexameters, and another of epigrams, all considered together, may equal him with the most learned princes in story.

Being thus arrived at the highest point of the Roman attainments, it cannot be unpleasant to look about us, and to take a short survey of the productions in every kind. Eloquence indeed will appear at some distance, rather in the Augustan age, than in Augustus's reign, ending in Cicero, at the dissolution of the commonwealth. Not that his death was properly the ruin of his profession; for the philosopher might have lived much longer; and yet the orator have been gone, when once the ancient liberty was taken away, which inspired him with all his lofty thoughts, and was the very soul of his harangues. But then the bounds of history and poesy were fixed under the emperor's protection, by Livy, Virgil, and Horace. And if we desire a view of philosophy, the two poets will account for that as well as for their own province.

I think none will deny Horace the elogy given him by a celebrated writer, " that he was the greatest master of life, and " of true sense in the conduct of it *." Especially since the author of that judgment is one of those whom (had he lived then) Horace himself would have willingly chose for his judge; and inserted in that short catalogue of men of wit and honour, whom he desired should approve his labours †.

Whether or no the common saying be true, that, if all arts and sciences were lost, they might be found in Virgil, it is plain he dived very deep into the mysteries of natural science, which he sets forth in all its ornaments, in several parts of his sublime work. And in that admirable place of his second Georgic, when he expresseth, in a sort of transport, his inclinations to poesy, he seems to direct its whole end towards the speculations of the philosophers, and to make the muses hand-maids to nature:

Me verò primùm dulces ante omnia Musæ,
Quarum sacra fero ingenti perculsus amore,
Accipiant; cœlique vias & sydera monstrent,
Defectus solis varios, Lunæque labores:

Unde

---

* Sir *Will. Temple's Miscellen.* p. 2. Essay 2.   † Book I. Sat. 10.

ESSAY I.

Unde tremor terris: quâ vi maria alta tumescant
Obicibus ruptis, rursusque in seipsa residant:
Quid tantum Oceano properent se tingere soles
Hyberni: vel quæ tardis mora noctibus obstet.

For me, the first desire, which does controul
All the inferior wheels that move my soul,
Is, that the muse me her high-priest would make;
Into her holy scenes of mystery take,
And open there, to my mind's purged eye,
Those wonders which to sense the gods deny;
How in the moon such change of shapes is found;
The moon, the changing world's eternal bound:
What shakes the solid earth: what strong disease
Dares trouble the far centre's ancient ease:
What makes the sea retreat, and what advance;
Varieties too regular for chance:
What drives the chariot on of winter's light,
And stops the lazy waggon of the night.

Mr COWLEY.

After Augustus, the Roman muses, as well as the eagles, stooped from their former height; and perhaps one of these misfortunes might be a necessary consequence of the other. I am very sorry when I find either of them attributed to the change of government, and the settlement of the monarchy: For, had the maxims and the example of Augustus been pursued by his successors, the empire, in all probability, might have been much more glorious than the commonwealth. But while a new scheme of politics was introduced by Tiberius, and the Cæsars began to act what the Tarquins would have been ashamed of, the learning might very well be corrupted, together with the manners and the discipline, and all beyond any hopes of a recovery.

It cannot be denied, that some of the worst princes were the most passionate affecters of learning, particularly Tiberius, Claudius, and Nero: But this rather deterred other men from such attempts, than encouraged them in their pursuits; while an applauded scholar was as much envied as a fortunate commander; and a rival in wit accounted as dangerous as a contender for the empire; the first being certainly the more hard combatant, who dared challenge his masters at their own weapons.

Whatever

Whatever essays were made to recover the languishing art under Vespasian, Titus, and Domitian, (for this last too was an encourager of poesy, though he banished the philosophers) scarce served to any better purpose than to demonstrate the poor success of study and application, while the ancient genius was wanting.

In the six next reigns immediately following Domitian, learning seems to have enjoyed a sort of lucid interval, and the banished favourite was again admitted to the court, being highly countenanced and applauded by the best set of princes Rome ever saw.

Not to inquire after the productions of the other reigns, the useful labours of Tacitus, Suetonius, and Pliny junior, will make the government of Trojan more famous than all his feats of arms. If they are less happy in their language than the ancients, in other respects, perhaps, they have overmatched them; the historians in the delicacy of their politics, and the sincere truth of their relations; and the orator in his wit and good sense. If we add to these Plutarch, who wrote most of his works in Rome, and was honoured by Trajan with the consulship; and Quintilian, who flourished a very little time before; they may pass for the twilight of learning after the sun-set of the Augustan age, or rather be resembled to a glimmering taper, which casts a double light when it is just on the point of expiring.

It is an observation of Sir William Temple, That all the Latin books which we have 'till the end of Trajan, and all the Greek 'till the end of Marcus Antoninus, have true and very estimable value; but that all, written since that time, owe their price purely to our curiosity, and not their own worth and excellence.

But the purity of the tongue was long before corrupted, and ended, in Sir William Temple's judgment, with Velleius Paterculus under Tiberius. The reason he assigns for this decay is, the strange resort of the ruder nations to Rome, after the conquest of their own country.

Thus the Gauls and Germans flocked in multitudes both to the army and the city, after the reducing of those parts by Julius Cæsar, Augustus, and Tiberius, as many Spaniards and Syrians had done before on the like account; but the greatest confluence of foreigners followed upon the victories of Trajan in the east, and his establishment of the three new provinces, Armenia, Assyria, and Mesopotamia. And though Adrian voluntarily

luntarily relinquished these new acquisitions, yet the prodigious swarms of the natives, who had waited on his predecessors triumphs, were still obliged to live in Rome in the condition of slaves.

The greatest part of the succeeding princes, who found it so hard an enterprize to defend their own territories, had little leisure or concern to guard the possessions of the muses. And therefore Claudian in those verses of his panegyric on Stilico,

Hinc priscæ redeunt artes, felicibus inde
Ingeniis aperitur iter, despectaque Musæ
Colla levant ;

is guilty of a great piece of flattery, in making that minister the restorer of polite studies, when it is plain, that in his time (under Honorius) were the last strugglings of the Roman state.

The Goths and Vandals, who soon carried all before them, might easily fright learning and sciences off the stage, since they were already so much out of countenance ; and thus render the conquerors of the universe as rough and illiterate as their first progenitors.

In this manner, the inundations of the barbarous people proved equally fatal to arts and empire ; and Rome herself, when she ceased to be the mistress of the world, in a little time quite forgot to speak Latin.

ESSAY II.

Of the ROMAN *Education.*

IT is an obvious remark, that the strongest body owes its vigor, in a great measure, to the very milk it received in its infancy, and to the first knitting of the joints: That the most stately trees, and the fairest herbs and flowers, are beholden for their shade and beauty to the hand that first fixed them in an agreeable soil; an advantage, which, if they happen to want, they seldom fail to degenerate into wildness, and to assume a nature quite different from their proper species. Every one knows how to apply the same observation to morals, who has the sense to discover it in naturals. Hence the most renowned people in story are those whose lawgivers thought it their noblest and most important work, to prescribe rules for the early institution of youth. On this basis, Lycurgus founded the glorious discipline of the Spartans, which continued for five hundred years without any considerable violation. " The Indian Brachmans had a strain beyond all the " wit of Greece, beginning their care of mankind even before " their birth, and employing much thought and diligence a- " bout the diet and etertainment of their breeding women; " so far as to furnish them with pleasant imaginations, to com- " pose their minds and their sleep with the best temper, du- " ring the time they carried their burthen *."

Plutarch severely reprehends the conduct of Numa, that, in his settlement of the Roman state, he did not in the first place provide

---

* Sir *Will. Temple*'s *Miscell.* P. 2. Essay 1.

provide and conftitute rules for the education of children, and makes the remiffnefs in this early difcipline the chief caufe of the feditious and turbulent temper of that people, and what contributed highly to the ruin of the commonwealth *. Thus much, indeed, feems to be agreed on by the latter hiftorians, that, in the loofer times of the empire, the fhameful negligence of parents and inftructors, with its neceffary confequence, the corruption and decay of morality and good letters, ftruck a very great blow towards the diffolving of that glorious fabric. But in the rifing ages of Rome, while their primitive integrity and virtue flourifhed with their arms and command, the training up of youth was looked on as a moft facred duty; and they thought themfelves in the higheft manner obliged to leave fit fucceffors to the empire of the world. So that, upon a fhort furvey of the whole method of difcipline, from the birth to the entrance on public bufinefs, they will appear fo far to have exceeded the wifdom and care of other nations, as to contend for this glory even with the ancient Spartans, whom Plutarch has magnified fo much beyond them: efpecially, if we agree with a great judge, that the taking no care about the learning, but only about the lives and manners of children, may be juftly thought a defect in Lycurgus's inftitution †.

Quintilian (or Tacitus) in the Dialogue *de Oratoribus*, gives an excellent account of the old way of breeding children, and fets it off with great advantage, by comparing it with the modern.

" As foon as the child was born, he was not given in charge
" to an hired nurfe, to live with her in fome pitiful hole that
" ferved her for lodgings, but was brought up in the lap and
" bofom of the mother, who reckoned it among her chief com-
" mendations, to keep the houfe, and attend on the children.
" Some ancient matron was pitched on out of the neighbours,
" whofe life and manners rendered her worthy of that office,
" to whofe care the children of every family were committed;
" before whom it was reckoned the moft heinous thing in the
" world to fpeak an ill word, or to do an ill action. Nor had
" fhe an eye only on their inftruction, and the bufinefs that
" they were to follow, but with an equal modefty and gravity
" fhe regulated their very divertifements and recreations. Thus
" Cornelia,

---

* *Plutarch.* Compar. of *Numa* and *Lycurg.*   † Archbifhop *Tillotfon's* Sermon of Education.

" Cornelia, Aurelia, and Attica, mothers to the Gracchi, Ju-
" lius Cæsar, and Augustus, are reported to have undertaken
" the office of governesses, and to have employed themselves
" in the education of noblemen's children. The strictness and
" severity of such an institution had this very good design,
" that the mind, being thus preserved in its primitive inno-
" cence and integrity, and not debauched by ill custom or ill
" example, might apply itself with the greatest willingness to
" liberal arts, and embrace them with all its powers and fa-
" culties. That, whether it was particularly inclined either to
" the profession of arms, or to the understanding of the law,
" or to the practice of eloquence, it might make that its only
" business, and greedily drink in the whole knowledge of the
" favourite study.

" But now the young infant is given in charge to some poor
" Græcian wench, and one or two of the serving-men, per-
" haps, are joined in the commission ; generally the meanest
" and most ill-bred of the whole pack, and such as are unfit
" for any serious business. From the stories and tattle of such
" fine companions, the soft and flexible nature must take its
" first impression and bent. Over the whole family there is not
" the least care taken of what is said or done before the child ;
" while the very parents, instead of inuring their dear little
" ones to virtue and modesty, accustom them, on the quite
" contrary, to licentiousness and wantonness, the natural re-
" sult of which, is a settled impudence, and a contempt of
" those very parents, and every body else."

Thus, although the care and instruction of youth, among
the old Romans, had been provided for by the public laws, as
in the Spartan state, yet the voluntary diligence of parents
would have made all such regulations superfluous.

Among the domestic cares, it will not be from the purpose
to take particular notice of one, which required little trouble
or difficulty, and yet proved as beneficial and serviceable as any
other institution : I mean the using children to speak the language purely at first, by letting them hear nothing but the truest and most proper phrase. By this only advantage several
persons arrived at the ordinary repute in the forum, who were
so unhappy as to want many other qualifications.

Tully says, that the Gracchi were educated, *non tam in gremio quàm in sermone matris*: and the report of Laelia, who
was reckoned the third orator
no poet, had read no books of

collections, and had no knowledge of the public or private part of the law. The only thing which gained him his applause was a clean shining phrase, and a sudden quickness and fluency of expression. This he got purely by the benefit of his private education; being used to such a correct and polished way of speaking in the house where he was brought up *.

For masters, in the first place, they had the *Literatores*, or Γραμματισται, who taught the children to read and write: To these they were committed about the age of six or seven years †. Being come from under their care, they were sent to the grammar schools, to learn the art of speaking well, and the understanding of authors; or more frequently, in the house of great men, some eminent grammarian was entertained for that employment.

It is pleasant to consider, what prudence was used in these early years to instil into the children's minds a love and inclination to the forum, whence they were to expect the greatest share of their honours and preferments. For Cicero tells Atticus, in his second book *de Legibus*, that when they were boys, they used to learn the famous laws of the twelve tables by heart in the same manner as they did an excellent poem. And Plutarch relates in his life of the younger Cato, that the very children had a play, in which they acted pleadings of causes before the judges; accusing one another, and carrying the condemned party to prison.

The masters already mentioned, together with the instructors in the several sorts of manly exercises, for the improving of their natural strength and force, do not properly deserve that name, if set in view with the rhetoricians and philosophers; who, after that reason had displayed her faculties, and established her command, were employed to cultivate and adorn the advantages of nature, and to give the last hand toward the forming of a Roman citizen. Few persons made any great figure on the scene of action in their own time, or in history afterwards, who, besides the constant frequenting of public lectures, did not keep with them in the house some eminent professor of oratory or wisdom.

I have often thought, that one main reason of the prodigious progress made by young gentlemen under these private tutors, was the perfect love and endearment which we find

to

* *Cic. in Brut.* † *Dacier in Horat.* Sat. 1. Lib. 1.

to have been between master and scholar, by which means government and instruction proceeded in the sweetest and easiest way. All persons in the happy ages of Rome had the same honour and respect for their teachers as Persius had for his master, Cornutus the stoic, to whom, addressing himself in his first satyr, he thus admirably describes his own love and piety to his governor, and the strict friendship that was between them.

Cumque iter ambiguum est, & vitæ nescius error
Diducit trepidas ramosa in compita mentes,
Me tibi supposui: teneros tu suscipis annos
Socratico, Cornute, sinu; tunc fallere solers
Apposita intortos extendit regula mores;
Et premitur ratione animus, vincique laborat,
Artificemque tuo ducit sub pollice vultum.
Tecum etenim longos memini consumere soles;
Et tecum primas epulis decerpere noctes.
Unum opus, & requiem pariter disponibus ambo,
Atque verecundâ laxamus seria mensâ.
Non equidem hoc dubites amborum fœdere certo
Consentire dies, & ab uno sidere duci.
Nostra vel æquali suspendit tempora librâ
Parca tenax veri, seu nata fidelibus hora
Dividit in Geminos concordia fata duorum;
Saturnumque gravem nostro Jove fregimus unâ.
Nescio quod, certè est quod me tibi temperat astrum.

Just at the age when manhood set me free,
I then depos'd myself, and left the reins to thee:
On thy wise bosom I repos'd my head,
And by my better Socrates was bred.
Then thy straight rule set virtue in my sight,
The crooked line reforming by the right.
My reason took the bent of thy command,
Was form'd and polish'd by thy skilful hand.
Long summer days thy precepts I rehearse,
And winter nights were short in our converse.
One was our labour, one was our repose;
One frugal supper did our studies close.
Sure on our birth some friendly planet shone,
And, as our souls, our horoscope was one:

Whether

Whether the mounting twins did heav'n adorn,
Or with the rising balance we were born;
Both have the same impression from above,
And both have Saturn's rage repell'd by Jove.
What star I know not, but some star, I find,
Has giv'n thee an ascendant o'er my mind.
MR DRYDEN.

Nor was the reverence paid by the public to the informers of youth less remarkable than the esteem and duty of their scholars. Which makes Juvenal break out into that elegant rapture:

Dii majorum umbris tenuem & sine pondere terram,
Spirantesque crocos, & in urnâ perpetuum ver,
Qui præceptorem sancti voluere parentis
Esse loco *.

In peace, ye shades of our great grandsires, rest;
No heavy earth your sacred bones molest.
Eternal springs and rising flow'rs adorn
The reliques of each venerable urn:
Who pious rev'rence to their tutors paid,
As parents honour'd, and as gods obey'd.
MR CHARLES DRYDEN.

At the age of seventeen years, the young gentlemen, when they put on the *manly gown*, were brought in a solemn manner to the forum, and entered in the study of pleading: Not only if they designed to make this their chief profession, but altho' their inclinations lay rather to the camp: For we scarce meet with any famous captain who was not a good speaker, or any eminent orator, who had not served some time in the army. Thus it was requisite for all persons, who had any thoughts of rising in the world, to make a good appearance, both at the bar and in the field; because, if the success of their valour and conduct should advance them to any considerable post, it would have proved almost impossible, without the advantage of eloquence, to maintain their authority with the senate and people; or, if the force of their oratory should in time procure them

---

* *Sat.* 7.

them the honourable office of Prætor or Conful, they would not have been in a capacity to undertake the government of the provinces (which fell to their fhare at the expiration of thofe employments) without fome experience in military command.

Yet becaufe the profeffion of arms was an art which would eafily give them an opportunity of fignalizing themfelves, and in which they would almoft naturally excel, as occafions fhould be afterwards offered for their fervice; their whole application and endeavours were directed at prefent to the ftudy of law and rhetoric, as the foundations of their future grandeur. Or, perhaps, they now and then made a campaign, as well for a diverfion from feveral labours, as for their improvement in martial difcipline.

In the Dialogue *de Oratoribus*, we have a very good account of this admiffion of young gentlemen into the forum, and of the neceffity of fuch a courfe in the commonwealth; which, coming from fo great a mafter, cannot fail to be very pertinent and inftructive.

"Among our anceftors," fays the author, "the youth who was defigned for the forum, and the practice of eloquence, being now furnifhed with the liberal arts, and the advantage of a domeftic inftitution, was brought by his father or near relations to the moft celebrated orator in the city. Him he conftantly ufed to attend, and to be always prefent at his performance of any kind, either in judicial matters, or in the ordinary affemblies of the people: So that by this means he learned to engage in the laurels and contentions of the bar, and to approve himfelf a man at arms in the wars of the pleaders.

"For in that ancient conftitution of a mixed ftate, when the differences were never referred to one fupreme perfon, the orators determined matters as they pleafed, by prevailing on the minds of the ignorant multitude. Hence came the ambition of popular applaufe; Hence the great variety of laws and decrees: Hence the tedious fpeeches and harangues of the magiftrates, fometimes carried on whole nights in the roftra: Hence the frequent indictment and impleading of the powerful criminals, and the expofing of houfes to the violence and fury of the rabble: Hence the factions of the nobility, and the conftant heats and bickerings between the fenate and people. All which, though in great meafure they diftracted the commonwealth, yet had this good effect, that they exercifed and improved the eloquence of thofe times, by propofing the

"higheft

"highest rewards of that study. Because the more excellent
"any person appeared in the art of speaking, the more easily he
"arrived at honours and employments; the more he surpassed
"his colleague in the same office, the greater was his favour
"with the leading men of the city, his authority with the
"senate, and his renown and esteem among the commons.
"These men were courted and waited on by clients even of
"foreign nations: These, when they undertook the command
"of provinces, the very magistrates reverenced at their depart-
"ure, and adored at their return: These the highest offices
"of prætor or consul seemed to require and call for, and court
"their acceptance: These, when in a private station, abated
"very little of their authority, while they guided both the se-
"nate and the people by their counsel. For they took this for
"an infallible maxim, that without eloquence it was impossi-
"ble either to attain or to defend a considerable trust in the
"commonwealth: And no wonder, when they were drawn
"to business even against their will, and compelled to shew
"their parts in public. When it was reckoned but an ordina-
"ry matter to deliver one's opinion in short before the senate,
"unless a man could maintain and improve it with the en-
"gaging ornaments of wit and elegance. When if they had
"contracted an envy or suspicion, they were to answer the
"accuser's charge in person. When they could not so much
"as give their evidence, as to public matters, in writing, but
"were obliged to appear in court, and deliver it with their own
"mouth: So that there was not only a vast encouragement,
"but even a necessity of eloquence. To be a fine speaker
"was counted brave and glorious; on the other hand, to act
"only a *mute person* on the public stage was scandalous and
"reproachful. And thus a sense of honour, and desire of
"avoiding infamy, was a main incitement to their endeavours
"to these studies; lest they should be reckoned among the cli-
"ents rather than among the patrons; lest the numerous de-
"pendences transmitted to them from their ancestors should
"now at last pass into other families for want of an able sup-
"porter; lest, like a sort of useless and unprofitable creatures,
"they should either be frustrated in their pretensions to ho-
"nour and preferments, or else disgrace themselves and their
"office by the miscarriages of their administration."

Crassus and Antonius, the two chief managers of the discourse in Tully's first book *de Oratore*, are represented as very
opposite in their judgments, concerning the necessary improvements

ments of an accomplished orator. The former denies any person the honour of his name, who does not possess, in some degree, all the qualities, both native and acquired, that enter into the composition of a general scholar. The force of his argument lies in this, That an orator ought to be able to deliver himself copiously on all manner of subjects; and he does not see how any one can answer this character, without some excellency in all the mysteries of arts and learning, as well as in the happy endowments of nature. Yet he would not have these acquisitions sit so loose about him, as to be laid open to the bottom on every occasion; but that (as a great man expresseth it) they should rather be enamelled in his mind, than embossed upon it. That, as the critics in gaits and gestures will easily discover, by the comportment of a man's body, whether he has learned to dance, though he does not practise his art in his ordinary motion; so an orator, when he delivers himself on any subject, will easily make it appear whether he has a full understanding of the particular art or faculty on which the cause depends, though he does not discourse of it in the manner of a philosopher or a mechanic. Antonius, on the other hand, reflecting on the shortness of human life, and how great a part of it is commonly taken up in the attainment of but a few parts of knowledge, is inclined to believe, that oratory does not require the necessary attendance of its sister arts; but that a man may be able to prosecute a theme of any kind, without a train of sciences, and the advantages of a learned institution. That as few persons are to seek in the cultivating of their land, or the contrivance and elegance of their gardens, though they never read *Cato de Re Rustica*, or *Mago the Carthaginian*; so an orator may harangue, with a great deal of reason and truth, on a subject taken from any part of knowledge, without any further acquaintance with the nicer speculations, than his common sense and understanding, improved by experience and conversation, shall lead him to: " For who ever (says he) when he comes
" to move the affections of the judges or people, stops at this,
" that he hath not philosophy enough to dive into the first
" springs of the passions, and to discover their various na-
" tures and operations? Besides, at this rate we must quite
" lay aside the way of raising pity in the audience, by repre-
" senting the misery of a distressed party, or describing (per-
" haps) the slavery which he endures; when philosophy tells
" us,

"us, That a good man can never be miserable, and that virtue is always absolutely free."

Now as Cicero, without doubt, sat himself for the picture, which, in Crassus's name, he there draws of an orator, and therefore strengthens his arguments by his own example as well as his judgment; so Antonius, in the next dialogue, does not stick to own, that his former assertion was rather taken up for the sake of disputing and encountering his rival, than to deliver the just sentiments of his mind. And therefore, the genteel education, in the politer ages of Rome, being wholly directed to the bar, it seems probable, that no part of useful knowledge was omitted, for the improving and adorning of the main study; and that all the other arts were courted, though not with an equal passion. And upon the whole it appears, that a strange assiduity, and unwearied application, were the very life and soul of their designs. When their historians describe an extraordinary man, this always enters into his character as an essential part of it, that he was *incredibili industriâ, diligentiâ singulari;* " of incredible industry, " of singular diligence *." And Cato, in Sallust, tells the Senate, that it was not the arms so much as the industry of their ancestors, which advanced the grandeur of Rome: So that the founders and regulators of this state, in making diligence and labour necessary qualifications of a citizen, took the same course as the poets will have Jupiter to have thought on, when he succeeded to the government over the primitive mortals:

——————— *Pater ipse colendi*
Haud facilem esse viam voluit; primusque per artem
Movit agros, curis acuens mortalia corda,
Nec torpere gravi passus sua regna veterno †.

To confirm the opinion of their extreme industry and perpetual study and labour, it may not seem impertinent to instance in the three common exercises of translating, declaiming, and reciting.

Translation, the ancient orators of Rome looked on as a most useful, though a most laborious employment. All persons that applied

---

* Archbishop *Tillotson's* Sermon of Education.   † *Virg. Georg.* I.

applied themselves to the bar, commonly proposed some one orator of Greece for their constant pattern; either Lysias, Hyperides, Demosthenes, or Æschines, as their genius was inclined. Him they continually studied, and, to render themselves absolutely masters of his excellencies, were always making him speak their own tongue. This Cicero, Quintilian, and Pliny *junior*, enjoin as an indispensable duty, in order to the acquiring any talent in eloquence. And the first of these great men, besides his many versions of the orators for his private use, obliged the public with the translation of several parts of Plato and Xenophon in prose, and of Homer and Aratus in verse.

As to declaiming, this was not the only main thing at which they laboured under the masters of rhetoric, but what they practised long after they undertook real causes, and had gained a considerable name in the forum. Suetonius, in his book of Famous Rhetoricians, tells us, that Cicero declaimed in Greek till he was elected Prætor, and in Latin till near his death: That Pompey the Great, just at the breaking out of the civil war, resumed his old exercise of declaiming, that he might the more easily be able to deal with Curio, who undertook the defence of Cæsar's cause, in his public harangues: That Mark Anthony and Augustus did not lay aside this custom, even when they were engaged in the siege of Mutina: And that Nero was not only constant at his declamations, while in a private station, but for the first year after his advancement to the empire.

It is worth remarking, that the subject of these old declamations was not a mere fanciful Thesis, but a case which might probably be brought into the courts of judicature. The contrary practice, which crept into some schools after the Augustan age, to the great debasing of eloquence, is what Petronius inveighs so severely against, in the beginning of his Satyricon, in a strain so elegant, that it would lose a great part of the grace and spirit in any translation.

When I speak of recitation, I intend not to insist on the public performances of the poets in that kind, for which purpose they commonly borrowed the house of some of their noblest patrons, and carried on the whole matter before a vast concourse of people, and with abundance of ceremony. For, considering the ordinary circumstances of men of that profession, this may be thought not so much the effect of an industrious temper, as the necessary way of raising a name among the wits, and getting a tolerable livelihood. And it is evident, that, under some princes, the most celebrated of this tribe, for all their trouble and pains in proclaiming their parts to the multitude, could hardly keep themselves from starving, as Juvenal observes of Statius:

———*Sed cùm fregit subsellia versu,*
Esurit, intactam Paridi nisi vendit Agaven.

I would mean, therefore, the rehearsal of all manner of compositions in prose or verse, performed by men of some rank and quality, before they obliged the world with their publication. This was ordinarily done in a meeting of friends and acquaintance, and now and then with the admission of a more numerous audience. The design they chiefly aimed at was the correction and improvement of the piece. For the author, having a greater awe and concern upon him on these occasions than at other times, must needs take more notice of every word and sentence, while he spoke them before the company, than he did in the composure, or in the common supervisal. Besides, he had the advantage of all his friends judgments, whether intimated to him afterwards in private conference, or tacitly declared at the recital by their looks and nods, with many other tokens of dislike and approbation. In the fuller auditories he had the benefit of seeing what took or what did not take with the people; whose common suffrage was of so great authority, in this case, that Pomponius Secundus, a celebrated author of tragedies, when he consulted with his friends about the polishing any of his writings, if they happened to differ in their opinion about the elegance, justness, and propriety of any thought or expression, used always to say, *AD POPULUM PROVOCO,* I APPEAL TO THE PEOPLE, as the best deciders of the controversy [*].

The example of the young Pliny, in this practice, is very observable, and the account which we have of it is given us by himself. "I omit," says he, "no way or method that may seem "proper for correction: And first I take a strict view of what

"I

---

[*] *Plin.* Lib. 7. Epist. 17.

"I have written, and consider thoroughly of the whole piece.
"In the next place, I read it over to two or three friends;
"and soon after send it to others for the benefit of their ob-
"servations. If I am in any doubt concerning their criticisms,
"I take in the assistance of one or two besides myself to judge
"and debate the matter. Last of all, I recite before a great
"number; and this is the time that I furnish myself with the
"severest emendations *."

It might be a farther pleasure on this subject, to describe the whole institution and course of study of the most famous Romans, with their gradual advances to those virtues and attainments, which we still admire in their story. But the account which Cicero gives of himself in his Brutus, and some hints from other parts of his works, will excuse, if not commend the omission of all the rest. And it is no ordinary happiness, that we are obliged with the history of that excellent person from his own hand, whom we must certainly pitch upon for the first and greatest example, if we were beholden only to the relations of other men.

For some time after his admission to the forum, he was a constant auditor of the best pleaders, whenever they spoke in public. Every day he spent several hours in writing, reading, and improving his invention, besides the exercises he performed in the art of oratory. For the knowledge of the civil law, he applied himself with all imaginable diligence to Q. Scævola, the most celebrated professor of that science, who, though he did not make it his business to procure scholars, yet he was very ready and willing to assist such persons in this study as desired his advice and directions. It was to this Scævola that Cicero's father, when he put him on his *manly gown*, committed his son, with a strict charge never to stir from him, but on extraordinary accounts.

About the 19th year of his age, in the heat of the contention between Marius and Sylla, when the courts of judicature were shut up, and all things in confusion, Philo the prince of the academy leaving Athens, on occasion of the Mithridatic war, took up his residence in Rome. Cicero wholly resigned himself to his institution, having now fixed the bent of his thoughts and inclinations to philosophy, to which he gave the

more

* *Plin.* Lib. 7. Epist. 17.

more diligent attendance, becaufe the diſtractions of the time gave him little reaſon to hope, that the judicial procefs, and the regular courſe of the laws, would ever be reſtored to their former vigour. Yet not entirely to forſake his oratory, at the ſame time he made his applications to Molo the Rhodian, a famous pleader and maſter of rhetoric.

Sylla being now the ſecond time advanced againſt Mithridates, the city was not much diſturbed with arms for three years together. During this interval, Cicero, with unwearied diligence, made his advances day and night in all manner of learning, having now the benefit of a new inſtructor, Diodotus the ſtoic, who lived and died in his houſe. To this maſter, beſides his improvement in other uſeful parts of knowledge, he was particularly obliged for keeping him continually exerciſed in logic, which he calls a *concife and compact kind of eloquence.*

But, though engaged at the ſame time in ſo many and ſuch different faculties, he let no day ſlip without ſome performance in oratory; declaiming conſtantly with the beſt antagoniſts he could light on among the ſtudents. In this exerciſe he did not ſtick to any one language, but ſometimes made uſe of Latin, ſometimes of Greek; and indeed more frequently of the latter, either becauſe the beauties and ornaments of the Greek ſtile would by this means grow ſo natural, as eaſily to be imitated in his own tongue; or becauſe his Græcian maſters would not be ſuch proper judges of his ſtile and method, nor ſo well able to correct his failures, if he delivered himſelf in any other than their native language.

Upon Sylla's victorious return, and his ſettlement of the commonwealth, the lawyers recovered their practice, and the ordinary courſe of judicial matters was revived: And then it was that Cicero came to the bar, and undertook the patronage of public and private cauſes. His firſt oration, in a *public judgment*, was the defence of Sextus Roſcius, proſecuted by no leſs a man than the dictator himſelf, which was the reaſon that none of the old ſtaunch advocates dared appear in his behalf. Cicero carried the cauſe, to his great honour, being now about ſix or ſeven-and-twenty; and having behaved himſelf ſo remarkably well in his firſt enterpriſe, there was no buſineſs thought too weighty or difficult for his management.

He found himſelf at this time to labour under a very weak conſtitution, to which was added the natural default in his make

make, of a long and thin neck: So that in probability the labour and straining of the body, required in an orator, could not consist but with manifest danger of his life. This was especially to be feared in him, because he was observed in his pleadings to keep his voice always at the highest pitch, in a most vehement and impetuous tone, and at the same time to use a proportionable violence in his gesture and action. Upon this consideration, the physicians and his nearest friends were continually urging him to lay aside all thoughts of a profession which appeared so extremely prejudicial to his health. But Cicero shewed himself equally inflexible to the advice of the one, and to the intreaties of the other; and declared his resolution rather to run the risque of any danger that might happen, than deprive himself of the glory which he might justly challenge from the bar.

Confirming himself in this determination, he began to think, that upon altering his mode of speaking, and bringing his voice down to a lower and more moderate key, he might abate considerably of the heat and fury which now transported him, and by that means avoid the damage which seemed now to threaten his design.

For the effecting of the cure, he concluded on a journey into Greece: And so, after he had made his name very considerable in the forum, by two years pleading, he left the city. Being arrived at Athens, he took up his residence for six months with the philosopher Atticus, the wisest and most noble assertor of the old academy: And here, under the direction of the greatest master, he renewed his acquaintance with that part of learning which had been the constant entertainment of his youth, at the same time performing his exercises in oratory under the care of Demetrius the Syrian, an eminent professor of the art of speaking. After this, he made a circuit round all Asia, with several of the most celebrated orators and rhetoricians, who voluntarily offered him their company.

But not satisfied with all these advantages, he sailed to Rhodes, and there entered himself once more among the scholars of the famous Molo, whom he had formerly heard at Rome: One that, besides his admirable talent at pleading and penning, had a peculiar happiness in marking and correcting the defaults in any performance. It was to his institution that Cicero gratefully acknowledges he owed the retrenching of his juvenile heat and unbounded freedom of thought, which did not consist with the just rules of an exact and severe method.

Returning

Returning to Rome, after two years abſence, he appeared quite another man; for his body, ſtrengthened by exerciſe, was come to a tolerable habit: His way of ſpeaking ſeemed to have grown cool; and his voice was rendered much eaſier to himſelf, and much ſweeter to the audience. Thus, about the one-and-thirtieth year of his age, he arrived at that full perfection, which had ſo long taken up his whole wiſhes and endeavours, and which hath been, ever ſince, the admiration or envy of the world.

THE
Antiquities of ROME.

PART I.   BOOK I.

The Original, Growth, *and* Decay, *of the* ROMAN Commonwealth.

CHAP. I.

Of the BUILDING *of the* CITY.

WHILE we view the original of states and kingdoms, (the most delightful and surprising part of history) we easily discern, as the first and fairest prospect, the rise of the Jewish and Roman commonwealths; of which, as the former had the honour always to be esteemed the Favourite of Heaven, and the peculiar care of Divine Providence, so the other had very good pretensions to stile herself the Darling of Fortune, who seemed to express a more than ordinary fondness for this her youngest daughter, as if she had designed the three former monarchies purely for a foil to set off this latter. Their own historians rarely begin without a fit of wonder; and, before they proceed to delineate the glorious scene, give themselves the liberty of standing still some time to admire at a distance.

For the founder of the city and republic, authors have long since agreed on Romulus, the son of Rhea Sylvia, and descendant of Æneas, from whom his pedigree may be thus in short derived,

Upon

Upon the final ruin and destruction of Troy by the Græcians, Æneas, with a small number of followers, had the good fortune to secure himself by flight. His escape was very much countenanced by the enemy, inasmuch as upon all occasions he had expressed his inclinations to a peace, and to the restoring of Helen, the unhappy cause of the mischief. Sailing thus from Troy, after a tedious voyage, and great variety of adventures, he arrived at last at Latium, a part of Italy so called, *à latendo*, or from *lying hid;* being the place that Saturn had chose for his retirement, when expelled the kingdom of Crete by his rebellious son Jupiter. Here applying himself to the king of the country, at that time Latinus, he obtained his only daughter, Lavinia, in marriage; and, upon the death of his father-in law, was left in possession of the crown. He removed the imperial seat from Laurentum to Lavinium, a city which he had built himself in honour of his wife; and upon his decease soon after, the right of succession rested in Ascanius; whether his son by a former wife, and the same he brought with him from Troy, or another of that name, which he had by Lavinia, Livy leaves undetermined. Ascanius being under age, the government was entrusted in the hands of Lavinia: But as soon as he was grown up, he left his mother in possession of Lavinium; and removing with part of the men, laid the foundation of a new city along the side of the mountain Albanus, called from thence *Longa Alba*. After him, by a succession of eleven princes, the kingdom devolved at last to Procas. Procas at his death left two sons, Numitor and Amulius; of whom Amulius over-reaching his elder brother, obliged him to quit his claim to the crown, which he thereupon secured to himself; and to prevent all disturbance that might probably arise to him or his posterity from the elder family, making away with all the males, he constrained Numitor's only daughter, Rhea Sylvia, to take on her the habit of a vestal, and consequently a vow of perpetual virginity. However, the princess was soon after found with child, and delivered of two boys, Romulus and Remus. The tyrant being acquainted with the truth, immediately condemned his niece to strait imprisonment, and the infants to be exposed, or carried and left in a strange place, where it was very improbable they should meet with any relief. The servant, who had the care of this inhuman office, left the children at the bottom of a tree, by the bank of the river Tiber. In this sad condition, they were casually discovered by Faustulus, the king's shepherd; who being wholly ignorant of the plot, took the infants up, and carried them

home

home to his wife Laurentia, to be nurfed with his own children *. This wife of his had formerly been a common proftitute, called in Latin *Lupa*, which word likewife fignifying a fhe-wolf, gave occafion to the ftory of their being nurfed by fuch a beaft; tho' fome take the word always in a literal fenfe, and maintain that they really fubfifted fome time by fucking this creature, before they had the good fortune to be relieved by Fauftulus †. The boys as they grew up difcovering the natural greatnefs of their minds and thoughts, addicted themfelves to the generous exercifes of hunting, racing, taking of robbers, and fuch-like; and always expreffed a great defire of engaging in any enterprife that appeared hazardous and noble ‡. Now there happening a quarrel betwixt the herdfmen of Numitor and Amulius, the former lighting cafually on Remus, brought him before their mafter to be examined. Numitor, learning from his own mouth the ftrange circumftance of his education and fortune, eafily gueffed him to be one of his grandfons who had been expofed. He was foon confirmed in this conjecture upon the arrival of Fauftulus and Romulus; when the whole bufinefs was laid open, upon confultation had, gaining over to their party a fufficient number of the difaffected citizens, they contrived to furprife Amulius, and re-eftablifh Numitor. This defign was foon after very happily put in execution, the tyrant flain, and the old king reftored to a full enjoyment of the crown §. The young princes had no fooner re-feated their grandfather in his throne but they began to think of procuring one for themfelves. They had higher thoughts than to take up with the reverfion of a kingdom; and were unwilling to live in Alba, becaufe they could not govern there: So taking with them their fofter-father, and what others they could get together, they began the foundation of a new city, in the fame place where in their infancy they had been brought up ‖. The firft walls were fcarce finifhed when, upon a flight quarrel, the occafion of which is varioufly reported by hiftorians, the younger brother had the misfortune to be flain. Thus the whole power came into Romulus's hands; who carrying on the remainder of the work, gave the city a name in allufion to his own, and hath been ever accounted the founder and patron of the Roman commonwealth.

G 2   CHAP.

---

* Livy, *lib.* 1.   † Dempfter's note to Rofinus's antiquities, *lib.* 1. *cap.* 1.
‡ Plutarch in the life of Romulus.   § *Ibid.* and Livy, *lib.* 1.   ‖ Plutarch as before, and Livy, *lib.* 1.

CHAP. II.

Of the ROMAN *Affairs under the Kings.*

THE witty historian * had very good reason to entitle the reign of the kings the Infancy of Rome; for it is certain, that under them she was hardly able to find her own legs, and at the best had but a very feeble motion. The greatest part of Romulus's time was taken up in making laws and regulations for the commonwealth: Three of his state designs, I mean the asylum, the rape of the Sabine virgins, and his way of treating those few whom he conquered, as they far exceeded the politics of those times, so they contributed in an extraordinary degree to the advancement of the new empire. But then Numa's long reign served only for the establishment of priests and religious orders; and in those three-and-forty years † Rome gained not so much as one foot of ground. Tullus Hostilius was wholly employed in converting his subjects from the pleasing amusements of superstition to the rougher institution of martial discipline: Yet we find nothing memorable related of his conquests; only that, after a long and dubious war, the Romans entirely ruined their old mother Alba ‡. After him Ancus Martius, laying aside all thoughts of extending the bounds of the empire, applied himself wholly to strengthen and beautify the city §; and esteemed the commodiousness and magnificence of that the noblest design he could possibly be engaged in. Tarquinius Priscus, though not altogether so quiet as his predecessor, yet consulted very little else besides the dignity of the senate, and the majesty of the government; for the increase of which, he appointed the ornaments and badges of the several officers, to distinguish them from the common people ‖. A more peaceful temper appeared in Servius Tullius, whose principal study was to have an exact account of the states of the Romans; and, according to those, to divide them into tribes +, that so they might contribute with justice and proportion to the public expences of the state. Tarquin the Proud, though perhaps more engaged

---

* Florus in the preface to his history.   † Plutarch in the life of Numa.
‡ Florus, l. 1. cap. 3.   § *Idem*, l. 1. cap. 4.   ‖ *Idem*, l. 1. cap. 5.
+ Florus, l. 1. cap. 6.

engaged in wars than any of his predecessors *, yet he had in his nature such a strange composition of the most extravagant vices, as must necessarily have proved fatal to the growing tyranny; and had not the death of the unfortunate Lucretia administered to the people an opportunity of liberty, yet a far slighter matter would have served them for a specious reason, to endeavour the assertion of their rights. However, on this accident all were suddenly transported with such a mixture of fury and compassion, that, under the conduct of Brutus and Collatinus, to whom the dying lady had recommended the revenge of her injured honour †, rushing immediately upon the tyrant, they expelled him and his whole family. A new form of government was now resolved on; and, because to live under a divided power carried something of complacency in the prospect ‡, they unanimously conferred the supreme command on the two generous assertors of their liberties §. Thus ended the royal administration, after it had continued about two hundred and fifty years.

Florus, in his reflections on this first age of Rome, cannot forbear applauding the happy fate of his country, that it should be blessed, in that weak age, with a succession of princes so fortunately different in their aims and designs; as if heaven had purposely adapted them to the several exigencies of the state ‖. And the famous Machiavel is of the same opinion ╪. But a judicious author ╫ hath lately observed, that this difference of genius in the kings, was so far from procuring any advantage to the Roman people, that their small increase, under that government, is referable to no other cause. However, thus far we are assured, that those seven princes left behind them a dominion of no larger extent than that of Parma or Mantua, at present.

CHAP.

---

* *Florus*, l. 1. c. 7. † *Idem*, lib. 1. cap. 9. ‡ *Plutarch* in the Life of *Poplicola*. § *Ibid.* & *Florus*, lib. 1. cap 9. ‖ *Idem*, cap. 8. ╪ *Machiavel's* Discourses on *Livy*, lib. 2. cap. 12. ╫ Monsieur St *Evremont's* Reflections on the *Genius* of the *Roman* people, *cap.* 1.

CHAP. III.

Of the ROMAN *Affairs, from the Beginning of the Consular Government, to the first Punic War.*

THE tyrant was no sooner expelled, but, as it usually happens, there was great plotting and designing for his restoration. Among several other young noblemen, Brutus's two sons had engaged themselves in the association: But the conspiracy being happily discovered, and the traitors brought before the consuls, in order to their punishment, Brutus only addressing himself to his sons, and demanding whether they had any defence to make against the indictment, upon their silence, ordered them immediately to be beheaded; and staying himself to see the execution, committed the rest to the judgment of his colleague *. No action among the old Romans has made a greater noise than this. It would be exceeding difficult to determine, whether it proceeded from a motion of heroic virtue, or the hardness of a cruel or unnatural humour; or whether ambition had not as great a share in it as either. But though the flame was so happily stifled within the city, it soon broke out with greater fury abroad: For Tarquin was not only received with all imaginable kindness and respect by the neighbouring states, but supplied too with all necessaries, in order to the recovery of his dominions. The most powerful prince in Italy was at that time Porsenna, king of Hetruria or Tuscany; who, not content to furnish him with the same supplies as the rest, approached with a numerous army in his behalf, to the very walls of Rome †. The city was in great hazard of being taken, when an admiration of the virtue and gallant disposition of the Romans induced the besieger to a peace ‡. The most remarkable instances of this extraordinary courage, were Cocles, Mutius, and Clælia. Cocles, when the Romans were beaten back in an unfortunate sally, and the enemy made good their pursuit to the very bridge, only with the the assistance of two persons defended it against their whole power, till his own party broke it down behind; and then cast himself in his armour into the river, and swam over to the other

---

* *Plutarch.* in vita *Poplicola.* † *Idem, & Florus,* lib. I. ‡ *Plut.* in *Poplicol.*

other side *. Mutius having failed in an attempt upon Porsenna's person, and being brought before the king to be examined, thrust his right-hand, which had committed the mistake, into a pan of coals that stood ready for the sacrifice. Upon which generous action he was dismissed without farther injury. As for Clælia, she, with other noble virgins, had been delivered to the enemy for hostages, on account of a truce; when obtaining liberty to bathe themselves in the Tiber, she, getting on horseback before the rest, encouraged them to follow her thro' the water to the Romans; though the consul generously sent them back to the enemy's camp. Porsenna had no sooner drawn off his army, but the Sabines and Latins joined in a confederacy against Rome; and tho' they were extremely weakened by the desertion of Appius Claudius, who went over with five thousand families to the Romans; yet they could not be entirely subdued, till they received a fatal overthrow from Valerius Poplicola †. But the Æqui and the Volsci, the most obstinate of the Latins, and the continual enemies of Rome, carried on the remainder of the war for several years, till it was happily concluded by Lucius Quintius, the famous Dictator taken from the plough, in less than fifteen days time: Upon which Florus has this remark, That *he made more than ordinary haste to his unfinished work* ‡. But they that made the greatest opposition were the inhabitants of Veii, the head of Tuscany, a city not inferior to Rome either in store of arms, or multitude of soldiers. They had contended with the Romans, in a long series of battles, for glory and empire; but having been weakened and brought down in several encounters, they were obliged to secure themselves within their walls: And, after a ten years siege, the town was forced and sacked by Camillus §. In this manner were the Romans extending their conquests, when the irruption of the Gauls made a strange alteration in the affairs of Italy. They were at this time besieging Clusium, a Tuscan city. The Clusians sent to the Romans, desiring them to interpose by ambassadors on their behalf. Their request was easily granted; and three of the Fabii, persons of the highest rank in the city, dispatched for this purpose to the Gallic camp. The Gauls, in respect to the name of Rome, received them with all imaginable civility; but could by no means be prevailed on to quit the siege. Whereupon the ambassadors going into the town, and encouraging the Clusians to a sally, one of them was seen personally

* *Plut. ibid.* † *Ibid.* ‡ *Florus*, lib. I. cap. 11. § *Plutarch* in his Life.

sonally engaging in the action. This being contrary to the received law of nations, was resented in so high a manner by the enemy, that, breaking up from before Clusium, the whole army marched directly toward Rome. About eleven miles from the city, they met with the Roman army commanded by the military tribunes, who engaging without any order or discipline, received an entire defeat. Upon the arrival of this ill news, the greatest part of the inhabitants immediately fled: Those, that resolved to stay, fortified themselves in the capitol. The Gauls soon appeared at the city-gates; and destroying all with fire and sword, carried on the siege of the capitol with all imaginable fury. At last, resolving on a general assault, they were discovered by the cackling of geese that were kept for that purpose; and as many as had climbed the rampart were driven down by the valiant Manlius; when Camillus, setting upon them in the rear with twenty thousand men he got together about the country, gave them a total overthrow. The greatest part of those, that escaped out of the field, were cut off in straggling parties, by the inhabitants of the neighbouring towns and villages. The city had been so entirely demolished, that, upon the return of the people, they thought of removing to Veii, a city ready built, and excellently provided of all things: But being diverted from this design, by an omen (as they thought) they set to the work with such extraordinary diligence and application, that within the compass of a year the whole city was rebuilt. They had scarce gained a breathing-time after their troubles, when the united powers of Æqui, Volsci, and other inhabitants of Latium, at once invaded their territories. But they were soon overreached by a stratagem of Camillus, and totally routed *.

Nor had the Samnites any better fate, tho' a people very numerous, and of great experience in war. The contention with them lasted no less than fifty years †, when they were finally subdued by Papirius Cursor ‡. The Tarentine war that followed, put an end to the entire conquest of Italy. Tarentum, a city of great strength and beauty, seated on the Adriatic sea, was especially remarkable for the commerce it maintained with most of the neighbouring countries, as Epirus, Illyricum, Sicily, &c §. Among other ornaments of their city, they had a spacious theatre for public sports, built hard by the sea-shore. They happened to be engaged in the celebration of some such solemnity,

* *Plut.* in vit. *Camill.* † *Florus*, lib. I. cap. 16.   ‡ *Liv.* lib. 10.   § *Flor.* lib. I. cap. 18.

solemnity, when, upon sight of the Roman fleet that casually sailed by their coasts, imagining them to be enemies, they immediately set upon them, and, killing the commander, rifled the greatest part of the vessels. Ambassadors were soon dispatched from Rome to demand satisfaction: But they met with as ill a reception as the fleet, being disgracefully sent away without so much as a hearing. Upon this, a war was soon commenced between the states. The Tarentines were increased by an incredible number of allies from all parts: But he that made the greatest appearance in their behalf, was Pyrrhus, king of Epirus, the most experienced general of his time. Besides the choicest of his troops that accompanied him in the expedition, he brought into the field a considerable number of elephants, a sort of beasts scarce heard of till that time in Italy. In the first engagement, the Romans were in fair hopes of a victory, when the fortune of the day was entirely changed upon the coming up of the elephants; who made such a prodigious destruction in the Roman cavalry, that the whole army was obliged to retire. But the politic general, having experienced so well the Roman courage, immediately after the victory sent to offer conditions for a peace, but was absolutely refused. In the next battle the advantage was on the Roman side, who had not now such dismal apprehensions of the elephants as before. However, the business came to another engagement, when the elephants, over-running whole ranks of their own men, enraged by the cry of a young one that had been wounded, gave the Romans an absolute victory *. Twenty-three thousand of the enemy were killed †, and Pyrrhus finally expelled Italy. In this war the Romans had a fair opportunity to subdue the other parts that remained unconquered, under the pretext of allies to the Tarentines. So that at this time, about the 477th year of the building of the city ‡, they had made themselves the entire masters of Italy.

H CHAP.

* Florus, *ibid.*   † Eutropius, *lib.* 2.   ‡ *Ibid.*

CHAP. IV.

Of the ROMAN *Affairs from the Beginning of the first Punic War, to the first Triumvirate.*

BUT the command of the continent could not satisfy the Roman courage; especially while they saw so delicious an isle as Sicily almost within their reach: They only waited an occasion to pass the sea, when fortune presented as fair an one as they could wish. The inhabitants of Messina, a Sicilian city, made grievous complaints to the senate of the daily encroachments of the Carthaginians, a people of vast wealth and power, and that had the same design on Sicily as the Romans *. A fleet was soon manned out for their assistance; and, in two years time, no less than fifty cities were brought over †. The entire conquest of the island quickly followed; and Sardinia and Corsica were taken in about the same time by a separate squadron. And now, under the command of Regulus and Manlius, the consuls, the war was translated into Africa. Three hundred forts and castles were destroyed in their march, and the victorious legions encamped under the very walls of Carthage. The enemy, reduced to such straits, were obliged to apply themselves to Xantippus, king of the Lacedæmonians, the greatest captain of the age; who immediately marched to their assistance with a numerous and well-disciplined army. In the very first engagement with the Romans, he entirely defeated their whole power: Thirty thousand were killed on the spot, and fifteen thousand, with their consul Regulus, taken prisoners. But as good success always encouraged the Romans to greater designs, so a contrary event did but exasperate them the more. The new consuls were immediately dispatched with a powerful navy, and a sufficient number of land forces. Several campaigns were now wasted, without any considerable advantage on either side: Or if the Romans gained any thing by their victories, they generally lost as much by shipwrecks; when, at last, the whole power of both states being drawn together on the sea, the Carthaginians were finally defeated, with the loss of 125 ships sunk

in

---

* Florus, *lib.* 2. *cap.* 2. † Eutrop. *lib.* 2.

in the engagement, 73 taken; 32,000 men killed, and 13,000 prisoners. Upon this they were compelled to sue for a peace; which, after much intreaty, and upon very hard conditions, was at last obtained *.

But the Carthaginians had too great spirits to submit to such unreasonable terms any longer than their necessities obliged them. In four years time † they had got together an army of 80,000 foot and 20,000 horse ‡, under the command of the famous Hannibal; who forcing a way through the Pyrenæan mountains and the Alps, reputed till that time impassable, descended with his vast army into Italy. In four successive battles he defeated the Roman forces; in the last of which, at Cannæ, 40,000 of the latter were killed ∥; and had he not been merely cast away by the envy and ill-will of his own countrymen, it is more than possible that he must have entirely ruined the Roman state §: But supplies of men and money being sometimes absolutely denied him, and never coming but very slowly, the Romans had such opportunities to recruit, as they little expected from so experienced an adversary. The wise management of Fabius Maximus was the first revival of the Roman cause. He knew very well the strength of the enemy; and therefore marched against him without intending to hazard a battle, but to wait constantly upon him, to straiten his quarters, intercept his provisions, and so make the victorious army pine away with penury and want. With this design, he always encamped upon the high hills, where the horse could have no access to him: When they marched, he did the same; but at such a distance, as not to be compelled to an engagement. By this policy he so broke Hannibal's army, as to make him absolutely despair of getting any thing in Italy ┼. But the conclusion of the war was owing to the conduct of Scipio: He had before reduced all Spain into subjection; and, now taking the same course as Hannibal at first had done, he marched with the greatest part of the Roman forces into Africa; and, carrying all before him to the very walls of Carthage, obliged the enemy to call home their general out of Italy for the defence of the city. Hannibal obeyed; and both armies coming to an engagement, after a long dispute, wherein the commanders and soldiers of both sides are reported to have outdone themselves, the victory fell to the Romans,

H 2

* Eutrop. *lib.* 2.   † Florus, *lib.* 2. *cap.* 6.   ‡ Eutrop. *lib.* 3.   ∥ *Ibid.*
§ Cornelius Nepos *in vit* Hannibal.   ┼ Plutarch, *in vit.* Fab. Max.

mans. Whereupon the enemy were obliged once more to sue for a peace, which was again granted them, though upon much harder conditions than before.

The Romans, by the happy conclusion of this war, had so highly advanced themselves in the opinion of the neighbouring states, that the Athenians, with the greatest part of Greece, being at this time miserably enslaved by King Philip of Macedon, unanimously petitioned the senate for assistance. A fleet, with a sufficient number of land forces, was presently dispatched to their relief; by whose valour the tyrant, after several defeats, was compelled to restore all Greece to their ancient liberties, obliging himself to pay an annual tribute to the conquerors *.

Hannibal, after his late defeat, had applied himself to Antiochus, king of Syria, who at this time was making great preparations against the Romans. Acilius Glabrio was first sent to oppose him, and had the fortune to give him several defeats; when Cornelius Scipio, the Roman admiral, engaging with the king's forces at sea, under the command of Hannibal, entirely ruined the whole fleet. Which victory being immediately followed by another as signal at land, the effeminate prince was contented to purchase a peace at the price of almost half his kingdom †.

The victorious Romans had scarce concluded the public rejoicings on account of the late success, when the death of king Philip of Macedon presented them with an occasion of a more glorious triumph. His son Perses, that succeeded, resolving to break with the senate, applied himself wholly to raising forces, and procuring other necessaries for a war. Never were greater appearances on the field than on both sides, most of the considerable princes in the world being engaged in this quarrel. But fortune still declared for the Romans, and the greatest part of Perses's prodigious army was cut off by the consul Æmilius, and the king obliged to surrender himself into the hands of the conqueror ‡. Authors that write of the four monarchies, here fix the end of the Macedonian empire.

But Rome could not think herself secure amongst all these conquests, while her old rival Carthage was yet standing: So that, upon a slight provocation, the city, after three years siege, was taken, and utterly razed, by the valour of Publius Scipio, grandson, by adoption, to him that conquered Hannibal ‖.

Not

---

* Eutrop. *l.* 4.   † Florus, *l.* 2. *cap.* 8.   ‡ Vell. Paterc. *l.* 1.   ‖ *Ibid.*

Not long after, Attalus, king of Pergamus, dying without issue, left his vast territories to the Romans *. And what of Africa remained unconquered, was for the most part reduced in the Jugurthine war that immediately followed; Jugurtha himself, after several defeats, being taken prisoner by Marius, and brought in triumph to Rome †.

And now after the defeat of the Teutones and Cimbri, that had made an inroad into Italy, with several lesser conquests in Asia and other parts, the Mithridatic war, and the civil war between Marius and Sylla, broke out both in the same year ‡. Sylla had been sent general against Mithridates king of Pontus, who had seized on the greatest part of Asia and Achaia in an hostile manner; when, before he was got out of Italy, Sulpicius, the tribune of the people, and one of Marius's faction, preferred a law to recal him, and to depute Marius in his room. Upon this, Sylla, leading back his army, and overthrowing Marius and Sulpicius in his way, having settled affairs at Rome, and banished the authors of the late sedition, returned to meet the foreign enemy ‖. His first exploit was the taking of Athens, and ruining the famous mole in the haven § Piræus. Afterwards, in two engagements, he killed and took near 130,000 of the enemy, and compelled Mithridates to sue for a truce ⊹. In the mean time, Marius, being called home by the new consuls, had exercised all manner of cruelty at Rome; whereupon, taking the opportunity of the truce, Sylla once more marched back towards Italy. Marius was dead before his return ++; but his two sons, with the consuls, raised several armies to oppose him. But some of the troops being drawn over to his party, and the others routed, he entered the city, and disposed all things at his pleasure, assuming the title and authority of a perpetual dictator. But having regulated the state, he laid down that office, and died in retirement =.

Mithridates had soon broke the late truce, and invaded Bithynia and Asia with as great fury as ever; when the Roman general, Lucullus, routing his vast armies by land and sea, chased them quite out of Asia; and had infallibly put an happy conclusion to the war, had not fortune reserved that glory for Pompey ↶. He being deputed in the room of Lucullus, after the defeat of the new forces of Mithridates, compelled him to fly

---

* Eutrop. *lib.* 4. † *Ibid.* ‡ Eutrop. *lib.* 5. ‖ *Ibid.* § Vell. Paterc. *lib.* 2. ⊹ Eutrop. *lib.* 5. ++ Vell. Patrec. *lib.* 2. = Aurelius Victor. *in vit.* Sylla. ↶ Vell. Paterc. *ibid.*

fly to his father-in-law Tigranes, king of Armenia. Pompey followed with his army; and struck such a terror into the whole kingdom, that Tigranes was constrained, in a humble manner, to present himself to the general, and offer his realm and fortune to his disposal. At this time the Catilinarian conspiracy broke out, more famous for the obstinacy than the number of the rebels; but this was immediately extinguished by the timely care of Cicero, and the happy valour of Antony. The senate, upon the news of the extraordinary success of Pompey, were under some apprehension of his affecting the supreme command at his return, and altering the constitution of the government. But when they saw him dismiss his vast army at Brundusium, and proceed in the rest of his journey to the city, with no other company than his ordinary attendants, they received him with all the expressions of complacency and satisfaction, and honoured him with a splendid triumph *.

C H A P. V.

Of the ROMAN *Affairs, from the Beginning of the first Triumvirate, to the End of the Twelve Cæsars.*

THE three persons that at this time bore the greatest sway in the state, were Crassus, Pompey, and Cæsar. The first, by reason of his prodigious wealth; Pompey, for his power with the soldiers and senate; and Cæsar, for his admirable eloquence, and a peculiar nobleness of spirit. When now taking advantage of the consulship of Cæsar, they entered into a solemn agreement to let nothing pass in the commonwealth without their joint approbation †. By virtue of this alliance, they had in a little time procured themselves the three best provinces in the empire, Crassus Asia, Pompey Spain, and Cæsar Gaul. Pompey, for the better retaining his authority in the city, chose to manage his province by deputies ‡; the other two entered on their governments in person. But Crassus soon after, in an expedition he undertook against the Parthians, had the ill fortune to lose the greatest part of his army, and was himself treacherously

* Vell. Paterc. *ib.* † Suet. in Jul. Cæs. *cap.* 19. ‡ Paterc. *lib.* 2. *cap.* 48.

rously murdered *. In the mean time, Cæsar was performing wonders in Gaul. No less than 40,000 of the enemy he had killed, and taken more prisoners; and nine years together (which was the whole time of his government) deserved a triumph for the actions of every campaign †. The senate, amazed at the strange relation of his victories, were easily inclined to suspect his power: So that taking the opportunity when he petitioned for a second consulship, they ordered him to disband his army, and appear as a private person at the election ‡. Cæsar endeavoured by all means to come to an accommodation: But finding the senate violently averse to his interest, and resolved to hear nothing but what they first proposed ‖, he was constrained to march towards Italy with his troops, to terrify or force them into a compliance. Upon the news of his approach, the senate, with the greatest part of the nobility, passing over into Greece, he entered the city without opposition, and, creating himself consul and dictator, hasted with his army into Spain; where the troops under Pompey's deputies were compelled to submit themselves to his disposal. With this reinforcement he advanced towards Macedonia, where the senate had got together a prodigious army under the command of Pompey. In the first engagement he received a considerable defeat: But the whole power on both sides being drawn up on the plains of Thessaly, after a long dispute the victory fell to Cæsar, with the entire ruin of the adverse party. Pompey fled directly towards Egypt, and Cæsar with his victorious legions immediately followed. Hearing at his arrival that Pompey had been killed by order of King Ptolemy, he laid close siege to Alexandria, the capital city; and having made himself absolute master of the kingdom, committed it to the care of Cleopatra, sister to the late king §. Scipio and Juba he soon after overcame in Africa, and Pompey's two sons in Spain ╪. And now being received at his return with the general applause of the people and senate, and honoured with the glorious titles of *Father of his country*, and *Perpetual Dictator*, he was designing an expedition into Parthia, when, after the enjoyment of the supreme command no more than five months, he was murdered in the senate-house ⁕; Brutus and Cassius, with most of the other conspirators, being his particular friends, and such as he had obliged in the highest manner.

A civil

* Plutarch in Crasso. † Paterc. l. 2. ‡ Ibid. c. 49. ‖ Ibid. c. eod.
§ Suet. in Jul. Cæs. c. 35. ╪ Ibid. c. eod. ⁕ Paterc. l. 2. c. 56.

A civil war necessarily followed, in which the senate, consisting for the most part of such as had embraced the faction of Pompey, declared in favour of the assassins, while Mark Antony the consul undertook the revenge of Cæsar. With this pretence, he exercised all manner of tyranny in the city, and had no other design but to secure the chief command to himself. At last the senate were obliged to declare him an enemy to the state; and, in pursuance of their edict, raised an army to oppose him, under the command of Hirtius and Pansa the new consuls, and Octavius, nephew and heir to Cæsar *. In the first engagement Antony was defeated; but Hirtius being killed in the fight, and Pansa dying immediately after, the sole command of the army came into the hands of Octavius †. The senate, before the late victory, had expressed an extraordinary kindness for him, and honoured him with several marks of their particular esteem: But now being freed from the danger they apprehended from Antony, they soon altered their measures; and, taking little notice of him any longer, decreed to the two heads of the late conspiracy, Brutus and Cassius, the two provinces of Syria and Macedonia, whither they had retired upon commission of the fact ‡. Octavius was very sensible of their designs, and thereupon was easily induced to conclude a peace with Antony; and soon after entering into an association with him and Lepidus, as his uncle had done with Crassus and Pompey, he returned to Rome, and was elected consul when under twenty years of age ‖. And now, by the power of him and his two associates, the old senate was for the most part banished, and a law preferred by his colleague Pedius, That all who had been concerned in the death of Cæsar should be proclaimed enemies to the commonwealth, and proceeded against with all extremity §. To put this order into execution, Octavius and Antony advanced with the forces under their command toward Macedonia, where Brutus and Cassius had got together a numerous army to oppose them; both parties meeting near the city Philippi, the traitors were defeated, and the two commanders died soon after by their own hands ⸸. And now for ten years all affairs were managed by the Triumviri; when Lepidus, setting up for himself in Sicily, was contented, upon the arrival of Octavius, to compound for his life, with the dishonourable resignation of his share in the government ⁑. The friend-

---

* Paterc. *l.* 2. *c.* 61. † Suet. in August. *c.* 11. ‡ Florus, *l.* 4. *c.* 7.
‖ Paterc. *l.* 2. *c.* 65. § Ibid. ⸸ Florus, *l.* 2. *c.* 7. ⁑ Paterc. *l.* 2. *c.* 80.

friendship of Octavius and Antony was not of much longer continuance: For the latter being, for several enormities, declared an enemy to the State, was finally routed in a sea-engagement at Actium; and, flying thence with his mistress Cleopatra, killed himself soon after, and left the sole command in the hands of Octavius. He, by his prudence and moderation, gained such an entire interest in the Senate and people, that when he offered to lay down all the authority he was invested with above the rest, and to restore the commonwealth to the ancient constitution, they unanimously agreed in this opinion, That their liberty was sooner to be parted with, than so excellent a Prince. However, to avoid all offence, he rejected the very names he thought might be displeasing, and above all things, the title of *Dictator*, which had been so odious in Sylla and Cæsar. By this means he was the founder of that government which continued ever after in Rome. The new acquisitions to the empire were, in his time, very considerable; Cantabria, Aquitania, Panonia, Dalmatia, and Illyricum being wholly subdued: The Germans were driven beyond the river Albis, and two of their nations, the Suevi and Sicambri, transplanted into Gaul *.

Tiberius, though in Augustus's time he had given proofs of an extraordinary courage in the German war †, yet, upon his own accession to the crown, is memorable for no exploit but the reducing of Cappadocia into a Roman province ‡; and this was owing more to his cunning than his valour. And at last, upon his infamous retirement into the island Capreæ, he grew so strangely negligent of the public affairs, as to send no lieutenants for the government of Spain and Syria, for several years; to let Armenia be over-run by the Parthians, Mœsia by the Dacians and the Sarmatians, and almost all Gaul by the Germans; to the extreme danger as well as dishonour of the empire §. Caligula, as he far exceeded his predecessor in all manner of debauchery, so, in relation to martial affairs, was much his inferior. However, he is famous for a mock-expedition that he made against the Germans; when, arriving in that part of the Low Countries which is opposite to Britain, and receiving into his protection a fugitive prince of the island, he sent glorious letters to the Senate, giving an account of the happy conquest of the whole kingdom ||. And soon after making his soldiers fill their helmets with cockle-shells and pebbles,

which

---

* Sueton. in August. *c.* 21.   † Paterc. *l.* 2. *cap.* 106. &c.   ‡ Eutrop. *l.* 7.
§ Sueton. in Tib. *cap.* 41. || Sueton. in Calig. *cap.* 46.

which he called, *The Spoils of the Ocean* *, returned to the city to demand a triumph. And when that honour was denied him by the Senate, he broke out into such extravagant cruelties, that he even compelled them to cut him off, for the security of their own persons †. Nay, he was so far from entertaining any desire of benefiting the public, that he often complained of his ill fortune, because no signal calamity happened in his time, and made it his constant wish, That either the utter destruction of an army, or some plague, famine, earthquake, or other extraordinary desolation, might continue the memory of his reign to succeeding ages ‡.

Caligula being taken off, the Senate assembled in the capitol, to debate about the extinguishing the name and family of the Cæsars, and restoring the commonwealth to the old constitution §. When one of the soldiers, that were ransacking the palace, lighting casually upon Claudius, uncle to the late emperor, where he had hid himself in a corner behind the hangings, pulled him out to the rest of his gang, and recommended him as the fittest person in the world to be emperor. All were strangely pleased at the motion; and, taking him along with them by force, lodged him among the guards ‖. The Senate, upon the first information, sent immediately to stop their proceedings: But not agreeing among themselves, and hearing the multitude call out for one governor, they were at last constrained to confirm the election of the soldiers; especially since they had pitched upon such an easy prince as would be wholly at their command and disposal ╪. The conquest of Britain was the most memorable thing in his time; owing partly to an expedition that he made in person, but chiefly to the valour of his lieutenants Osorius, Scapula, Aulus Plautius, and Vespasian. The bounds of the empire were in his reign as followeth; Mesopotamia in the east, the Rhine and Danube in the north, Mauritania in the south, and Britain in the West ⁑.

The Roman arms cannot be supposed to have made any considerable progress under Nero; especially when Suetonius tells us, he neither hoped nor desired the enlargement of the empire ↺. However, two countries were in his time reduced into Roman provinces; the kingdom of Pontus, and the Cottian Alps, or that part of the mountains which divides Dauphiné and Piedmont. Britain and Armenia were once both lost ⚌, and not

without

---

* *Idem, cap.* 45. † *Idem, cap.* 47. ‡ *Idem, cap.* 49 & 56. § *Idem, cap.* 31. ‖ *Idem, cap.* 60. ╪ *Idem,* in Claud. *cap.* 10. ⁑ *Aurelius Victor de Cæsaribus in Caligula.* ↺ *Aurelius Victor de Cæsaribus in Claud.* ⚌ *Sueton. in Nerone, cap.* 18.

without great difficulty recovered. And indeed, his averseness to the camp made him far more odious to the soldiers, than all his other vices to the people: So that when the citizens had the patience to endure him for fourteen years, the army under Galba, his lieutenant in Spain, were constrained to undertake his removal.

Galba is acknowledged on all hands for the great reformer of martial discipline; and though, before his accession to the empire, he had been famous for his exploits in Germany, and other parts *, yet the shortness of his reign hindered him from making any advancements afterwards. His age and severity were the only causes of his ruin: The first of which rendered him contemptible, and the other odious. And the remedy he used to appease these dissatisfactions did but ripen them for revenge. For immediately upon his adopting Piso, by which he hoped to have pacified the people, Otho, who had ever expected that honour, and was now enraged at his disappointment †, upon application made to the soldiers, easily procured the murder of the old prince and his adopted son; and by that means was himself advanced to the imperial dignity.

About the same time the German army under Vitellius having an equal aversion to the old emperor with those of Rome, had sworn allegiance to their own commander. Otho, upon the first notice of their designs, had sent to offer Vitellius an equal share in the government with himself ‡. But all proposals for an accommodation being refused, and himself compelled, as it were, to march against the forces that were sent towards Italy, he had the good fortune to defeat them in three small engagements. But having been worsted in a greater fight, at Bebriacum, though he had still sufficient strength for carrying on the war, and expected daily a reinforcement from several parts §, yet he could not, by all the arguments in the world, be prevailed with to hazard another battle; but, to end the contention, killed himself with his own hands. On this account Pagan authors, though they represent his life as the most exact picture of unmanly softness, yet they generally confess his death equal to the noblest of antiquity; and the same poet ‖, that has given him the lasting title of Mollis Otho, has yet set him in competition with the famous Cato, in reference to the final action of his life.

It

---

* Suet. in Galb. cap. 8. † Idem, cap. 17. ‡ Sueton. in Otho. cap. 8.
§ Ibid. cap. 9. ‖ Martial.

It has been observed of Vitellius, that he obtained the empire by the sole valour of his lieutenants, and lost it purely on his own account. His extreme luxury and cruelty were for this reason the more detestable, because he had been advanced to that dignity, under the notion of the patron of his country, and the restorer of the rights and liberties of the people. Within eight months time the provincial armies had unanimously agreed on Vespasian * for their emperor; and the tyrant, after he had been strangely mangled by the extreme fury of the soldiers and rabble, was at last dragged into the river Tyber †.

The republic was so far from making any advancement under the disturbances of the three last reigns, that she must necessarily have felt the fatal consequences of them, had she not been seasonably relieved by the happy management of Vespasian. It was a handsome turn of some of his friends, when, by order of Caligula, his bosom had, by way of punishment, been stuffed with dirt, to put this interpretation on the accident, that the commonwealth being miserably abused, and even *trodden under foot*, should hereafter *fly to his bosom* for protection ‡. And indeed, he seems to have made it his whole care and design to reform the abuses of the city and state, occasioned by the licentiousness of the late times. Nine provinces he added to the empire §, and was so very exact in all circumstances of his life and conduct, that one, who has examined them both with all the niceness imaginable, can find nothing in either that deserves reprehension, except an immoderate desire of riches ‖. And he covertly excuses him for this, by extolling at the same time his extraordinary magnificence and liberality ┴.

But perhaps he did not more oblige the world by his own reign, than by leaving so admirable a successor as his son Titus; the only prince in the world that has the character of never doing an ill action. He had given sufficient proof of his courage in the famous siege of Jerusalem, and might have met with as good success in other parts, had he not been prevented by an untimely death, to the universal grief of mankind.

But then Domitian so far degenerated from the two excellent examples of his father and brother, as to seem more emulous

of

---

* Sueton. in Vitell. *cap*. 15.   † *Id. ib. cap.* 17.   ‡ Sueton. in Vespas. *cap*. 5.
§ Eutrop. *lib.* 7.   ‖ *Id. ib. cap.* 16.   ┴ *Id. ib. cap.* 17. 18.

of copying Nero and Caligula. However, as to martial affairs, he was as happy as most of his predecessors, having, in four expeditions, subdued the Catti, Daci, and the Sarmatians, and extinguished a civil war in the first beginning *. By this means, he had so entirely gained the affections of the soldiers, that when we meet with his nearest relations, and even his very wife engaged in his murder †, yet we find the army so extremely dissatisfied, as to have wanted only a leader to revenge his death ‡.

* Sueton. in Domit. *cap.* 6   † *Id ib. cap.* 14.   ‡ *Id. ib. cap.* 23.

C H A P. VI.

Of the ROMAN *Affairs from Domitian to the End of Constantine the Great.*

THE two following emperors have been deservedly stiled the restorers of the Roman grandeur; which, by reason of the viciousness or negligence of the former princes, had been extremely impaired.

Nerva, though a person of extraordinary courage and virtue, yet did not enjoy the empire long enough to be on any other account so memorable, as for substituting so admirable a successor in his room as Trajan.

It was he, that for the happiness which attended his undertakings, and for his just and regular administration of the government, has been set in competition even with Romulus himself. It was he that advanced the bounds of the empire farther than all his predecessors; reducing into Roman provinces the five vast countries of Dacia, Assyria, Armenia, Mesopotamia, and Arabia *. And yet his prudent management in peace has been generally preferred to his exploits in war; his justice, candour, and liberality having gained him such an universal esteem and veneration, that he was even deified before his death.

Adrian's

* Eutrop. *lib.* 8.

Adrian's character was generally more of the scholar than the soldier; upon which account, as much as out of envy to his predecessor, he slighted three of the provinces that had been taken by Trajan, and was contented to fix the bounds of the empire at the river Euphrates *. But perhaps he is the first of the Roman emperors that ever took a circuit round his dominions, as we are assured he did †.

Antoninus Pius studied more the defence of the empire than the enlargement of it. However, his admirable prudence, and strict reformation of manners, rendered him perhaps as serviceable to the commonwealth as the greatest conquerors.

The two Antonini, Marcus and Lucius, were they that made the first division of the empire. They are both famous for a successful expedition against the Parthians: And the former, who was the longest liver, is especially remarkable for his extraordinary learning, and strict profession of Stoicism; whence he has obtained the name of *the Philosopher*.

Commodus was as noted for all manner of extravagancies, as his father had been for the contrary virtues, and, after a very short enjoyment of the empire, was murdered by one of his mistresses ‡.

Pertinax too was immediately cut off by the soldiers, who found him a more rigid exactor of discipline than they had been lately used to. And now claiming to themselves the privilege of choosing an emperor, they fairly exposed the dignity to sale §.

Didius Julian was the highest bidder, and was thereupon invested with the honour. But as he only exposed himself to ridicule, by such a mad project, so he was in an instant made away with, in hopes of another bargain. Zosimus makes him no better than a sort of an emperor in a dream ‖.

But the Roman valour and discipline were in a great measure restored by Severus. Besides a famous victory over the Parthians, the old enemies of Rome, he subdued the greatest part of Persia and Arabia, and marching into this island, Britain, delivered the poor natives from the miserable tyranny of the Scots and Picts; which an excellent historian ‡ calls the greatest honour of his reign.

Antoninus Caracalla had as much of a martial spirit in him as his father, but died before he could design any thing memorable,

---

* Eutrop. *lib.* 8.   † *Id. ibid.*   ‡ Zosimus, Hist. lib. 1.   § *Ibid.*   ‖ *Ibid.*
‡ Ælius Spartan. in Sever.

rable, except an expedition against the Parthians, which he had just undertaken.

Opilius Macrinus and his son Diadumen had made very little noise in the world, when they were cut off without much disturbance, to make room for Heliogabalus, son of the late emperor.

If he was extremely pernicious to the empire by his extravagant debaucheries, his successor Alexander Severus was as serviceable to the state in restoring justice and discipline. His noblest exploit was an expedition against the Persians, in which he overcame their famous king Xerxes *.

Maximin, the first that from a common soldier aspired to the empire, was soon taken off by Pupienus, and he, with his colleague Balbinus, quickly followed, leaving the supreme command to Gordian, a prince of great valour and fortune, and who might probably have extinguished the very name of the Persians †, had he not been treacherously murdered by Philip, who, within a very little time, suffered the like fortune himself.

Decius, in the former part of his reign, had been very successful against the Scythians and other barbarous nations; but was at last killed, together with his son, in an unfortunate engagement ‡.

But then Gallus not only struck up a shameful league with the Barbarians, but suffered them to over-run all Thrace, Thessally, Macedon, Greece, §, &c.

They were just threatning Italy, when his successor Æmilian chaced them off with a prodigious slaughter: And, upon his promotion to the empire, promised the Senate to recover all the Roman territories that had been entirely lost, and to clear those that were over-run ‖. But he was prevented after three months reign, by the common fate of the emperors of that time.

After him Valerian was so unfortunate as to lose the greater part of his army in an expedition against the Persians, and to be kept prisoner himself in that country till the time of his death ╪.

Upon the taking of Valerian by the Persians, the management of affairs was committed to his son Gallienus; a prince so extremely negligent and vicious, as to become the equal scorn

---

* Eutrop. *lib.* 8.   † Pompon. Laetus in Gordian.   ‡ *Idem*, in Decio.
§ *Idem*, in Gallo.   ‖ *Idem*, *ibid*.   ╪ *Idem*, in Valeriano.

scorn and contempt of both sexes * : The loosenefs of his government gave occasion to the usurpation of the thirty tyrants, of whom some indeed truly deserved that name ; others were persons of great courage and virtue, and very serviceable to the commonwealth †. In his time the Almains, after they had wasted all Gaul, broke into Italy. Dacia, which had been gained by Trajan, was entirely lost ; all Greece, Macedon, Pontus, and Asia, over-run by the Goths. The Germans too had proceeded as far as Spain, and taken the famous city Tarraco, now Tarragona in Catalonia ‡.

This desperate state of affairs was in some measure redressed by the happy conduct of Claudius, who, in less than two years time, routed near three hundred thousand Barbarians, and put an entire end to the Gothic war : Nor were his other accomplishments inferior to his valour ; an elegant historian § having found in him the virtue of Trajan, the piety of Antoninus, and the moderation of Augustus.

Quintilius was, in all respects, comparable to his brother ; whom he succeeded, not on account of his relation, but his merits ‖. But reigning only seventeen days, it was impossible he could do any thing more than raise an expectation in the world.

If any of the Barbarians were left within the bounds of the empire by Claudius, Aurelian entirely chaced them out. In one single war he is reported to have killed a thousand of the Sarmatians with his own hands ┼. But his noblest exploit was, the conquering the famous Zenobia, queen of the East (as she styled herself) and the taking her capital city Palmyra. At his return to Rome there was scarce any nation in the world, out of which he had not a sufficient number of captives to grace his triumph : The most considerable were the Indians, Arabians, Goths, Franks, Suevians, Saracens, Vandals, and Germans ++.

Tacitus was contented to shew his moderation and justice, in the quiet management of the empire, without any hostile design : Or, had he expressed any such inclinations, his short reign must necessarily have hindered their effect.

Probus, to the wise government of his predecessor, added the valour and conduct of a good commander : It was he that obliged the barbarous nations to quit all their footing in Gaul, Illyricum,

---

* Trebell. Pollio in Tyran.   † *Id.* in Gallieno.   ‡ Eutrop. *l.* 9.   § Trebell. Pollio in Claud.   ‖ *Ibid.*   ┼ Flavius Vopisc. in Aureliano.   ++ *Ibid.*

uch, that
g the dif-
inſt their
eace *.
arus, ex-
ertook an
gements,

oppoſite a
lt, the o-
cherouſly
emperor
y fortune
erors; ſo
and Ar-
pare him
ercules.
than moſt
moſt part

very re-
r, as the
of his two
empire to
iniſtration
EAT, an
reſpect he
e imperial
to the ut-

HAP.

ponius Lætus in

Illyricum, and several provinces of the empire; insomuch, that the very Parthians sent him flattering letters, confessing the dismal apprehensions they entertained of his designs against their country, and beseeching him to favour them with a peace *.

There was scarce any enemy left to his successor Carus, except the Persians; against whom he accordingly undertook an expedition: But, after two or three successful engagements, died with the stroke of a thunderbolt †.

His two sons, Carinus and Numerian, were of so opposite a genius, that one is generally represented as the worst, the other as the best of men. Numerian was soon treacherously murdered by Aper; who, together with the other emperor Carinus, in a very little time gave way to the happy fortune of Dioclesian, the most successful of the latter emperors; so famous for his prodigious exploits in Egypt, Persia, and Armenia, that a Roman author ‡ has not stuck to compare him with Jupiter, as he does his son Maximinian with Hercules.

Constantius Chlorus, and Galerius, were happier than most of their predecessors, by dying, as they had for the most part lived, in peace.

Nor are Severus and Maximilian on any account very remarkable, except for leaving so admirable a successor, as the famous *CONSTANTINE;* who, ridding himself of his two competitors, Licinius and Maxentius, advanced the empire to its ancient grandeur. His happy wars and wise administration in peace, have gained him the surname of *The GREAT*, an honour unknown to former emperors: Yet in this respect he is justly reputed unfortunate, that, by removing the imperial seat from Rome to Constantinople, he gave occasion to the utter ruin of Italy.

CHAP.

---

* *Flavius Vopisc.* in *Probo.* vita ejus. † *Idem* in *Caro.* ‡ *Pomponius Lætus* in

CHAP. VII.

Of the ROMAN *Affairs from* Constantine *the Great, to the taking of* ROME *by* Odoacer, *and the Ruin of the Western Empire.*

THOUGH the three sons of Constantine at first divided the empire into three distinct principalities, yet it was afterwards re-united under the longest survivor, Constantius. The wars between him and Magnentius, as they proved fatal to the tyrant, so were they extremely prejudicial to the whole state; which at this time was involved in such unhappy difficulties, as to be very unable to bear so excessive loss of men, no less than 54,000 being killed on both sides *. And perhaps this was the chief reason of the ill success which constantly attended that emperor in the eastern wars: For the Persians were all along his superiors; and when at last a peace was concluded, the advantage of the conditions lay on their side.

Julian, as he took effectual care for the security of the other bounds of the empire, so his designs against the most formidable enemies, the Persians, had all appearance of success; but that he lost his life before they could be fully put in execution.

Jovian was no sooner elected emperor, but, being under some apprehension of a rival in the west, he immediately struck up a most dishonourable peace with the Persians, at the price of the famous city Nisibis, and all Mesopotamia. For which base action, as he does not fail of an invective from every historian, so particularly Ammianus Marcellinus † and Zosimus have taken the pains to show, that he was the first Roman governor who resigned up the least part of their dominions upon any account.

Valentinian the First has generally the character of an excellent prince: But he seems to have been more studious of obliging his subjects, by an easy and quiet government, than desirous of acting any thing against the encroaching enemies.

Gratian

---

* *Pompon. Lætus.* † *Lib.* 25.

Gratian too, tho' a prince of great courage and experience in war, was able to do no more than to settle the single province of Gaul: But he is extremely applauded by historians for taking such extraordinary care in the business of a successor: For being very sensible how every day produced worst effects in the empire, and that the state, if not at the last gasp, yet was very nigh beyond all hopes of recovery; he made it his whole study to find out a person that should, in all respects, be capacitated for the noble work of the deliverance of his country. The man he pitched upon was Theodosius, a native of Spain; who, being now invested with the command of the east, upon the death of Gratian, remained sole emperor. And, indeed, in a great measure, he answered the expectation of the world, proving the most resolute defender of the empire in its declining age. But for his colleague Valentinian the Second, he was cut off without having done any thing that deserves our notice.

Under Honorius things returned to their former desperate state, the barbarous nations getting ground on all sides, and making every day some diminution in the empire; 'till, at last, Alaric, king of the Goths, wasting all Italy, proceeded to Rome itself; and being contented to set a few buildings on fire, and rifle the treasuries, retired with his army * : So that this is rather a disgrace than a destruction of the city. And Nero is supposed to have done more mischief when he set it on fire in jest, than it now suffered from the barbarous conqueror.

Valentinian the Third, at his accession to the empire, gave great hopes of his proving the author of a happy revolution † ; and he was very fortunate in the war against the famous Attilla the Hun; but his imprudence, in putting to death his best commander Ætius, hastened very much the ruin of the Roman cause, the barbarous nations now carrying all before them, without any considerable opposition.

By this time the state was given over as desperate; and what princes followed 'till the taking of the city by Odoacer, were only a company of miserable, short-lived tyrants, remarkable for nothing but the meanness of their extraction, and the poorness of their government; so that historians generally pass them over in silence, or at most with the bare mention of their names.

---

* *Paul. Diacon. & Pompon. Let.*   † *Pompon. Let.*

The best account of them we can meet with is as follows: Maximus, who, in order to his own promotion, had procured the murder of Valentinian, soon after compelled his widow Eudoxia to accept of him as a husband; when the empress, entertaining a mortal hatred for him on many accounts, sent to Genseric, a famous king of the Vandals, and a confederate of the late emperor's, desiring his assistance for the deliverance of herself and the city, from the usurpation of the tyrant. Genseric easily obeyed; and, landing with a prodigious army in Italy, entered Rome without any opposition; where, contrary to his oath and promise, he seized on all the wealth, and carried it, with several thousands of the inhabitants, into Africa *.

Avitus, the general in Gaul, was the next that took upon him the name of emperor, which he resigned within eight months †.

Majorianus succeeded; and after three years left the honour to Severus, or Severian; who had the happiness, after four years reign, to die a natural death ‡.

After him, Anthemius was elected emperor, who lost his life and dignity in a rebellion of his son-in-law Ricimer §. And then Olybrius was sent from Constantinople too, with the same authority; but died within seven months ‖.

Liarius, or Glycerius, who had been elected in his room by the soldiers, was immediately almost deposed by Nepos; and he himself quickly after by Orestes ╪; who made his son Augustus, or Augustulus, emperor. And now Odoacer, king of the Heruli, with an innumerable multitude of the barbarous nations, ravaging all Italy, approached to Rome, and entering the city without any resistance, and deposing Augustulus, secured the imperial dignity to himself; and though he was forced afterwards to give place to Theodoric the Goth, yet the Romans had never after the least command in Italy.

THE

---

* Paul. Diacon. & Evagrius Hist. Eccles. lib. 2. cap. 7   † Id ibid.
‡ Paul. Diacon. lib. 16.   § Ibid.   ‖ Ibid.   ╪ Jornandes de Regn. Success.

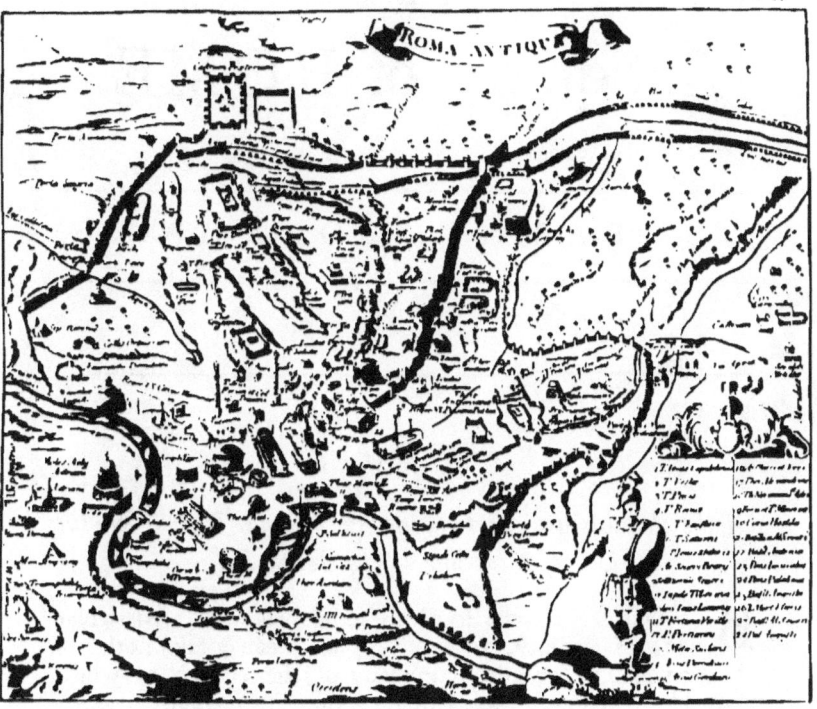

THE
Antiquities of ROME.

PART II. BOOK I.

Of the CITY.

CHAP. I.

Of the Pomœrium, *and of the Form and Bigness of the* CITY, *according to the Seven Hills.*

BEFORE we come to please ourselves with a particular view of the city, we must, by all means, take notice of the Pomœrium, for the singularity of the custom to which it owed its original. Livy defines the Pomœrium, in general, to be the space of ground, both within and without the walls, which the augurs, at the first building of cities, solemnly consecrated, and on which no edifices were suffered to be raised *. But the account which Plutarch gives us of this matter, in reference to Rome itself, is sufficient to satisfy our curiosity; and is delivered by him to this purpose: Romulus having sent for some of the Tuscans, to instruct him in the ceremonies to be observed in laying the foundations of his new city, the work was begun in this manner:

First, They dug a trench, and threw into it the first-fruits of all things, either good by custom, or necessary by nature: And every man taking a small turf of earth of the country from whence he came, they all cast them in promiscuously together; making this trench their centre, they described the city in a circle round it: Then the founder fitted to a plough
a brasen

* *Liv.* lib. 1.

a brasen plough-share; and yoking together a bull and a cow, drew a deep line or furrow round the bounds; those that followed after taking care that all the clods fell inwards toward the city. They built the wall upon this line, which they called *Pomœrium,* from *Pone Mœnia* *. Though the phrase of *Pomœrium proferre* be commonly used in authors to signify the enlarging of the city, yet it is certain the city might be enlarged without that ceremony. For Tacitus and Gellius declare no person to have had a right of extending the Pomœrium, but such an one as had taken away some part of an enemy's country in war; whereas it is manifest, that several great men, who never obtained that honour, increased the buildings with considerable additions.

It is remarkable, that the same ceremony, with which the foundations of their cities were at first laid, they used too in destroying and rasing places taken from the enemy; which we find was begun by the chief commander's turning up some of the walls with a plough †.

As to the form and bigness of the city, we must follow the common direction of the seven hills, whence came the phrase of *Urbs Septicollis,* and the like, so frequent with the poets.

Of these Mons Palatinus has ever had the preference; whether so called from the people Palantes, or Palatini; or from the bleating and strolling of cattle, in Latin, *Balare* and *Palare;* or from *Pales,* the pastoral goddess; or from the burying-place of *Pallas,* we find disputed, and undetermined among the authors. It was in this place that Romulus laid the foundations of the city, in a quadrangular form; and here the same king and Tullus Hostilius kept their courts, as did afterwards Augustus, and all the succeeding emperors; on which account, the word *Palatium* came to signify a royal seat ‡.

This hill to the east has Mons Cœlius; to the south, Mons Aventinus; to the west, Mons Capitolinus; to the north, the Forum §.

In compass twelve hundred paces ||.

Mons Tarpeius took its name from *Tarpeia,* a Roman virgin, who betrayed the city to the Sabines in this place ╪. It was called too *Mons Saturni* and *Saturnius,* in honour of Saturn, who is reported to have lived here in his retirement, and was ever reputed

---

* *Plutarch.* in *Romul.*   † *Dempster. Paralipom. ad Rosin.* lib. I. cap. 3.
‡ *Rosin. Antiq.* lib. I. cap. 4.   § *Fabricii Roma,* cap. 3. || *Marlian. Topograph.*
Antiq. Romæ, lib. I. cap. 14.   ╪ *Plutarch.* in *Romul.*

puted the tutelar deity of this part of the city. It had afterwards the denomination of *Capitolinus*, from the head of a man casually found there in digging for the foundations of the famous temple of Jupiter *, called *Capitolium*, for the same reason. This hill was added to the city by Titus Tatius, king of the Sabines, when, having been first overcome in the field by Romulus, he and his subjects were permitted to incorporate with the Romans †. It has, to the east, Mons Palatinus and the Forum; to the south, the Tyber; to the west, the level part of the city; to the north, Collis Quirinalis ‡.

In compass seven stadia or furlongs ‖.

Collis Quirinalis was so called, either from the temple of Quirinus, another name of Romulus, or, more probably, from the Curetes, a people that removed hither with Tatius from Cures, a Sabine city §. It afterwards changed its name to Caballus, Mons Caballi, and Caballinus, from the two marble horses, with each a man holding him, which are set up here. They are still standing; and, if the inscriptions on the pilasters be true, were the work of Phidias and Praxiteles ٭; made by those famous masters, to represent Alexander the Great and his Bucephalus, and sent to Nero for a present by Tiridates, king of Armenia. This hill was added to the city by Numa ┼.

To the east, it has Mons Esquilinus and Mons Viminalis; to the south, the Forums of Cæsar and Nerva; to the west, the level part of the city; to the north, Collis Hortulorum, and the Campus Martius ┼.

In compass almost three miles ┼┼.

Mons Cœlius owes its name to Cœlius, or Cœles, a famous Tuscan general, who pitched his tents here, when he came to the assistance of Romulus against the Sabines ═. Livy ↶ and Dionysius ** attribute the taking of it in to Tullius Hostilius; but Strabo †† to Ancus Martius. The other names by which it was sometimes known, were Querculanus, or Quercetulanus, and Augustus: The first occasioned by the abundance of oaks growing there; the other imposed by the emperor Tiberius, when he had raised new buildings upon it after a fire ‡‡.

One part of this hill was called Cœliolus, and Minor Cœlius ‖‖‖.

To

* *Liv.* lib. 1. cap. 55. † *Dionysius.* ‡ *Fabricii Roma*, cap. 3. ‖ *Marlian.* lib. 1. cap. 1. § *Sext. Pomp. Festus.* ٭ *Fabricii Roma*, cap. 3. ┼ *Dionys. Halic.* lib. 2. ┼ *Fabricii Roma*, cap. 3. ┼┼ *Marlian.* l. 1. c. 1. ═ *Varro de Ling. Lat.* lib. 4. ↶ Lib. 1. cap. 30. ** Lib. 3. †† *Georg.* lib. 5. ‡‡ *Tacit. Ann.* 4. *Suet.* in *Tib.* cap. 48. ‖‖‖ *Fabricii Roma*, cap. 3.

To the east, it has the city walls; to the south, Mons A-
ventinus; to the west, Mons Palatinus; to the north, Mons
Esquilinus *.

In compass about two miles and a half †.

Mons Esquilinus was anciently called Cispius and Oppius ‡:
The name of Esquilinus was varied for the easier pronunciation,
from Exquilinus, a corruption of Excubinus, *ab Excubiis*, from
the watch that Romulus kept there ‖. It was taken in by Servius Tullius §, who had here his royal seat ⁎. Varro will
have the Esquiliæ to be properly two mountains ╪; which o-
pinion has been since approved of by a curious observer +.

To the east, it has the city-walls; to the south, the Via
Labicana; to the west, the valley lying between Mons Cœlius
and Mons Palatinus; to the north, Collis Viminalis ++.

In compass about four miles =.

[*] *Vimina*. Mons Viminalis derives its name from the [*]
osiers that grew there in great plenty. This hill
was taken in by Servius Tullius ∽.

To the east, it has the Campus Esquinalis; and to the south,
part of the Suburra and the Forum; to the west, Mons Quirinalis; to the north, the Vallis Quirinalis **.

In compass two miles and a half ††.

The Name of Mons Aventinus has given great cause of dispute among the critics, some deriving the word from Aventinus, an Alban king ‡‡.; some from the river Avens ‖‖‖; and
others *ab avibus*, from the birds which used to fly thither in great
flocks from the Tyber §§. It was called too *Murcius*, from
Murcia, the goddess of sleep, who had there a *facellum*, or little temple ⁎⁎; *Collis Dianæ*, from the temple of Diana ‡‡;
and *Remonius*, from Remus, who would have had the city begun in this place, and was here buried ╪. A. Gellius affirms ╫, that this hill, being all along reputed sacred, was never inclosed within the bounds of the city till the time of Claudius. But Eutropius ≡ expressly attributes the taking of it
in to Ancus Martius; and an old epigram inserted by Cuspi-
nian, in his comment on Cassiodorus, confirms the same.

To the east, it has the city-walls; to the south, the Campus

* *Ibid.* † *Marlian.* lib. 1. cap. 1. ‡ *Fabricii Roma*, cap. 3. ‖ *Propert.*
lib. 2. *Eleg.* 8. § *Liv.* lib. 1. cap. 44. ⁎ *Ibid.* ╪ *De Ling. Latin.* l. 4.
+ *Marlian.* lib. 1. cap. 1. ++ *Fabricii Roma*, cap. 3. ∽ *Marlian.* l. 1. c. 1.
∽ *Dionys.* lib. 4. ** *Fabricii Roma*, cap. 3. †† *Marlian.* lib. 1. cap. 1.
‡‡ *Varro de Ling. Lat.* lib. 4. ‖‖‖ *Ibid.* §§ *Ibid.* ⁎⁎ *Sext. Pomp. Festus.*
‡‡ *Martial.* ╪ *Plut.* in *Romul.* ╫ *Lib.* 13. cap. 14. ≡ *Lib.* 1.

pus Figulinus; to the weſt, the Tyber; to the north, Mons Palatinus (a).

In circuit eighteen ſtadia, or two miles and a quarter (b).

Beſides theſe ſeven principal hills, three other of inferior note were taken in in later times.

Collis Hortulorum, or Hortorum, had its name from the famous gardens of Salluſt adjoining to it (c). It was afterwards called *Pincius*, from the Pincii, a noble family who had here their ſeat (d). The emperor Aurelian firſt encloſed it within the city-walls (e).

To the eaſt and ſouth, it has the plaineſt part of Mons Quirinalis; to the weſt, the Vallis Martia; to the north, the walls of the city (f).

In compaſs about eighteen ſtadia (g).

Janiculum, or Janicularis, was ſo called, either from an old town of the ſame name, ſaid to have been built by Janus; or, becauſe Janus dwelt and was buried there (h); or, becauſe it was a ſort of * gate to the Romans, whence they iſſued out upon the Tuſcans (i).   * *Janua*.

The ſparkling ſands have at preſent given it the name of *Mons Aureus*, and by corruption *Montorius* (k). We may make two obſervations about this hill from an epigram of Martial: That it is the fitteſt place to take one's ſtanding for a full proſpect of the city; and that it is leſs inhabited than the other parts, by reaſon of the groſſneſs of the air (l). It is ſtill famous for the ſepulchres of Numa, and Statius the poet (m).

To the eaſt and ſouth, it has the Tyber; to the weſt, the fields; to the north, the Vatican (n).

In circuit (as much of it as ſtands within the city-walls) five ſtadia (o).

Mons Vaticanus owes its name to the anſwers of the *vates*, or prophets, that uſed to be given there; or from the god *Vaticanus*, or *Vagitanus* (p). It ſeems not to have been incloſed within the walls till the time of Aurelian.

This hill was formerly famous for the ſepulchre of Scipio Africanus, ſome remains of which are ſtill to be ſeen (q). But it is more celebrated at preſent on account of St Peter's

---

(a) *Fabricii Roma*, cap. 3.   (b) *Marlian*. lib. 1. cap. 1.   (c) *Roſin*. l. 1. c. 11.
(d) *Ibid*.   (e) *Ibid*.   (f) *Fabricii Roma*, cap. 3.   (g) *Marlian*. lib. 1. cap. 1.
(h) *Roſin*. lib. 1. cap. 11.   (i) *Feſtus*.   (k) *Fabricii Roma*. cap. 3.   (l) *Martial*. *Epig*. lib. 4. Ep. 64.   (m) *Fabricii Roma*, lib. 1. cap. 3.   (n) *Ibid*.   (o) *Marlian*. lib. 1. cap. 1.   (p) *Feſtus*.   (q) *Warcup*'s Hiſt. of *Italy*, Book II.

ter's church, the Pope's palace, and the noblest library in the world.

To the east, it has the Campus Vaticanus and the River; to the south, the Janiculum; to the west, the Campus Figulinus, or Potters Field; to the north, the Prata Quintia (*a*).

It lyes in the shape of a bow drawn up very high, the convex part stretching almost a mile (*b*).

As to the extent of the whole city, the greatest we meet with in history was in the reign of Valerian, who enlarged the walls to such a degree as to surround the space of fifty miles (*c*).

The number of inhabitants, in its flourishing state, Lipsius computes at four millions (*d*).

At present the compass of the city is not above thirteen miles (*e*).

(*a*) *Fabricii Roma*, cap. 3.   (*b*) *Marlian*. lib. 1. cap. 1.   (*c*) *Vopisc.* in *Aureliano*.   (*d*) *De Magnitud. Rom.*   (*e*) *Fabricii Roma*, cap. 2.

CHAP. II.

Of the Division of the City into Tribes *and* Regions, *and of the Gates and Bridges.*

ROMULUS divided his little city into three tribes; and Servius Tullius added a fourth; which division continued till the time of Augustus. It was he first appointed the fourteen regions or wards: An account of which, with the number of temples, baths, &c. in every region, may be thus taken from the accurate Panvinius.

REGION I. *PORTA CAPENA.*

Streets 9.
Luci 3.
Temples 4.
Ædes 6.
Public Baths 6.
Arches 4.
Barns 14.
Mills 12.
Great Houses 121.

The whole compass 13223 feet.

REGION II. *COELIMONTIUM.*

Streets 12.
Luci 2.
Private Baths 80.
The great Shambles.

Temples

Book I.   *Of the* CITY.   35

Temples 5.
The public Baths of the City.
Barns 23.
Mills 23.
Great Houses 133.
The compass 13200 feet.

REGION III. *ISIS* and *SERAPIS.*

Streets 8.
Temples 2.
The Amphitheatre of Vespasian.
The Baths of Titus, Trajan, and Philip.
Barns 29, or 19.
Mills 23.
Great Houses 160.
The compass 12450 feet.

REGION IV. *VIA SACRA,* or *TEMPLUM PACIS.*

Streets 8.
Temples 10.
The Colossus of the Sun, 120 feet high.
The Arches of Titus, Severus, and Constantine.
Private Baths 75.
Barns 18.
Mills 24.
Great Houses 138.
The compass 14000; as some say, only 8000 feet.

REGION V. *ESQUILINA.*

Streets 15.
Luci 8.
Temples 6.
Ædes 5.
Private Baths 75.
Barns 18.
Mills 22.
Great Houses 180.
The compass 15950 feet..

REGION VI. *ACTA SEMITA.*

Streets 12, or 13.
Temples 15.
Porticos 2.
Circi 2.
Fora 2.
Private Baths 75.
Barns 19.
Mills 23.
Great Houses 155.
The compass 15600 feet.

REGION VII. *VIA LATA.*

Streets 40.
Temples 4.
Private Baths 75.
Arches 3.

Mills 17.
Barns 25.
Great Houses 120.

The compass 23700 feet.

REGION VIII. *FORUM ROMANUM.*

Streets 12.
Temples 21.
Private Baths 66.
Ædes 10.
Porticos 9.
Arches 4.
Fora 7.

Curiæ 4.
Basilicæ 7.
Columns 6.
Barns 18.
Mills 30.
Great Houses 150.

The compass 14867 feet.

REGION IX. *CIRCUS FLAMINIUS.*

Streets 20.
Temples 8.
Ædes 20.
Porticos 12.
Circi 2.
Theatres 4.
Basilicæ 3.

Curiæ 2.
Thermæ 5.
Arches 2.
Columns 2.
Mills 32.
Barns 32.
Great Houses 189.

The compass 30560 feet.

REGION X. *PALATIUM.*

Streets 7.
Temples 10.
Ædes 9.
Theatre 1.
Curiæ 4.

Private Baths 15.
Mills 12.
Barns 16.
Great Houses 109.

The compass 11600 feet.

REGION XI. *CIRCUS MAXIMUS.*

Streets 8.
Ædes 22.
Private Baths 15.

Barns 16.
Mills 12.
Great Houses 189.

The compass 11600 feet.

REGION XII. *PISCINA PUBLICA.*

Streets 12.
Ædes 2.
Private Baths 68.

Barns 28.
Mills 25.
Great Houses 128.

The compass 12000 feet.

REGION XIII. *AVENTINUS.*

Streets 17.
Luci 6.
Temples 6.
Private Baths 74.

Barns 36.
Mills 30.
Great Houses 155.

The compass 16300 feet.

REGION XIV. *TRANSTIBERINA.*

Streets 23.
Ædes 6.
Private Baths 136.

Barns 20.
Mills 32.
Great Houses 150.

The compass 33409 feet.

As to the gates, Romulus built only three, or (as some will have it) four at most. But, as the buildings were enlarged, the gates were accordingly multiplied; so that Pliny tells us, there were thirty-four in his time.

The most remarkable were,

Porta Flumentana, so called, because it stood near the river.

Porta Flaminia, owing its name to the Flaminian way, which begins there.

Porta Carmentalis, built by Romulus, and so called from Carmenta the prophetess, mother of Evander.

Porta Nævia, which Varro derives *à nemoribus*, from the woods which formerly stood near it.

Porta

Porta Saliana, deriving its name from the falt which the Sabines ufed to bring in at that gate from the fea, to fupply the city.

Porta Capena, called fo from Capua, an old city of Italy, to which the way lay through this gate. It is fometimes called Appia, from Appius the cenfor; and Triumphalis, from the triumphs in which the proceffion commonly paffed under there; and Fontinalis, from the aquæducts which were raifed over it: Whence Juvenal calls it, Madida Capena; and Martial, Capena, *grandi Porta quæ pluit guttâ.*

The Tyber was paffed over by eight bridges; the names of which are thus fet down by Marlian, Milvius, Ælius, Vaticanus, Janiculenfis, Ceftius, Fabricius, Palatinus, and Sublicius.

CHAP. III.

Of the Places of Worfhip; particularly of the TEMPLES *and* LUCI.

BEFORE we proceed to take a view of the moft remarkable places fet apart for the celebration of divine fervice, it may be proper to make a fhort obfervation about the general names under which we meet with them in authors.

Templum then was a place which had not been only dedicated to fome deity, but withal formerly confecrated by the Augurs.

Ædes Sacræ, were fuch as wanted that confecration; which, if they afterwards received, they changed their names to temples. Vid. *Agell.* L. XIV. C. 7.

Delubrum, according to Servius, was a place that, under one roof, comprehended feveral deities.

Ædicula is only a diminutive, and fignifies no more than a little *Ædes*.

Sacellum may be derived the fame way from *Ædes Sacræ*. Feftus tells us, it is a place facred to the gods without a roof.

It were endlefs to reckon up but the bare names of all the temples we meet with in authors. The moft celebrated on all accounts were the Capitol and Pantheon.

The

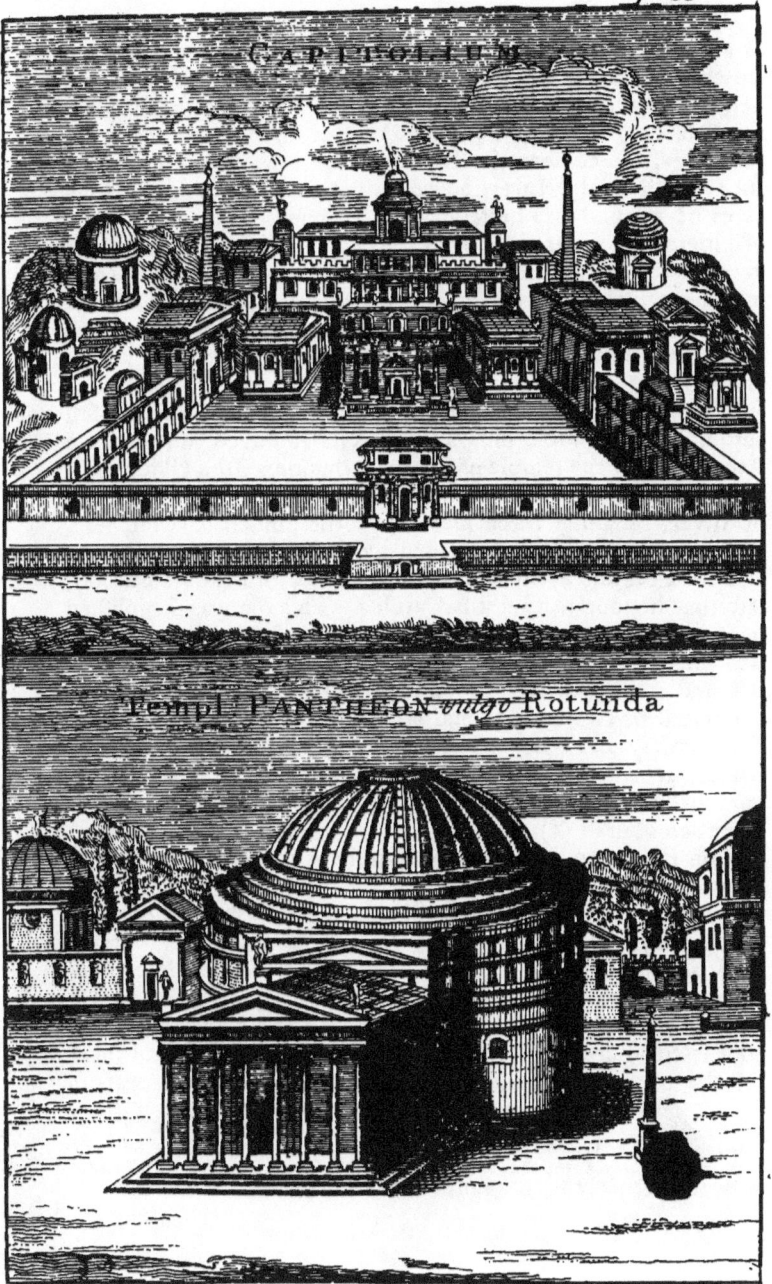

The Capitol, or temple of Jupiter Capitolinus, was the effect of a vow made by Tarquinius Priscus in the Sabine war (*a*). But he had scarce laid the foundations before his death. His nephew, Tarquin the Proud, finished it with the spoils taken from the neighbouring nations (*b*). But upon the expulsion of the kings, the consecration was performed by Horatius the consul (*c*). The structure stood on a high ridge, taking in four acres of ground. The front was adorned with three rows of pillars, the other sides with two (*d*). The ascent from the ground was by a hundred steps (*e*). The prodigious gifts and ornaments, with which it was at several times endowed, almost exceed belief. Suetonius (*f*) tells us, that Augustus gave at one time two thousand pounds weight of gold: And in jewels and precious stones, to the value of five hundred sestertia. Livy and Pliny (*g*) surprise us with accounts of the brasen thresholds, the noble pillars that Sylla removed thither from Athens out of the temple of Jupiter Olympius; the gilded roof, the gilded shields, and those of solid silver; the huge vessels of silver, holding three measures; the golden chariot, &c. This temple was first consumed by fire in the Marian war, and then rebuilt by Sylla; who dying before the dedication, left that honour to Quintus Catulus. This too was demolished in the Vitellian sedition. Vespasian undertook a third, which was burnt about the time of his death. Domitian raised the last and most glorious of all; in which the very gilding amounted to twelve thousand talents (*h*). On which account Plutarch (*i*) has observed of that emperor, that he was, like Midas, desirous of turning every thing into gold. There are very little remains of it at present; yet enough to make a Christian church (*k*).

The Pantheon was built by Marcus Agrippa, son-in-law to Augustus Cæsar; and dedicated either to Jupiter Ultor, or to Mars and Venus, or, more probably, to all the gods in general, as the very name (*quasi* Τῶν πάντων Θιῶν) implies. The structure, according to Fabricius (*l*), is a hundred and forty feet high, and about the same breadth. But a later author has increased the number of feet to a hundred and fifty eight. The roof is curiously vaulted, void places being left here and there for the greater strength. The rafters were pieces of brass of

forty

(*a*) [...] 1. (*b*) *Ibid.* (*c*) *Plutarch,* in *Poplicol.* (*d*) *Dionys. Halicar.* (*e*) *Tacitus.* [...] *August.* cap. 30. (*g*) *Liv.* l. 35. 38. *Plin.* l. 33. &c. (*h*) *Plutarch.* in *Poplicola.* (*i*) *Ibid.* (*k*) *Fabricii Roma.* cap. 9. (*l*) *Ibid.*

forty feet in length. There are no windows in the whole edifice, only a round hole at the top of the roof, which serves very well for the admission of the light. Diametrically under, is cut a curious gutter to receive the rain. The walls on the inside are either solid marble, or incrusted (*a*). The front on the outside was covered with brasen plates gilt, the top with silver plates, which are now changed to lead (*b*). The gates were brass, of extraordinary work and bigness (*c*).

This temple is still standing, with little alterations besides the loss of the old ornament, being converted into a Christian church by Pope Boniface III. (or, as Polydore Virgil (*d*) has it, by Boniface IV.) dedicated to St Mary and all saints, though the general name be St Mary de Rotonda (*e*). The most remarkable difference is, that, whereas heretofore they ascended by twelve steps, they now go down as many to the entrance (*f*).

The ceremony of the consecration of temples (a piece of superstition very well worth our notice,) we cannot better apprehend, than by the following account which Tacitus gives us of that solemnity in reference to the Capitol, when repaired by Vespasian: Though, perhaps, the chief rites were celebrated upon the entire raising of the structure, this being probably intended only for the hallowing the floor.

Undecimo Kalendas Julias (*g*). &c. 'Upon the 21st of June, 'being a very clear day, the whole plot of ground designed for 'the temple was bound about with fillets and garlands. Such 'of the soldiers as had lucky names, entered first with boughs 'in their hands, taken from those trees which the gods more 'especially delighted in. Next came the vestal virgins, with 'boys and girls whose fathers and mothers were living, and 'sprinkled the place with brook-water, river-water, and 'spring-water. Then Helvidius Priscus the prætor (Plautus 'Ælian, one of the chief priests, going before him) after he 'had performed the solemn sacrifice of a swine, a sheep, and a 'bullock, for the purgation of the floor, and laid the entrails 'upon a green turf, humbly besought Jupiter, Juno, Minerva, 'and the other deities protectors of the empire, that they 'would be pleased to prosper their present undertaking, and 'accomplish, by their divine assistance, what human piety had 'thus begun. Having concluded this prayer, he put his hand to 'the fillets, to which the robes, with a great stone fastened in 'them,

(*a*). Marlian. Topograph. Rom. Antiq. lib. 6. cap. 6. (*b*) Ibid. &c. cap. 9. (*c*) Marlian. Ibid. (*d*) Lib. 6. cap. 8. (*e*) Fa.ric. cap. 9. (*f*) Ibid. (*g*) Histor. lib. 4.

'them, had been tied for this occasion; when immediately the
'whole company of priests, senators, and knights, with the
'greatest part of the common people, laying hold together on
'the rope, with all the expressions of joy, drew the stone
'into the trench designed for the foundation, throwing in
'wedges of gold, silver, and other metals which had never
'endured the fire.'

Some curious persons have observed this similitude between the shape of these old temples and our modern churches: That they had one apartment more holy than the rest, which they termed *Cella*, answering to our chancel or choir: That the porticos in the sides were in all respects like to our isles; and that our *navis*, or body of the church, is an imitation of their *basilica* (*a*).

There are two other temples particularly worth our notice; not so much for the magnificence of the structure, as for the customs that depend upon them, and the remarkable use to which they were put. These are the temples of Saturn and Janus.

The first was famous upon account of serving for the public treasury: The reason of which some fancy to have been, because Saturn first taught the Italians to coin money; or, as Plutarch conjectures, because in the golden age under Saturn, all persons were honest and sincere, and the names of *fraud* and *covetousness* unknown to the world (*b*). But, perhaps, there might be no more in it, than that this temple was one of the strongest places in the city, and so the fittest for that use. Here were preserved all the public registers and records, among which were the *Libri Elephantini*, or great ivory tables, containing a list of all the tribes, and the schemes of the public accounts.

The other was a square piece of building, (some say of entire brass) so large as to contain a statue of Janus five feet high; with brazen gates on each side, which used always to be kept open in war, and shut in time of peace (*c*).

But the Romans were so continually engaged in quarrels, that we find the last custom but seldom put in practice.

First, all the long reign of Numa. Secondly, *A. U. C.* 519, upon the conclusion of the first Punic war. Thirdly, by Augustus, *A. U. C.* 725. and twice more by the same emperor, *A. U. C.* 729, and again about the time of our Saviour's birth. Then by Nero, *A. U. C.* 811. Afterwards by Vespasian, *A. U. C.* 824. And lastly by Constantius, when, upon Magnentius's

(*a*) *Polletus* Hist. Roman. Flori, lib. 1. cap. 3.   (*b*) *Plutarch.* in Problem.
(*c*) *Marlian.* Topog. Rom. Antiq. lib. 6. cap. 8.

tius's death, he was left sole possessor of the empire, *A. U. C.* 1105 (*a*).

Of this custom Virgil gives a noble description:

Sunt geminæ belli portæ, sic nomine dicunt,
Religione sacræ, & sævi formidine Martis:
Centum ærei claudunt vectes æternaque ferri
Robora; nec custos absistit limine Janus.
Has, ubi certa sedet patribus sententia pugnæ;
Ipse, Quirinali trabeâ cinctuque Gabino
Insignis, reserat stridentia limina consul;
Ipse vocat pugnas (*b*).

Sacred to Mars two stately gates appear,
Made awful by the dread of arms and war;
A hundred brasen bolts from impious pow'r
And everlasting bars the dome secure,
And watchful Janus guards his temple door.
Here, when the fathers have ordain'd to try
The chance of battle by their fix'd decree,
The consul, rich in his Gabinian gown,
And regal pall, leads the procession on;
The sounding hinges gravely turn about,
Rouse the imprison'd god, and let the furies out.

Near the temple of Janus there was a street which took the same name, inhabited for the most part by bankers and usurers. It was very long, and divided by the different names of *Janus Summus, Janus Medius,* and *Janus Imus.* The first and the last of these partitions are mentioned by Horace, lib. 1. epist. 1.

———— *Hoc Janus Summus ab imo*
Perdocet.

The other Tully speaks of in several places of his works (*c*):
The superstition of consecrating groves and woods to the honour of the deities, was a practice very usual with the ancients: For, not to speak of those mentioned in the holy scriptures, Pliny assures us, That *trees in old time served for the temples of the gods.* Tacitus reports this custom of the old Germans; Q. Curtius of the Indians, and almost all writers
of

———

(*a*) *Casaubon.* Not Id. *Sueton. August.* cap. 22. (*b*) *Virg. Æn.* 7. (*c*) Lib. 2. *de Offic. Philip.* 8, *&c.*

THEATRUM CORNELII BALBI GADITANI

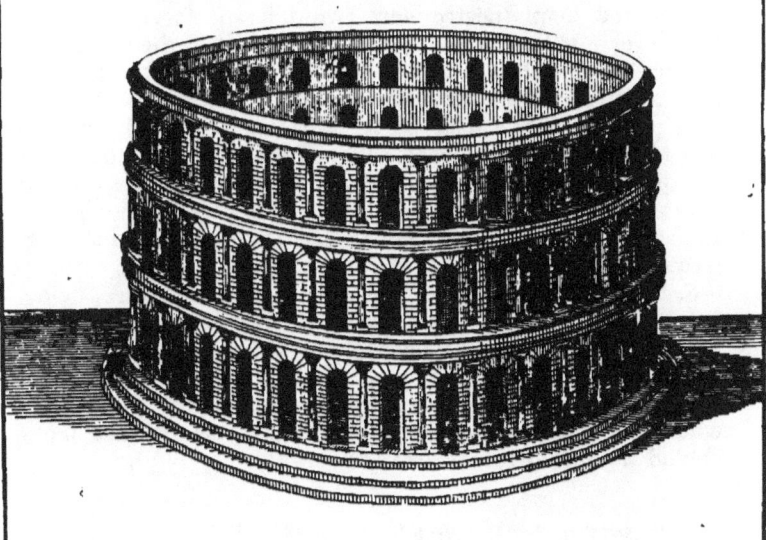

AMPHITHEATRUM CLAUDII

of the old Druids. The Romans too were great admirers of this way of worship, and therefore had their Luci, in most parts of the city, generally dedicated to some particular deity.

The most probable reason that can be given for this practice is taken from the common opinion, that fear was the main principle of devotion among the ignorant heathens. And therefore such darksome and lonely seats putting them into a sudden horror and dread, made them fancy that there must necessarily something of divinity inhabit there, which could produce in them such an awe and reverence at their entrance.

CHAP. IV.

Of the Theatres, Amphitheatres, Circi, Naumachiæ, Odea, Stadia, *and* Xysti, *and of the* Campus Martius.

THEATRES, so called from the Greek θιάομαι, *to see*, owe their original to Bacchus (*a*). They were usual in several parts of Greece; and at last, after the same manner as other institutions, were borrowed thence by the Romans. That the theatre and amphitheatre were two different sorts of edifices was never questioned, the former being built in the shape of a semicircle, the other generally oval, so as to make the same figure as if two theatres should be joined together (*b*) Yet the same place is often called by these names in several authors. They seem too to have been designed for quite different ends; the theatres for stage plays, the amphitheatres for the greater shows of gladiators, wild beasts, &c. The parts of the theatre and amphitheatre best worth our observation, by reason of their frequent use in classics, are as follow:

Scena was a partition reaching quite cross the theatre, being either *versatilis* or *ductilis*, either to turn round or to draw up, for the presenting a new prospect to the spectators, as Servius has observed (*c*).

Proscenium was the space of ground just before the scene, where the *pulpitum* stood, into which the actors came from behind the scenes to perform (*d*).

(*a*) Polydor. Virg. de Rer. invent. lib. 3. cap. 13. (*b*) Ibid. (*c*) In Georg. 3. (*d*) Rosin. lib. 5. cap. 4.

The middle part, or area, of the amphitheatre, was called *Cavea*, because it was considerably lower than the other parts; whence perhaps the name of *pit* in our play houses was borrowed; and *Arena*, because it used to be strown with sand, to hinder the performer from slipping. Lipsius has taken notice, that the whole amphitheatre was often called by both these names (*a*). And the Veronese still call the theatre, which remains almost entire in that city, the *Arena* (*b*).

There was a threefold distinction of the seats, according to the ordinary division of the people into senators, knights, and commons; the first range was called *Orchestra*, from ὀρχεῖσθαι, because in that part of the Græcian theatres the dances were performed; the second *Equestria*; and the other *Popularia* (*c*).

Theatres, in the first ages of the commonwealth, were only temporary, and composed of wood, which sometimes tumbled down with a great destruction, as Dio (*d*) and Pliny (*e*) speak of one particularly. Of these temporary theatres, the most celebrated was that of M. Scaurus, mentioned by Pliny (*f*); the scenes of which were divided into three partitions, one above another; the first consisting of 120 pillars of marble; the next of the like number of pillars, curiously wrought in glass: The top of all had still the same number of pillars adorned with gilded tablets. Between the pillars were set 3000 statues and images of brass. The cavea would hold 80,000 men. The structure which Curio afterwards raised at the funeral of his father, tho' inferior to the former in magnificence, yet was no less remarkable upon account of the admirable artifice and contrivance. He built two spacious theatres of wood, so ordered with hinges and other necessaries, as to be able to turn round with very little trouble. These he set at first back to back, for the celebration of the stage-plays and such like diversions, to prevent the disorder that might otherwise arise by the confusion of the scenes. Toward the latter end of the day, pulling down the scenes, and joining the two fronts of the theatres, he composed an exact amphitheatre, in which he again obliged the people with a show of gladiators (*g*).

Pompey the Great was the first that undertook the raising of a fixed theatre, which he built very nobly with square stone; on which account, Tacitus (*h*) tells us he was severely reprehended for introducing a custom so different from that of their forefathers, who

---

(*a*) *Lips* in Amphitheat. (*b*) *Warcup*'s History of *Italy*. (*c*) *Casalius* de Urb. Rom. & Imp. Splendore, lib. 2. cap. 5. (*d*) Lib. 37. (*e*) Lib. 36. c. 15. (*f*) Ibid. (*g*) Ibid. (*h*) *Ann.* 14.

who were contented to see the like performances, in seats built only for the present occasion, and in ancient times standing only on the ground. To this purpose I cannot omit an ingenious reflection of Ovid, upon the luxury of the age he lived in, by comparing the honest simplicity of the old Romans with the vanity and extravagance of the modern in this particular:

> *Tunc neque marmoreo pendebant vela Theatro,*
>   *Nec fuerant liquido pulpita rubra croco.*
> *Illic quas tulerant, nemoroso Palatia, frondes*
>   *Simpliciter positæ: Scena sine arte fuit.*
> *In gradibus sedit populus de cespite factis*
>   *Qualibet hirsutas fronde tegente comas* (a).

> No pillars then of Egypt's costly stone,
> No purple sails hung waving in the sun,
> No flowers about the scented seats were thrown.
> But Sylvan bowers and shady palaces,
> Brought by themselves, secur'd them from the rays.
> Thus guarded and refresh'd with humble green,
> Wond'ring they gaz'd upon the artless scene:
> Their seats of homely turf the crowd would rear,
> And cover with green boughs their more disorder'd hair.

Juvenal intimates, that this good old custom remained still uncorrupted in several parts of Italy:

> ——————————————*ipsa dierum*
> *Festorum herboso colitur si quando Theatro*
> *Majestas; tandemque redit ad pulpita notum*
> *Exodium, cum personæ pallentis hiatum*
> *In gremio matris formidat rusticus infans;*
> *Æquales habitus illic, similemque videbis*
> *Orchestram & populum*——— (b).

> On theatres of turf, in homely state,
> Old plays they act, old feasts they celebrate;
> The same rude song returns upon the crowd,
> And by tradition is for wit allow'd.
> The mimic yearly gives the same delights,
> And in the mother's arms the clownish infant frights.
> Their habits (undistinguish'd by degree)
> Are plain alike; the same simplicity
> Both on the stage, and in the pit you see.

Mr Dryden.

(a) *Ovid, de Arte Amandi.*   (b) *Juv. Sat.* 3.

Some remains of this Theatre of Pompey are still to be seen at Rome, as also of those other of Marcellus, Statilius Taurus, Tiberius, and Titus, the second being almost entire (*a*).

The Circi were places set apart for the celebration of several sorts of games, which we will speak of hereafter. They were generally oblong, or almost in the shape of a bow (*b*), having a wall quite round (*c*), with ranges of seats for the convenience of the spectators. At the entrance of the Circi stood the carceres, or lists, whence they started; and just by them one of the metæ, or marks; the other standing at the farther end to conclude the race.

There were several of these Circi in Rome, as those of Flaminius, Nero, Caracalla, and Severus: But the most remarkable, as the very name imports, was Circus Maximus, first built by Tarquinius Priscus (*d*). The length of it was four stadia, or furlongs, the breadth the like number of acres; with a trench of ten feet deep, and as many broad, to receive the water; and seats enough for 150,000 men (*e*). It was extremely beautified and adorned by succeeding princes, particularly by Julius Cæsar, Augustus, Caligula, Domitian, Trajan, and Heliogabalus! and enlarged to such a prodigious extent, as to be able to contain, in their proper seats, 260,000 spectators (*f*).

The Naumachiæ, or places for the shows of sea engagements, are no where particularly described; but we may suppose them to be very little different from the Circus and Amphitheatres, since those sort of shows, for which they were designed, were often exhibited in the aforementioned places (*g*).

Odeum was a public edifice, much after the manner of a Theatre (*h*), where the musicians and actors privately exercised before their appearance on the stage (*i*). Plutarch has described one of their Odeums at Athens (whence to be sure the Romans took the hint of theirs) in the following words: " For the " contrivance of it, in the inside it was full of seats and ranges " of pillars; and, on the outside, the roof or covering of it " was made from one point at top, with a great many bend- " ings, all shelving downward, in imitation of the king of Per- " sia's pavilion (*k*)."

The Stadia were places in the form of Circi, for the running

(*a*) *Fabric. Rom.* cap. 12.   (*b*) *Marlian. Topog. Rom. Ant.* lib. 4. cap. 10.
(*c*) *Polydor. Virg.* de Rer. invent. lib. 2. cap. 14.   (*d*) *Liv. & Dionys. Halic.*
(*e*) *Dionys.* lib. 3.   (*f*) *Plin.* lib. 36.   (*g*) *Marlian. Topog. Ant.* lib. 4. cap. 13.
(*h*) *Fabric. Rom.* cap. 12.   (*i*) *Rosin.* lib. 5. cap. 4.   (*k*) In *Pericle*.
(*l*) *Fabric. Rom.* cap. 12.   (*m*) In *Domitian*.

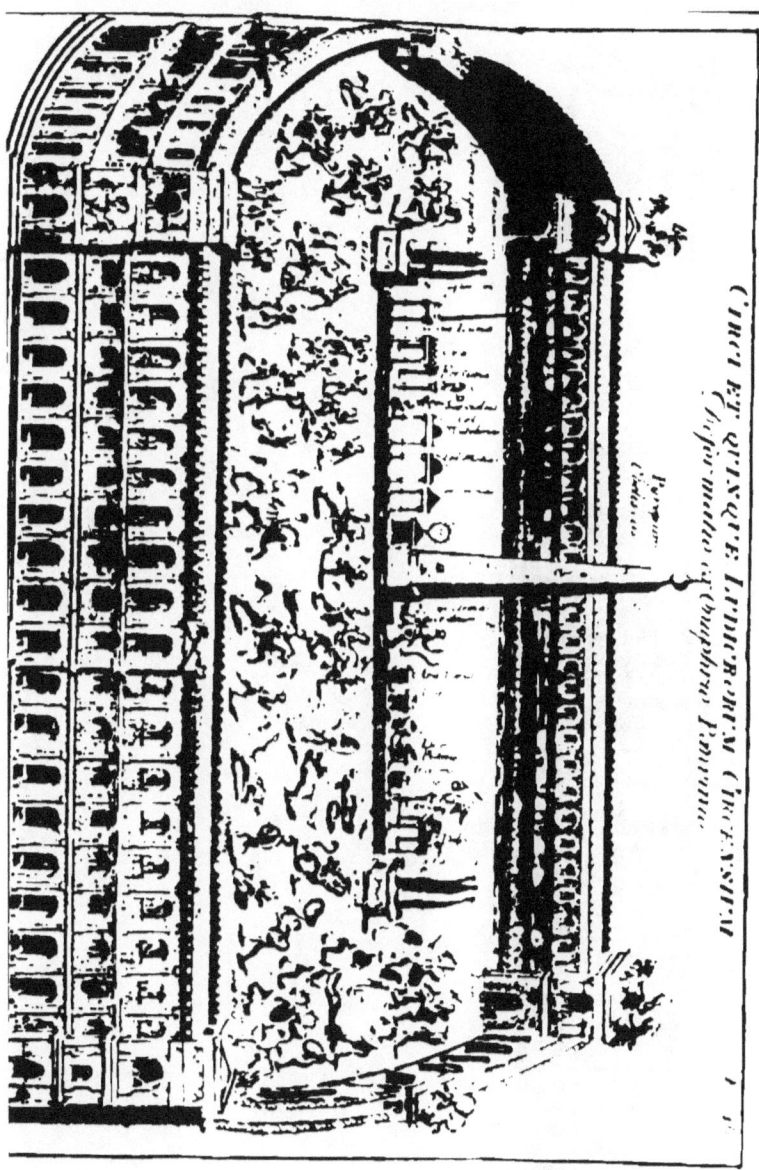

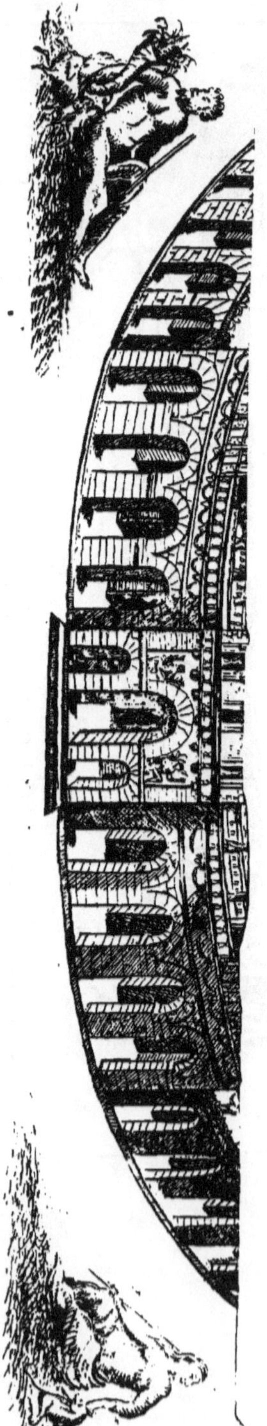

y
ı)
s,
a
e-
e-
s.
s,
ıe
of
s.
re
es
ıd
ɔr
rs
y.
ɔr
ed
ıe
s,
e,
a
of
f.
–
ı.
of
ıd
e-
ıe
of
a
a,

ning of men and horses (*l*). A very noble one Suetonius (*m*) tells us was built by Domitian.

The Xysti were places built, after the fashion of porticos, for the wrestlers to exercise in (*a*).

The Campus Martius, famous on so many accounts, was a large plain field, lying near the Tyber, whence we find it sometimes under the name of *Tyberinus*; it was called Martius, because it had been consecrated by the old Romans to the god Mars.

Besides the pleasant situation, and other natural ornaments, the continual sports and exercises performed here made it one of the most diverting sights near the city. For,

Here the young noblemen practised all manner of feats of activity; learned the use of all sorts of arms and weapons. Here the races, either with chariots or single horse, were undertaken. Besides this, it was nobly adorned with the statues of famous men, and with arches, columns, and porticos, and other magnificent structures. Here stood the Villa Publica, or palace for the reception and entertainment of ambassadors from foreign states, who were not allowed to enter the city. Several of the public Comitia were held in this field; and for that purpose were the Septa or Ovilia, an apartment inclosed with rails, where the Tribes or Centuries went in one by one to give their votes. Cicero, in one of his epistles to Atticus, intimates a noble design he had to make the Septa of marble, and to cover them with a high roof, with the addition of a stately portico or piazza all round. But we hear no more of this project, and therefore may reasonably suppose he was disappointed by the civil wars which broke out presently after.

(*a*) *Fabric. Rom*, cap. 12.

CHAP. V.

Of the Curiæ, Senacula, Basilicæ, Fora, *and* Comitium.

THE Roman Curia (it signifies a public edifice) was of two sorts, divine and civil: In the former, the priests and religious orders met for the regulations of the rites and ceremonies belonging to the worship of the gods: In the other, the Senate used to assemble, to consult about the public concerns of the commonwealth. (*a*) The Senate could not meet in such a Curia,

(*a*) *Alex.* ab *Alex.* 1. cap. 16.

Curia, unless it had been solemnly consecrated by the Augurs (*a*), and made of the same nature as a temple. Sometimes (at least) the Curiæ were no distinct building, but only a room or hall in some public place; as particularly Livy (*b*) and Pliny (*c*) speak of a Curia in the Comitium, though that itself were no entire structure. The most celebrated Curiæ were,

Curia Hostilia, built by Tullus Hostilius, as Livy (*d*) informs us: And,

Curia Pompeii, where the Senate assembled for the effecting the death of Julius Cæsar (*e*).

Senaculum is sometimes the same as Curia (*f*): To be sure it could be no other than a meeting-place for the senate, the same as the Græcians called γερυσία. Sext. Pomp. Festus (*g*) tells us of three Senacula; two within the city-walls for ordinary consultations; and one without the limits of the city, where the Senate assembled to give audience to those ambassadors of foreign states, whom they were unwilling to honour with an admission into the city.

Lampridius (*h*) informs us, that the emperor Heliogabalus built a Senaculum purposely for the use of the women, where, upon high days, a council of grave matrons were to keep court.

The Basilicæ were very spacious and beautiful edifices, designed chiefly for the Centumviri, or the judges to sit in and hear causes, and for the counsellors to receive clients. The bankers too had one part of it allotted for their residence (*i*). Vossius (*k*) has observed, that these Basilicæ were exactly in the shape of our churches, oblong almost like a ship; which was the reason that, upon the ruin of so many of them, Christian churches were several times raised on the old foundations; and very often a whole Basilica converted to such a pious use. And hence, perhaps, all our great domes or cathedrals are still called Basilicæ.

The Roman Forums were public buildings, about three times as long as they were broad. All the compass of the Forum was surrounded with arched porticos, only some passages being left for places of entrance. They generally contrived to have the most stately edifices all round them, as Temples, Theatres, Basilicæ, &c. (*l*).

They

(*a*) *A Gell.* l. 14. c. 7. (*b*) Lib. 1. (*c*) Lib. 1. (*d*) Lib. 1. (*e*) *Sueton.* in *Jul. Cæs.* c. 80. (*f*) *Marlian.* Topog. Ant. Rom. lib. 3. c. 27. (*g*) In voce *Senaculum.* (*h*) In vit. *Heliogab.* (*i*) *Rosin.* Ant. l. 9. c. 7. (*k*) In voce *Basilica.* (*l*) *Lipf.* de Mag. Rom.

They were of two sorts; *Fora Civilia*, and *Fora Venalia*: The first were designed for the ornaments of the city, and for the use of public courts of justice; the others were intended for no other end but the necessities and conveniencies of the inhabitants, and were no doubt equivalent to our markets. I believe Lipsius, in the description that has been given above, means only the former. Of these there were five very considerable in Rome.

Forum Romanum, built by Romulus, and adorned with porticos on all sides by Tarquinius Priscus. It was called *Forum Romanum*, or simply *Forum*, by way of eminence, on account of its antiquity, and of the most frequent use of it in public affairs. Martial (*a*) and Statius (*b*), for the same reason, give it the name of *Forum Latium*; Ovid the same (*c*), and of *Forum Magnum* (*d*); and Herodian (*e*) calls it τὴν ἀρχαίαν ἀγοράν *Forum Vetus*.

Statius the poet (*f*) has given an accurate description of the Forum, in his poem upon the statue of Domitian on horseback, set up there by that emperor.

Forum Julium, built by Julius Cæsar with the spoils taken in the Gallic war. The very area, Suetonius (*g*) tells us, cost 100,000 Sesterces; and Dio (*h*) affirms it to have much exceeded the Forum Romanum.

Forum Augusti, built by Augustus Cæsar, and reckoned by Pliny among the wonders of the city. The most remarkable curiosity was the statues in the two porticos on each side of the main building. In one, were all the Latin kings, beginning with Æneas; in the other, all the kings of Rome, beginning with Romulus, and most of the eminent persons in the commonwealth, and Augustus himself among the rest; with an inscription upon the pedestal of every statue, expressing the chief actions and exploits of the person it represented (*i*).

This Forum, as Spartian (*k*) informs us, was restored by the emperor Hadrian.

Forum Nervæ, begun by Domitian, as Suetonius (*l*) relates; but finished and named by the emperor Nerva. In this Forum, Alexander Severus set up the statues of all the emperors that had been canonized (*m*), in imitation of the contrivance of Augustus, mentioned but now. This Forum was called *Transitorium*,

---

(*a*) *Epig.* lib. 2. (*b*) *Sylvan.* lib. 1. cap. 1. (*c*) *Fast.* 4. (*d*) *Fast.* 3.
(*e*) 5. vit. *M. Antonin.* (*f*) *Syl.* lib. 1. cap. 1. (*g*) In *Jul. Cæs.* cap. 26.
(*h*) *Dio.* lib. 43. (*i*) *Lips.* de Magnitud. Rom. (*k*) In vit. *Hadriani*;
(*l*) In *Domit.* cap. In. (*m*) Spartian in *Severo.*

rium becaufe it lay very convenient for a paffage to the other three; and *Palladium,* from the ftatue of Minerva, the tutelar deity of Auguftus (*a*); upon which account, perhaps, Fabricius (*b*) attributes the name of *Palladium* to the Forum of that emperor.

There is fcarce any thing remaining of this Forum, except an old decayed arch, which the people, by a ftrange corruption, inftead of Nerva's Arch, call Noah's Ark (*c*).

But the moft celebrated for the admirable ftructure and contrivance, was the *Forum Trajani,* built by the emperor Trajan with the foreign fpoils he had taken in the wars. The covering of this edifice was all brafs, the porticos exceedingly beautiful and magnificent, with pillars of more than ordinary height, and chapiters of exceffive bignefs (*d*).

Ammianus Marcellinus, in the defcription of Conftantius's triumphal entrance into Rome, when he has brought him, with no ordinary admiration, by the Baths, the Pantheon, the Capitol, and other noble ftructures, as foon as ever he gives him a fight of this Forum of Trajan, he puts him into an ecftafy, and cannot forbear making an harangue upon the matter (*e*). We meet in the fame place with a very fmart repartee which Conftantius received at this time from Ormfdas, a Perfian prince. The emperor, as he ftrangely admired every thing belonging to this noble pile, fo he had a particular fancy for the ftatue of Trajan's horfe, which ftood on the top of the building, and expreffed his defire of doing as much for his own beaft: " Pray " Sir," fays the prince, " before you talk of getting fuch a horfe, " will you be pleafed to build fuch a ftable to put him in (*f*).

The chief *Fora Venalia*, or markets, were,

Boarium, for oxen and beef

Propertius (*g*) has a pretty fancy about this forum, that it took its name from Hercules's oxen, which he brought from Spain, and refcued them here, after they had been ftolen by Cacus.

Suarium, for fwine.

Piftorium, for bread.

Cupedinarium, for dainties.

Holitorium, for roots, falads, and fuch like.

The *Comitium* was only a part of the Forum Romanum, which ferved fometimes for the celebration of the Comitia, which will be defcribed hereafter.

In

(*a*) Lipf. in *Magn. Rom.* (*b*) *Roma,* cap. 7 (*c*) *Marlian.* lib. 3. cap. 14.
(*d*) *Idem,* lib. 3. c. 13. (*e*) *Ammian Marcellin.* Hift. lib. 16. (*f*) *Ibid.*
(*g*) Lib. 4. Eleg. 10. ver. 20.

In this part of the Forum stood the *Rostra*, being a *Suggestum*, or sort of pulpit, adorned with the beaks of ships taken in a sea-fight from the inhabitants of Antium in Italy, as Livy (*a*) informs us. In this the causes were pleaded, the orations made, and the funeral panegyrics spoke by persons at the death of their relations, which pious action they termed *Defuncti pro rostris laudatio*.

Hard by was fixed the *Puteal*, of which we have several and very different accounts from the critics; but none more probable than the opinion of the ingenious Monsieur Dacier (*b*), which he delivers to this purpose:

" The Romans, whenever a thunderbolt fell upon a place
" without a roof, took care, out of superstition, to have a
" sort of cover built over it, which they properly called *Puteal*.
" This had the name of *Puteal Libonis*, and *Scribonium Puteal*,
" because Scribonius Libo erected it by order of the senate.
" The prætor's tribunal standing just by, is often signified in
" authors by the same expression."

(*a*) Lib. 8.   (*b*) *Dacier*, Notes on *Horace*, lib. 2. Sat. 6. verse 35.

CHAP. VI.

Of the Porticos, Arches, Columns, *and* Trophies.

IN accounts of the eminent buildings of the city, the PORTICOS have ever had an honourable place. They were structures of curious work and extraordinary beauty, annexed to public edifices, sacred and civil, as well for ornament as use. They generally took their names either from the temples that they stood near, as *Porticus Concordiæ, Quirini, Herculis*, &c. or from the authors, as *Porticus Pompeia, Octavia, Livia* &c; or from the nature and form of the building, as *Porticus curva, stadiata, porphyretica;* or from the shops that were kept in them, as *Margaritaria* and *Argentaria;* or from the remarkable paintings in them, as *Porticus Isidis, Europæ,* &c. or else from the places to which they joined, as *Porticus Amphitheatri, Porticus Circi,* &c. (*a*).

These porticos were sometimes put to very serious uses, serving for the assemblies of the senate on several accounts. Sometimes the jewellers, and such as dealt in the most precious wares, took up here their standing to expose their goods to sale:

(*a*) *Fabricii Roma*, cap. 13.

But the general use that they were put to, was the pleasure of walking or riding in them; in the shade in summer, and in winter in the dry, like the present piazzas in Italy. Velleius Paterculus (a), when he deplores the extreme corruption of manners that had crept into Rome upon the otherwise happy conclusion of the Carthaginian war, mentions particularly the vanity of the noblemen, in endeavouring to outshine one another in the magnificence of their porticos, as a great instance of their extravagant luxury.

And Juvenal, in his seventh Satyr, complains:

Balnea sexcentis, & pluris porticus, in quâ
Gestetur dominus quoties pluit : Anne serenum
Expectet, spargatque luto jumenta recenti ?
Hic potius ; namque hic mundæ nitet ungula mulæ.

On sumptuous baths the rich their wealth bestow,
Or some expensive airy portico ;
Where safe from show'rs they may be borne in state,
And, free from tempests, for fair weather wait :
Or rather not expect the clearing sun :
Thro' thick and thin their equipage must run :
Or staying, 'tis not for their servants sake,
But that their mules no prejudice may take.
Mr CHARLES DRYDEN.

Arches were public buildings, designed for the reward and encouragement of noble enterprises, erected generally to the honour of such eminent persons as had either won a victory of extraordinary consequence abroad, or had rescued the commonwealth at home from any considerable danger. At first they were plain and rude structures, by no means remarkable for beauty or state. But in latter times no expences were thought too great for the rendering them in the highest manner splendid and magnificent : Nothing being more usual than to have the greatest actions of the heroes they stood to honour curiously expressed, or the whole procession of the triumph cut out on the sides. The arches built by Romulus were only of brick; that of Camillus of plain square stone ; but then those of Cæsar, Drusus, Titus, Trajan, Gordian, &c. were all entirely marble (b).

As to their figure, they were at first semicircular, whence probably they took their names. Afterwards they were built four-

---

(a) Lib. 2. cap. 1.   (b) *Fabricii Roma*, cap. 14.

four square, with a spacious arched gate in the middle, and little ones on each side. Upon the vaulted part of the middle gate hung little winged images, representing victory, with crowns in their hands, which, when they were let down, they put upon the conqueror's head as he passed under in triumph (a).

The COLUMNS, or pillars, were none of the meanest beauties of the city. They were at last converted to the same design as the arches, for the honourable memorial of some noble victory or exploit, after they had been a long time in use for the chief ornaments of the sepulchres of great men; as may be gathered from Homer, Iliad 16. where Juno, when she is foretelling the death of Sarpedon, and speaking at last of carrying him into his own country to be buried, has these words:

"Ενϑα ἑ ταρχύουσι κασίγνητοί τε, ἔται τε,
Τύμϐῳ τε σήγη τε, τὸ γὰρ γέρας ἐσὶ θανόντων.

There shall his brothers and sad friends receive
The breathless corpse, and bear it to the grave.
A pillar shall be rear'd, a tomb be laid,
The noblest honour earth can give the dead.

The pillars of the emperors Trajan and Antoninus have been extremely admired for their beauty and curious work, and therefore deserve a particular description.

The former was set up in the middle of Trajan's forum, being composed of 24 great stones of marble, but so curiously cemented, as to seem one entire natural stone. The height was 144 feet, according to Eutropius (b); tho' Marlian (c) seems to make them but 128: Yet they are easily reconciled, if we suppose one of them to have begun the measure from the pillar itself, and the other from the basis. It is ascended on the inside by 185 winding stairs, and has 40 little windows for the admission of the light. The whole pillar is incrusted with marble; in which are expressed all the noble actions of the emperor, and particularly the Decian war. One may see all over it the several figures of forts, bulwarks, bridges, ships, &c. and all manner of arms, as shields, helmets, targets, swords, spears, daggers, belts, &c. together with the several offices and employments of the soldiers; some digging trenches, some measuring out a place for the tents, and others making a triumphal

(a) *Fabricii Roma.* cap. 15.   (b) *Hist.* lib. 8.   (c) Lib. 3. cap. 13.

triumphal proceſſion (*a*). But the nobleſt ornament of this pillar, was the ſtatue of Trajan on the top, of a gigantic bigneſs, being no leſs than twenty feet high. He was repreſented in a coat of armour proper to the general, holding in his left hand a ſceptre, in his right a hollow globe of gold, in which his own aſhes were depoſited after his death (*b*).

The column of Antoninus was raiſed in imitation of this, which it exceeded only in one reſpect, that it was 176 feet high (*c*); for the work was much inferior to the former, as being undertaken in the declining age of the empire. The aſcent on the inſide was by 106 ſtairs, and the windows in the ſides 56. The ſculpture and the other ornaments were of the ſame nature as thoſe of the firſt; and on the top ſtood a Coloſſus of the emperor naked, as appears from ſome of his coins (*d*).

Both theſe columns are ſtill ſtanding at Rome, the former moſt entire. But Pope Sixtus the Firſt, inſtead of the two ſtatues of the emperor, ſet up St Peter's on the column of Trajan, and St Paul's on that of Antoninus (*e*).

Among the columns, we muſt not paſs by the *Milliarium aureum*, a gilded pillar in the forum, erected by Auguſtus Cæſar, at which all the high ways of Italy met, and were concluded (*f*). From this they counted their miles, at the end of every mile ſetting up a ſtone; whence came the phraſe of *Primus ab urbe lapis*, and the like. This pillar, as M. Laſſels informs us, is ſtill to be ſeen.

Nor muſt we forget the *Columna Bellica*, thus deſcribed by Ovid:

> *Proſpicit à tergo ſummum brevis area circum,*
>   *Eſt ibi non parvæ parva columna notæ :*
> *Hinc ſolet haſta manu, belli prænuncia, mitti*
>   *In regem & gentem, cùm placet arma capi* (*g*).

> Behind the circus, on the level ground,
> Stands a ſmall pillar, for its uſe renown'd:
> Hence 'tis our herald throws the fatal ſpear,
> Denotes the quarrel, and begins the war.

But thoſe who admire antiquity, will think all theſe inferior to the *Columna Roſtrata*, ſet up to the honour of C. Duillius, when he had gained ſo famous a victory over the Carthaginian and Sicilian fleets, *A. U. C.* 493, and adorned with the beaks of the veſſels taken in the engagement. This is ſtill to be ſeen in Rome, and

---

(*a*) *Fabricius* cap. 7. (*b*) *Caſalius* Par. 1. c. 11. (*c*) *Marlian.* lib. 6. cap. 13.
(*d*) *Id.* (*e*) *Caſal.* Par. 1. c. 11. (*f*) *Marlian.* l. 3. c. 18. (*g*) *Ovid. Faſt.* 6.

Book I.　　　*Of the* CITY.　　　55

and never fails of a visit from any curious stranger. The inscription on the basis is a noble example of the old way of writing, in the early times of the commonwealth. Besides this ancient and most celebrated one, there were several other *Columnæ rostratæ* erected on like occasions; as particularly four by Augustus Cæsar after the Actium defeat of Antony: To these virgil alludes:

Addam & navali surgentes ære columnas (a).

The design of the trophies is too well known to need any explication: The shape of them cannot be better understood than by the following description of the poet:

Ingentem quercum decisis undique ramis
Constituit tumulo, fulgentiáque induit arma,
Mezenti ducis exuvias; tibi magne trophæum
Bellipotens: Aptat rorantes sanguine Cristas,
Telaque trunca viri, & his sex thoraca petitum
Perfossumque locis: clypeumque ex ære sinistræ
Subligat, atque ensem collo suspendit eburnum (b).

And first he lopp'd an oak's great branches round;
The trunk he fasten'd in a rising ground:
And here he fix'd the shining armour on,
The mighty spoil from proud Mezentius won;
Above the crest was plac'd, that dropp'd with blood,
A grateful trophy to the warlike god;
His shatter'd spears stuck round: The corslet too,
Pierc'd in twelve places, hung deform'd below:
While the left side his massy target bears,
The neck the glittering blade he brandish'd in the wars.

Of those trophies which Marius raised after the Cimbric war, still remaining at Rome, we have this account in Fabricius: "They are two trunks of marble hung round with spoils: One of them is covered with a scaly corslet, with shields and other military ornaments: Just before it is set a young man in the posture of a captive, with his hands behind him, and all round were winged images of victory. The other is set out with the common military garb, having a shield of an unequal round, and two helmets, one open and adorned with crests, the other close without crests. On the same trophy is the shape of a soldier's coat, with several other designs, which, by reason of the decay of the marble, are very difficult to be discovered (c)."

CHAP.

(a) *Georg.* 3.　　(b) *Virg. Æneid.* 11.　　(c) *Fabricius,* cap. 14.

CHAP. VII.

Of the Bagnios, Aquæducts, Cloacæ, *and* Public Ways.

THERE cannot be a greater instance of the magnificence, or rather luxury of the Romans, than their noble Bagnios. Ammianus Marcellinus observes (*a*), that they were built *in modum Provinciarum*, as large as provinces: But the great Valesius (*b*) judges the word *Provinciarum* to be a corruption of *Piscinarum*. And though this emendation does in some measure extenuate one part of the vanity, which has been so often alledged against them, from the authority of that passage of the historian; yet the prodigious accounts we have of their ornaments and furniture, will bring them, perhaps, under a censure no more favourable than the former. Seneca, speaking of the luxury of his countrymen in this respect, complains, That they were arrived to such a pitch of niceness and delicacy, as to scorn to set their feet on any thing but precious stones (*c*); and Pliny wishes good old Fabricius were but alive to see the degeneracy of his posterity, when the very women must have their seats in the baths of solid silver (*d*). But a description from a poet may, perhaps, be more diverting; and this Statius has obliged us with in his poem upon the baths of Claudius Etruscus, steward to the emperor Claudius:

> *Nil ibi plebeium : nusquam Temesæa videbis*
> *Æra, sed argento felix propellitur unda,*
> *Argentoque cadit labrisque nitentibus instat*
> *Delicias mirata suas, & abire recusat.*

> Nothing there's vulgar; not the fairest brass
> In all the glittering structure claims a place.
> From silver pipes the happy waters flow,
> In silver cisterns are receiv'd below.

See

(*a*) *Ammian. Marcell.* lib. 16.   (*b*) *Nota ad locum.*   (*c*) *Epist.* 86.
(*d*) Lib. 33, cap. 12.

> See where with noble pride the doubtful stream
> Stands fix'd in wonder on the shining brim;
> Surveys its riches, and admires its state,
> Loth to be ravish'd from the glorious seat.

The most remarkable bagnios were those of the emperors Dioclesian and Antonius Caracalla, great part of which are standing at this time; and with the vast high arches, the beautiful and stately pillars, the extraordinary plenty of foreign marble, the curious vaulting of the roofs, the prodigious number of spacious apartments, and a thousand other ornaments and conveniencies, are as pleasing a sight to a traveller as any other antiquities in Rome.

To these may be added the *Nymphæ*, a kind of grottos sacred to the nymphs, from whose statues which adorned them, or from the waters and fountains which they afforded, their name is evidently derived. A short essay of the famous Lucas Holstenius, on the old picture of a *Nymphæum* dug up at the foundation of the palace of the Barbarini, is to be met with in the fourth tome of Grævius's *Thesaurus*, p. 1800.

The *Aquæducts* were, without question, some of the noblest design of the old Romans. Sextus Julius Frontinus, a Roman author, and a person of consular dignity, who has compiled a whole treatise on this subject, affirms them to be the clearest token of the grandeur of the empire. The first invention of them is attributed to Appius Claudius, *A. U. C.* 441. who brought water into the city by a channel of eleven miles in length. But this was very inconsiderable to those that were afterwards carried on by the emperors and other persons; several of which were cut through the mountains, and all other impediments, for above forty miles together; and of such a height, that a man on horseback, as Procopius informs us, might ride thro' them without the least difficulty (*a*). But this is meant only of the constant course of the channel, for the vaults and arches were in some places 109 feet high (*b*). Procopius (*c*) makes the *Aquæducts* but fourteen: Victor (*d*) has enlarged the number to twenty: In the names of them the waters only were mentioned, as *Aqua Claudia, Aqua Appia,* &c.

The noble poet Rutilius thus touches on the aquæducts, in his ingenious itinerary:

O   Quid

(*a*) *Procopius de Bell. Goth.* lib. 1.   (*b*) *Sext. Tul. Fronton.*   (*c*) *De Bell. Goth.* lib. 1.   (*d*) *Descrip. Urb. Region.*

Quid loquar aerio pendentes fornice rivos,
Qua vix imbriferas tolleret Iris aquas?
Hos potius dicas crevisse in sidera montes,
Tale giganteum Græciæ laudat opus (a).

What, should I sing how lofty waters flow
From airy vaults, and leave the rain below,
While conquer'd Iris yields with her unequal bow?
Bold Typhon here had spar'd his strength and skill,
And reach'd Jove's walls from any single hill.

But that which Pliny calls *Opus omnium maximum* were the *Cloacæ*, or common gutters for the conveyance of dirt and filth. And because no authority can be better than his, we may venture to borrow the whole account of them from the same place, *Cloacæ, opus omnium maximum*, &c.

"The *Cloacæ*, the greatest of all the works, he contrived by undermining and cutting through the seven hills upon which Rome is seated, making the city hang, as it were, between heaven and earth, and capable of being sailed under. M. Agrippa, in his ædileship, made no less than seven streams meet together under ground in one main channel, with such a rapid current, as to carry all before them that they met with in their passage. Sometimes, when they are violently swelled with immoderate rains, they beat with excessive fury against the paving at the bottom, and on the sides. Sometimes, in a flood, the Tyber waters oppose them in their course; and then the two streams encounter with all the fury imaginable; and yet the works preserve their old strength, without any sensible damage. Sometimes huge pieces of stone and timber, or such like materials, are carried down the channel, and yet the fabric receives no detriment. Sometimes the ruins of whole buildings, destroyed by fire or other casualties, press heavily upon the frame. Sometimes terrible earthquakes shake the very foundations, and yet they still continue impregnable, almost 800 years since they were first laid by Tarquinius (b)."

Very little inferior to the works already mentioned were the public ways, built with extraordinary charge, to a great distance from the city on all sides. They were generally paved with flint, though sometimes, and especially without the city, with

(a) *Rutil. Itinerar.* lib. 1. (b) *Plin.* lib 36. cap. 15.

with pebbles and gravel. The moſt noble, in all reſpects, was the *Via Appia*, taking its name from the author Appius, the ſame that invented the aquæducts, *vide* p. 57, 58. This was carried to ſuch a vaſt length, that Procopius (*a*) reckons it a very good five days journey to reach the end ; and Lipſius (*b*) computes it at 350 miles. An account of as much of this way as lyes between Rome and Naples, the right reverend the preſent Lord Biſhop of Sarum has obliged us with in his letters (*c*) : He tells us, it is twelve feet broad, all made of huge ſtones, moſt of them blue ; and they are generally a foot and a half large on all ſides. And preſently after, admiring the extraordinary ſtrength of the work, he ſays, that though it has laſted above 1800 years, yet, in moſt places, it is for ſeveral miles (*d*) together as entire as when it was firſt made. And as to the *Via Flaminia*, the next cauſeway of note, the ſame author obſerves, that though it be not indeed ſo entire as the former, yet there is enough left to raiſe a juſt idea of the Roman greatneſs.

I muſt deſire leave to conclude this ſubject with the ingenious epigram of Janus Vitalis, an Italian poet.

> *Quid Romam in media quæris novus advena Roma,*
> *Et Romæ in Roma nil reperis media ?*
> *Aſpice murorum moles, præruptaque ſaxa,*
> *Obrutaque horrenti vaſta theatra ſitu :*
> *Hæc ſunt Roma : Viden' velut ipſa cadavera tantæ*
> *Urbis adhuc ſpirent imperioſa minas ?*
> *Vicit ut hæc mundum, niſa eſt ſe vincere : vicit,*
> *A ſe non victum ne quid in orbe foret.*
> *Hinc victa in Roma victrix Roma illa ſepulta eſt,*
> *Atque eadem victrix victaque Roma fuit.*
> *Albula Romani reſtat nunc nominis index,*
> *Qui quoque nunc rapidis fertur in æquor aquis.*
> *Diſce hinc quod poſſit fortuna ; immota lavaſcunt,*
> *Et quæ perpetuo ſunt agitata, manent.*

To ſeek for Rome, vain ſtranger ! art thou come,
And find'ſt no mark, within Rome's walls, of Rome ?
See here the craggy walls, the tow'rs defac'd,
And piles that frighten more than once they pleas'd :
See the vaſt theatres, a ſhapeleſs load,
And ſights more tragic than they ever ſhow'd.

(*a*) *De Bell. Goth.* lib. 1.   (*b*) *De Magn. Rom.*   (*c*) *Letter* 4th.   (*d*) *Ibid.*

This, this is Rome: Her haughty carcafe fpread,
Still awes in ruin, and commands when dead.
The fubject world firft took from her their fate;
And when fhe only ftood unconquer'd yet,
Herfelf fhe laft fubdu'd, to make the work complete.
But ah! fo dear the fatal triumph coft,
That conqu'ring Rome is in the conquer'd loft.
Yet rolling Tyber ftill maintains his ftream,
Swell'd with the glories of the Roman name.
Strange pow'r of fate! unfhaken moles muft wafte,
While things that ever move for ever laft.

PART

PART II. BOOK II.

Of the RELIGION of the Romans.

CHAP. I.

Of the Religion and Morality of the ROMANS in General.

THAT RELIGION is absolutely necessary for the establishing of civil government, is a truth so far from being denied by any sort of persons, that we meet with too many who are unwilling to allow any other design in sacred institutions. As to the Romans, it has been universally agreed, That virtue and fortune were engaged in a sort of noble contention for the advancement of the grandeur and happiness of that people. And a judge, not suspected of partiality in that case, has concluded the latter to be only a consequence of the former, "For religion," says he, (a), "produced good laws, "good laws good fortune, and good fortune a good end, in "whatever they undertook." Nor, perhaps, has he strained the panegyric much too high, when he tells us, That, "for several ages together, never was the fear of God more "eminently conspicuous than in that republic (b)." It was this consideration which made the great St Austin observe (c), That God would not give heaven to the Romans, because they were heathens; but he gave them the empire of the world, because they were virtuous. And, indeed, in their more

general

(a) *Machiavel's* Discourse on *Livy*, lib. I. cap. II.   (b) *Ibid.*
(c) *Civitate Dei*, lib. 4. cap. 5.

general virtues, their practice inclined rather to the excess than the defect: Thus were they devout to superstition; valiant to a contempt of life, and an inconsiderate courting of danger: Frugal and temperate in the first ages, to a voluntary abstinence from agreeable pleasures and conveniencies; constant, several times, to the occasion of their own ruin, and rather rigorous than just. A tedious account of the Decii, Regulus, Fabricius, Curius, Scævola, &c. would be needless even to a school-boy, who is seldom unfurnished with a stock of such histories.

But we must by no means omit a most noble saying of Cicero to this purpose, in his oration about the answer of the *Aruspices: Quam volumus licet, Patres Conscripti, nos amemus: tamen nec numero Hispanos, nec robore Gallos, nec calliditate Pœnos, nec artibus Græcos; nec denique hoc ipso hujus Gentis & Terræ domestico nativoque sensu Italos ipsos & Latinos, sed Pietate ac Religione, atque hac una sapientia quod Deorum immortalium Numine omnia regi gubernarique perspeximus, omnes Gentis Nationesque superavimus.*

But it will naturally be objected, that whatever harangues we make upon the justice, temperance, and other celebrated virtues of the old Romans, they at last degenerated into the most luxurious and extravagant people in the world. Every page of their own satyrists is a very good argument for this opinion; besides the numerous complaints of their historians and other writers. Now tho' Lipsius has undertaken to bring them off clear from all such imputations, yet I think we must be forced to allow, that they did indeed debase the noble and generous spirit of their ancestors; and this corruption was, without doubt, the only cause of the declension and final ruin of the empire. But as we are not to give over the cause of virtue, on account of the debauchery of latter times, so we have little reason to exalt the eminent qualities of the old Romans to so high a pitch as some imagine. There is no necessity of making a hero of every consul, or fancying every one, who was eminently serviceable to the republic, to have been a person of consummate virtue. So that when we meet in Roman authors with such extravagant encomiums of their ancestors, we may conclude, that what Horace had observed with reference to poetry, will hold altogether as well in this case: The generality of people being so strangely transported with the love and admiration of antiquity, that nothing was more usual than to meet with such a person as he describes.

Qui

Qui redit ad Faftos, & virtutem æftimat annis,
Miraturque nihil nifi quod Libitina facravit.

That, when he tried a man's pretence to fame,
Runs to his chronicle to find his name:
Thinks virtue better for its age, like wine;
And only likes what death has made divine.

For we may often obferve, that their very panegyrics upon the honeft people of the firft ages of the commonwealth reprefent them rather as a fort of rude, unpolifhed mortals, than as perfons eminent for any noble endowments. So Juvenal, Sat. 14:

———Saturabat glebula talis
Patrem ipfum turbamque cafæ; quâ fæta jacebat
Uxor, & infantes ludebant quatuor, unis
Vernula, tres domini: Sed magnis fratribus horum
A fcrobe vel fulco redeüntibus altera cœna
Amplior, & grandes fumabant pultibus ollæ.

———This little fpot of earth, well till'd,
A numerous family with plenty fill'd.
The good old man and thrifty houfewife fpent
Their days in peace, and fatten'd with content;
Enjoy'd the dregs of life, and liv'd to fee
A long-defcending healthful progeny.
The men were fafhion'd in a larger mould:
The women fit for labour, big and bold.
Gigantic hinds, as foon as work was done,
To their huge pots of boiling pulfe would run,
Fell to, with eager joy, on homely food,
And their large veins beat ftrong with wholefome blood.
Mr JOHN DRYDEN, Jun.

But the account which Perfius gives us of Titus Quintius, the old country Dictator, has fomething more of the ridiculous in it;

Unde Remus, fulcoque terens dentalia, Quinti,
Quem trepida ante boves Dictatorem induit uxor,
Et tua Aratra domum Lictor tulit (a).

Where

(a) *Perf. Sat.* 1.

> Where Romulus was bred, and Quintius born,
> Whose shining plough-share was in furrows worn,
> Met by his trembling wife returning home,
> And rustically joy'd as chief of Rome.
> She wip'd the sweat from the Dictator's brow;
> And o'er his back his robe did rudely throw;
> The lictors bore in state the Lord's triumphant plow.
> Mr DRYDEN.

We must therefore allow every age its proper character and commendation; and conclude with the ingenious Monsier St Evremont, "That the excellent citizens lived among "the ancient Romans, and the most accomplished generals a- "mong the latter (a)."

(a) Reflect. upon the Genius of the Roman People, cap. 4.

CHAP. II.

Of the Luperci, Lupercalia, *&c. Of the* Potitii *and* Pinarii, *and of the* Arval *Brothers.*

THE places of worship having been already described, the chief subjects that still remain, relating to religion, are the priests, the sacrifices, and the festivals: For it would be very needless and impertinent to enter into a disquisition about the deities; a matter that is involved in so many endless fictions, and yet has employed so many pens to explain it.

Luperci.] The most ancient order of the priests were the *Luperci*, sacred to Pan the god of the country, and particularly of shepherds. They had their name from the deity they attended on, called in Greek λύκαιος, probably from λύκος, a wolf, in Latin *Lupus;* because the chief employment of Pan was the driving away such beasts from the sheep that he *Lupercalia,* protected. The *Lupercalia,* as Plutarch observes, appear to have been a feast of *Purification,* being solemnized on the *Dies Nefasti,* or non-court-days of the month February, which derives its name from *februo* to purify:
And

and the very day of the celebration was anciently called *Februaca* (*a*).

The ceremony was very singular and strange.

In the first place, there was a sacrifice killed of goats and a dog. Then two children, noblemens sons, being brought thither, some of the Luperci stained their foreheads with the bloody knife, while others wiped it off with locks of wool dipped in milk; the boys must always laugh after their foreheads had been wiped: This done, having cut the goat-skins into thongs, they ran about the streets all naked but their middle, and lashed all that they met in their procession. The young women never took any care to avoid the strokes, but rather offered themselves of their own accord, fancying them to be great helpers of conception and delivery (*b*) They ran naked, because Pan is always painted so. They sacrificed a goat, because the same deity was supposed to have goat's feet; which gave occasion to his common epithet of *Capripes*. As for the dog we meet with in the sacrifice, it was added as a necessary companion of a shepherd, and because of the natural antipathy between them and wolves.

Some have fancied with Plutarch, that these Lupercalia were instituted in honour of the wolf that preserved Romulus and Remus. Others carry their original much higher, and tell us, that they were brought into Italy by Evander, before the time of Æneas.

There were two companies of the Luperci, the *Fabiani* and *Quintiliani*; one for Romulus, the other for Remus: They took their names from Fabius and Quintilius, two of their masters or chief priests (*c*). Dion Cassius tells us, that a third sort of priests, designed for the celebration of the Lupercalia, were instituted by the Senate to the honour of Julius Cæsar (*d*).

Suetonius(*e*)reckons the Lupercalia among the ancient rites and ceremonies restored by Augustus: And Onuph. Panvinius assures us they continued in Rome till the time of the emperor Anastasius.

2. *Potitii* and *Pinarii*.] The Potitii and Pinarii were of equal antiquity with the former. They owe their institution to the same author, upon the following account:

After the killing of Cacus, a giant that had stole some of Hercules's cattle, the booty that he brought through Italy, from Spain, the shepherds and ignorant people of the country gathering in great flocks about the stranger, at last brought him before Evander. The king, after examination, finding him to be

---

(*a*) *Plutarch* in *Romul.* (*b*) *Ibid.* (*c*) *Sext. Pomp. Festus, & Ovid, Fast.* (*d*) *Ibid.* 44. (*e*) In *August.* cap. 31.

be in all respects the same person that his mother the prophetess Carmenta had told him should come into Italy, and be afterwards a god, immediately erected an altar to his honour, and offered for a sacrifice a young bullock that never bore the yoke; ordaining that the same ceremony should be repeated in a solemn manner every year. The performance of these rites he committed to the care of the Potitii and Pinarii, two of the noblest families, and of best repute in those parts. There goes a story, that the Pinarii happening to come too late to the sacrifice, so as to lose their share in the intrails, they were, by way of punishment, debarred from ever tasting them for the future: And hence some derive their name from πεῖνα, Hunger. But this I take to be but a trifling fancy; for we may as well derive Potitii from *Potiri*, because they enjoyed the intrails, as Pinarii from πεῖνα, because they wanted them.

We meet with something very remarkable of the Potitii in Livy (*a*), and Valerius Maximus (*b*).

That when, upon application made to Appius Claudius the Censor, they got leave to have their hereditary ministry discharged by servants, in the compass of one year the whole family was entirely extinct, though no less than thirty of them were lusty young men. And Appius Claudius lost his eyes, as a judgment for his part in the offence.

Acca Laurentia, Romulus's nurse, had a custom once a year to make a solemn sacrifice for a blessing upon the fields; her twelve sons assisting her always in the solemnity. At last she had the ill fortune to lose one of her sons; when Romulus, to show his gratitude and respect, offered himself to fill up the number in his room, and gave the company the name of *Fratres Arvales*. This order was in great repute at Rome; they held the dignity always for their lives, and never lost it upon account of imprisonment, banishment, or any other accident (*c*). They wore on their heads, at the time of their solemnity, crowns made of ears of corn, upon a tradition that Laurentia at first presented Romulus with such an one (*d*). Some will have it, that it was their business to take care of the boundaries, and the divisions of lands, and to decide all controversies that might happen about them: The processions, or perambulations made under their guidance, being termed *Ambarvalia*: Others make a different order instituted for that purpose, and called *Sodales Arvales*, on the same account as the *Fratres Arvales*.

CHAP.

(*a*) Lib. 9. (*b*) Lib. 1. c. 1. (*c*) *Plin.* l. 17. c. 2. (*d*) *Pomp. Lat. de Sacerd.*

CHAP. III.

Of the Augurs, Auguries, *&c.*

THE invention of soothsaying is generally attributed to the Chaldeans; from them the art passed to the Grecians; the Grecians delivered it to the Tuscans, and they to the Latins and the Romans. The name of *Augur* is derived by some, *ab Avium gestu*, by others, *ab Avium gerritu*; either from the motion and actions, or from the chirping and chattering of birds. Romulus was himself an extraordinary proficient in this art (*a*), and therefore, as he divided the city into three tribes, so he constituted three Augurs, one for every tribe. There was a fourth added some time after, probably by Servius Tullius, who increased the tribes to that number. These four being all chosen out of the patricii, or nobility, in the year of the city 454, the tribunes of the people, with much difficulty, procured an order, that five persons, to be elected out of the commons, should be added to the college (*b*). Afterwards Sylla, the Dictator, *A. U. C.* 671, made the number up fifteen (*c*). The eldest of these had the command of the rest, and was honoured with the title of *Magister Collegii* (*d*).

Their business was to interpret dreams, oracles, prodigies, &c. and to tell whether any action should be fortunate or prejudicial to any particular persons, or to the whole commonwealth. Upon this account, they very often occasioned the displacing of magistrates, the deferring of public assemblies, &c. whenever the omens proved unlucky.

Before we proceed to the several kinds of auguries, it may not be improper to give an account of the two chief terms by which they are distinguished in authors, *Dextra* and *Sinistra*. These being differently applied by the Greeks and Latins, and very often by the Latins themselves, (who sometimes speak agreeably to the Grecian customs, sometimes according to their own) have given occasion to many mistakes, which may be all cleared up by this easy observation, That the Greeks and Romans both deriving the happiness of their omens from the eastern quarter, the former turned towards the north, and so had the east on the right hand; the latter towards the south,

and

(*a*) *Plutarch.* in *Romul.* (*b*) *Liv.* lib 10. (*c*) *Florus* Epitom. *Liv.* lib. 89.
(*d*) *Alex. ab Alex.* lib. 5, cap. 19.

and therefore had the east on their left. *Vide* Bullenger, de Augur. & Auspic. L. 2. C. 2.

There are five sorts of auguries mentioned in authors.

1. From the appearances in heaven; as thunder, lightning, comets, and other meteors. As suppose of thunder, whether it came from the right or the left; whether the number of strokes were even or odd, &c. Only the master of the college could take this sort of augury (a).

2. From birds; whence they had the names of *Auspices*, of *avis* and *specio*. Some birds furnished them with observations from their chattering and singing, others from their flying. The former they called *Oscines*, the latter *Præpetes*. Of the first sort, were crows, pies, owls, &c. of the other, eagles, vultures, buzzards, and the like.

For the taking of both these sorts of auguries, the observer stood upon a tower, with his head covered in a gown peculiar to his office, called *Læna*, and turning his face towards the east, marked out the heavens into four templa, or quarters, with his lituus, a short straight rod, only a little turning at one end: This done, he staid waiting for the omen, which never signified any thing, unless confirmed by another of the same sort.

3. From chickens kept in a coop or pen for this purpose. The manner of divining from them was as follows: Betimes in the morning the augur that was to make the observation, called from hence *Pullarius* (tho' perhaps the keeper of the chickens had rather that name) in the first place commanding a general silence, ordered the pen to be opened, and threw down a handful of crumbs or corn. If the chickens did not immediately run fluttering to the meat; if they scattered it with their wings; if they went by without taking notice of it, or if they flew away, the omen was reckoned unfortunate, and to protend nothing but danger or mischance: But if they leaped presently out of the pen, and fell to so greedily as to let some of their meat drop out of their mouths upon the pavement, there was all the assurance in the world of happiness and success (b). This augury was called *Tripudium quasi Terripavium*, from striking the earth; the old word *pavire* signifying as much as *ferire*. We meet with *Tripudium Solistimum*, and *Tripudium Sonivium* in Festus, both derived from the crumbs falling to the ground.

4. From beasts. These, as Rosinus reckons them up, were wolves, foxes, goats, heifers, asses, rams, hares, weesels, and mice. The general observations about them were, Whether they appeared in a strange place, or crossed the way; or whether they ran to the right or the left, &c. 5. The

(a) *Alex. ab Alex.* lib. 5. cap. 19. (b) *Idem*, lib. 9. cap. 29.

5. The last sort of divination was from what they called *Diræ*, or unusual accidents to any person or place; as sneezing, stumbling, seeing apparitions, hearing strange voices, the falling of salt upon the table, the spilling of wine upon one's cloathes, the meeting a wolf, a fox, a hare, a bitch with whelp, &c.

We may observe, that though any augur might take an observation, yet the judging of the omen was left to the decision of the whole college (a).

Cicero has sufficiently exposed these auguries, especially that about the chickens, in his second book of divination.

The learned Mr O W. has taken notice, that the emperors assumed the office of augurs as well as pontiffs, as appears from several coins of Julius, Augustus, Vespasian, Verus, &c. which have the augurs ensigns upon them.

CHAP. IV.
Of the Aruspices *and* Pontifices.

THE Aruspices had this name *ab aris aspiciendis*, from looking upon the altars; as *ab extis inspiciendis*, they were called *Extispices:* They owe their original to Romulus, who borrowed the institution from the Tuscans. The Tuscans received it, as the general tradition goes, from a boy that they strangely ploughed up out of the ground, who obliged them with a discovery of all the mysteries belonging to this art (b). At first, only the natives of Tuscany exercised this office at Rome; and therefore the senate made an order, that twelve of the sons of the principal nobility should be sent into that country to be instructed in the rites and ceremonies of their religion, of which this secret was a chief part (c). The business of the Aruspices was to look upon the beasts offered in sacrifice, and by them to divine the success of any enterprise. They took their observations from four appearances:

1. From the beasts before they were cut up.
2. From the intrails of those beasts after they were cut up.
3. From the flame that used to rise when they were burning.
4. From the flour or bran, from the frankincense, wine, and water that they used in the sacrifice.

In the beasts, before they were cut up, they took notice, whether they were forcibly dragged to the altar; whether they got loose

(a) *Alex. ab Alex.* l. 1. c. 29.   (b) *Cicero de Div.* l. 2.   (c) *Id. de Liv.* l. 1.

loose out of the leaders hands; whether they escaped the stroke, or bounded up, and roared very loud when they received it; whether they died with a great deal of difficulty; all which, with several other omens, were counted unfortunate: Or whether, on the other side, they followed the leader without compulsion; received the blow without struggling and resistance; whether they led easily, and sent out a great quantity of blood, which gave equal assurance of a prosperous event.

In the beast, when cut up, they observed the colour of the parts, and whether any were wanting. A double liver was counted highly unfortunate: A little or a lean heart was always unlucky: If the heart was wholly missing, nothing could be thought more fatal and dreadful; as it happened in two oxen together, offered by Julius Cæsar, a little before his murder: If the intrails fell out of the priest's hands; if they were besmeared more than ordinarily with blood; if they were of a pale livid colour, they portended sudden danger and ruin.

As to the flame of the sacrifice, it furnished them with a good omen, if it gathered up violently, and presently consumed the sacrifice; if it was clear, pure, and transparent, without any mixture of smoke, and not discoloured with red, pale, or black; if it was quiet and calm, not sparkling or crackling, but ran up directly in the shape of a pyramid. On the contrary, it always portended misfortunes, if at first it required much pains to light it; if it did not burn upright, but rolled into circles, and left void spaces between them; if it did not presently catch hold on the whole sacrifice, but crept up by degrees from one part to another; if it happened to be spread about by the wind, or to be put out by sudden rain, or to leave any part unconsumed.

In the meal, frankincense, wine and water, they were to observe, whether they had their due quantity, their proper taste, colour, smell, &c.

There were several lesser signs which supplied them with conjectures, too insignificant to be here mentioned.

Most of those ill omens are hinted at by Virgil, *Geor.* 3. *v.* 486.

Sæpe in honore Deûm medio stans hostia ad aram,
Lanea dum niveâ circumdatur insulâ vittâ,
Inter cunctantes cecidit moribunda ministros.
Aut si quam ferro mactaverat antè Sacerdos,
Inde neque impositis ardent altaria fibris,
Nec responsa potest consultus reddere vates:
Ac vix suppositi tinguntur sanguine cultri,
Summaque jejunâ sanie infuscatur arena.

> The victim ox that was for altars press'd,
> Trim'd with white ribbons, and with garlands dress'd,
> Sunk of himself without the gods command,
> Preventing the slow sacrificer's hand:
> Or, by the wooly butcher if he fell,
> Th' inspected intrails could no fate foretell:
> Nor laid on altars, did pure flames arise,
> But clouds of smouldring smoke forbade the sacrifice.
> Scarcely the knife was redden'd with his gore,
> Or the black poison stain'd the sandy floor.
>
> Mr DRYDEN.

Yet the business of the Aruspices was not restrained to the altars and sacrifices, but they had an equal right to the explaining all other portents and monsters. Hence we find them often consulted by the Senate on extraordinary occasions; or if the Roman Aruspices lay under a disrepute, others were sent for out of Tuscany, where this craft most flourished, as it was first invented.

The college of Aruspices, as well as those of the other religious orders, had their particular registers and records, such as the memorials of thunders and lightenings, the Tuscan histories and the like.

There are but two accounts of the derivation of the name of the *Pontifices*, and both very uncertain; either from *Pons*, and *facere*; because they first built the Sublician bridge in Rome, and had the care of its repair; or from *Posse* and *facere*, where *facere* must be interpreted to signify the same as *Offere* and *Sacrificare*. The first of these is the most received opinion; and yet Plutarch himself hath called it absurd (a). At the first institution of them by *Numa*, the number was confined to four, who were constantly chosen out of the nobility, 'till the year of the city 454, when five more were ordered to be added of the commons, at the same time that the Augurs received the like addition. And as the Augurs had a college, so the Pontifices too were settled in such a body. And as Sylla afterwards added seven Augurs, so he added as many Pontifices to the college: The first eight bearing the name of *Pontifices, majores*, and the rest of *minores*.

The offices of the Pontifices were to give judgment in all causes relating to religion; to inquire into the lives and manners of the inferior priests, and to punish them if they saw occasion; to prescribe rules for public worship; to regulate the feasts, sacrifices,

---

(a) In *Numa*.

crifices, and all other sacred institutions. Tully, in his oration to them for his house, tells them, that the honour and safety of the commonwealth, the liberty of the people, the houses and fortunes of the citizens, and the very gods themselves were all entrusted to their care, and depended wholly on their wisdom and management.

The master or superintendant of the Pontifices was one of the most honourable offices in the commonwealth. Numa, when he instituted the order, invested himself first with this dignity, as Plutarch informs us; tho' Livy attributes it to another person of the same name. Festus's definition of this great priest is, *Judex atque Arbiter Rerum Humanarum, Divinarumque,* the Judge and Arbitrator of Divine and Human Affairs. Upon this account all the emperors, after the examples of Julius Cæsar and Augustus, either actually took upon them the office, or at least used the name. And even the Christian emperors, for some time, retained this in the ordinary enumeration of their titles, 'till the time of Gratian, who (as we learn from (*a*) Zosimus) absolutely refused it.

Polydore Virgil (*b*) does not question but this was an infallible omen of the authority which the Bishop of Rome enjoys to this day, under the name of *pontifex maximus*.

(*a*) *Histor.* lib. 4.   (*b*) *De rerum invent.* lib. 4. cap. 14.

CHAP. V.

Of the Flamines, Rex Sacrorum, Salii, Feciales *and* Sodales.

THE name of *Flamines* is not much clearer than the former. Plutarch makes it a corruption of *Pilamines* from *Pileus*, a sort of cap proper to the order. Varro, Festus, and Servius will have it to be a contradiction of *Filamines*, from *Filum*; and tell us, that, finding their caps too heavy and troublesome, they took up a lighter fashion, only binding a parcel of thread about their heads. Others derive the word from *Flamina* or *Flameum*, a sort of Turban, which they make them to have worn; tho' this generally signifies a woman's veil. Rosinus and Mr Dodwell declare for the second of these opinions; Polydore Virgil has given his judgment in favour of the third (*a*).

Numa

(*a*) *De invent. rer.* lib. 4. cap. 14.

Numa at first discharged several offices of religion himself, and designed that all his successors should do the like; but because he thought the greatest part of them would partake more of Romulus's genius than his own, and that their being engaged in warlike enterprises might incapacitate them for this function, he instituted these Flamines to take care of the same services which by right belonged to the kings (*a*).

The only three constituted at first was Flamen Dialis, Martialis, and Quirinalis. The first was sacred to Jupiter, and a person of the highest authority in the commonwealth. He was obliged to observe several superstitious restraints, as well as honoured with several eminent privileges beyond other officers; which are reckoned up at large by Gellius (*b*). The same author tells us, that the wife of this Flamen had the name of *Flaminica*, and was entrusted with the care of several ceremonies peculiar to her place.

But, to be sure, the greatness of the dignity was sufficiently diminished in succeeding times, otherwise we cannot imagine that Julius Cæsar should have been invested with it at seventeen years of age, as Suetonius (*c*) informs us he was; or that Sylla should have so easily driven him from his office, and from his house.

The other two were of less, yet of very eminent authority; ordained to inspect the rites of Mars and Romulus. All three were chosen out of the nobility. Several priests of the same order, tho' of inferior power and dignity, were added in latter times; the whole number being generally computed at fifteen. Yet Fenestella (or the author under his name) assures us from Varro, that the old Romans had a particular Flamen for every deity they worshipped (*d*).

Though the Flamen Dialis discharged several religious duties that properly belonged to the kings, yet we meet with another officer of greater authority, who seems to have been purely designed for that employment: And this was the *Rex Sacrificulus*, or *Sacrorum*. Dionysius gives us the original of this institution as follows: "Because the kings had in a great many respects been very serviceable to the state, the establishers of the commonwealth thought it very proper to keep always the name of King in the city. Upon this account they ordered the Augurs and Pontifices to choose out a fit person, who should engage never to have the least hand in civil affairs, but devote himself wholly to the care of the public worship " and

(*a*) Liv. lib. 1.   (*b*) Noct. Att. lib. 10. cap. 15.   (*c*) Cap. 1.
(*d*) De Sacerdotiis, cap. 15.   (*e*) Antiq. lib. 5.

"and ceremonies of religion, with the title of *Rex Sacrorum* (a)." And Livy informs us, that the office of *Rex Sacrorum* was therefore made inferior to that of *Pontifex Maximus*, for fear that the name of King, which had been formerly so odious to the people, might, for all this restraint, be still, in some measure, prejudicial to their liberty (b).

Salii.] The original of Salii may be thus gathered from Plutarch. In the eight year of Numa's reign a terrible pestilence spreading itself over Italy, among other places miserably infested Rome. The citizens were almost grown desperate, when they were comforted on a sudden by the report of a brasen target, which (they say) fell into Numa's hands from heaven. The king was assured by the conference he maintained with the nymph Egeria and the Muses, that the target was sent from the gods for the cure and safety of the city; and this was soon verified by the miraculous ceasing of the sickness. They advised him too, to make eleven other targets, so like in their dimensions and form to the original, that, in case there should be a design of stealing it away, the true might not be distinguished or known from those which were counterfeited; by which means it would be more difficult to defeat the counsels of fate, in which it had been determined, that, while this was preserved, the city should prove happy and victorious. This difficult work one Veturius Mamurius very luckily performed, and made eleven others that Numa himself could not know from the first. They were worked into an oval form, with several folds or plaits closing one over another; they exactly fitted the elbow by their figure, and were thence called *Anclya*, from Ἀγκύη, which signifies a crooked javelin; or from the *Cubit* (Ἀγκών) that part of the arm between the wrist and the elbow upon which they carried the Anclya (c): For the keeping of these, Numa instituted an order of priests, called *Salii, à saliendo*, from leaping or dancing. They lived all in a body, and composed a college consisting of the same number of men with the bucklers which they preserved. The three seniors governed the rest; of whom the first had the name of *Præsul*, the second of *Vates*, and the other of *Magister* (d). In the month of March was their great feast, when they carried their sacred charge about the city. At this procession they were habited in a short scarlet cassoc, having round them a broad belt clasped with brass buckles. On their head they wore a sort of copper helmet. In this manner they went on with a nimble motion, keeping just measures with their feet and

(a) *Antiq.* lib. 5. (b) *Liv.* lib. 2.   (c) *Plutarch.* in *Numa.*   (d) *Alex. ab Alex.* lib. 1. cap. 26.

and demonstrating great strength and agility by the various and handsome turns of their body (*a*). They sung all along a set of old verses, called the *Carmen Saliere*, the original form of which was composed by Numa. They were sacred to Mars, (the ancylia, or targets, being parts of armour) who from them took the name of *Salisubsulus:* And therefore, upon account of the extraordinary noise and shaking that they made in their dances, Catullus, to signify a strong bridge, has used the phrase,

In quo vel Salisubsuli Sacra fiunto (*b*),

unless the conjecture of Vossius be true, that *Salisubsulus* is here a corruption from *Salii ipsulis:* The performers in those dances bearing with them, among other superstitious trifles, a sort of thin plates worked into the shapes of men and women, which they called *ipsiles*, or *subsiles;* and *ipsulæ*, or *subsulæ*. Upon admitting this opinion, Mars must lose his name of *salisubsulus;* and Pacuvius cannot relieve him; because the verse with this word in it commonly cited from that old poet, is thought (by Vossius at least) to be a mere fiction of Muretus's, who was noted for this kind of forgery. See Voss. in Catull. p. 46.

Tho' the month of March (dedicated to that god) was the proper time for carrying about the Ancylia, yet if at any time a just and lawful war had been proclaimed by order of the senate against any state or people, the Salii were in a solemn manner to move the Ancylia; as if by that means they roused Mars from his seat, and sent him out to the assistance of their arms (*c*).

Tullus Hostillus afterwards increased the college with twelve more Salii, in pursuance of a vow he made in the battle with the Sabines: And therefore, for distinction-sake, the twelve first were generally called *Salii Palatini*, from the Palatine mountain, whence they began their procession; the other *Salii Collini*, or *Agonenses*, from the Quirinal hill, sometimes called *Mons Agonalis*, where they had a chapel on one of the highest eminences of the mountain (*d*).

Alexander ab Alexandro has observed, that the entertainments of these priests, upon their solemn festivals, were exceeding costly and magnificent, with all the variety of music, garlands, perfumes, &c. (*e*): And therefore Horace uses *dapes saliares* (*f*) for delicate meats, as he does *pontificum cœnæ* (*g*) for great regalios.

Feciales.]

(*a*) *Plutarch.* in *Num.* (*b*) *Catull. Carm.* 17. (*c*) *Alex. ab Alex.* lib. 1. cap. 26. (*d*) *Dionys. Halic.* lib. 3. (*e*) *Gen. Dier.* lib. 1. cap. 6. (*f*) Lib. 1. Od. 37. (*g*) Lib. 1. Od. 14.

Feciales.] The *Feciales* Varro derives from *Fides*, because they had the care of the public faith in leagues and contracts. Others bring the word *à fœdere faciendo* on the same account. Their original in Italy was very ancient. Dionysius Halicarn. finds them among the Aborigines under the name of σπονδοφόροι, *libaminum latores:* And Virgil intimates as much in several places. Numa first instituted the order at Rome (*a*), consisting of twenty persons (*b*), chosen out of the most eminent families in the city, and settled in a college. It is probable he ranked them among the officers of religion, to procure them the more deference and authority, and to make their persons more sacred in the commonwealth.

Their office was to be the arbitrators of all controversies relating to war and peace; nor was it lawful on any account to take up arms, till they had declared all means and expedients that might tend to an accommodation to be insufficient. In case the republic had suffered any injury from a foreign state, they dispatched these feciales, who were properly heralds, to demand satisfaction; who, if they could procure no restitution or just return, calling the gods to witness against the people and country, immediately denounced war; otherwise they confirmed the alliance that had been formerly made, or contracted a new one (*c*). But the ceremonies used upon both these occasions will fall more properly under another head. It is enough to observe here, that both the affairs were managed by these officers with the consent of the senate and people.

As to the *Pater Patratus*, it is not easy to determine whether he was a constant officer, and the chief of the feciales, or whether he was not a temporary master, elected upon account of making a peace or denouncing war, which were both done by him. Rosinus makes him the constant governor or master of the feciales (*d*). Fenestella (or the author under his name) a distinct officer altogether (*e*). Pomponius Lætus (*f*) and Polydore Virgil (*g*) tells us, that he was only chosen by one of the feciales out of their own body, upon such occasions as we mentioned but now. The latter opinion may be defended by the authority of Livy, who, in order to the treaty with the Albans before the triple combat of the Horatii and Curiatii, makes one of the feciales chuse a Pater Patratus to perform that ceremony (*h*). The person to be entrusted with this office must have been one, who

(*a*) Dionys. Liv. (*b*) Alex. ab Alex. lib. 5. cap. 3. (*c*) Plutarch in Num.
(*d*) Lib. 3. cap. 21. (*e*) De Sacerdot. Rom. cap. 6. (*f*) Ibid. (*g*) De invent.
Rer. lib. 4. cap. 14. (*h*) Lib. 1. cap. 24.

who had a father and a son both alive; and therefore Pater Patratus is no more than a more perfect sort of father; as they imagined him to be, whose own father was still living after he himself had been a father for some time. Perhaps too they might fancy him to be the fittest judge in affairs of such consequence, who could see as well behind as before him (*a*).

Tho' the members of any collegiate body, and particularly the free tradesmen of the several companies, are often called *Sodales,* yet those who challenged that name by way of eminence, were religious officers, instituted to take care of the festivals and annual honours of great persons deceased. The first of this order were the *Sodales Tatii,* created to supervise the solemnities in memory of Tatius the Sabine King. Tiberius founded a college of the same nature, and gave the members the title of *Sodales Augustales;* their business was to inspect the rites paid to Augustus Cæsar after his death; and to perform the same good offices to the whole Julian family, as the old Sodales Tatii preserved the sacred memorials of all the Sabine race.

Afterwards we meet with the *Sodales Antoniniani, Helviani, Alexandrini,* &c. instituted on the like accounts, but so restrained to the service of the particular emperors that the Antoniniani, for example, were divided into the Pii, Lucii, Marci, &c. according to the proper name of the prince on whose honours they were to attend. Vid. Dodwell. Prælect. 1. ad Spartian. Hadrian. S. 5.

(*a*) *Plutarch.* in *Quæstion. Roman.*

CHAP. VI.

Of the VESTALS.

THE institution of the *Vestal Virgins* is generally attributed to Numa; tho' we meet with the *Sacred Fire* long before, and even in the time of Æneas. But perhaps Numa was the first who settled the order, and built a temple to the Goddess in Rome (*a*). Their office was to attend upon the rites of Vesta, the chief part of it (*b*) being the preservation of the holy fire, which

(*a*) *Virgil. Æneid.* lib. 2. carm. 297. (*b*) *Plutarch. & Dionysius.*

which Numa, fancying fire to be the firſt principle of all things, committed to their charge. Ovid tells us, that they underſtood nothing elſe but fire by Veſta herſelf:

Nec tu aliud Veſtam quam vivam intellige flammam (a).

Though ſometimes he makes her the ſame as the earth:

————*Tellus Veſtaque numen idem eſt* (b).

Polydore Virgil reconciles the two names, by obſerving that fire, or the natural heat by which all things are produced, is encloſed in the earth (c).

They were obliged to keep this fire with all the care in the world; and, if it happened to go out, it was thought impiety to light it at any common flame, but they made uſe of the pure and unpolluted rays of the ſun (d). Every year, on the firſt of March, whether it had gone out or no, they always lighted it a-new (e). There were other relics and holy things under their care, of which we have very uncertain accounts; particularly the famous *Palladium* brought from Troy by Æneas; for Ulyſſes and Diomedes ſtole only a counterfeit one, a copy of the other, which was kept with leſs care.

Dionyſius and Plutarch aſſure us, that Numa conſtituted only four virgins for this ſervice; and that the ſame number remained ever after. And therefore a great antiquary is certainly miſtaken, when he makes the number increaſed to twenty (f).

They were admitted into this ſociety between the years of ſix and ten; and were not properly ſaid to be elected or created, but *Captæ*, taken; the Pontifex Maximus taking her that he liked by the hand, and leading her, as it were by force, from her parents (g).

The chief rules preſcribed them by their founder, were to vow the ſtricteſt chaſtity for the ſpace of thirty years. The firſt ten they were only novices, obliged to learn the ceremonies, and perfect themſelves in the duties of their religion. The next ten years they actually diſcharged the ſacerdotal function; and ſpent the remaining ten in teaching and inſtructing others.

After

(a) *Faſt*. 6. v. 231.   (b) *Faſt*. 6. v. 460.   (c) *De invent. Rer.* lib. 1. cap. 14.
(d) *Plutarch*, in *Numa*.   (e) *Alex. ab Alex.* l. 5. c. 12. *Macrob. Saturnal.* l. 1. c. 12.
(f) *Alex. ab Alex. Ibid.*   (g) *A. Gell.* lib. 1. cap. 12.

After this term was completed, they had liberty to leave the order, and chuse any condition of life that beſt ſuited with their inclinations; tho' this was counted unlucky, and therefore ſeldom put in practice. Upon commiſſion of any leſſer faults, they were puniſhed as the Pontifex Maximus (who had the care of them) thought fit. But if they broke their vow of virginity, they were conſtantly buried alive in a place without the city-wall allotted for that particular uſe (*a*), and thence called *Campus Sceleratus*, as Feſtus informs us.

But this ſevere condition was recompenſed with ſeveral privileges and prerogatives. When they went abroad, they had the faſces carried before them (*b*), a conſul or prætor being obliged to give them the way (*c*). And if in their walk they caſually lighted upon a malefactor leading to execution, they had the favour to deliver him from the hands of juſtice, provided they made oath that their meeting was purely accidental, without any compact or deſign (*d*).

(*a*) *Plutarch*. in *Num*.   (*b*) *Ibid*.   (*c*) *Alex. ab Alex*. lib. 5. cap. 12.
(*d*) *Plutarch*. in *Num*.

C H A P. VII.

Of the Duumviri, Decemviri, *and* Quindecemviri, *Keepers of the* Sibylline *Writings; and of the* Corybantes, *or Prieſts of* Cybele, *and the* Epulones.

THE firſt of theſe orders, famous only on account of the relics they preſerved, owe their original to this occaſion.

A ſtrange old woman came once to Tarquinius Superbus with nine books, which, ſhe ſaid, were the oracles of the Sibyls, and proffered to ſell them. But the king making ſome ſcruple about the price, ſhe went away and burnt three of them; and returning with the ſix, aſked the ſame ſum as before. Tarquin only laughed at the humour: Upon which the old woman left him once more; and after ſhe had burnt three others, came again with them that were left, but ſtill kept to her old terms. The king begun now to wonder at her obſtinacy, and thinking

there

there might be something more than ordinary in the business, sent for the augurs to consult what was to be done. They, when their divinations were performed, soon acquainted him what a piece of impiety he had been guilty of, by refusing a treasure sent to him from heaven, and commanded him to give whatever she demanded for the books that remained. The woman received her money, and delivered the writings, and, only charging them by all means to keep them sacred, immediately vanished. Two of the nobility were presently after chosen to be the keepers of these oracles, which were laid up with all imaginable care in the capitol, in a chest under ground. They could not be consulted without a special order of the senate, which was never granted, unless upon the receiving some notable defeat, upon the rising of any considerable mutiny or sedition in the state, or upon some other extraordinary occasion (*a*); several of which we meet with in Livy (*b*).

The number of priests in this, as in most other orders, were several times altered. The Duumviri continued till about the year of the city 388, when the tribunes of the people preferred a law, that there should be ten men elected for this service, part out of the nobility, and part out of the commons. We meet with the Decemviri all along from hence, till about the time of Sylla the Dictator, when the Quindecemviri occur; which addition of five persons, may, with very good reason, be attributed to him, who increased so many of the other orders. It were needless to give any farther account of the Sibyls, than that they are generally agreed to have been ten in number; for which we have the authority of Varro; tho' some make them nine, some four, some three, and some only one (*c*). They all lived in different ages and countries, were all prophetesses, and, if we believe the common opinion, foretold the coming of our Saviour. As to the writing, Dempster tells us it was in linen (*d*). But one would think the common phrase of *Folia Sibyllæ*, used by Virgil, Horace, and other credible authors, should argue, that they wrote their prophecies on leaves of trees; especially if we consider the great antiquity which is generally allowed them, and that we are assured at the same time by Pliny (*e*), that this was the oldest way of writing.

Solinus

They had the common name of *Duumviri* (*Decemviri*, or *Quindecemviri*) *Sacris faciundis*.

(*a*) *Dionys. Antiq.* lib. 4. lib. 7. cap. 28. lib. 4. cap. 21. (*e*) Lib. 33. cap. 11.   (*b*) Particularly lib. 3. cap. 10. lib. 5. cap 13. (*c*) *Dempster ad Rosin.* lib. 3. cap. 24.   (*d*) *Ibid.*

Solinus acquaints us, that these books which Tarquin bought were burnt in the conflagration of the capitol the year before Sylla's dictatorship (a). Yet there were others of their inspired writings, or at least copies of extracts of them, gathered up in Greece and other parts, upon a special search made by order of the Senate; which were kept with the same superstition, as the former, till about the time of Theodosius the Great, when, the greatest part of the Senate having embraced the Christian faith, such vanities began to grow out of fashion; till at last Stilico burnt them all, under Honorius, for which he is so severely censured by the noble poet Rutilius, in his ingenious itinerary:

> *Nec tantum Geticis graffatus proditor armis,*
>   *Ante Sibyllinæ fata cremavit Opis.*
> *Odimus Althæam confumpto funere torris;*
>   *Nifæum crinem flere putantur aves.*
> *At Stilico æterni fatalia pignora libri,*
>   *Et plenas voluit præcipitare colus.*

> Nor only Roman arms the wretch betray'd
> To barbarous foes; before that cursed deed,
> He burnt the writings of the sacred maid.
> We hate Althæa for the fatal brand;
> When Nisus fell, the weeping birds complain'd:
> More cruel he than the revengeful fair;
> More cruel he than Nisus' murderer;
> Whose impious hands into the flames have thrown
> The heav'nly pledges of the Roman crown,
> Unravelling all the doom that careful fate had spun.

Among all the religious orders, as we meet with none oftener in authors, so there were none of such an extravagant constitution as the priests of Cybele. We find them under the different names of (b) *Curetes, Corybantes, Galli,* and *Idæi Dactyli;* but can scarce get one tolerable etymology of either. As for Cybele herself, she is generally taken for the earth, and is the same with *Rhea, Ops, Berecynthia,* the *Idæan Mother,* the *Mother of the Gods,* and the *Great Goddess.* She was invited and received into Rome, from Persinus in Galatia, with great solemnity, upon advice of the Sibylline oracles (c).

R But

(a) *Polyhistor.* c. 8.   (b) *Dionyf. Antiq.* lib. 4.   (c) *Liv.* lib. 29, cap. 14.

But to return to her priests: We find little of any certainty about them, only that they were all eunuchs, and by nation Phrygians; and that in their solemn processions they danced in armour, making a confused noise with timbrels, pipes, and cymbals, howling all the while as if they were mad, and cutting themselves as they went along. One would little think that this was the goddess who required such a sacred silence in her mysteries, as Virgil (a) would persuade us she did. And the best we could suppose at the sight of this bawling retinue is, that they were going to settle a swarm of bees; for which service the same poet recommends the use of the cymbals of Cybele (b).

But we cannot have a better relation of the original, and the manner of their strange solemnity, than what Lucretius has given us in his second book:

> *Hanc variæ gentes, antiquo more sacrorum,*
> *Idæam vocitant Matrem Phrygiasque catervas*
> *Dant Comites; qui primum ex illis finibus edunt*
> *Per terrarum orbem fruges cœpisse creari.*
> *Gallos attribuunt quia, numen qui volârint*
> *Matris & ingrati genitoribus inventi sunt,*
> *Significare volunt indignos esse putandos,*
> *Vivam progeniem qui in oras luminis edant.*
> *Tympana tenta tonant palmis & cymbala circum*
> *Concava raucisonoque minantur cornua cantu,*
> *Et Phrygio stimulat numero cava tibia mentes;*
> *Telaque præportant violenti signa furoris,*
> *Ingratos animos, atque impia pectora volgi*
> *Conterrere metu quæ possint numine divæ.*
>
> *Hic armata manus (Curetas nomine Graii*
> *Quos memorant Phrygios) inter se fortè catervis*
> *Ludunt, in numerumque exsultant sanguine læti; &*
> *Terrificas capitum quatientes numine cristas.*
> *Dictæos referunt Curetas; qui Jovis illum*
> *Vagitum in Cretâ quondam occultâsse feruntur,*
> *Cum pueri circum puerum pernice chorea*
> *Armati in numerum pulsarent artibus æra,*
> *Ne Saturnus eam malis mandaret adeptus,*
> *Æternumque daret matri sub pectore vulnus.*

Concerning her, fond superstition frames
A thousand odd conceits, a thousand names,
And gives her a large train of Phrygian dames:

Because

(a) *Æneid.* 3.   (b) *Georg.* 4.

Because in Phrygia corn at first took birth,
And thence was scatter'd o'er the other earth.
They eunuch all their priests; from whence 'tis shown,
That they deserve no children of their own,
Who or abuse their sires, or disrespect,
Or treat their mothers with a cold neglect;
Their mothers whom they should adore———
Amidst her pomp fierce drums and cymbals beat,
And the hoarse horns with rattling notes do threat;
The pipe with Phrygian airs disturbs their souls,
Till, reason overthrown, mad passion rules.
They carry arms, those dreadful signs of war,
To raise in th' impious rout religious fear.

Here some in arms dance round among the crowd,
Look dreadful gay in their own sparkling blood,
Their crests still shaking with a dreadful .od.
These represent those armed priests who strove
To drown the tender cries of infant Jove:
By dancing quick, they made a greater sound,
And beat their armour as they danc'd around,
Lest Saturn should have found, and eat the boy,
And Ops for ever mourn'd her prattling joy.
Mr CREECH.

But we must not omit a more comical, though a shorter account that we have of them in Juvenal:

——— *Matrisque deûm chorus intrat, & ingens*
Semiver obscœno facies reverenda minori,
Mollia qui raptâ fecuit genitalia testâ,
Jampridem cui ranca cohors, cui tympana cedunt
Plebeia——— (*a*).

And Cybele's priests, an eunuch at their head,
About the streets a mad procession lead;
The venerable gelding, large and high,
O'erlooks the herd of his inferior fry.
His aukward clergymen about him prance,
And beat their timbrels to the mystic dance.
Mr DRYDEN.

The Epulones, at their first creation, Livy (*b*) assures us, were only three: Soon after they were increased to seven; whence they

(*a*) *Sat.* 6.   (*b*) Lib. 33.

they are commonly called *Septemviri Epulonum*, or barely *Septemviri*, or the *Septemviratus*; and some report, that Julius Cæsar, by adding three more, changed them to a *Decemvirate*; tho' it is certain they kept their old name. They had their name from a custom which obtained among the Romans, in time of public danger, of making a sumptuous feast in their temples, to which they did, as it were, invite the deities themselves: For their statues were brought on rich beds, with their *pulvinarii* too, or pillows, and placed at the most honourable part of the table, as the principal guests. These regalios they called *Epula*, or *Lectisternia*; the care of which belonged to the Epulones. This priesthood is by Pliny *junior* set on an equal foot with that of Augurs; when, upon a vacancy in each order, he supplicates his master Trajan to be admitted to either. The whole epistle ought to be set down for an example of modesty and wit.

PLINIUS TRAJANO.

Cum sciam, Domine, ad testimonium laudemque morum meorum pertinere tam boni principis judicio exornari, rogo, dignitati, ad quam me provexit indulgentia tua, vel auguratum, vel septemviratum, quia vacant, adjicere digneris: ut jure sacerdotii precari deos pro te publicè possem, quos nunc precor pietate privata.

CHAP. VIII.

Of the ROMAN Sacrifices.

THE word *Sacrificium* more properly signifies the thing offered than the action of offering. The two common words to express the former, were *Victima* and *Hostia*; which, though they are very often confounded, yet by the first word are properly meant the greater sort of sacrifices, by the other the less.

Though every deity had some peculiar rites and institutions, and consequently different sorts of sacrifices, in which the greatest part of the public worship then consisted, yet there were some standing rules and ceremonies to be observed in all.

The priest (and sometimes the person that gave the victim) went before in a white garment free from spots and figures: For Cicero tells us, that white is the most acceptable colour to the gods; I suppose, because it seems to denote purity and innocence. The

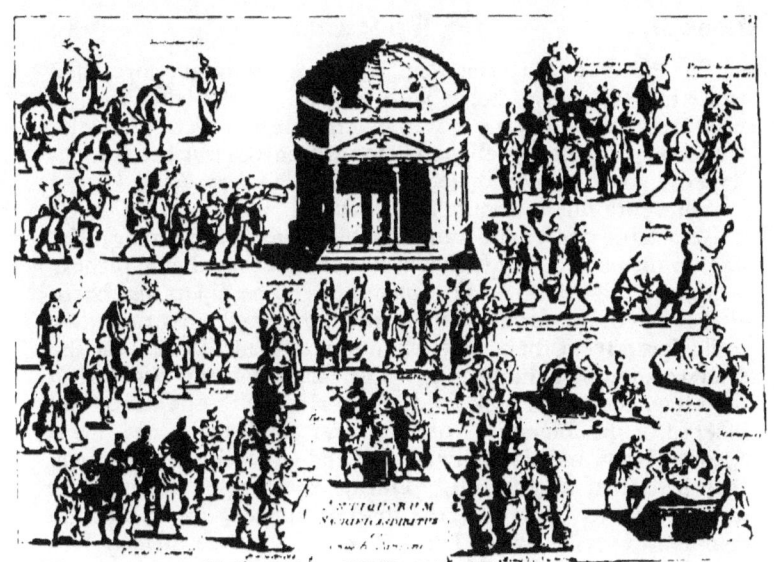

The beaft to be facrificed, if it was of the larger fort, ufed to be marked on the horns with gold; if of the leffer fort, it was crowned with the leaves of that tree which the deity was thought moft to delight in, for whom the facrifice was defigned. And, befides thefe, they wore the *Infulæ* and *Vitæ*, a fort of white fillets, about their head.

Before the proceffion went a public crier, proclaiming, *Hoc age*, to the people; to give them notice that they fhould forbear working, and attend to the folemnity. The pipers and harpers too, were the forerunners of the fhow; and what time they could fpare from their inftruments was fpent in affifting the crier to admonifh the people. The facrifice being brought to the altar, the prieft took hold of the altar with one hand, and ufhered in the folemnity with a prayer to all the gods; mentioning Janus and Vefta always firft and laft, as if through them they had accefs to the reft. During the prayer, fome public officer was to command the ftricteft filence, for which the common expreffion was, *Favete Linguis*, a phrafe ufed by Horace (*a*), Juvenal (*b*), Tibullus (*c*), &c. And the piper played all the while, to hinder the hearing of any unlucky noife. After his prayer, the prieft began the facrifice with what they called *Immolatio* (though, by fynecdoche, the word is often taken for the whole act of facrificing) the throwing fome fort of corn and frankincenfe, together with the mola, *i. e.* bran or meal mixed with falt, upon the head of the beaft. In the next place, he fprinkled wine between the horns; a cuftom very often taken notice of by the poets; fo Virgil:

> *Ipfa tenens dextrâ pateram pulcherrima Dido,*
> *Candentis vaccæ media inter cornua fundit* (*d*).

O'er the white heifer's horns the beauteous queen
Holds the rich plate, and pours the wine between.

And Ovid more exprefsly:

> *Rode caper vitem; tamen hinc cum flabis ad aras,*
> *In tuo quod fundi cornua poffit, erit* (*e*).

Go, wanton goat, about the vineyard browze
On the young fhoots, and ftop the rifing juice;
You'll leave enough to pour between your horns,
When for your fake the hallow'd altar burns.

But

(*a*) Lib. 3. Od. 1. (*b*) Sat. 12. (*c*) Lib. 2. Eleg. 1. (*d*) Aeneid. 4. v. 60. (*e*) Faft. 1.

But before he poured the wine on the beast, he put the plate to his own mouth, and just touched it with his lips, giving it to those that stood near him to do the like. This they termed *Libatio*.

In the next place, he plucked off some of the roughest hairs growing between the horns of the beast, and threw them into the fire, as the *prima Libamina:*

Et summas capiens media inter cornua setas,
Ignibus imponit sacris, libamina prima (a).

The bristling hairs that on the forehead grew,
As the first offering on the fire she threw.

And now turning himself to the east, he only made a sort of crooked line with his knife from the forehead to the tail; and then delivered the beast to the public servants to kill. We find these inferior officers under the several names of *Popæ, Agones, Cultrarii,* and *Victimarii:* Their business, besides the killing of the beast, was to take off his skin, to bowel him, and to wash the whole body. Then the Aruspex's duty came in place, to search the intrails for good and bad omens. When this was over, the priests had nothing else to do but to lay what parts they thought fittest for the gods upon the altar, and to go and regale themselves upon the rest. *See* Alex. ab Alex. *lib.* 4. *cap.* 17.

(*a*) *Aeneid.* 6. v. 246.

C H A P. IX.

Of the ROMAN *Year.*

WE meet with three accounts in use at several times among the Romans; which owe their original to Romulus, Numa, and Julius Cæsar. Romulus divided his year into ten months, which Plutarch would persuade us had no certain or equal term; but consisted, some of twenty days, some of thirty-five, and some of more (*a*). But he is generally allowed to have

(*a*) *Plut.* in *Num.*

have settled the number of days with a great deal more equality, allotting to March, May, Quintilis, and October, one-and-thirty days; to April, June, Sextilis, November, and December, thirty, making up in all three hundred and four days (*a*):

> *Scilicet arma magis quàm sidera, Romule, noras.*

Scaliger, indeed, is very angry, that people should think the Romans had ever any other account than by twelve months (*b*). But it is probable, that the testimonies of Varro, Macrobius, Censorinus, Ovid, &c. will over-rule the bare words of Licinius, Macer, and Fenestella, which are all he produces. As to the names of Romulus's months, the first, to be sure, was consecrated to Mars, the father of the state. The next, too, may be fetched from Venus, the other guardian parent of the Romans, if we admit of the allusion between the word *Aprilis* and 'Αφροδίτη, her name in Greek: Tho' it is generally derived from *Aperio*, to open, because this is the chief part of the spring in which the buds and flowers open and disclose themselves (*c*). May he named so from *Maia*, the mother of Mercury, according to Plutarch (*d*); tho' Macrobius makes the Maia, to whom May was dedicated, the same as Rhea, Ops, or the earth, and different from Mercury's mother (*e*). Ovid brings it *à Senibus*, i.e. *à Majoribus* (*f*). Juno either comes from *Juventus*, because this is the youthful and gay part of the year (*g*), or else it is a contraction of *Junonius*, and dedicated to the goddess Juno (*h*). The other months he denominated as they stood in order: So Quintilis is no more than the fifth month, Sextilis than the sixth, and so on: But these two afterwards changed their names to July and August, in honour of Julius Cæsar and his successor Augustus. As Nero had afterwards called April *Neronius* (*i*), so Plutarch tells us, that Domitian too, in imitation of them, gave the two months immediately following the names of *Germanicus* and *Domitianus*; but he being slain, they recovered their old denominations (*k*).

Numa was a little better acquainted with the celestial motions than his predecessor; and therefore undertaking to reform the kalendar, in the first place he added the two months of January

---

(*a*) *Macrob. Saturn.* lib. 1. cap. 12. *Censor. de die Natal.* c. 20, &c. (*b*) *De Emendat. Tempor.* l. 2. (*c*) *Plut.* in *Num. Macrob. Sat.* l. 1. c. 12. (*d*) In *Numa.* (*e*) *Sat.* l. 1. c. 12. (*f*) *Fast.* 1. v. 41. (*g*) *Plut.* in *Numa.* (*h*) *Macrob. ubi supra.* (*i*) *Suet.* in *Ner.* c. 55. (*k*) *Plut.* in *Numa.*

nuary and February; the firſt of which he dedicated to the god Janus; the other took its name from *Februo*, to purify, becauſe the feaſts of purification were celebrated in that month (*a*). To compoſe theſe two months, he put fifty days to the old three hundred and four, to make them anſwer the courſe of the moon; and then took ſix more from the ſix months that had even days, adding one odd day more than he ought to have done, merely out of ſuperſtition, and to make the number fortunate. However, he could but get eight-and-twenty days for February, and therefore that month was always counted unlucky (*b*). Beſides this, he obſerved the difference between the ſolar and the lunar courſe to be eleven days; and, to remedy the inequality, he doubled thoſe days after every two years, adding an interſtitial month to follow February, which Plutarch calls in one place *Mercedinus* (*c*), and in another *Mercedonius* (*d*). But the care of this intercalation being left to the prieſts, they clapped in, or left out the month whenever they pleaſed, as they fancied it lucky or unlucky, and ſo made ſuch mad work, that the feſtivals and ſolemn days for ſacrifice were removed by little and little, till at laſt they came to be kept at a ſeaſon quite contrary to what they had been formerly (*e*).

Julius Cæſar was the firſt that undertook to remedy this diſorder; and to this purpoſe, he called in the beſt philoſophers and mathematicians of his time to ſettle the point. In order to bring matters right, he was forced to make one confuſed year of fifteen months, or four hundred and forty-five days; but, to preſerve a due regulation for the future, he took away the intercalary months; and adding ten days to Numa's three hundred and fifty-five, equalled them to the courſe of the ſun, except ſix odd hours. The ten days he diſtributed among thoſe ſeven months that had before but nine-and-twenty; and as for the ſix hours, he ordered them to be let alone till they made up a whole day; and this every fourth year he put in the ſame place where the month uſed to be inſerted before (*f*); and that was juſt five days before the end of February, or next before the ſixth of the calends of March. For this reaſon, the ſupernumerary day had the name of *Dies Biſſextus*; and thence the leap-year came to be called *Annus Biſſextilis*.

But

(*a*) *Ibid.* (*b*) *Cenſorin. de die Natali,* cap. 20. (*c*) *In Numa.* (*d*) *In Jul. Cæſ.* (*e*) *Ibid.* (*f*) *Cenſorin.* cap. 20.

But the priests, who had been the authors of the old confusion, committed as great a blunder in the new computation, by interposing the leap-day at the beginning of every fourth year instead of the end; 'till Augustus Cæsar brought it into the right course again (*a*), in which it has continued ever since, and is followed by a great part of Europe at this day.

Yet because there wanted eleven minutes in the six odd hours of Julius's year, the equinoxes and solstices, losing something continually, were found, about the year 1582, to have run back ten whole days; for which reason, Pope Gregory at that time undertook a new reformation of the kalendar, cutting off ten days to bring them to their proper places. This account they call the *Gregorian*, or *New Style*, which is observed too in many parts of Europe.

(*a*) *Macrob. Sat.* lib. I. cap. 14. *Sueton.* in *August.* cap. 31.

CHAP. X.

The Distinction of the ROMAN *Days*.

WHEN Numa divided the year into twelve months, he made a distinction too in the days, ranking them in these three orders: *Dies Festi, Profesti,* and *Intercisi:*

The first sort was consecrated to the gods:

The second allotted for the civil business of men:

The third divided between sacred and ordinary employments.

The *Dies Festi* were set apart for the celebration of these four solemnities, *Sacrificia, Epulæ, Ludi,* and *Feriæ*.

Sacrificia were no more than public sacrifices to the gods.

Epulæ were a sort of banquets celebrated to the honour of the deities.

Ludi were public sports instituted with the same design.

Feriæ were either public or private.

The public were of four sorts; *Stativæ, Conceptivæ, Imperativæ,* and *Nundinæ*.

Feriæ Stativæ were public feasts kept by the whole city, according to the set time appointed in the kalendar for their observation; as the *Agonalia, Carmentalia, Lupercalia,* &c

Feriæ Conceptivæ were such as the magistrates, or priests, appointed annually to be celebrated upon what days they pleased, as the *Latinæ, Paganalia, Compitalia*, &c.

Feriæ Imperativæ were such as the consuls, prætors, or dictators, instituted by virtue of their own authority, and commanded to be observed upon solemn occasions, as the gaining of a victory, and the like.

Nundinæ were days set apart for the concourse of the people out of the country and neighbouring towns to expose their commodities to sale, the same as our greater markets or fairs. They had the name of *Nundinæ*, because they were kept every ninth day, as Ovid informs us (*a*). It must be remembered, that though the *Nundinæ* at first were of the number of the *Feriæ*, yet they were afterwards by a law declared to be *Dies Fasti*; that the country people might not be hindered in their work, but might at the same time perform their business of market and sale, and also have their controversies and causes decided by the prætor; whereas otherwise they must have been forced to come to town again upon the usual court-days.

Feriæ Privatæ were holy-days observed by particular persons or families upon several accounts, as birth-days, funerals, and the like.

Thus much for the *Dies Festi*.

The *Profesti* were *Fasti, Comitiales, Comperendini, Stati*, and *Præliares*.

Dies Fasti were the same as our court-days; upon which it was lawful for the prætor to sit in judgment, and consequently *Fari tria verba*, to say those three solemn words, *Do, Dico, Addico*, "I sit here to give laws, declare rights, adjudge los-"ses." All other days (except the *intercisi*) were called *Nefasti*; because it was not lawful to say these three words upon them; that is, the courts were not open. But we may observe, from a phrase of Horace (*b*), that *Dies Nefastus* signifies an unlucky day, as well as a non-court-day.

Dies Comitiales were such days as the *Comitia*, or public assemblies of the people, were held upon; or, as Ovid styles them,

———— *Quies populum jus est includere septis* (*c*).

Days when people are shut up to vote.

Dies

(*a*) *Fast.* 1. *ver.* 54.   (*b*) Lib. 2. *Od.* 13.   (*c*) *Fast.* 1. *ver.* 53.

Dies Comperendini, were days when persons that had been sued might give bail, properly days of adjournment.

Dies Stati were days appointed for the decision of any cause between a Roman and a foreigner.

Dies Præliares were such days upon which they thought it lawful to engage in any action of hostility: For, during the time of some particular feasts, as the *Saturnalia*, the *Latinæ*, and that which they called *Cùm Mundus patet*, consecrated to *Dis* and *Proserpina*, they reckoned it a piece of impiety to raise, march, or exercise their men, or to encounter with the enemy, unless first attacked.

If we make a division of the Roman days into fortunate and unfortunate; *Dies Postriduani, i. e.* the next day after the Kalends, Nones, or Ides, were always reckoned of the latter sort; and therefore had the names of *Dies Atri*.

A. Gellius gives us the reason of this observation from *Verrius Flaccus*, because they had taken notice for several ages, that those days had proved unlucky to the state in the loss of battles, towns, and other casualties (*a*).

He tells us in the same place, that the day before the fourth of the Kalends, Nones, or Ides, was always reckoned unfortunate; but he does not know for what reason, unless that he finds the great overthrow at Cannæ to have happened on such a day.

(*a*) *Noct. Attic.* lib. 5. cap. 17.

CHAP. XI.

Of the Kalends, Nones, *and* Ides.

THE way the Romans used to reckon the days of their months was by the Kalends, Nones, and Ides. Romulus began his months always upon the first day of the moon, and was followed in this by the authors of the other accounts, to avoid the altering of the immoveable feasts. Therefore every new moon, one of the inferior priests used to assemble the people in the capitol, and *call* over as many days as there were between that and the Nones: And so from the old word *Calo*, or the Greek καλῶ, to call, the first of these days had the name of *Kalendæ*. But we must remember, that this custom of *calling* the days continued no longer than the year of the city 450, when C. Flavius, the *Curule Ædile*, ordered the *Fasti*, or kalendar, to be set up in public places, that every body might know the difference of times, and the return of the festivals (*a*).

The *Nones* were so called, because they reckoned nine days from the *Ides*.

The *Ides* were generally about the middle of the month, and then we may derive the word from *Iduare*, an obsolete verb, signifying to divide.

The *Kalends* were always fixed to the first day of every month, but the Nones and the Ides in four months were on different days than in the other eight. For March, May, July and October had six Nones a piece, the others only four. Therefore in the first, the Nones were the 7th, and the Ides the 15th; in the last, the Nones the 5th, and the Ides the 13th.

In reckoning these, they always went backwards, thus, January 1, was the first of the kalends of January: December 31, *Prid. Kal. Jan.* Decemb. 30. *tertio Kal Jan.* and so on to the 13th; and that was *Idus Decembris*; and then the 12th *Prid. Iduum. Decem.* the 11th, 3 *Iduum Decemb.* and so on to the 5th day, and that was *Nonæ Decemb.* And then again the 4th *Prid. Nonarum Decemb.* the third, 3 *Non. Decemb.* the second, 4 *Non. Decemb.* and the first *Kalendæ Decemb.*

We must observe, That when we meet with *Kalendas Nonas*, or *Idus* in the accusative case, the preposition *ante* is always understood: as *tertio Kalendas, Idus,* or *Nonas,* is the same as *tertio Die ante Kal. Non.* or *Idus.*

(*a*) Liv. lib. 5. cap. 46. &c.

C H A P. XII.

The most remarkable Festivals *of the* ROMANS, *as they stand in the* Kalendar.

THE kalends, or the first day of January, was noted for the entering of the magistrates on their office; and for the wishing of good fortune, and sending presents to one another among friends (*a*).

(*a*) Ovid. Fast. 1. v. 71.

The ninth (or *quint. Id.*) was the feast of the *Agonalia*, instituted by Numa Pompilius, in honour of Janus, and attended with the ἀγῶνες, the solemn exercises and combats; whence, in Ovid's judgment (*a*), it took its name.

The eleventh (or *tert. Id*) was the feast of the *Carmentalia*, in memory of Carmenta, Evander's mother.

February the fifteenth, or the fifteenth of the kalends of March, was the feast of the *Lupercalia*, when the *Luperci* make their wild procession (*b*), which has been described before.

February the eleventh, or the third of the Ides, was the *Feralia*, or feast in honour of the ghosts; when people carried some little sort of offering to the graves of their deceased friends. Ovid gives us so handsome an account of it, that we must not pass it by:

Est honor & tumulis; animas placare paternas (*c*),
 Parvaque in extructas munera ferre pyras:
Parva petunt manes: pietas pro divite grata est
 Munere; non avidos Styx habet ima Deos.
Tegula porrectis satis est velata corionis;
 Est sparsæ fruges, parvaque mica salis.

Tombs have their honours too: Our parents crave
Some slender present to adorn the grave.
Slender the present which the ghosts we owe;
Those powers observe not what we give, but how.
No greedy souls disturb the happy seats below.
They only ask a tile with garlands crown'd,
And fruit and salt to scatter on the ground.

The day after the Feralia was the *Charistia*, or festival of love, when all the relations in every family met together, and had a feast.

On the 22d or 23d (according to the different length of this month) were the *Terminalia*, sacred to Terminus, the guardian of boundaries and land-marks; on which they now offered to him cakes and fruits, and sometimes sheep and swine, notwithstanding the ancient prohibition of bloody sacrifices in this case; the reason of which prohibition Plutarch (*d*) supposes to have

---

(*a*) *Ovid. Fast.* lib. 1. (*b*) *Ovid. Fast.* 2. v. 267, &c. (*c*) *Ibid.* 533, &c.
(*d*) *Quæst. Rom.*

have been left they should violate the tokens of peace and agreement, by staining them with blood.

On the kalends of March were the *Matronalia*, a feast kept by the Roman matrons to the honour of Mars; to whom they thought themselves obliged for the happiness of bearing good children; a favour which he first conferred on his own mistress, Rhea (*a*).

This feast was the subject of Horace's ode,

Martiis cœlebs quid agam calendis, &c.

On the same day began the solemn feast of the Salii, and their procession with the Ancylia, which have been spoken of before.

The Ides of March was the feast of *Anna Perenna*; in honour either of the sister of Dido, who fled into Italy to Æneas, or of one Anna, an old gentlewoman, that, in a great dearth at Rome, for some time furnished the common people with corn out of her own store. The celebration of this day consisted in drinking and feasting largely among friends. The common people met for this purpose in the fields near the Tyber, and, building themselves boothes and arbours, kept the day with all manner of sports and jollity, wishing one another to live as many years as they drank cups (*b*).

The same day was, by a decree of the senate, ordered to be called *Parricidium*, for the murder of Julius Cæsar, which happened on it (*c*). Appian, in his second book, tells us of a very different law that Dolabella the consul would have preferred upon this occasion; and that was, to have the day called ever after *Natalis urbis*, the birth-day of the city; as if their liberty had revived upon the death of Cæsar.

March the 19th, or the 14th of the kalends of April, began the *Quinquatrus*, or *Quinquatria*, the feast of Minerva, continuing five days. It was during this solemnity that the boys and girls used to pray to the goddess for wisdom and learning, of which she had the patronage: To which custom Juvenal alludes:

Eloquium & famam Demosthenis aut Ciceronis
Incipit optare, & totis quinquatribus optat (*d*).

To

(*a*) Ovid. Fast. 3. v. 233. cap. 88.   (*b*) Ibid. v. 523, &c.   (*c*) Sueton. in Jul.
(*d*) Sat. 10.

> To rival Tully or Demosthenes,
> Begins to with in the Quinquatrian days,
> And wishes all the feast.———

At the same time the youths carried to their masters their fee, or present, termed *Minerval*.

April the 19th, or the 13th of the kalends of May, was the *Cerealia*, or feast of Ceres, in which solemnity the chief actors were the women. No person that mourned was allowed to bear a part in this service; and therefore it is very remarkable, that, upon the defeat at Canæ, there was such an universal grief in the city, that the anniversary feast of Ceres was forced to be omitted (a).

April the 21st, or the 11th of the kalends of May, was the *Palilia*, or feast of Pales, goddess of shepherds. This is sometimes called *Parilia, à pariendo*, because prayers were now made for the fruitfulness of the sheep. Ovid tells us a very tedious course of superstition that the shepherds ran through upon this day. They always contrived to have a great feast at night; and, when most of them were pretty merry, they concluded all with dancing over the fires that they made in the field with heaps of stubble (b).

The same day was called *Urbis Natalis*, being the day on which the city was built (c).

April the 25th, or the 7th of the kalends of May, was the *Robigalia*, a feast of the goddess Robigo, or the god Robigus, who took care to keep off the mildew and blasting from the corn and fruit (d).

April the 27th, or the 5th of the kalends of May, was the *Floralia*, or feast of Flora, goddess of flowers (e), when the public sports were celebrated that will be hereafter described (f).

In the remaining part of the year we meet with no festival of extraordinary note, except the *Poplifugium* and the *Saturnalia*.

The original of the famous *Nonæ Caprotinæ*, or *Poplifugium*, is doubly related by Plutarch, according to the two common opinions. First, because Romulus disappeared on that day, when an assembly being held in the *Palus Capreæ*, or Goat's-marsh,

on

(a) *Liv.* lib. 22.   (b) *Ovid. Fast.* v. 721, &c.   (c) *Ibid.* v. 806.
(d) *Ibid.* v. 901.   (e) *Ibid.* v. 943.   (f) See Book. v. cap. 7.

on a sudden happened a most wonderful tempest, accompanied with terrible thunder, and other unusual disorders in the air. The common people fled all away to secure themselves; but, after the tempest was over, could never find their kings (a).

Or else from *Caprificus* a wild fig-tree, because, in the Gallic war, a Roman virgin, who was prisoner in the enemies camp, taking the opportunity when she saw them one night in disorder, got up into a wild fig-tree, and holding out a lighted torch toward the city, gave the Romans a signal to fall on; which they did with such good success as to obtain a considerable victory (b).

The original of the *Saturnalia*, as to the time, is unknown, Macrobius assuring us, that it was celebrated in Italy long before the building of Rome (c); the story of Saturn, in whose honour it was kept, every body is acquainted with. As to the manner of the solemnity, besides the sacrifices and other parts of public worship, there were several lesser observations worth our notice. As first, the liberty now allowed to servants to be free and merry with their masters, so often alluded to in authors. It is probable this was done in memory of the liberty enjoyed in the golden age under Saturn, before the names of servant and master were known to the world. Besides this, they sent presents to one another among friends: No war was to be proclaimed, and no offender executed: The schools kept a vacation, and nothing but mirth and freedom was to be met with in the city. They kept at first only one day, the 14th of the kalends of January; but the number was afterwards increased to three, four, five, and some say, seven days (d).

(a) *Plutarch. in Romulo. Macrob. Saturn.* lib. I. cap. 7.   (b) *Plutarch. in Romulo, & in Camillo.*   (c) *Macrob. Saturn.* lib. I. cap. 7.   (d) *Lipf. Saturnal.* lib. I. cap. 3.

PART

PART II. BOOK III.

Of the Civil Government of the ROMANS.

CHAP. I.

Of the General Division of the People.

ROMULUS, as soon as his city was tolerably well filled with inhabitants, made a distinction of the people according to honour and quality; giving the better sort the name of *Patres*, or *Patricii*, and the rest the common title of *Plebeii*. To bind the two degrees more firmly together, he recommended to the Patricians some of the Plebeians to protect and countenance; the former being styled *Patroni*, and the latter *Clientes*. The patrons were always their clients counsellors in difficult cases, their advocates in judgments; in short, their advisers and overseers in all affairs whatever. On the other side, the clients faithfully served their patrons, not only paying them all imaginable respect and deference, but, if occasion required, assisting them with money towards the defraying of any extraordinary charges. But afterwards, when the state grew rich and great, though all other good offices continued between them, yet it was thought a dishonourable thing for the better sort to take any money of their inferiors (*a*).

T   The

(*a*) Vide *Dionys*. lib. 2. *Liv.* lib. 1. *Plutarch*. in *Romulo*.

The division of the people into the three distinct orders, of Senators, Knights, and Commons, took its rise about the time of Tarquin's expulsion. The Senators were such persons as had been promoted to sit in the supreme council of state, either out of the nobility or commons. If out of the latter order, they had the honour of a gold ring, but not of a horse kept at the public charge, as Manutius hath nicely observed. The Knights were such persons as were allowed a gold ring and a horse at the public charge. The Commons were all the rest of the people, besides these two orders, including not only the inferior populacy, but such of the nobility too as had not yet been elected Senators, and such of the gentry as had not a complete knight's estate: For persons were admitted into the two higher ranks according to their fortunes; one that was worth eight hundred sestertia, was capable of being chosen Senator: One that had four hundred, might be taken into the Equestrian order. Augustus afterwards altered the Senatorian estate to twelve hundred sesterces, but the Equestrian continued the same.

The three common terms by which the knights are mentioned in Roman authors, are *Eques, Equestris ordinis,* and *Equestri loco natus.* Of which the two former are, in all respects, the very same. But the latter is properly applied to those Equites, whose fathers were indeed of the same order, but had never reached the senatorian dignity. For, if their fathers had been senators, they would have been said to have been born of the Senatorian, and not of the Equestrian rank (*a*).

When we find the *Optimates,* and the *Populares* opposed in authors, we must suppose the former to have been those persons, of what rank soever, who stood up for the dignity of the chief magistrates, and the rigorous grandeur of the state; and who cared not if the inferior members suffered for the advancement of the commanding powers. The latter we must take likewise for those persons, of what rank soever, who courted the favour of the commons, by encouraging them to sue for greater privileges, and to bring things nearer to a level. For it would be unreasonable to make the same distinction between these parties, as Sigonius and others lay down,
" That the *Populares* were those who endeavoured, by their
" words and actions, to ingratiate themselves with the multitude; and the *Optimates* those who so behaved themselves in
" all

(*a*) Vid. P. Manut, *de Civ. Rom.* p. 5.

"all affairs, as to make their conduct approved by every good "man." This explication agrees much better with the found of the words, than with the sense of the things; for, at this rate, the *Optimates* and the *Populares* will be only other terms for the virtuous and the vicious; and it would be equally hard, in such large divisions of men, to acknowledge one side to have been wholly honest, and to affirm the other to have been entirely wicked. I know that this opinion is built on the authority of Cicero; but if we look on him not only as a prejudised person, but as an orator too, we shall not wonder, that in distinguishing the two parties, he gave so infamous a mark to the enemies side, and so honourable a one to his own: Otherwise the murderers of Cæsar (who were the *Optimates*) must pass for men of the highest probity; and the followers of Augustus (who were of the opposite faction) must seem in general a pack of profligate knaves. It would therefore be a much more moderate judgment, to found the difference rather on policy, than on morality; rather on the principles of government, than of religion and private duty.

There is another common division of the people into *Nobiles*, *Novi*, and *Ignobiles*, taken from the right of using pictures, or statues; an honour only allowed to such whose ancestors or themselves had borne some *Curule* office, that is, had been *Curule Ædile*, Censor, Prætor, or Consul. He that had the pictures or statues of his ancestors, was termed *Nobilis*; he that had only his own, *Novus*; he that had neither, *Ignobilis*. So that *Jus imaginis* was much the same thing among them, as the right of bearing a coat of arms among us: And their *Novus Homo* is equivalent to our upstart gentleman.

For a great while none but the Patricii were the Nobiles, because no person, unless of that superior rank, could bear any Curule office. Hence in many places of Livy, Sallust, and other authors, we find *Nobilitas* used for the Patrician order, and so opposed to *Plebs*; but in after-times, when the Commons obtained a right of enjoying those Curule honours, they by the same means procured the title of *Nobiles*, and left it to their posterity (*a*).

Such persons as were free of the city are generally distinguished into *Ingenui*, *Liberti*, and *Libertini*. The *Ingenui* were such as had been born free, and of parents that had been always

(*a*) Vide Sigon. de Jur. Civ. Rom. lib. 2. cap. 20.

ways free. The *Libertini* were the children of such as had been made free : *Liberti*, such as had been actually made free themselves.

The two common ways of conferring freedom were by *Testament* and by *Manumission*. A slave was said to be free by testament, when his master, in consideration of his faithful service, had left him free in his last will: Of which custom we meet with abundance of examples in every historian.

These kind of *Liberti* had the title of *Orcini*, because their masters were gone to Orcus. In allusion to which custom, when, after the murder of Julius Cæsar, a great number of unworthy persons had thrust themselves into the senate, without any just pretensions, they were merrily distinguished by the term of *Senatores Orcini* (a).

The ceremony of manumission was thus performed: The slave was brought before the consul, and in after-times before the prætor, by his master; who laying his hand upon his servant's head, said to the prætor, *Hunc hominem liberum esse volo;* and with that, let him go out of his hand, which they termed *è manu emittere*. Then the prætor, laying a rod upon his head, called *Vindicta*, said, *Dico eum liberum esse more Quiritum*. Hence Persius,

   Vindicta postquam meus à Pretore recessi.

After this the lictor taking the rod out of the prætor's hand, struck the servant several blows on the head, face, and back; and nothing now remained but *Pileo donari*, to receive a cap in token of liberty, and to have his name entered in the common roll of freemen, with the reason of his obtaining that favour.

There was a third way of bestowing freedom, which we do not so often meet with in authors; it was when a slave, by the consent and approbation of his master, got his name to be inserted in the censor's roll : Such a man was called *liber censu;* as the two already mentioned were *liber testamento,* and *liber manumissione*.

(a) *Sueton.* in *Octav.* cap. 55.

CHAP.

CHAP. II.
Of the SENATE.

THE chief council of state, and, as it were, the body of magistrates, was the *Senate*; which, as it has been generally reckoned the foundation and support of the Roman greatness, so it was one of the earliest constitutions in the republic: For Romulus first chose out a hundred persons of the best repute for birth, wisdom, and integrity of manners, to assist him in the management of affairs, with the name of *Senatores*, or *Patres*, from their age and gravity (*vel ætate, vel curæ similitudine* Patres *appellabantur*, says Sallust:) a title as honourable, and yet as little subject to envy, as could possibly have been pitched upon. After the admission of the Sabines into Rome, an equal number of that nation were joined to the former hundred (*a*). And Tarquinius Priscus, upon his first succession to the crown, to ingratiate himself with the commons, ordered another hundred to be selected out of that body, for an addition to the senate (*b*), which before had been ever filled with persons of the higher ranks. Sylla the dictator made them up above four hundred; Julius Cæsar nine hundred; and, in the time of the second Triumvirate, they were above a thousand; no distinction being made with respect to merit or quality. But this disorder was afterwards rectified by Augustus, and a reformation made in the senate, according to the old constitution (*c*).

The right of naming senators belonged at first to the kings; afterwards the consuls chose, and referred them to the people for their approbation: But, at last, the censors engrossed the whole privilege of conferring this honour. He that stood first in the censor's roll, had the honourable title of *Princeps Senatûs* (*d*): Yet the chief magistrates, as the consuls, dictator, &c. were always his superiors in the house.

Besides the estate of eight hundred, or, after Augustus, of twelve hundred sestertia, no person was capable of this dignity, but one who had already borne some magistracy in the commonwealth. And that there was a certain age (even in latter times) required, is plain, from the frequent use of *Ætas Senatoria*

(*a*) *Dionys.* lib. 2.   (*b*) *Idem.* lib. 3.   (*c*) *Sueton.* in *August.* cap. 35.
(*d*) *A. Gell.* lib. 3. cap. 18.

toria in authors. Dio Caffius pofitively limits it to five and twenty (*a*), which was the fooneft time any one could have difcharged the Quæftorfhip, the firft office of any confiderable note: Yet we meet with very many perfons promoted to this order, without any confideration had to their years; as it ufually happened in all other honours whatever.

As to the general title of *Patres Confcripti* given them in authors, it was taken as a mark of diftinction, proper to thofe fenators who were added to Romulus's hundred either by Tarquinius Prifcus, or by the people upon the eftablifhment of the commonwealth: But in after-times, all the number were promifcuoufly ftiled *Patres*, and *Patres Confcripti* (*b*).

We may take a further view of the Senators, confidered all together as a council or body.

The magiftrates, who had the power of affembling the fenators, were only the Dictator, the Confuls, the Prætors, the Tribunes of the commons, and the Interrex. Yet upon extraordinary accounts, the fame privilege was allowed to the *Tribuni Militum invefted with confular power*, and to the Decemvirs, created for the regulating the laws; and to the other magiftrates chofen upon fome unufual occafion. In the firft times of the ftate, they were called together by a public crier; but when the city grew larger, an edict was publifhed to command their meeting (*c*).

The places where they affembled were only fuch as had been formerly confecrated by the Augurs, and moft commonly within the city; only they made ufe of the temple of Bellona without the walls for the giving audience to foreign ambaffadors, and to fuch provincial magiftrates as were to be heard in open fenates, before they entered the city; as when they petitioned for a triumph, and the like cafes. Pliny too has a very remarkable obfervation, that whenever the Augurs reported that *an ox had fpoke*, which we often meet with among the ancient prodigies, the fenate was prefently to fit *fub dio*, or in the open air (*d*).

As for the time of their fitting, we muft have recourfe to the common diftinction of *Senatus legitimus*, and *Senatus indictus*.

The former was when the fenate met of courfe, upon fuch days as the laws or cuftom obliged them to. Thefe were the kalends, nones, and ides in every month, till the time of Auguftus, who confined them to the kalends and ides. In the months

of

(*a*) Liv. 52.   (*b*) P. Manut. de Senat. & C. Sigon. de Antiq. Jur. C. R.
(*c*) P. Manut. de Senat. Rom.   (*d*) Plin. Nat. Hift. lib. 8. cap. 45.

of September and October, by an order of the same emperor, the senators were discharged from their necessary attendance; except so many of them as made a quorum, a number sufficient by law to dispatch business; and therefore all that time they drew lots for their *appearance or excuse*, as Suetonius informs us (*a*). We may observe, from the same author, that the ides of March (called *Parricidium*, from the murder of Julius Cæsar, which happened on it) was particularly excepted; and a decree passed, that the senate should never meet on that day for the future (*b*).

Senatus Indictus, was a senate called for the dispatch of any business upon any other day; except the *Dies Comitiales*, when the senators were obliged to be present at the comitia.

As soon as the senate was sat, the consul, or other supreme magistrate, in the first place performed some divine service, and then proposed the business to the house; both which actions they called *referre ad senatum* (*c*).

When he had opened the cause, he went round in order (beginning with the *princeps senatus*, and the *designed consuls*) and asked every body's opinion; upon which, all that pleased stood up, and gave their judgment upon the point.

It is very remarkable, that when any senator was asked his opinion, he had the privilege of speaking as long as he pleased, as well about other concerns as about the matter in hand; and therefore when any particular member had a design to hinder the passing of any decree, it was a common practice to protract his speech till it was too late to make any determination in the house.

When as many as thought fit had given their judgments at large, the supreme magistrate made a short report of their several opinions, and then, in order to the passing their decree, ordered the senators to divide, one party to one side of the house, and the opposite to the other. The number being now told, the major part determined the case; and a *senatus-consultum* was accordingly wrote by the public notaries at the feet of the chief magistrate, being subscribed by the principal members that promoted it.

But in cases of little concern, or such as required expedition, the formality of asking opinions, and debating the business, was laid aside, and a decree passed upon the bare division of the house, and the counting of the numbers on both sides. This

was

(*a*) *In Octav.* c. 35.   (*b*) *Id. in Jul. Cæs.* c. 88.   (*c*) *P. Manut. de senat. Rom.*

was called *senatus-consultum per discessionem factum*, the former simply *senatus-consultum* (a).

Julius Capitolinus speaks of a sort of *senatus-consulta*, not described by any other author, which he calls *senatus consulta tacita*; and tells us they were made in reference to affairs of great secrecy, without the admittance of the very public servants; but all the business was done by the senators themselves, after the passing of an oath of secrecy, till their design should be effected (b).

There were several things that might hinder the passing of a decree in senate, as in case of an *intercessio*, or interposing. This was commonly put in practice by the tribunes of the commons, who reckoned it their privilege: But it might be done too by any magistrate of equal authority with him that proposed the business to the house; or else when the number required by law for the passing of any bill was not present: For that there was such a fixed number is very evident, though nothing of certainty can be determined any farther about it.

In both these cases, the opinion of the major part of the senators was not called *senatus-consultum*, but *authoritas senatus*; their *judgment*, not their *command*; and signified little, unless it was afterwards ratified, and turned into a *senatus-consultum*, as usually happened (c). Yet we must have a care of taking *authoritas senatus* in this sense every time we meet with it in authors: For unless, at the same time, there be mention made of an *intercessio*, it is generally to be understood as another term for a *senatus consultum*; and so Tully frequently uses it: Sometimes both the names are joined together; as the usual inscription of the decrees was in these initial letters, S. C. A. *i. e* Senatus Consulti Authoritas.

Besides these two impediments, a decree of senate could not pass after sun-set, but was deferred till another meeting.

All along, till the year of the city 304, the written decrees were in the custody of the consul, who might dispose of them as he thought proper, and either suppress or preserve them: But then a law passed, that they should be carried always for the future to the *Ædiles Plebis*, to be laid up in the temple of Ceres (d); yet we find, that afterwards they were for the most part preserved in the public treasury (e).

It may be further observed, that, besides the proper senators, any magistrates might come into the house during their honour,

and

(a) P. Manut. de Sen. (b) Jul. Capit. in Gordian. (c) P. Manut. de Sen.
(d) Liv. lib. 3. (e) Cicer. Philip. 5. Sueton. in August. Tacit. Annal. 3.

and they who had borne any *Curule* office, after its expiration. But then none of those who came into the House, purely upon account of their magistracy, were allowed the privilege of giving their judgment upon any matter, or of being numbered among the persons who had votes. Yet they tacitly expressed their mind by going over to those senators whose opinions they embraced; and upon this account they had the name of *Senatores Pedarii*.

This gave occasion to the joke of Laberius the mimic:

Caput sine lingua pedaria sententia est.

There was an old custom too, in the commonwealth, that the sons of senators might come into the House, and hear the proceedings. This, after it had been abrogated by a law, and long disused, was at last revived by Augustus, who, in order to the bringing in the young noblemen the sooner to the management of affairs, ordered that any senator's son, at the time of his putting on the *Toga Virilis*, should have the privilege of using the *Latus Clavus*, and of coming into the senate (*a*).

(*a*) Sueton. in *August*. cap. 38.

CHAP. III.

Of the general Divisions of the Magistrates; and of the Candidates for Offices.

NOT to speak of the different forms of government which obtained among the Romans, or to decide the case of pre-eminency between them, we may in the next place take a short view of the chief magistrates under them all. Of those we meet with many general divisions; as in respect of time, *Magistratus Ordinarii*, and *Etraordinarii;* with reference to the persons, *Patricii, Plebeii,* and *Mixti;* from their quality, *Majores* and *Minores;* from their manner of appearing in public, *Curules* and *Non Curules;* and lastly, from the place of their residence, *Urbani,* and *Provinciales* (*a*). If we would pitch upon the clearest and most compendious method, we must rank them according to the last distinction, and describe in order the most remarkable of the civil offices at home and abroad. But it will

(*a*) Lipsius de *Magistrat*. cap. 1.

be expected, that we first give some account of the persons that stood candidates for these honours. They borrowed the name of *Candidati* from the *Toga Candida*, in which they were habited at the time of their appearing for a place. They wore this loose gown open and ungirded, without any close garment under; which some interpret as done with design to avoid any suspicion the people might have of bribery and corruption: But Plutarch (a) thinks it was either to promote their interest the better, by suing in such an humble habit; or else, that such as had received wounds in the service of their country might the more easily demonstrate those tokens of their courage and fidelity; a very powerful way of moving the affections of the people. But he disallows the reason above mentioned, because this custom prevailed in Rome many ages before gifts and presents had any influence on the public suffrages; a mischief to which he attributed, in a great measure, the ruin of the commonwealth.

They declared their pretensions generally about a year before the election; all which time was spent in gaining and securing of friends. For this purpose, they used all the arts of popularity, making their circuits round the city very often; whence the phrase, *Ambire Magistratum*, had its rise. In their walks, they took the meanest persons by the hands; and not only used the more familiar terms of father, brother, friend, and the like, but called them too by their own proper names. In this service they had usually a *Nomenclator*, or *Monitor*, to assist them, who whispered every body's name in their ears. For though Plutarch tells us of a law which forbade any candidate to make use of a prompter; yet at the same time he observes, that Cato the younger was the only person who conformed to it, discharging the whole business by the help of his own memory (b).

They had reason to be very nice and cautious in the whole method of their address and canvass; for an affront, or perhaps a jest, put upon the most inconsiderable fellow, who was master of a vote, might sometimes be so far resented by the mob, as to turn the election another way. There is a particular story told of Scipio Nasica, which may confirm this remark: When he appeared for the place of *Curule Ædile*, and was making his circuit to increase his party, he lighted upon an honest plain countryman, who was come to town, to give his vote among the rest, and finding, as he shook him by the hand, that the flesh was very hard and callous, "Pr'ythee, friend," (says

(a) *In Coriolan.*   (b) *Plut. in Catone Uticens.*

says he, "doſt uſe to walk upon thy hands?" The clown was ſo far from being pleaſed with this piece of wit, that he complained of the affront, and loſt the gentleman the honour which he ſued for.

Such perſons as openly favoured their deſigns have been diſtinguiſhed by the names of *Salutatores, Deductores,* and *Sectatores* (*a*). The firſt ſort only paid their compliments to them at their lodgings in the morning, and then took their leave. The ſecond waited upon them from thence as far as the forum. The laſt compoſed their retinue thro' the whole circuit. Pliny has obliged us with a farther remark, that not only the perſon who ſtood for an office, but ſometimes too the moſt conſiderable men of their party, went about in the ſame formal manner, to beg voices in their behalf: And therefore when he would let us know his great diligence in promoting the intereſt of one of his friends, he makes uſe of the ſame phraſes which are commonly applied to the candidates themſelves; as *Ambire domos, Prenſare amicos, Circumire ſtationes,* &c. (*b*).

The proceedings in the elections will fall more properly under the account of the aſſemblies where they were managed.

(*a*) *Roſin.* lib. 7. cap. 8.　　(*b*) *Plin. Epiſt.* lib. 2. ep. 9.

CHAP. IV.

Of the CONSULS.

THE conſular office began upon the expulſion of the Tarquins, in the year of the city 244. There are ſeveral derivations given of the word, that of *Cicero à Conſulendo* (*a*) is generally followed. Their power was at firſt the ſame as that of the king's, only reſtrained by plurality of perſons and ſhortneſs of time; therefore Tully calls it *Regum Imperium* (*b*), and *Regia Poteſtas* (*c*). In war they commanded in chief over citizens and aſſociates, nor were they leſs abſolute in peace, having the government of the ſenate itſelf, which they aſſembled or diſmiſſed at their pleaſure. And though their authority was very much impaired, firſt by the tribunes of the people, and afterwards upon the eſtabliſhment of the empire; yet they were ſtill employed in conſulting the ſenate, adminiſtering juſtice,

(*a*) *Cicero de leg.* lib. 3.　　(*b*) *Ibid.*　　(*c*) *Idem de Petitione Conſulatus.*

managing public games, and the like; and had the honour to characterize the year by their own names.

At the firſt inſtitution this honour was confined to the nobility; but in the year of the city 387, the commons obtained the privilege of having one of their own body always an aſſociate in this office. Sometimes, indeed, the populacy were ſo powerful, as to have both conſuls choſe out of their order; but, generally ſpeaking, one was a nobleman, and the other a commoner.

No perſon was allowed to ſue for this office, unleſs he was preſent at the election, and in a private ſtation; which gave occaſion to the civil wars between Pompey and Cæſar, as has been already obſerved. The common age required in the candidates was forty-two years. This Cicero himſelf acquaints us with, if we allow a little ſcope to his way of ſpeaking, when he ſays, that Alexander the Great, dying in the thirty-third year, came ten years ſhort of the conſular age (a). But ſometimes the people diſpenſed with the law, and the emperors took very little notice of the reſtraint.

The time of the conſul's government, before Julius Cæſar, was always a complete year: But he brought up a cuſtom of ſubſtituting conſuls at any time for a month or more, according as he pleaſed. Yet the conſuls, who were admitted the firſt of January, denominated the year, and had the title of *Ordinarii;* the others being ſtiled *Suffecti* (b).

The chief ornaments and marks of their authority were the white robe edged with purple, called *Prætexta;* which in aftertimes they changed for the *Toga Palmata,* or *Picta,* before proper only to ſuch perſons as had been honoured with a triumph; and the twelve lictors, who went before one of them one month, and the other the next, carrying the faſces and the ſecuris, which, though Valerius Poplicola took away from the faſces, yet it was ſoon after added again.

Their authority was equal; only in ſome ſmaller matters he had the precedency, according to the Valerian law, who was oldeſt; and he, according to the Julian law, who had moſt children.

CHAP.

(a) *Ciceron. Philip.* 5.   (b) *Dio.* lib. 43. *Sueton. in Julio,* cap. 76. &c.

CHAP. V.

Of the Dictator *and his Master of Horse.*

THE office of *Dictator* was of very early original: For the Latins entering into a confederacy against Rome to support Tarquin's cause after his expulsion, the senate were under great apprehensions of danger, by reason of the difficulty they found in procuring levies to oppose them: While the poorer commons, who had been forced to run themselves into debt with the Patricians, absolutely refused to list themselves, unless an order of senate might pass for a general remission. Now the power of life and death being lately taken from the consuls by the Valerian law, and liberty given for an appeal from them to the people, they could not compel any body to take up arms. Upon this account, they found it necessary to create a magistrate, who for six months should rule with absolute authority, even above the laws themselves. The first person pitched upon for this honour was Titus Largius Flavius, about *A. U. C.* 253, or 255 (*a*).

This supreme officer was called *Dictator*, either because he was dictus, named of the consul, or else from his dictating and commanding what should be done (*b*): Tho' we sometimes meet with the naming of a dictator upon a smaller account, as the holding the comitia for the election of consuls, the celebration of public games, the *fixing* the *nail* upon Jove's temple, (which they called *clavum pangere*, and which was used in the times of primitive ignorance, to reckon the number of the years, and in the times of later superstition, for the averting or driving away pestilences and seditions) and the like; yet the true and proper dictator was he who had been invested with this honour upon the occasion of dangerous war, sedition, or any such emergency as required a sudden and absolute command (*c*). And therefore he was not chosen with the usual formalities, but only named in the night, *viva voce*, by the consul (*d*), and confirmed by the divination from birds (*e*). The time assigned for the duration of the office was never lengthened, except out of mere necessity:

(*a*) *Dionys. Antiq.* lib. 5. *Liv.* lib. 2.   (*b*) *Ibid.*   (*c*) *Lips. de Magistrat.* cap. 17.   (*d*) *Liv.* lib. 4.   (*e*) *Cicero de Leg.* lib. 3.

necessity: And as for the perpetual dictatorships of Sylla and Julius Cæsar, they are confessed to have been notorious violations of the laws of their country. There were two other confinements which the dictator was obliged to observe. First, he was never to stir out of Italy, for fear he should take advantage of the distance of the place to attempt any thing against the common liberty (*a*). Besides this, he was always to march on foot; only upon account of a tedious or sudden expedition, he formally asked leave of the people to ride (*b*). But setting aside these restraints, his power was most absolute. He might proclaim war, levy forces, lead them out, or disband them, without any consultation had with the senate: He could punish as he pleased, and from his judgment lay no appeal (*c*), at least not till in latter times. To make the authority of his charge more awful, he had always twenty four bundles of rods, and as many axes, carried before him in public, if we may believe Plutarch (*d*) and Polybius (*e*). Tho' Livy attributes the first rise of this custom to Sylla (*f*). Nor was he only invested with the joint authority of both the consuls, (whence the Grecians called him Δικτάτως, or *Double Consul*) but, during his administration, all other magistrates ceased, except the tribunes, and left the whole government in his hands (*g*).

This office had the repute to be the only safeguard of the commonwealth in times of danger four hundred years together; till Sylla and Cæsar having converted it into a tyranny, and rendered the very name odious: Upon the murder of the latter, a decree passed in the senate, to forbid the use of it upon any account whatsoever for the future (*h*).

The first thing the dictator did, was to chuse a *Magister Equitum*, or Master of the Horse, (he himself being in ancient times, by a more general name, termed *Magister Populi*) who was to be his lieutenant-general of the army, but could act nothing without his express order. Yet in the war with Hannibal, when the slow proceedings of Fabius Maximus created a suspicion in the commons, they voted, that Minutius, his master of the horse, should have an equal authority with Fabius himself, and be, as it were, another dictator (*i*). The like was afterwards practised in the same war upon the defeat at Cannæ, when the dictator, M. Junius, being with the army, Fabius Buteo

---

(*a*) *Dio. Hist.* lib. 36. (*b*) *Plut. in Fab. Max.* (*c*) *Dionys. Antiq.* lib. 8.
(*d*) *In Fab. Max.* (*e*) *Hist.* l. 3. (*f*) *Epitom.* l. 89. (*g*) *Plut. in Fab. Max.*
(*h*) *Dio*, lib. 44. *Appian,* lib. 3. (*i*) *Plutarch. in Fab. Max. Polybius,* lib. 3.

Buteo was chose a second dictator at Rome, to create new senators for the supplying of their places who had been killed in the battle: Though, as soon as ever the ceremony was over, he immediately laid down his command, and acted as a private person (a).

There was another expedient used in cases of extreme emergency, much like this custom of creating a dictator; and that was, to invest the consuls, sometimes the other chief magistrates, as the prætors, tribunes, &c. with an absolute and uncontroulable power. This was performed by that short yet full decree of senate, *Dent operam Consules*, &c. *ne quid Detrimenti capiat Respublica.* " Let the Consuls, &c. take care that " the Commonwealth suffer no damage."

(a) *Plutarch. Ibid.*

CHAP. VI.

Of the PRÆTORS.

THE original of this office, instituted in the year of the city 389, is owing to two occasions: Partly because the consuls being very often wholly taken up with foreign wars, found the want of some person to administer justice in the city; and partly because the nobility, having lost their appropriation of the consulship, were ambitious of procuring to themselves some new honour in its room (a). At the first, only one was created, taking his name *à præundo*; and for the same reason most of the old Latins called their commanders *Prætores*: And the consuls are supposed to have used that title at their first institution. *A. U. C.* 501 another prætor was added; and then one of them applied himself wholly to the preserving of justice among the citizens, with the name of *Prætor Urbanus*, while the other appointed judges in all matters relating to foreigners. But upon the taking in of Sicily and Sardinia, *A. U. C.* 520, two more prætors, were created to assist the consuls in the government of the provinces; and as many more upon the entire conquest of Spain, *A. U. C.* 551. Sylla increased the number to

(a) *Liv. lib.* 7. *circa Princip.*

to eight; Julius Cæsar first to ten, and then to sixteen; the second Triumviri, after an extravagant manner, to sixty-four.

After this, sometimes we meet with twelve prætors, sometimes fixteen or eighteen; but, in the declension of the empire, they fell as low again as three.

When the number of the prætors was thus increased, and the *Quæstiones*, or inquiries into crimes, made perpetual, and not committed to officers chosen upon such occasions, Prætor Urbanus (and, as Lipsius thinks, the Prætor Peregrinus) undertook the cognizance of private causes, and the other Prætors that of crimes. The latter therefore were sometimes called *Quæsitores quia quærebant de Crimine*; the first barely *jus dicebat*. Here we must observe the difference between *jus dicere* and *judicare*; the former relates to the prætor, and signifies no more than the allowing an action, and granting judices for determining the controversy; the other is the proper officer of the judices allowed by the prætor, and denotes the actual hearing and deciding of a cause (*a*).

(*a*) P. Manut. de legibus, p. 826.

CHAP. VII.

Of the CENSORS.

THE Census, or survey of the Roman citizens and their estates (from *Censeo*, to rate, or value) was introduced by Servius Tullius the sixth king, but without the assignment of any particular officer to manage it: And therefore he took the trouble upon himself, and made it a part of the regal duty. Upon the expulsion of the Tarquins, the business fell to the consuls, and continued in their care, till their dominions grew so large as to give them no leisure for its performance. Upon this account, it was wholly omitted seventeen years together, till *A. U. C.* 311, when they found the necessity of a new magistracy for that employment, and thereupon created two censors: Their office was to continue five years, because, every fifth year, the general survey of the people used to be performed: But when they grew to be the most considerable persons in the state, for fear they should abuse their authority, *A. U. C.* 420. a

law

law passed, by which their place was confined to a year and a half; and therefore, for the future, though they were elected every five years, yet they continued to hold the honour no longer than the time prefixed by that law.

After the second Punic war, they were always created out of such persons as had been Consuls, though it sometimes happened otherwise before. Their station was reckoned more honourable than the Consulship, though their authority, in matters of state, was not so considerable. And the badges of the two officers were the same, only that the Censors were not allowed the Lictors to walk before them, as the Consuls had.

Lipsius divides the duty of the Censors into two heads; the survey of the people, and the censure of manners. As to the former, they took an exact account of the estates and goods of every person, and accordingly divided the people into their proper classes and centuries. Besides this, they took care of the public taxes, and made laws in reference to them. They were inspectors of the public buildings and ways, and defrayed the charges of such sacrifices as were made upon the common account.

With respect to the latter part of their office, they had the power to punish an immorality in any person, of what order soever. The Senators they might *expel the House*, which was done by omitting such a person when they called over the names. The Equites they punished by *taking away the horse* allowed them at the public charge. The Commons they might either *remove* from a higher tribe to a less honourable; or quite *disable* them to give their votes in the assemblies; or set a *fine* upon them to be paid to the treasury. And sometimes when a Senator, or *Eques*, had been guilty of any notorious irregularity, he suffered two of these punishments, or all three at once.

Senatus ejicere.

Equum adimere.

Tribu movere.

In Æritum Tabulas referre, & Ærarium facere.

The greatest part of the *Censor's* public business was performed every fifth year, when, after the survey of the people, and inquisition into their manners, taken anciently in the forum, and afterwards in the Villa Publica, the Censors made a solemn lustration, or expiatory sacrifice, in the name of all the people. The sacrifice consisted of a sow, a sheep, and a bull, whence it took the name of *Suovetaurilia*. The ceremony of performing it they called *Lustrum condere*; and upon this account the space of five years came to be signified by the word *Lustrum*.

It is very remarkable, that, if one of the Censors died, nobody was substituted in his room till the next lustrum, and his partner was obliged to quit his office; because the death of a Censor happened just before the sacking of Rome by the Gauls, and was ever after accounted highly ominous and unfortunate (*a*).

This office continued no longer than to the time of the Emperors, who performed the same duty at their pleasure: And the Flavian family, *i. e.* Vespasian and his sons, took a pride (as Mr Walker (*b*) observes) to be called *Censors*, and put this among their other titles upon their coins. Decius the Emperor entered on a design of restoring the honour to a particular magistrate, as heretofore, but without any success (*c*).

(*a*) Liv. lib. 4. cap. 9.   Plut. Probl. 59.   (*b*) *Of Coins and Medals.*
(*c*) Trebel. Poll. in Decio.

CHAP. VIII.

Of the QUÆSTORS.

THE original of the *Quæstors* (*à quærendo*, from getting in the revenues of the State) Dionysius (*a*) and Livy (*b*) place about *A. U. C.* 269. Plutarch, indeed, with some small difference, refers their institution to the time of Valerius Poplicola, when he allotted the temple of Saturn for the treasury, (to which use it always served afterwards) and granted the people the liberty of chusing two young men for the treasurers (*c*). This was the whole number at the beginning; but afterwards two others were created, *A. U. C.* 332, to take care of the payment of the armies abroad, of the selling plunder and booty, &c. For which purpose, they generally accompanied the Consuls in their expeditions; and upon this account were distinguished from the other Quæstors by the name of *Peregrini*, and gave them occasion to assume the title of *Urbani*. This number continued till the entire conquest of Italy; and then it was again doubled, *A. U. C.* 439. The four that were now added had their residence with the Proconsuls and Proprætors in the provinces, where they employed themselves in regulating the taxes and customs due from thence to the State.

Sylla

(*a*) Lib. 8.   (*b*) Lib. 3.   (*c*) Plut. in Poplicol.

Sylla the Dictator, as Tacitus informs us (a), created twenty Quæstors to fill up the Senate, and Dio (b) mentions the creating of forty by Julius Cæsar upon the same design.

The chief offices of the Quæstors were the receiving, lodging, and carrying out ambassadors, and the keeping the decrees of the Senate appointed them by Augustus (c), which before had been under the care of the Ædiles and Tribunes.

From hence came the two offices of *Quæstor Principis*, or *Augusti*, called sometimes *Candidatus Principis*, described by Brissonius (d), and resembling the office of our Secretary of State, and *Quæstor Palatii*, instituted by Constantine the Great; answering in most respects to the place of the Lord Chancellor amongst us. Perhaps we ought not here to make a distinction of offices; the Quæstores Candidati being honoured by Constantine with the new title of *Quæstores Palatii*, and admitted to greater trust, and more important business (e).

The Quæstorship was the first office any person could bear in the Commonwealth, and might be undertaken at the age of twenty-four or twenty-five years.

(a) *Annal.* lib. 1. lib. 1. cap. 16. (b) Lib. 43. (c) Dio. lib. 54. (d) *Select. Antiq.*
(e) *Notit. Dignitat. Imp. Orient.* c. 73.

CHAP. IX.

Of the Tribunes *of the People.*

THIS office owes its original to a quarrel between the nobility and commons, about *A. U. C.* 260; when the latter making a defection, could not be reduced into order, till they had obtained the privilege of choosing some magistrates out of their own body, for the defence of their liberties, and to interpose in all grievances and impositions offered by their superiors (a). At first only two were elected; but three more were quickly added; and about *A. U. C.* 297, the number was made up ten, which continued ever after.

Their authority was extraordinary: For, tho' at first they pretended only to be a sort of protectors of the Commons, and redressers of public grievances, yet afterwards they usurped the power of doing almost whatever they pleased, having the whole

(a) *Dionys.* lib. 9. *Liv.* lib. 2, &c.

whole populacy to back and secure them: And therefore they assembled the people, preferred laws, made decrees, and executed them upon the magistrates themselves; and sometimes commanded the very Consuls to be carried to prison: And were, without question, the authors of far greater animosities between the nobles and commons than they were at first created to appease.

That which gained them the greater security was their repute of being *Sacro-sancti*, which they confirmed by a law: So that it was reckoned the highest act of impiety to offer them the least injury, or so much as to interrupt them when they were speaking. Their interposing in matters determined by the Senate, or other magistrates, was called *Intercessio*, and was performed by standing up, and pronouncing only one word, *VETO*.

As for the ensigns of their office, they had no Pretexta, Lictors, nor Curule chair; and only a sort of a beadle, whom they called Viator, went before them.

Sylla the Dictator was the first who dared to put a stop to the encroachments of the Tribunes; but they soon recovered their old power again, till the time of the Emperors, who left them very little but the name and shadow of magistrates: This they effected as by several means, so particularly by obliging the people to confer the same power and authority on themselves: Whence they were said to be *Tribunitiâ Potestate donati :* For they could not be directly Tribuni, unless their family had been Plebeian.

CHAP. X.
Of the ÆDILES.

THE Commons had no sooner prevailed with the Senate to confirm the office of Tribunes, but they obtained further the privilege to choose yearly, out of their own body, two more officers, to assist those magistrates in the discharge of some particular services (*a*), the chief of which was the care of public edifices, whence they borrowed their name. Rosinus, for distinction's sake, calls them *Ædiles Plebis*. Besides the duty mentioned above, they had several other employments of lesser note; as to attend on the Tribunes of the people, and to judge
some

(*a*) *Dionys.* lib. 6.

some inferior causes by their deputation, to rectify the weights and measures, prohibit unlawful games, and the like.

A. U. C. 389, two more Ædiles were elected out of the nobility, to inspect the public games (a). They were called *Ædiles Curules*, because they had the honour of using the *Sella Curulis*; the name of which is generally derived *à curru* (b), because they sat upon it as they rode in their chariots; but Lipsius fancies it owes its name, as well as its invention, to the *Curetes*, a people of the Sabines.

The *Curules Ædiles*, besides their proper office, were to take care of the building and reparation of temples, theatres, baths, and other noble structures; and were appointed judges in all cases relating to the selling or exchanging of estates.

Julius Cæsar, A. U. C. 710, added two more Ædiles out of the nobility, with the title of *Ædiles Cerealis*, from *Ceres*, because their business was to inspect the public stores of corn and other provisions; to supervise all the commodities exposed in the markets, and to punish delinquents in all matters concerning buying and selling (c).

(a) *Liv.* lib. 6. & 7.   (b) *Agell.* lib. 3. cap. 18.   (c) *Dio.* lib. 43. & *Pompon.* lib. 2. F. *de Orig. Juris*.

CHAP. XI.

Of the DECEMVIRI.

ABOUT the year of Rome 291, the people thinking themselves highly wronged, that though they had freed themselves from the government of the kings, yet still the whole decision of equity and justice should lie in the breast of the supreme magistrates, without any written statute to direct them, proposed to the Senate by their Tribunes, that standing laws might be made which the City should use for ever. The business hung in suspense several years; at last it was concluded to send ambassadors to Athens, and other Græcian cities, to make collections out of the best of their constitutions, for the service of their country in the new design. Upon the return of the commissioners, the Tribunes claiming the promise of the Senate, to allow them a new magistracy for the putting the project in execution, it was agreed, that ten men out of the chief Senators

tors should be elected: That their power should be equal to that of the Kings, or Consuls, for a whole year: And that, in the mean time, all other offices should cease. The Decemviri having now taken the government upon them, agreed that only one of them should at any time enjoy the fasces and other consular ornaments, should assemble the Senate, confirm decrees, and act in all respects as supreme magistrate. To this honour they were to succeed by turns, till the year was out; and the rest were obliged to differ very little in their habits from private persons, to give the people the less suspicion of tyranny and absolute government.

At length, having drawn up a model out of such laws as had been brought from Greece, and the customs of their own country, they exposed it to the public view in ten tables, liberty being given for any person to make exceptions. Upon the general approbation of the citizens, a decree passed for the ratification of the new laws, which was performed in the presence of the priests and augurs, in a most solemn and religious manner.

This year being expired, a farther continuance of this office was voted necessary, because something seemed yet to be wanting for the perfecting of the design. The Decemviri, who had procured themselves the honour in the new election, quickly abused their authority; and, under pretence of reforming the commonwealth, showed themselves the greatest violators of justice and honesty. Two more tables, indeed, they added to the first, and so seemed to have answered the intent of their institution: Yet they not only kept their office the remaining part of that year, but usurped it again the next, without any regard to the approbation of the Senate or people. And tho' there was some stir made in the city for putting a stop to their tyranny, yet they maintained their absolute power, till an action of their chief leader Appius gave a final ruin to their authority: For he, falling desperately in love with Virginia, the daughter of a Plebeian, and prosecuting his passion by such unlawful means, as to cause the killing of her by her own father (the story of which is told at large by Livy) gave an occasion of a mutiny in the army, and a general dislike through the whole city; so that it was agreed in the Senate, to let the same form of government return which was in force at the creation of the Decemviri (*a*).

(*a*) *Liv.* lib. 3. *Dionyf.* lib. 8.

CHAP.

CHAP. XII.

Tribuni Militum Confulari Poteſtate.

UPON the concluſion of the Decemvirate, the firſt Conſuls that were elected, appearing highly inclined to favour the Commons, gave them ſuch an opportunity of getting a head in the State, that, within three years afterwards, they had the confidence to petition for the privilege of being made capable of the Conſulſhip, which had hitherto been denied them. The ſtiffeſt of the Patricians violently oppoſed their requeſt, as a fair means to ruin their honour and authority, and to bring all perſons, of whatever quality, upon the ſame level. But a war caſually breaking out at the ſame time in the confederate countries, which the Romans were obliged to aſſiſt, the Conſuls, by reaſon of the diſſentions upon this account in the city, could not, with all their diligence, procure any levies to be made, becauſe the Tribunes of the commons oppoſed all their orders, and would let no ſoldiers be liſted, till their petition had been canvaſſed in the Senate. In this exigency, the Fathers were called together; and, after the buſineſs had been a long time debated with great heat and tumult, at laſt pitched upon this expedient; that three magiſtrates ſhould be elected out of each order, who being inveſted with the whole conſular power, at the end of the year it ſhould be in the liberty of the Senate and people to have that office or Conſuls for the following year.

Both parties readily embraced this propoſal, and accordingly proceeded to an election; where, tho' the whole deſign of this ſtir had been purely to increaſe the honour of the Commons, yet, when the matter came to be put to a vote, they choſe none of that order to the new magiſtracy, but conferred the honour on three of the moſt eminent Patricians, with the title of *Tribuni Militum Conſulare Poteſtate*, about *A. U. C.* 310.

The firſt Tribunes, having held their dignity no longer than ſeventy days, were obliged to quit it, by reaſon that the Augurs had diſcovered ſome flaw in their election; and ſo the government returned to its former courſe, the ſupreme command reſting

resting in the hands of the Consuls (*a*). Afterwards they were some years chose, and some years passed by, having risen from three to six, and afterwards to eight, and the Plebeians being admitted to a share of the honour; till about *A. U. C.* 388, when they were entirely laid aside.

(*a*) *Liv.* lib. 4. *Dionyf.* lib. 11.

C H A P. XIII.

Civil Officers of less Note, or of less frequent Occurrence in Authors, together with the public Servants.

THERE are several officers behind, who deserve little more than to be named; some by reason of their low station in the commonwealth, others because they are very seldom mentioned in our ordinary classics. Among whom we may take notice of these that follow:

Interrex, the supreme magistrate, who governed between the death of one king, and the election of another. This office was taken by turns by the Senators, continuing in the hands of every man five days (*a*), or, if we may believe Plutarch (*b*), only twelve hours at a time. We sometimes meet with an Interrex under the consular government, created to hold assemblies, when the ordinary magistrates were either absent, or disabled to act by reason of their undue election.

Tribunes, or *Præfectus Celerum*, the captain of Romulus's life-guard, which consisted of three hundred of the stoutest young men, and of the best families in the city, under the name of *Celeres*, or light-horse. After the expulsion of the kings, the *Magister Equitum* held the same place and command under the Dictators, and the *Præfectus Prætorio* under the Emperors.

Præfectus Urbis, a sort of Mayor of the city, created by Augustus, by the advice of his favourite Mæcenas, upon whom at first he conferred the new honour (*c*). He was to precede all other city magistrates, having power to receive appeals from the inferior courts, and to decide almost all causes within the limits

(*a*) *Dionyf.* l. 2. *Liv.* l. 1. (*b*) *In Numa.* (*c*) *Dio.* l. 52. *Tacit. Annal.* 4, 5.

limits of Rome, or a hundred miles round. Before this there was sometimes a *Præfectus Urbis* created, when the Kings, or greater officers, were absent from the city, to administer justice in their room (*a*).

Præfectus Ærarii; an officer chosen out of such persons as had discharged the office of Prætor by Augustus, to supervise and regulate the public fund, which he raised for the maintenance of the army (*b*). This project was revived by several of his successors.

Præfectus Prætorio; created by the same Emperor, to command the Prætorian cohorts, or his life-guard, who borrowed their name from the Prætorium, or General's tent, all commanders in chief being anciently stiled Prætores. His office answered exactly to that of the *Magister Equitum* under the old Dictators; only his authority was of greater extent, being generally the highest person in favour with the army. And therefore, when the soldiers once came to make their own Emperors, the person they commonly pitched upon was the *Præfectus Prætorio*.

Præfectus Frumenti, and *Præfectus Vigilum;* both owing their institution to the same Augustus. The first was to inspect and regulate the distribution of corn, which used to be often made among the common people. The other commanded in chief all the soldiers appointed for a constant watch to the city, being a cohort to every two regions. His business was to take cognizance of thieves, incendiaries, idle vagrants, and the like; and had the power to punish all petty misdemeanors which were thought too trivial to come under the care of the *Præfectus Urbis*.

In many of these inferior magistracies, several persons were joined in commission together; and then they took their name from the number of men that composed them. Of this sort we meet with the

Triumviri, or *Tresviri Capitales;* the keepers of the public goal; they had the power to punish malefactors, like our masters of the houses of correction, for which service they kept eight lictors under them, as may be gathered from Plautus:

> *Quid faciam nunc si Tresviri me in carcerem compegerint?*
> *Inde cras é promptuariâ cellâ depromar ad flagrum:*
> *Ita quasi incudem me miserum octo homines validi cædent* (*c*).

Triumviri Nocturni; mentioned by Livy (*d*) and Tacitus (*e*), instituted for the prevention of fires in the night.

Y   *Triumviri*

(*a*) *Ibid.*   (*b*) *Dio.* l. 55.   (*c*) *In Amphitr.*   (*d*) Lib. 9.   (*e*) *Annal.* l. 5.

Triumviri Monetales; the masters of the mint: Sometimes their name was wrote, *Triumviri A. A. Æ. F. F.* standing for *Auro. Argento, Ære, Flando, Feriendo.*

Quatuor Viri Viarum curandarum; persons deputed by the Censor to supervise the public ways.

Centumviri, and *Decemviri Litibus judicandis;* the first were a body of men chose, three out of every tribe, for the judging of such matters as the Prætors committed to their decision; which are reckoned up by Cicero in his first book de Oratore. The *Decemviri* seem to have been the principal members of the *Centumvirate,* and to have presided under the Prætor in the *Judicia Centumviralia.* These were some of the first steps to preferment for persons of parts and industry; as was also the *Vigintiviratus,* mentioned by Cicero, Tacitus, and Dio, which, perhaps, was no more than a select part of the *Centumviri.* The proper sign of authority, when these judges acted, was the setting up a *spear* in the forum:

> *Seu trepidos ad jura decem citat hasta virorum,*
> *Seu firmare jubet centeno judice causam.* LUCAN.

The learned Grævius observes, that a *spear* was the common badge and ensign of power among the ancients, and therefore given to the gods in their statues, and to kings and princes, till it was succeeded by the *sceptre* (a). A spear was likewise set up at the collections of the taxes by the Censors; and at all auctions, public or private, to signify that they were done by a lawful commission; whence the phrase, *Sub hasta vendi.*

There are other officers of as little note behind, who had no fixed authority, but were constituted upon some particular occasions; such as the

Duumviri Perduellionis, sive Capitales, officers created for the judging of traitors. They were first introduced by Tullus Hostilius; continued as often as necessity required under the rest of the Kings, and sometimes under the consular government, at its first institution. But after they had been laid down many years as unnecessary, Cicero, in the latter times of their commonwealth, complains of their revival by Labienus, Tribune of the Commons (b).

Quæstores, or *Quæstores Parricidii, vel Rerum capitalium;* magistrates chosen by the people to give judgment in capital causes, after

---

(a) *Præfat. II. Tom. Thesaur. Antiq. Rom.* (b) *Cicero. Orat. pro C. Rabirio Perduellionis reo.*

after the Confuls were denied that privilege, and before the Quæſtiones were made *perpetual*.

The public ſervants of the magiſtrates had the common name of *Apparitores*, from the word *Appareo*, becauſe they always ſtood ready to execute their maſter's orders. Of theſe, the moſt remarkable were the

Scribæ; a ſort of public notaries, who took an account of all the proceedings in the courts: In ſome meaſure too they anſwered to our attornies, inaſmuch as they drew up the papers and writings which were produced before the judges; *Notarius* and *Actuarius* ſignifying much the ſame office.

Accenſi and *Præcones*, the public criers, who were to call witneſſes, ſignify the adjournment of the court, and the like. The former had the name from *Accieo*, and the other from *Præcieo*. The *Præcones* ſeem to have had more buſineſs aſſigned them than the *Accenſi*; as, the proclaiming things in the ſtreet; the aſſiſting at public ſales, to declare how much every one bids; whereas the *Accenſi* more nearly attended on the magiſtrates: And, at the bench of juſtice, gave notice, every three hours, what it was o'clock.

Lictores: The ſerjeants, or beadles, who carried the faſces before the ſupreme magiſtrates; as the *Interreges*, Dictators, Conſuls, and Prætors. Beſides this, they were the public executioners in ſcourging and beheading.

The *Lictors* were taken out of the common people, whereas the *Accenſi* generally belonged to the body of the *Libertini*, and ſometimes to that of the *Liberti* (a).

The *Viatores* were little different from the former, only that they went before the officers of leſs dignity, and particularly before the Tribunes of the Commons.

In ancient times they were uſed to call the plain Senators out of the country, whence Tully in his Cato Major derives their name; as if they were to ply about the roads and picks, and to pick up an aſſembly of rural fathers, who perhaps were then employed in driving, or keeping their own ſheep.

We muſt not forget the *Carnifex*, or common hangman, whoſe buſineſs lay only in crucifixions. Cicero has a very good obſervation concerning him: That, by reaſon of the odiouſneſs of his office, he was particularly forbid by the laws to have his dwelling-houſe within the city.

(a) *Sigon. de Antiq. Jur Civ. Rom.* cap.

CHAP. XIV.

Of the Provincial Magistrates; and first of the PROCONSULS.

THE chief of the provincial officers were the *Proconsuls*. Whether the word ought to be written *Proconsul*, and declined, or *Proconsule*, and undeclined,

Grammatici certant, & adhuc sub judice lis est.

We may divide these magistrates into four sorts;

First, Such as being Consuls had their office prolonged beyond the time prefixed by law.

Secondly, Such as were invested with this honour, either for the government of the provinces, or the command in war, who before were only in a private station.

Thirdly, Such as immediately, upon the expiration of their consulship, went Proconsuls into the provinces, in the time of the commonwealth.

Fourthly, Such governors as in the times of the empire were sent into those provinces which fell to the share of the people.

Proconsuls of the two former sorts we meet with very rarely, only Livy gives us an example of each (*a*).

The third kind more properly enjoyed the name and dignity, and therefore deserve to be described at large, with reference to their creation, administration, and return from their command.

They were not appointed by the people, but when at the *Comitia Centuriata* new Consuls were designed for the following year; one of the present Consuls proposed to the Senate what province they would declare consular, and what prætorian, to be divided among the *designed* Consuls and Prætors. According to their determination, the *designed* Consuls, or Consuls *elect*, presently agreed what provinces to enter upon at the expiration of their office in the city, the business being generally decided by casting lots.

Afterwards,

(*a*) Liv lib. 8, cap. 26.

Afterwards, in the time of their confulfhip, they formally got leave of the people to undertake the military command, which could not be otherwife obtained. Befides this, they procured a decree of the Senate, to determine the extent of their provinces, the number of their forces, the pay that fhould be allowed them, with all other neceffaries for their journey and fettlement.

By the paffing of this decree, they were faid *Ornari Provincia;* and Cicero ufes in the fame fenfe *Ornari Apparitoribus, Scribus,* &c. who made a part of the Proconful's retinue.

Nothing now remained, but at the end of the year to fet forward for their new government. But we muft obferve, that tho' the Senate had given them leave to depart, yet the Tribunes of the Commons had power to ftop their journey; and therefore, becaufe Craffus went Proconful into Parthia, contrary to the exprefs order of the Tribune, he was generally believed to have loft the Roman army and his own life, as a judgment on him for defpifing the authority of that officer, whom they always counted *facro-fanctus.*

At their firft entrance on their province, they fpent fome time in conference with their immediate predeceffors, to be informed of the ftate of things, though their adminiftration began the very day of their arrival.

Their authority, both civil and military, was very extraordinary. The winter they generally fpent in the execution of the firft, and the fummer in the difcharge of the latter.

They decided cafes of equity and juftice either privately in their prætorium, or palace; where they received petitioners, heard complaints, granted writs under their feals, and the like; or elfe publicly in the common-hall, with the ufual ceremonies and formalities obferved in courts of judicature, the proceffes being in all refpects the fame as thofe at Rome.

Befides this, by virtue of their edicts they had the power of ordering all things relating to the Tribunes; taxes, contributions, and provifions of corn and money, and whatever elfe belonged to the chief adminiftration of affairs.

Their return from the command was very remarkable: They either met their fucceffor at his arrival, and immediately delivered into his hands the charge of the army, being obliged to leave the province in thirty days; or elfe they came away beforehand, and left a deputy in their room to perform the folemnity of a refignation, having firft made up their accompts, and left them in writing in the two chief cities of their feveral provinces.

Upon their arrival at Rome, if they had no thoughts of a triumph, they presently difmiffed their train, and entered the city as private perfons. If they afpired to that honour, they ftill retained the fafces, and other proconfular ornaments, and gave the Senate, (affembled for that purpofe in the temple of Bellona) a relation of their actions and exploits, and petitioned for a triumph. But in both cafes they were obliged to give in their accompts into the public treafury within thirty days.

Tho' the Proconfuls ordered matters as they pleafed during their honour, yet at their return a very ftrict account was made into the whole courfe of their government; and upon the difcovery of any ill dealing, it was ufual to prefer bills againft them, and bring them to a formal trial. The crimes moft commonly objected againft them were *Crimen Peculatûs;* relating to the ill ufe of the public money, and the deficiency of their accompts: *Majeftatis,* of treachery and perfidioufnefs againft the commonwealth; or *Repetundarum,* of oppreffion or extortion exercifed upon the inhabitants of the provinces, whom, as their allies and confederates, the Romans were obliged to patronize and defend.

Auguftus, when, at the defire of the Senate and people, he affumed the fole government of the empire, among other conftitutions at the beginning of his reign, divided the provinces into two parts, one of which he gave wholly over to the people, and referved the other for himfelf. After which time, only the governors fent into the firft divifion bore the name of *Proconfuls,* though they were denied the whole military power, and fo fell fhort of the old Proconfuls.

To thefe four forts of Proconfuls we may add two more from Alexander of Naples:

Firft, fuch as the Senate created Proconfuls without a *province,* purely for the command of the army, and the care of the military difcipline: And, fecondly, fuch *defigned* Confuls as entered on their proconfular office, before they were admitted to the confulfhip.

CHAP.

CHAP. XV.

Of the Provincial Prætors *and* Proprætors; *of the* Legati, Quæstors, *and* Proquæstors.

IN the first times of the commonwealth, the provinces were governed by *Prætors*; and as the dominions of the State were enlarged, the number of those magistrates was accordingly increased; yet even in those times, if they continued in the command of the province beyond the time prefixed for the continuance of their prætorship, they took upon them the names of *Proprætors*, tho' they still kept the same authority as before.

About *A. U. C.* 604. the *designed* Prætors began to divide the prætorian, or lesser provinces, by lot, in the same manner as the Consuls did the consular; and when, at the end of the year, they repaired to their respective governments, assumed the title of *Proprætors.* As their creation was the same as that of the Proconsuls, so their entrance upon their office, and the whole course of their administration, was exactly answerable to theirs; only that they were allowed but six lictors, with an equal number of fasces, whereas the Proconsuls had twelve of each.

Now tho' before the time of Augustus the Proprætors, by reason of their presiding over the provinces of lesser note and importance, were always reckoned inferior to the Proconsuls, yet, upon his division of the provinces, the governors of those which fell to his share, bearing the name of *Proprætors*, got the preference of the Proconsuls, in respect of power and authority, being invested with the military command, and continuing in their office as long as the Emperor pleased.

The chief assistants of the Proconsuls and the Proprætors were the Legati and the provincial Quæstors. The former being different in number, according to the quality of the Governor whom they accompanied, served for the judging of inferior causes, and the management of all smaller concerns, remitting every thing of moment to the care of the governor, or president. But tho' instituted at first for counsel only (like the *deputies of the States* attending the Dutch armies) yet they were afterwards admitted to command; and therefore will be described as *general officers*, when we come to speak of military affairs (*a*).

Besides

(*a*) Lib. IV. cap. 8.

Besides the Legati, there went with every Proconsul, or Propraetor, one *Quaestor* or more, whose whole business was concerned in managing the public accounts, taking care of the supplies of money, corn, and other necessaries and conveniencies for the maintenance of the Roman army.

We seldom meet with Proquaestors in authors, they being only such as performed the office of Quaestor in the provinces, without the deputation of the Senate, which was requisite to the constitution of the proper Quaestors. This happened either when a Quaestor died in his office, or went to Rome without being succeeded by another Quaestor: For in both these cases, the governor of the province appointed another in his room, to discharge the same duties under the name of *Proquaestor*.

Of the like nature with the Quaestor were the *Procuratores Caesaris*, often mentioned by Tacitus and Suetonius; officers sent by the Emperors into every province, to receive and regulate the public revenue, and to dispose of it at the Emperor's command.

Such a magistrate was Pontius Pilate in Judea; and tho' the judging of capital causes did not properly belong to his office, yet because the Jews were always looked upon as a rebellious nation, and apt to revolt upon the least occasion; and because the President of Syria was forced to attend on other parts of his province; therefore, for the better keeping the Jews in order, the Procurator of Judea was invested with all the authority proper to the Proconsul, even with the power of life and death, as the learned Bishop Pearson observes (*a*).

(*a*) *Bishop Pearson on the Creed*, Art. 4.

CHAP. XVI.

Of the COMITIA.

THE Comitia, according to Sigonius's definition, were "general assemblies of the people, lawfully called by some "magistrates, for the enjoinment or prohibition of any thing "by their votes (*a*)."

The proper Comitia were of three sorts; *Curiata*, *Centuriata*, and *Tributa*; with reference to the three grand divisions of the city and people into *Curiae*, *Centuries*, and *Tribes:* For by Comitia

(*a*) *Sigon. de Antiq. Jur. Civ. Romanorum*, lib. 1. cap. 17.

Comitia Calata, which we sometimes meet with in authors, in elder times were meant all the comitia in general; the word *Calata*, from καλέω, or *Calo*, being their common epithet; tho' it was at last restrained to two sorts of assemblies, those for the creation of priests, and those for the inspection and regulation of last wills and testaments (*a*).

The *Comitia Curiata* owes their original to the division which Romulus made of the people into thirty Curiæ, ten being contained under every tribe. They answered, in most respects, to the parishes in our cities, being not only separated by proper bounds and limits, but distinguished too by their different places set apart for the celebration of divine service, which was performed by particular priests (one to every Curiæ) with the name of *Curiones*.

Dionysius Halicarnassus expressly affirms, that each Curia was again subdivided into Decuriæ, and these lesser bodies governed by Decuriones. And, upon the strength of this authority, most compilers of the Roman customs give the same account without any scruple. But it is the opinion of the learned Grævius (*b*), that since Dionysius is not seconded in this part of his relation, by an ancient writer, we ought to think it was a mistake in that great man; and that, by forgetfulness, he attributed such a division to the Curiæ as belonged properly to the Turmæ in the army.

Before the institution of the *Comitia Centuriata*, all the grand concerns of the State were transacted in the assembly of the Curiæ; as, the election of Kings, and other chief officers, the making and abrogating of laws, and the judging of capital causes. After the expulsion of the Kings, when the Commons had obtained the privilege to have Tribunes and Ædiles, they elected them for some time at these assemblies: But, that ceremony being at length transferred to the Comitia Tributa, the Curiæ were never convened to give their votes, except now and then upon account of making some particular law relating to adoptions, wills, and testaments, or the creation of officers for an expedition; or for the electing of some of the priests, as the Flamines, and the Curio Maximus, or Superintendant of the Curiones, who themselves were chose by every particular Curia.

The power of calling these assemblies belonged at first only to the Kings; but, upon the establishment of the democracy, the

(*a*) *A. Gell.* lib. 15. cap. 27.   (*b*) *Præf. ad* 1 *Vol. Thes. Antiq. Rom.*

the same privilege was allowed to most of the chief magistrates, and sometimes to the Pontifices.

The persons who had the liberty of voting here were such Roman citizens as belonged to the Curiæ, or such as actually lived in the city, and conformed to the customs and rites of their proper Curia; all those being excluded who dwelt without the bounds of the city, and retaining the ceremonies of their own country, though they had been honoured with the *Jus Civitatis*, or admitted free citizens of Rome (*a*).

The place where the Curiæ met was the Comitium, a part of the forum described before (*b*).

No set time was allotted for the holding of these or any of the other Comitia, but only as business required.

The people being met together, and confirmed by the report of good omens from the augurs (which was necessary in all the assemblies) the rogatio, or business to be proposed to them, was publicly read. After this, (if none of the magistrates interposed) upon the order of him that presided in the Comitia, the people divided into their proper Curiæ, and consulted of the matter; and then the Curiæ being called out, as it happened by lot, gave their votes, man by man, in ancient *Tabella*. times *vivâ voce*, and afterwards by tablets; the most votes in every Curia going for the voice of the whole Curia, and the most Curiæ for the general consent of the people (*c*).

In the time of Cicero, the *Comitia Curiata*, were so much out of fashion, that they were formed only by thirty lictors representing the thirty Curiæ; whence in his second oration against Rullus, he calls them *Comitia adumbrata*.

The *Comitia Centuriata* was instituted by Servius Tullius; who obliging every one to give a true account of what they were worth, according to those accounts divided the people into six ranks, or classes, which he subdivided into 193 centuries. The first classis containing the equites and richest citizens, consisted of ninety-eight centuries. The second, taking in the tradesmen and mechanics, made up two and twenty centuries. The third, the same number. The fourth, twenty. The fifth thirty. And the last, filled up with the poorer sort, had but one century (*d*).

And

(*a*) Sigon. de Antiq. jur. Provinc. lib. 2. cap. 1.   (*b*) See Part II. Book 1. cap. 5.   (*c*) Rosin. lib. 7. cap. 7.   (*d*) See Dionys. lib. 4.

And this, though it had the same name with the rest, yet was seldom regarded, or allowed by any power in public matters. Hence it is a common thing with the Roman authors, when they speak of the classes, to reckon no more than five, the sixth not being worth their notice. This last classis was divided into two parts, or orders, the *Proletarii*, and the *Capite Censi*. The former, as their name implies, were designed purely to stock the commonwealth with men, since they could supply it with so little money. And the latter, who paid the lowest tax of all, were rather counted and marshalled by their heads than their estates (*a*).

Persons of the first rank, by reason of their pre-eminence, had the name of *Classici*; whence came the phrase of *Classici Authores*, for the most approved writers. All others, of what classis soever, were said to be *infra Classem* (*b*).

The assembly of the people by centuries was held for the electing of Consuls, Censors, and Prætors; as also for the judging of persons accused of what they called *Crimen Perduellionis*, or actions by which the party had showed himself an enemy to the State; and for the confirmation of all such laws as were proposed by the chief magistrates, and which had the privilege of calling these assemblies.

The place appointed for their meeting was the Campus Martius; because in the primitive times of the commonwealth, when they were under continual apprehensions of enemies, the people, to prevent any sudden assault, went armed, in martial order, to hold these assemblies; and were for that reason forbid by the laws to meet in the city, because an army was upon no account to be marshalled within the walls : Yet, in latter ages, it was thought sufficient to place a body of soldiers as a guard in the janiculum, where an imperial standard was erected, the taking down of which denoted the conclusion of the comitia.

Tho' the time of these comitia for other matters was undetermined, yet the magistrates, after the year of the city 601, when they began to enter on their place on the kalends of January, were constantly *designed* about the end of July, and the beginning of August.

All the time between their election and confirmation they continued as private persons, that inquisition might be made into the election, and the other candidates might have time to enter objections, if they met with any suspicion of foul dealing.

(*a*) *A. Gell.* lib. 7. cap. 13.   (*b*) *A. Gell.* lib. 16. cap. 10.

Yet at the election of the Censors this custom did not hold; but as soon as they were pronounced elected, they were immediately invested with the honour (*a*).

By the institution of these Comitia, Servius Tullius secretly conveyed the whole power from the Commons: For the centuries of the first and richest class being called out first, who were three more in number than all the rest put together, if they all agreed, as they generally did, the business was already decided, and the other classes were needless and insignificant. However, the three last scarce ever came to vote (*b*).

The Commons, in the time of the free state, to rectify this disadvantage, obtained, that before they proceeded to voting any matter at these comitia, that century should give their suffrages first, upon whom it fell by lot, with the name of *Centuria Prærogativa*, the rest being to follow according to the order of their classes. After the constitution of the five-and-thirty tribes, into which the classes and their centuries were divided, in the first place, the tribes cast lots which should be the *prerogative* tribe; and then the centuries of the tribe, for the honour of being the *prerogative* century. All the other tribes and centuries had the appellation of *Jure vocatæ*, because they were called out according to their proper places.

The *Prerogative Century* being chose by lot, the chief magistrate sitting in a * tent in the middle of the

* *Tabernaculum.* Campus Martius, ordered that century to come out and give their voices; upon which they presently separated from the rest of the multitude, and came into an inclosed apartment, which they termed *Septa*, or *Ovilia*, passing over the pontes, or narrow boards, laid there for the occasion; on which account, *de Ponte dejici* is to be denied the privilege of voting, and persons thus dealt with are called *Depontani*.

At the hither end of the pontes stood the *Diribitores*, (a sort of under-officers, called so from dividing or marshalling the people) and delivered to every man, in the election

* *Tabellæ.* of magistrates, as many * tablets as there appeared candidates, one of whose names was written upon every tablet.

A fit number of great chests were set ready in the *Septa*, and every body threw in which tablet he pleased.

By

(*a*) *Liv.* lib. 40.   (*b*) *Dionys.* lib. 4.

By the chests were placed some of the public servants, who taking out the tablets of every century for every tablet, made a prick, or a point, in another tablet which they kept by them. Thus the business being decided by most points, gave occasion to the phrase of *Omne tulit punctum* (a), and the like.

The same method was observed in the judiciary processes at these comitia, and in the confirmation of laws; except that in both these cases only two tablets were offered to every person, on one of which was written *U. R.* and on the other *A.* in capital letters; the two first standing for *Uti Rogas*, or, *Be it as you desire*, relating to the magistrates who proposed the question; and the last for *Antiquo*, or, *I forbid it*.

It is remarkable, that though in the election of magistrates, and in the ratification of laws, the votes of that century whose tablets were equally divided signified nothing, yet in trials of life and death, if the tablets *pro* and *con* were the same in number, the person was actually acquitted (b).

The division of the people into tribes was an invention of Romulus, after he had admitted the Sabines into Rome; and tho' he constituted at that time only three, yet as the State increased in power, and the city in number of inhabitants, they rose by degrees to five-and-thirty. For a long time after this institution, a tribe signified no more than such a space of ground with its inhabitants. But at last the matter was quite altered, and a tribe was no longer *Pars Urbis*, but *Civitatis*; not a quarter of the city, but a company of citizens living where they pleased. This change was chiefly occasioned by the original difference between the tribes in point of honour. For Romulus having committed all sordid and mechanic arts to the care of strangers, slaves, and libertines, and reserved the more honest labour of agriculture to the freemen and citizens, who, by this active course of life, might be prepared for martial service; the *Tribus Rusticæ* were for this reason esteemed more honourable than the *Urbanæ*: And now all persons being desirous of getting into the more creditable division, and there being several ways of accomplishing their wishes, as by adoption, by the power of the Censors, and the like; that rustic tribe which had most worthy names in its roll, had the preference to all others, tho' of the same general denomination. Hence all of the same great family, bringing themselves by degrees into the same tribe, gave the name of their family to the tribe they honoured;

(a) *Hor. de Arte Poet.*   (b) *Dionys.* lib. 7.

noured; whereas at firſt, the generality of the tribes did not borrow their names from perſons, but from places (a).

The firſt aſſembly of the tribes we meet with is about the year of Rome 263, convened by Sp. Sicinius, Tribune of the Commons, upon account of the trial of Coriolanus. Soon after the Tribunes of the Commons were ordered to be elected here; and at laſt all the inferior magiſtrates and the collegiate prieſts. The ſame comitia ſerved for the enacting laws relating to war and peace, and all others propoſed by the Tribunes and Plebeian officers, though they had not properly the name of *Leges* but *Plebiſcita*. They were generally convened by Tribunes of the Commons; but the ſame privilege was allowed to all the chief magiſtrates.

They were confined to no place, and therefore ſometimes we find them held in the *Comitium*, ſometimes in the *Campus Martius*, and now and then in the capitol.

The proceedings were, in moſt reſpects, anſwerable to thoſe already deſcribed in the account of the other comitia, and therefore need not be inſiſted on; only we may further obſerve of the comitia in general, that when any candidate was found to have moſt tablets for a magiſtracy, he was declared to be *deſigned* or *elected* by the preſident of the aſſembly: And this they termed *renunciari Conſul, Prætor*, or the like: And that the laſt ſort of the comitia only could be held without the conſent and approbation of the Senate, which was neceſſary to the convening of the other two (b).

(a) Mr *Walker of Coins*, p. 126. (b) *Dionyſ.* lib. 9.

CHAP. XVII.

Of the ROMAN *Judgments; and firſt of Private Judgments.*

A Judgment, according to Ariſtotle's definition, is no more than Κρίσις τῦ δικαίυ καὶ ἀδίκυ, *the deciſion of right and wrong.*

The whole ſubject of the Roman judgments is admirably explained by Sigonius in his three books de Judiciis, from whom the following account is for the moſt part extracted:

Judgments,

Judgments, or determinations of a proper judge, were made either by a competent number of select judges, or by the whole people in a general assembly.

Judgments made by one or more select judges, may be divided into public and private; the first relating to controversies, the second to crimes.

The former will be sufficiently described, if we consider the matter or subjects of these judgments, the persons concerned in them, and the manner of proceeding.

The matter of private judgments takes in all sorts of causes that can happen between man and man; which being so vastly extended, and belonging more immediately to the civil law, need not here be insisted on.

The persons concerned, were the parties, the assistants, and the judges.

The parties, were the *Actor* and *Reus*, the plaintiff and defendant.

The assistants were the *Procuratores* and the *Advocati*, of whom, tho' they are often confounded, yet they first were properly such lawyers as assisted the plaintiff in proving, or the defendant in clearing himself from the matter of fact: The others, who were likewise called *Patroni*, were to defend their client's cause in matters of law (a).

Both these were selected out of the ablest lawyers, and had their names entered into the *Matriculation-Book* of the forum. This was one condition requisite to give them the liberty of pleading; the other was the being retained by one party, or the receiving a fee, which they termed *Mandatum* (b).

The judges, besides the Prætor, or supreme magistrate, who presided in the court, and allowed and confirmed them, were of three sorts; *Arbitri, Recuperatores,* and *Centumviri Litibus judicandis.*

Arbitri, whom they called simply *Judices,* were appointed to determine in some private causes of no great consequence, and of very easy decision.

Recuperatores were assigned to decide the controversies about receiving or recovering things which had been lost or taken away.

But the usual judges in private causes, were the *Centumviri*; three of which were taken out of every tribe, so that their number was five more than their name imported; and at length

---

(a) Zouch. Element. Jurisprud. p. 5. Sect. 3.   (b) Ibid.

length increased to a hundred and eighty. It is probable that the *Arbitri* and *Recuperatores* were assigned out of this body by the Prætor.

The manner of carrying on the private suits was of this nature: The difference failing to be made up between friends, the injured person proceeded, *in jus reum vocare*, to summon or cite the offending party to the court; who was obliged immediately to go with him, or else to give bond for his appearance, according to the common maxim, *In jus vocatus aut eat, aut satisdet*.

Both parties being met before the Prætor, or other supreme magistrate presiding in the court, the plaintiff proposed the action to the defendant, in which he designed to sue him: This they termed *Edere Actionem*, being performed commonly by writing it in a tablet, and offering it to the defendant, that he might see whether he had best compound, or stand the suit.

In the next place came the *Postulatio Actionis*, or the plaintiff's desiring leave of the Prætor to prosecute the defendant in such an action: This being granted, the plaintiff, *vadabatur reum*, obliged him to give sureties for his appearance on such a day in the court; and this was all that was done in public before the prefixed day for the trial.

In the mean time, the difference used very often to be made up, either *Transactione*, or *Pacto*, by letting the cause fall as dubious and uncertain; or by composition for so much damage to be ascertained by an equal number of friends.

On the day appointed for hearing, the Prætor ordered the several bills to be read, and the parties to be summoned by an *accensus* or beadle. Upon the default of either party, the defaulter lost his cause. The appearing of both they termed *se stetisse*; and then the plaintiff proceeded, *litem sive actionem intendere*, to prefer the suit; which was performed in a set form of words, varying according to the difference of the action. After this, the plaintiff desired judgment of the Prætor; that is, to be allowed a *Judix*, or arbiter, or else the *Recuperatores* or *Centumviri*, for the hearing and deciding the business; but none of these could be desired, unless both parties agreed. The Prætor, when he assigned them their judges, at the same time defined the number of witnesses, to hinder the protracting of the suit; and then the parties proceeded to give caution, that the judgment, whatever it was, should stand, and be performed on both sides. The judges always took a solemn oath to be impartial; and the parties swore they did not go to law with a design to abuse

one

one another: This they called *Juramentum Calumniæ*. Then began the *Disceptatio Causæ*, or disputing the case, managed by the lawyers on both sides; with the assistance of witnesses, writings, and the like; the use of which is so admirably taught in their books of oratory.

In giving sentence, the major part of the judges was required to overthrow the defendant. If the number was equally divided, the defendant was actually cleared; and if half condemned him in one sum to be paid, and half in another, the least sum always stood good (*a*).

The consequence of the sentence was either *in integrum Restitutio, Addictio, Judicium Calumniæ*, or *Judicium Falsi*.

The first was, when, upon petition of the party who was overthrown, the Prætor gave him leave to have the suit come on again, and allowed him another full hearing.

Addictio was, when the party who had been cast in such a sum, unless he gave surety to pay it in a little time, was brought by the plaintiff before the Prætor, who delivered him into his disposal, to be committed to prison, or otherwise secured, till satisfaction was made.

Judicium Calumniæ, was an action brought against the Plaintiff for false accusation.

Judicium falsi, was an action which lay against the judges for corruption and unjust proceedings.

(*a*) *Zouch. Element.* p. 5. Sect. 10.

CHAP. XVIII.

Of Public JUDGMENTS.

FOR the knowledge of public judgments, we may take notice of the crimes, of the punishments, of the quæsitores and judges, of the method of proceeding, and of the consequences of the trial.

The crimes, or the matter of the public judgments, were such actions as tended either mediately, or immediately, to the prejudice of the State, and were forbid by the laws. As if any person had derogated from the honour and majesty of the commonwealth; had embezzled or put to ill uses the public money, or any treasure consecrated to religion; or had corrupted

rupted the people's votes in an election; or had extorted contributions from the allies; or received money in any judgment; or had used any violent compulsion to a member of the commonwealth: These they termed *Crimina Majestatis, Peculatûs, Ambitûs, Reputundarum,* and *Vis publica.* Or if any person had killed another with a weapon, or effected the same with poison, or laid violent hands on his parents; or had forged a will; or counterfeited the public coin; or had corrupted another man's wife; or had bought, bound, or concealed a servant without the knowledge of his master: Whence these crimes took the names of *inter Sicarios, Veneficii, Parricidii, Falsi, Adulterii, Plagii.*

Besides these, any private cause, by virtue of a new law, might be made of public cognizance.

As to the punishments, they may be allowed a chapter by themselves hereafter.

The inquisition of criminal matters belonged at first to the Kings, and after the abrogation of the government, for some time, to the Consuls: But being taken from them by the Valerian law, it was conferred, as occasion happened, upon officers deputed by the people, with the title of *Quæsitores Parricidii.* But, about the year of the city 604, this power was made perpetual, and appropriated to the Prætors, by virtue of an order of the people at their annual election; the inquisition of such and such crimes being committed to such and such Prætors: Yet, upon extraordinary occasions, the people could appoint other Quæsitores, if they thought convenient.

Next to the Quæsitores, was the *Judex Quæstionis*; called also by Asconius, *Princeps Judicum*, who, though he is sometimes confounded with the Prætor, yet was properly a person of note, deputed by the Prætor, to manage the trial, of which the former magistrate performed only the main business.

After him were the *Judices selecti*, who were summoned by the Prætor to give their verdict in criminal matters, in the same manner as our juries. What alterations were made in different times as to the orders of the people whence the Judices were to be taken, will be observed when we speak of the particular laws on this head (*a*). No person could regularly be admitted into the number, unless five and twenty years of age (*b*).

As to the method of the proceedings, the first action, which they termed *in Jus Vocatio*, was much the same in public as in private

(*a*) Cap. 36. (*b*) Græv. *Præfat. ad Vol.* I. *Antiq. Rom.*

private causes: But then, as the *postulatio* of the plaintiff consisted in desiring leave of the Prætor to enter a suit against the defendant, so here the accuser desired permission to enter the name of the offender with the crime which he objected to him: This they called *Nominis Delatio;* being performed first *vivâ voce*, in a form of words, according to the nature of the crime, and then offered to the Prætor, being writ in a tablet; if approved by the Prætor, the accused party's name was entered in the roll of criminals; both persons having taken the *Oath of Calumny* already spoken of.

At the entrance of the name, the Prætor appointed a set day for the trial: And from that time the accused person changed his habit, going in black till the trial was over, and using in his dress and carriage all tokens of sorrow and concern.

Upon the appointed day, the court being met, and both parties appearing, the first thing that was done was the *Sortitio Judicum*, or impannelling the jury; performed commonly by the *Judex Quæstionis*, who took by lot such a number out of the body of the *Judices selecti*, as the particular law on which the accusation was founded had determined; liberty being given to both parties to reject (or, as we call it, to challenge) any that they pleased, the Prætor, or *Judex Quæstionis*, substituting others in their places.

The jury being thus chosen, was cited by the public servants of the court; and when the proper number appeared, they were sworn, and then took their places in the Subsellia, and heard the trial.

In this we may reckon four parts, *Accusatio, Defensio, Lauatio,* and *Latio sententiæ.*

Accusatio is defined, *Perpetua oratio ad crimina inferenda atque augenda artificiosè composita:* " A continued oration artificially composed for the making out, and heightening the " crimes alledged:" For it did not only consist in giving a plain narration of the matter of fact, and confirming it by witnesses and other evidences, but in bringing of other arguments too, drawn from the nature of the thing, from the character of the accused person, and his former course of life, from the circumstances of the fact, and several other topics, which the orators teach us to enlarge upon: Nor was the accuser limited in respect of time, being allowed commonly as many days as he pleased, to make good his charge.

Defensio belonged to the lawyers or advocates retained by the accused party, who in like manner were allowed to speak as many days as they pleased, towards the clearing of their client. The three common methods they took, were *Facti negatio, negatio nominis facti*, or *brobatio jure factum :* either plainly to deny the matter of fact, and endeavour to evince the contrary ; or else to acknowledge the fact, and yet to deny that it fell under the nature of the crime objected : Or, lastly, to prove the fact lawful.

The first way of defence was generally used when the person stood indicted of what they called *Crimen repetundarum*, and *Crimen ambitus ;* the next in the *Crimen Majestatis ;* and the last in cases of murder.

Cicero has given us an excellent example in every kind. Of the first in his orations for Fonteius, Flaccus, Muræna, and Plancius : Of the second in that for Cornelius ; and of the third in his admirable defence of Milo.

Laudatio was a custom, like that in our trials, of bringing in persons of credit to give their testimony of the accused person's good behaviour and integrity of life. The least number of the *Laudatores* used to be ten.

In the *Latio Sententiæ*, or pronouncing sentence, they proceeded thus: After the orators on both sides had said all they designed, the crier gave notice of it accordingly ; and then the Prætor sent out the jury to consult *(mittebat Judices in consilium)* delivering to every one three tablets covered with wax, one of absolution, another of condemnation, and a third of ampliation, or adjournment of the trial ; the first being marked with *A;* the second with *C ;* the other with *N. L.* or *non liquet.*

In the place where the jury withdrew was set a proper number of urns, or boxes, into which they threw what tablet they pleased ; the accused person prostrating himself all the while at their feet, to move their compassion.

The tablets being drawn, and the greatest number known, the Prætor pronounced sentence accordingly. The form of condemnation was usually *Videtur fecisse*, or *Non jure videtur fecisse :* Of absolution, *Non videtur fecisse :* Of amplification, *Amplius cognoscendum*, or rather the bare word *AMPLIUS :* This *Asconius* teaches us, *Mos veterum hic fuerat, ut si absolvendus quis esset, statim absolveretur ; si damnandus, statim damnaretur, si causa non esset idonea ad damnationem, absolvi tamen non posset, AMPLIUS pronunciaretur.* Sometimes he mentioned the punishment, and sometimes left it out, as being determined by the law on which the indictment was grounded.

The consequences of the trial in criminal matters, may be reduced to these four heads, *Æstimatio litis, Animadversio, Judicium calumniæ*, and *Judicium prævaricationis.*

Æstimatio

Æstimatio litis, or the rating of the damages, was in use only in cases of bribery, and abuse of the public money.

Animadversio, was no more than the putting the sentence in execution, which was left to the care of the Prætor.

But in case the party was absolved, there lay two actions against the accuser; one of calumny, the common punishment of which was *frontis inustio,* burning in the forehead; and the other of prevarication, when the accuser, instead of urging the crime home, seemed rather to hide or extenuate the guilt: Hence the Civilians define a prevaricator to be " one that be-
" trays his cause to the adversary, and turns on the criminal's
" side, whom he ought to prosecute."

CHAP. XIX.

Judgments of the whole People.

THE people were sometimes the judges, both in private and public causes; though of the first we have only one example in Livy; the other we frequently meet with in authors.

These judgments were made first at the Comitia Curiata, and afterwards at the Centuriata and Tributa; the proceedings in all which assemblies have been already shown: What we may further observe is this: when any magistrate designed to impeach a person of a crime before the whole people, he ascended the rostra, and calling the people together by a crier, signified to them, That, upon such a day, he intended to accuse such a person of such a crime: This they termed *Reo diem dicere:* The suspected party was obliged immediately to give sureties for his appearance on the day prefixed, and, in default of bail, was committed to prison.

On the appointed day, the magistrate again ascended the rostra, and cited the party by the crier; who, unless some other magistrate of equal authority interposed, or a sufficient excuse was offered, was obliged to appear, or might be punished at the pleasure of the magistrate who accused him. If he appeared, the accuser began his charge, and carried it on every other day for six days together; at the end of the indictment mentioning

mentioning the particular punishment specified in the law for such an offence. This intimation they termed *Inquisitio*. The same was immediately after expressed in writing, and then took the name of *Rogatio*, in respect of the people who were to be asked or consulted about it; and *Irrogatio*, in respect of the criminal, as it imported the mulct or punishment assigned him by the accuser. This rogatio was publicly exposed three *nundinæ*, or market-days together, for the information of the people. On the third market-day, the accuser again ascended the rostra, and, the people being called together, undertook the fourth turn of his charge, and, having concluded, gave the other party leave to enter upon his defence, either in his own person, or by his advocates.

At the same time as the accuser finished his fourth charge, he gave notice what day he would have the Comitia meet to receive the bill; the Comitia Tributa to consider of mulcts, and the Centuriata for capital punishments.

But, in the mean time, there were several ways by which the accused party might be relieved; as, first, if the Tribunes of the Commons interposed in his behalf; or if he excused himself by voluntary exile, sickness, or upon account of providing for a funeral; or if he prevailed with the accuser to relinquish his charge, or let the cause fall; or if upon the day appointed for the Comitia the augurs discovered any ill omens, and so forbade the assembly.

If none of these happened, the Comitia met, and proceeded as has been already described; and as for their animadversio, or putting sentence in execution, this was performed in the same manner as in the Prætorian judgments.

The forms of judgments, which have been thus described, must be supposed to have prevailed chiefly in the time of the free State: For as the Kings before, so the Emperors afterwards, were themselves judges in what causes, and after what manner they pleased, as Suetonius particularly informs us of almost all the twelve Cæsars. It was this gave occasion to the rise of the *Mandatores* and *Delatores*, a sort of wretches to be met with in every part of history. The business of the former was to mark down such persons as upon inquisition they pretended to have found guilty of any misdemeanor; and the latter were employed in accusing and prosecuting them upon the other's order. This mischievous tribe, as they were countenanced and rewarded by ill Princes, so were they extremely detested by the good Emperors. Titus prosecuted all that could

be

be found upon the most diligent search, with death or perpetual banishment (*a*): And Pliny reckons it among the greatest praises of Trajan, that he had cleared the city from the perjured race of informers (*b*).

(*a*) *Sueton. in Tit.* cap. 8.   (*b*) *Plin. in Panegyric.*

CHAP. XX.

Of the ROMAN *Punishments.*

THE accurate Sigonius has divided the punishments into eight sorts, *Damnum, Vincula, Verbera, Talio, Ignominia, Exilium, Servitus,* and *Mors*.

Damnum was a pecuniary mulct or fine set upon the offender, according to the quality of the crime.

Vinculum signifies the guilty person's being condemned to imprisonment and fetters, of which they had many sorts, as *Manicæ, Pedicæ, Nervi, Boiæ,* and the like. The public prison in Rome was built by Ancus Martius, hard by the forum (*a*); to which a new part was added by Servius Tullius, called thence *Tullianum:* Sallust describes the Tullianum as an apartment under ground (*b*), into which they put the most notorious criminals. The higher part, raised by Ancus Martius, had commonly the name of the *Robur,* from the oaken plants which composed it. For the keeping of the prison, besides the Triumviri, was appointed a sort of goaler, whom Valerius Maximus calls *Custos Carceris* (*c*), and Pliny *Commentariensis* (*d*).

Verbera, or stripes, were inflicted either with rods [*Virgæ*] or with batons [*Fustus*]: The first commonly preceded capital punishments properly so called: The other was most in use in the camp, and belonged to the military discipline.

Talio was a punishment by which the guilty person suffered exactly after the same manner as he had offended; as in cases of maiming, and the like. Yet A. Gellius informs us, that the criminal was allowed the liberty of compounding with the person

(*a*) *Liv.* lib. 1.   (*b*) *In Bello Catilinar.*   (*c*) Lib. 5.   (*d*) Lib. 7. cap. 7.

person he had injured; so that he needed not suffer the talio, unless he voluntarily chose it (*a*).

Ignominia, was no other than a public shame which the offending person underwent, either by virtue of the Prætor's edict, or more commonly by order of the Censor: This punishment, besides the scandal, took away from the party on whom it was inflicted the privilege of bearing any office, and almost all other liberties of a Roman citizen.

Exilium was not a punishment immediately, but by consequence; for the phrase used in the sentence and laws, was *Aquæ & ignis interdictio*, the forbidding the use of water and fire, which being necessary for life, the condemned person was obliged to leave his country. Yet in the times of the latter Emperors, we find it to have been a positive punishment, as appears from the civil law. *Relegatio* may be reckoned under this head, tho' it were something different from the former; this being the sending a criminal to such a place, or for such a time, or perhaps for ever, by which the party was not deprived of the privilege of a citizen of Rome, as he was in the first sort of banishment, which they properly called *Exilium*. Suetonius speaks of a new sort of *Relegatio* invented by the Emperor Claudius; by which he ordered suspected persons not to stir three miles from the city (*b*). Besides this relegatio they had two other kinds of banishment, which they termed *Deportatio* and *Proscriptio*; tho' nothing is more common than to have them confounded in most authors. *Deportatio*, or transportation, differed in these respects from *Relegatio*; that whereas the *Relegati* were condemned either to change their country for a set time, or for ever, and lost neither their estate and goods, nor the privilege of citizens: On the contrary, the *Deportati* were banished always for ever, and lost both their estates and privileges, being counted dead in the law (*c*). And as for the *Proscripti*, they are defined by the lawyers to be "such persons whose names were fixed up in ta-
"blets at the forum, to the end that they might be brought to
"justice; a reward being proposed to those that took them,
"and a punishment to those that concealed them (*d*)." Sylla was the first inventor of this practice, and gave himself the greatest example of it that we meet with, *proscribing* 2000 knights and senators at once (*e*). It is plain, that this was not

a positive

(*a*) *A. Gell.* lib. 11. cap. 1.   (*b*) *Suet.* in *Claud*, cap. 33.   (*c*) *Calvin. Lexicon. Jurisdic. in voc. Deportati & Relegati.*   (*d*) *Ibid. in voce Proscripti.* (*e*) *Florus,* lib. 2. cap. 28.

a positive banishment, but a forcing persons to make use of that security; so that we may fancy it of like nature with our outlawry.

Servitus was a punishment, by which the criminal's person, as well as goods, was publicly exposed to sale by auction: This rarely happened to the citizens, but was an usual way of treating captives taken in war, and therefore will be described hereafter.

Under the head of capital punishments the Romans reckoned extreme banishment, because those who underwent that sentence were in a civil sense dead. But because this punishment has been already described, we are only now to take notice of such as reached the offender's life. *Mors.*

The chief of these were *Percussio securi, Strangulatio, Præcipitatio de robore, Dejectio è rupe Tarpeiâ. In crucem Actio,* and *Projectio in profluentem.*

The first was the same as beheading with us.

The second was performed in the prison, as it is now in Turkey.

The third and fourth were a throwing the criminal headlong, either from that part of the prison called *Robur*, or from the highest part of the Tarpeian mountain.

The fifth punishment, namely crucifixion, was seldom inflicted on any but slaves, or the meanest of the Commons; yet we find some examples of a different practice; and Suetonius particularly relates of the Emperor Galba, that having condemned a Roman citizen to suffer this punishment for poisoning his ward, the gentleman, as he was carrying to execution, made a grievous complaint, that a citizen of Rome should undergo such a servile death, alledging the laws to the contrary: The Emperor, hearing his plea, promised to alleviate the shame of his sentence, and ordered a cross much larger, and more neat than ordinary, to be erected, and to be washed over with white paint, that the gentleman, who stood so much on his quality, might have the honour to be hanged in state (*a*).

The cross and the furca are commonly taken for the same thing in authors; tho', properly speaking, there was a great difference between them. The furca is divided by Lipsius into *Ignominiosa* and *Pœnalis:* The former Plutarch describes to be that piece of wood which supports the thill of a waggon: He adds, that it was one of the greatest penances for a servant who had offended to take this upon his shoulders, and carry it about

(*a*) *Sueton. in Galbâ.* cap. 9.

the neighbourhood; for whoever was seen with this infamous burden had no longer any credit or trust among those who knew it, but was called *Furcifer*, by way of ignominy and reproach (a). *Furca pœnalis* was a piece of wood, much of the same shape as the former, which was fastened about the convicted person's neck, he being generally either scourged to death under it, or lifted up by it upon the cross. Lipsius makes it the same with the *Patibulum*, and fancies, that for all the name, it might not be a forked piece of timber, but rather a straight beam, to which the criminal's arms, being stretched out, were tied, and which, being hoisted up at the place of execution, served for the transverse part of the cross.

Projectio in profluentem was a punishment proper to the crime of parricide (or the murder of any near relation:) The person convicted of this unnatural guilt was immediately hooded, as unworthy of the common light: In the next place he was whipped with rods, and then sewed up in a sack, and thrown into the sea; or, in inland countries, into the next lake or river. Afterwards, for an addition to the punishment, a serpent used to be put into the sack with the criminal; and by degrees, in latter times, an ape, a dog, and a cock. The sack which held the malefactor was termed *Culeus*; and hence the punishment itself is often signified by the same name. The reason of the addition of living creatures is thought to have been, that the condemned persons might be tormented with such troublesome company, and that their carcases might want both burial and rest. Juvenal expresly alludes to this custom in his eighth satyr:

> *Libera si dentur populo suffragia, quis tam*
> *Perditus, ut dubitet Senecam præferre Neroni,*
> *Cujus supplicio non debuit una parari*
> *Simia, non serpens unus, non culeus unus?*

Had we the freedom to express our mind,
There's not a wretch so much to vice inclin'd,
But will own Seneca did far excel
His pupil, by whose tyranny he fell.
To expiate whose complicated guilt,
With some proportion to the blood he spilt,
Rome should more serpents, apes, and sacks provide
Than one, for the compendious parricide.   Mr *Stepney*.

The

(a) *Plutarch. in Coriolan.*

The same poet in another place intimates, that this sack was made of leather.

Tully, in his defence of Sextus Roscius, who stood arraigned for parricide, has given an admirable account of this punishment, with the reason on which it was grounded; particularly, that the malefactor was thrown into the sea, sewed up in a sack, for fear he should pollute that element, which was reckoned the common purifier of all things.: With many the like ingenious reflections.

Besides the punishments mentioned by Sigonius, who seems to consider the Roman people as in a free state, we meet with abundance of others, either invented or revived in the times of the Emperors, and especially in latter ages: Among these, we may take notice of three, as the most considerable, *ad Ludos, ad Metalla, ad Bestias.*

The lawyers divide Ludus, when they take it for a punishment, into *Venatorius* and *Gladiatorius* (a). By the former the convicted persons (commonly slaves) were obliged to engage with the wild beasts in the amphitheatre; by the latter, they were to perform the part of gladiators, and satisfy justice by killing one another.

Ad Metalla, or condemning to work in the mines, Suidas would have to be invented by Tarquinius Superbus (b). Whatever reason he had for his assertion, it is certain we rarely find it mentioned till the times of the later Emperors; and particularly in the histories of the persecutions of the Christians, who were usually sent in great numbers to this laborious and slavish employment, with the name of *Metallici.*

The throwing of persons to wild beasts was never put in execution but upon the vilest and most despicable malefactors in crimes of the highest nature. This too was the common doom of the primitive Christians; and it is to the accounts of their sufferings we are beholden for the knowledge of it. It may be observed, that the phrase, *Ad Bestias dari* (c), affects as well such criminals as were condemned to fight with the beasts, as those who were delivered to them to be devoured: And the former of these were properly termed *Bestiarii* (d).

There is still one punishment behind worth our observation, and which seems to have been proper to incendiaries, and that was the wrapping up the criminal in a sort of coat, daubed

over

(a) Calvin. Lexicon. Juridic. (b) *In voce* Σ ἰατιρϘ⊛. (c) Calvin. in voce ad Bestias dari. (d) Ibid. in Bestiarii.

over with pitch, and then setting it on fire. Thus when Nero had burnt Rome, to satisfy his curiosity with the prospect, he contrived to lay the odium on the Christians, as a sort of men generally detested; and, seizing on all he could discover, ordered them to be lighted up in this manner, to serve for tapers in the dark; which was a much more cruel jest than the former, that occasioned it. Juvenal alludes to this custom in his eighth satyr:

Ausi quod liceat tunicâ punire molesta.

To recompense whose barbarous intent,
Pitch'd shirts would prove a legal punishment.

CHAP. XXI.

Of the ROMAN LAWS *in general.*

IN the beginning of the Roman State, we are assured all things were managed by the sole authority of the King, without any certain standard of justice and equity. But when the city grew tolerably populous, and was divided by Romulus into thirty Curiæ, he began to prefer laws at the assembly of those Curiæ, which were confirmed, and universally received. The like practice was followed by Numa, and several other Kings; all whose constitutions being collected in one body, by Sextus Papirius, who lived in the time of Tarquin the Proud, took from him the name of *Jus Papirianum*.

But all these were abrogated soon after the expulsion of the royal family, and the judicial proceedings for many years together depended only on custom, and the judgment of the court. At last, to redress this inconvenience, commissioners were sent into Greece, to make a collection of the best laws for the service of their country; and at their return, the Decemviri were created to regulate the business, who reduced them into twelve tables, as has been already shewn. The excellency of which institution, as it is sufficiently set forth by most authors, so it is especially beholden to the high encomium of Cicero, when he declares it as his positive judgment and opinion,

That

That "the laws of the twelve tables are juftly to be prefer-
"red to whole libraries of the philofophers (*a*)."

They were divided into three parts, of which the firft related to the concerns of religion; the fecond to the rights of the public; and the laft to private perfons.

Thefe laws being eftablifhed, it neceffarily followed, that there fhould be difputations and controverfies in the courts, fince the interpretation was to be founded upon the authority of the learned. This interpretation they called *Jus Civile*, though at prefent we underftand, by that phrafe, the whole fyftem of the Roman laws.

Befides, out of all thefe laws the learned men of that time compofed a fcheme of forms and cafes, by which the proceffes in the courts were directed. Thefe were termed *Actiones Leges*.

We may add to thefe the laws preferred at the public affemblies of the people; and the *Plebifcita*, made without the authority of the Senate, at the comitia tributa, which were allowed to be of equal force with other conftitutions, though they were not honoured with the title of *Leges*.

And then the *Senatus-confulta*, and edicts of the fupreme magiftrates, particularly of the Prætors, made up two more forts of laws, the laft of which they called *Jus Honorarium*.

And, laftly, when the government was intrufted in the hands of a fingle perfon, whatever he ordained, had the authority of a law, with the name of *Principalis Conftitutio*.

Moft of thefe daily increafing, gave fo much fcope to the lawyers for the compiling of reports and other labours, that, in the reign of Juftinian, there were extant two thoufand diftinct volumes on this fubject. The body of the law being thus grown unweildy, and rendered almoft ufelefs by its exceffive bulk, that excellent Emperor entered on a defign to bring it into juft dimenfions; which was happily accomplifhed in the conftituting thofe four tomes of the civil law, which are now extant, and have contributed, in a great meafure, to the regulating of all the ftates in Chriftendom: So that the old fancy of the Romans, about the eternity of their command, is not fo ridiculous as at firft fight it appears; fince, by their admirable fanctions, they are ftill like to govern for ever.

(*a*) *Cicero de Oratore*, lib. 1.

CHAP.

CHAP. XXII.

Of the LAWS *in particular; and first, of those relating to* RELIGION.

AS for the laws of the twelve tables, and other more ancient institutions, as it would require no ordinary stock of criticism barely to explain their words; so is the knowledge of them almost useless, since they are so seldom mentioned by the classics. Those which we generally meet with are such as were preferred by some particular magistrate, from whom they took their names; these, by reason of their frequent occurrence in the best writers, deserve a short explication, according to the common heads laid down by those authors, who have hitherto managed this subject; beginning with such as concerned the public worship, and the ceremonies of religion.

Sulpicia Sempronia Lex, the authors P. Sulpicius Saverrio and P. Sempronius Sophus, in their consulship, *A.* 449, ordaining, That no person should consecrate any temple, or altar, without the order of the Senate, and the major part of the Tribunes (*a*).

Papiria Lex, the author L. Papirius, Tribune of the commons; commanding, That no person should have the liberty of consecrating any edifice, place, or thing, without the leave of the Commons (*b*).

Cornelia Lex, the author L. Cornelius Sulla, defining the expences of funerals (*c*).

Sexta Licinia Lex, the authors L. Sextus and Licinius, Tribunes of the Commons, *A.* 385, commanding, That instead of the *Duumviri sacris faciundis,* a *Decemvirate* should be created, part out of the Patricians, and part out of the Commons (*d*).

Ogulnia Lex, the authors Q. and Cn. Ogulnius, Tribunes of the Commons, *A.* 453, commanding, That whereas there were then but four Pontifices, and four Augurs, five more should be added out of the Commons to each order (*e*).

Manlia

(*a*) Liv. lib. 9.   (*b*) *Cicero in Orat. pro Domo suâ.*   (*c*) *Plut. in Sylla.*
(*d*) Liv. lib. 6.   (*e*) Liv. lib. 10.

Manlia Lex, the author P. Manlius, Tribune of the Commons, *A.* 557, enacted for the revival of the *Tresviri Epulones*, an old institution of Numa's (*a*).

Clodia Lex, the author P. Clodius in his tribuneship, *A.* 664, divesting the priest of Cybele (or the Great Mother, who came from Pessinum) of his office, and conferring it on Brotigarus, a Gallo-Græcian (*b*).

Papia Lex, ordering the manner of chusing the vestal virgins (*c*), as has been already described.

The punishment of those holy recluses is grounded on the laws of Numa.

Licinia Lex, preferred by C. Licinius Crassus, Tribune of the Commons, *A.* 608, for the transferring the right of chusing priests from the college to the people (*d*); but it did not pass (*e*).

Domitia Lex, the author Cn. Domitius Ahenobarbus, Tribune of the Commons, *A.* 650, actually transferring the said right to the people (*f*).

Cornelia Lex, the author L. Cornelius Sylla, Dictator and Consul with Q. Metellus, *A.* 677, abrogating the former law of Domitius, and restoring the privilege there mentioned to the college (*g*).

Attia Lex, the author T. Attius Labienus, Tribune of the Commons, *A.* 690, repealing the Cornelian law, and restoring the Domitian (*h*).

Antonia Lex, the author M. Antony in his consulship with Julius Cæsar, *A.* 700, abrogating the Attian law, and restoring the Cornelian (*i*). Paulus Manutius has conjectured from several reasons, that this law of Antony was afterwards repealed, and the right of chusing priests entrusted in the hands of the people.

To this head is commonly referred the law about the exemption from military service, or *de Vacatione*, in which there was a very remarkable clause, *Nisi bellum Gallicum exoriatur;* " Unless in case of a Gallic insurrection." In which case, no persons, not the priests themselves, were excused; the Romans apprehending more danger from the Gauls than from any other nation, because they had once taken their city (*k*).

As also the three laws about the shows.

Licinia

(*a*) Cicer. de Orat. lib. 3.   (*b*) Idem. Orat. pro Sest. & de Harusp. Respons.
(*c*) A. Gellius.   (*d*) Cic. de Amicitiâ.   (*e*) Idem.   (*f*) Suet. in Ner. Patercul. lib. 2.   Cicer. Agrar. 2.   (*g*) Asconius in Divinatione.   (*h*) Dio. lib. 37.
(*i*) Dio. lib. 44.   (*k*) Plut. in Marcel. Cic. pro Fonteio & Philip. 8.

Licinia Lex, the author P. Licinius Varus, City-Prætor, *A.* 545, settling the day for the celebration of the Ludi Appollinares, which before was uncertain (*a*).

Roscia Lex Theatralis, the author L. Roscius Otho, Tribune of the Commons, *A.* 685, ordaining, That none should sit in the first fourteen seats of the theatre, unless they were worth four hundred sestertia, which was then reckoned the Census Equestris (*b*).

Augustus Cæsar, after several of the Equestrian families had impaired their estates in the civil wars, interpreted this law so as to take in all those whose ancestors ever had possessed the sum there specified.

(*a*) Liv. lib. 27. *Alex. Neapolitan.* &c. (*b*) *Cic. Philip.* 2. *Ascon. in Cornelian Javen.* Sat. 3. & 14. *Horat.* Epod. 4. Epist. 1.

CHAP. XXIII.

Laws *relating to the Rights and Privileges of the* Roman *Citizens.*

VALERIA Lex de Provocatione, the author P. Valerius Poplicola, sole Consul upon the death of his colleague Brutus, *A.* 243, giving liberty to appeal from any magistrate to the people, and ordering that no magistrate should punish a Roman citizen in case of such an appeal (*a*).

Valeria Horatio Lex, the authors L. Valerius and M. Horatius, Consuls, *A.* 304, reviving the former law, which had lost its force under the Decemvirate (*b*).

Valeria Lex Tertia, the author M. Valerius Corvinus, in his consulship with Q. Apuleius Pansa, *A.* 453, no more than a confirmation of the first Valerian law (*c*).

Porcia Lex, the author M. Porcius, Tribune of the Commons in the same year as the former, commanding, That no magistrate should execute, or punish with rods, a citizen of Rome; but, upon the sentence of condemnation, should give him permission to go into exile (*d*).

Sem-

(*a*) Liv. lib. 9. *Plut. in Poplicol.* &c. (*b*) Liv. lib. 3. (*c*) Liv. lib. 10.
(*d*) Liv. lib. 10. *Cic. pro Rabirio. Sallust, in Catilinar. Sueton. in Ner.* &c.

Sempronia Leges, the author C. Sempronius Gracchus, Tribune of the Commons, *A.* 630, commanding, That no capital judgment should pass upon a citizen, without the authority of the people, and making several other regulations in this affair (*a*).

Papia Lex de Peregrinis, the author C. Papius, Tribune of the Commons, *A.* 688, commanding, That all strangers should be expelled Rome (*b*).

Junia Lex, the author M. Junius Pennus, confirming the former law, and forbidding, that any strangers should be allowed the privilege of citizens (*c*).

Servilia Lex, the author C. Servilius Glaucia, ordaining, That if any Latin accused a Roman senator, so that he was convicted, the accuser should be honoured with the privilege of a citizen of Rome (*d*).

Licinia Mutia Lex, the authors L. Licinius Crassus and Q. Mutius Scævola, in their consulship, *A.* 658, ordering all the inhabitants of Italy to be enrolled in the list of citizens, in their own proper cities (*e*).

Livia Lex de Sociis: In the year of the city 662, M. Livius Drusus proposed a law to make all the Italians free denizens of Rome; but before it came to be voted, he was found murdered in his house, the author unknown (*f*).

Varia Lex: Upon the death of Drusus, the Knights prevailed with his colleague Q. Varius Hybrida, to bring in a bill for the prosecuting all such persons as should be discovered to have assisted the Italian people in the petition for the privilege of the city (*g*).

Julia Lex de Civitate: The next year, upon the revolt of several States in Italy (which they called the *Social War*) L. Julius Cæsar, the Consul, made a law, that all the people, who had continued firm to the Roman interest, should have the privilege of citizens (*h*): And in the year 664, upon the conclusion of that war, all the Italian people were admitted into the roll of free denizens, and divided into eight new tribes (*i*).

Sylvani & Carbonis Lex, the authors Sylvanus and Carbo, Tribunes of the Commons, in the year 664, ordaining, That any persons, who had been admitted free denizens of any of the confederate

---

(*a*) Cic. *pro Rabirio, pro domo suâ, pro Cluentio,* &c. (*b*) Cic. *pro Balbo.* (*c*) Cic. *de Offic.* l. 3. (*d*) Ascon. in Orat. *pro Scauro.* Cic. *pro Balbo.* (*e*) Cic. *de Offic.* l. 3. & *pro Balbo.* (*f*) Flor. lib. cap. 17. Cic. *de Leg.* lib. 3. (*g*) Cic. *in Bruto.* Val. Max. lib. 8. cap. 6. (*h*) Cic. *pro Balbo.* (*i*) Appian. lib. 1.

confederate cities, and had a dwelling in Italy at the time of the making of this law, and had carried in their name to the Prætor in sixty days time, should have the privilege of citizens of Rome (a).

Sulpicia Lex, the author P Sulpicius, Tribune of the Commons, *A.* 665, ordaining, That the new citizens, who composed the eight tribes, should be divided among the thirty-five old tribes, as a greater honour (b).

Cornelia Lex, the author L. Cornelius Sylla, *A.* 670, a confirmation of the former law, to please the Italian confederates (c).

Cornelia Lex de Municipiis, the author the same Sylla, in his dictatorship, taking away the privilege formerly granted to the corporate towns, from as many as had assisted Marius, Cinna, Sulpicius, or any of the contrary faction (d).

Gellia Cornelia Lex, the authors L. Gellius Poplicola, and Cn. Cornelius Lentulus, *A.* 681, ordaining, That all those persons whom Pompey, by his own authority, had honoured with the privilege of the city, should actually keep that liberty (e).

(a) *Cic. pro Acchia.* (b) *Plut. in Sylla, Epit. Liv.* 77. (c) *Epit. Liv.* 68.
(d) *Cic. pro Domo suâ.* (e) *Cic. pro Balbo.*

CHAP. XXIV.

LAWS *Concerning Meetings and Assemblies.*

ÆLIA Lex, ordaining, That, in all assemblies of the people, the augurs should make observations from the heavens; and that the magistrate should have the power of declaring against the proceedings, and of interposing in the decision of any matter.

Fusia Lex, ordaining, That upon some certain days, though they were fasti, it should be unlawful to transact any thing in a meeting of the people.

The authors of these two laws are unknown; but P. Manutius conjectures, that the first is owing to Q. Ælius Pætus, Consul with M. Junius Pennus, *A.* 586.; the other to P. Furius, or Fusius, Consul with S. Attilius Serranus, *A.* 617. The laws themselves occur frequently in writers.

Clodia Lex, the author P. Clodius, Tribune of the Commons, *A.* 695, containing an abrogation of the greatest part of the two former

former laws, and ordering, That no obfervation fhould be made from the heavens upon the days of the Comitia; and, That on any of the dies fafti, laws might be enacted in a public affembly (*a*).

Curia Lex, the author M. Curius Dentatus, Tribune of the Commons, *A.* 454, ordaining, That no Comitia fhould be convened for the election of magiftrates, without the approbation of the Senate ; *Ut ante Comitia Magiftratum Patres auctores fierent* (*b*).

Claudia Lex, the author M. Claudius Marcellus, Conful with Serv. Sulpicius Rufus, *A.* 702, ordering, That at the Comitia for the election of magiftrates, no account fhould be taken of the abfent (*c*).

Gabinia Lex, the author A Gabinius, Tribune of the Commons, *A.* 614, commanding That in the Comitia for the election of magiftrates, the people fhould not give their fuffrages *vivâ voce*, but by tablets, for the greater freedom and impartiality of the proceedings (*d*).

Caffia Lex, enacted about two years after, commanding, That in the courts of juftice, and in the *Comitia Tributa*, the votes fhould be given in a free manner, that is, by tablets (*e*).

Papyria Lex, the author C. Papyrius Carbo, Tribune of the Commons, *A.* 621, ordaining, That in the Comitia about the paffing or rejecting of laws, the fuffrages fhould be given by tablets (*f*).

Cœlia Lex, the author Cœlius, Tribune of the Commons, *A.* 635, ordaining, That in the judicial proceedings before the people, in cafes of treafon (which had been excepted by the Caffian law) the votes fhould be given by tablets (*g*).

Sempronia Lex, the author C. Sempronius Gracchus, in the fame year as the former, ordering, That the centuries fhould be chofen out by lot to give their votes, and not according to the order of the claffes (*h*).

Maria Lex, the author C. Marius, Tribune of the Commons, *A.* 634, ordering the bridges, or long planks, on which the people ftood in the Comitia to give their voices, to be made narrower, that no other perfons might ftand there, to hinder the proceedings by appeals, or other difturbances (*i*).

(*a*) *Afcon. in Pifon.* (*b*) *Cic. de claris Oratoribus.* (*c*) *Suet. in Julio.* (*d*) *Cic. de Amicit. & pro Plancio, & de Leg.* lib. 3. (*e*) *Cic. in Lælio.* (*f*) *Cic. de Leg.* lib. 3. (*g*) *Id. Ibid.* (*h*) *Salluft. in Orat.* 2. *ad Cæfarem.* (*i*) *Cic. de Leg.* lib. 3. *Plut. in Mario.*

Sempronia Lex, the author C. Sempronius Gracchus, Tribune of the Commons, *A.* 565, ordaining, That the Latin confederates should have the privilege of giving their suffrages as well as the Roman citizens (*a*).

Manilia Lex, the author C. Manilius, Tribune of the Commons, *A.* 687, ordaining, That the Libertini should have the privilege of voting in all the tribes (*b*).

Gabinia Lex, a confirmation of an old law of the twelve tables, making it a capital offence for any person to convene a clandestine assembly (*c*).

(*a*) *Cic. sæpissime.*   (*b*) *Cic. pro lege Manilia.*   (*c*) *Sallust. in Catilinar.*

CHAP. XXV.

Laws *relating to the* SENATE.

CASSIA Lex, the author L. Cassius Longinus, Tribune of the Commons, *A.* 649, ordaining, That no person, who had been condemned or deprived of his office by the people, should have the privilege of coming into the Senate (*a*).

Claudia Lex, the author Q. Claudius, Tribune of the Commons, *A.* 535, commanding, That no senator, or father of a senator, should possess a sailing vessel of above three hundred amphoræ; this was thought big enough for the bringing over fruits and other necessaries; and as for gain, procured by trading in merchandize, they thought it unworthy the dignity of that order (*b*).

Sulpicia Lex, the author Servius Sulpicius, Tribune of the Commons, *A.* 665, requiring, That no senator should owe above two thousand drachmæ (*c*).

Sentia Lex, the author (probably) C. Sentius, Consul with Q. Lucretius, *A.* 734, in the time of Augustus, ordering, That in the room of such noblemen as were wanting in the Senate, others should be substituted (*d*).

Gabinia Lex, the author A. Gabinius, Tribune of the Commons, *A.* 685, ordering, That the Senate should be convened from

(*a*) *Ascon. in Cornelian.*   (*b*) *Cic. Verrin.* 7.   (*c*) *Plut. in Sylla.*   (*d*) *Tacit. Ann.* 2.

from the kalends of February, to the kalends of March, every day, for the giving audience to foreign miniſters (a).

Pupia Lex, ordaining, That the Senate ſhould not be convened from the eighteenth of the kalends of February, to the kalends of the ſame month ; and that before the embaſſies were either accepted or rejected, the Senate ſhould be held on no other account (b).

Tullia Lex, the author M. Tullius Cicero, Conſul with C. Antony, *A.* 690, ordaining, That ſuch perſons to whom the Senate had allowed the favour of a *Libera Legatio*, ſhould hold that honour no longer than a year. *Libera Legatio* was a privilege that the Senators often obtained for the going into any province, or country, where they had ſome private buſineſs, in the quality of lieutenants ; though with no command, but only that the dignity of their titular office might have an influence on the management of their private concerns (c).

(a) *Cic. Epiſt. ad Quint. Fratr.* lib. 2. Ep. 12. (b) *Cic.* lib. 1. Ep. 4. *ad LentaL.* lib. 2. Ep. 2. *ad Quint. Fratr.* &c. (c) *Cic. de leg* lib. 3.

CHAP. XXVI.

Laws *relating to the* Magistrates.

LEX Villia Annalis, or *Annaria*, the author L. Villius (for whom we ſometimes find L. Julius, or Lucius Tullius) Tribune of the Commons, *A.* 574, defining the proper age requiſite for bearing of all the magiſtracies (a). Livy, who relates the making of this law, does not inſiſt on the particular ages; and learned men are much divided about that point. Lipſius ſtates the difference after this manner : The age proper to ſue for the Quæſtorſhip, he makes twenty-five years ; for the Ædiles and Tribunes, twenty-ſeven or twenty-eight ; thirty for the Prætor, and forty-two for the Conſuls.

Genutia Lex, the author L. Genutius, Tribune of the Commons *A.* 411, commanding, That no perſon ſhould bear the ſame magiſtracy within ten years diſtance, nor ſhould be inveſted with two offices in one year (b).

Cornelia Lex, the author Cornelius Sylla, the Dictator, *A.* 673, a repetition and confirmation of the former law (c).

Sem.

(a) *Liv.* lib. 40. (b) *Idem*, lib. 7. (c) *Appian.* lib. 1. *de Bell. Civil.*

Sempronia Lex, the author C. Sempronius Gracchus, Tribune of the Commons, *A.* 630, ordaining, That no person, who had been lawfully deprived of his magistracy, should be capable of bearing an office again. This was abrogated afterwards by the author (*a*).

Cornelia Lex, the author L. Cornelius Sylla, Dictator; ordaining, That such persons as had embraced his party in the late troubles, should have the privilege of bearing honours before they were capable by age; and that the children of those who had been proscribed should lose the power of standing for any office (*b*).

Hirtia Lex, the author A. Hirtius, ordaining, That none of Pompey's party should be admitted to any dignity (*c*).

Sextia Licinia Lex, the authors C. Licinius and L. Sextius, Tribunes of the Commons, *A.* 316, ordaining, That one of the Consuls should be chosen out of the body of the Commons (*d*).

Genutia Lex, the author L. Genutius, Tribune of the Commons, *A.* 411, making it lawful that both Consuls might be taken out of the Commons (*e*).

Cornelia Lex, the author L. Cornelius Sylla, Dictator, *A.* 673, ordaining, That the Prætors should always use the same method in judicial processes. For the Prætors used, upon the entrance on their office, to put up an edict to show what way they designed to proceed in all causes during their year: These edicts, which before commonly varied, were by this law ordered to be always the same, for the preserving a constant and regular course of justice (*f*).

Marcia Lex, the author Marcius Censorinus, forbidding any person to bear the Censorship twice (*g*).

Clodia Lex, the author P. Clodius, Tribune of the Commons, *A.* 695, ordering, That the Censors should put no mark of infamy on any person in their general surveys, unless the person had been accused and condemned by both the Censors; whereas before they used to punish persons, by omitting their names in their surveys, and by other means, whether they were accused or no: And what one Censor did, unless the other actually interposed, was of equal force, as if both had joined in the action (*h*).

Cæcilia Lex, the author Q. Cæcilius Metellus Pius, Consul with Pompey the Great, *A.* 701, restoring their ancient dignity and

---

(*a*) Plut. in Gracchis.   (*b*) Plin. lib. 7. Quintil. lib. 11. cap. 1. Cic. in Pison.
(*c*) Cic. Philip. 13.   (*d*) Liv. lib. 6.   (*e*) Idem, lib. 7.   (*f*) Cic. Philip. 2.
(*g*) Plut. in Coriol.   (*h*) Cic. in Pison. pro Milon, pro Sextio, &c.

and power to the Censors, which had been retrenched by the former law (a).

Antonia Lex, the author M. Antony, a member of the Triumvirate; ordaining, That for the future, no proposal should be ever made for the creation of a Dictator; and that no person should ever accept of that office, upon pain of incurring a capital penalty (b).

Titia Lex, the author P. Titius, Tribune of the Commons, A. 710, ordaining, That a Triumvirate of magistrates, invested with consular power, should be settled for five years, for the regulating the commonwealth; and that the honour should be conferred on Octavius, Lepidus, and Antony (c).

Valeria Lex, the author P. Valerius Poplicola, sole Consul, A. 243, ordaining, That the public treasure should be laid up in the temple of Saturn, and that two Quæstors should be created to supervise it (d).

Junia Sacrata Lex, the author L. Junius Brutus, the first Tribune of the Commons, A. 260, ordaining, That the persons of the Tribunes should be sacred: That an appeal might be made to them from the determinations of the Consuls: And, That none of the Senators should be capable of that office (e).

Atinia Lex, the author Atinius, Tribune of the Commons, ordaining, That any Tribune of the Commons should have the privilege of a Senator; and, as such, take his place in the house (f).

Cornelia Lex, the author L. Cornel. Sylla, Dictator, A. 673, taking away from the Tribunes the power of making laws, and of interposing, of holding assemblies and receiving appeals, and making all, that had borne that office, incapable of any other dignity in the commonwealth (g).

Aurelia Lex, the author C. Aurelius Cotta, Consul with L. Octavius, A. 678, an abrogation of some part of the former law, allowing the Tribunes to hold their other offices afterwards (h).

Pompeia Lex, the author Pompey the Great, Consul with M. Crassus, A. 683, restoring their full power and authority to the Tribunes, which had been taken from them by the Cornelian law (i).

CHAP.

(a) *Dio.* lib. 40. (b) *Appian. de Bell. Civ.* lib. 3. (c) *Flor. Epit. Liv.* lib. 120. (d) *Liv.* lib. 2. *Plut. in Poplicol.* (e) *Dionyf.* lib. 6. (f) *A. Gell.* lib. 14. cap. *ult.* (g) *Cic. de Leg.* lib. 3. *Cæfar. Comm. de Bell. Gall.* lib. 1. *Flor. Plut.* &c. (h) *Patercul.* lib. 2. *Afcon. in Cornel. in ver.* 1. (i) *Plut. in Pomp. Afcon. ver* 1. & 2. *Cæfar. de Bell. Civ.* lib. 1.

CHAP. XXVII.

Laws *relating to Public Constitutions, Laws, and Privileges.*

Hortensia Lex, the author Q. Hortensius, Dictator, *A.* 467, ordaining, That whatever was enacted by the Commons, should be observed by the whole Roman people; whereas the nobility had been formerly exempted from paying obedience to the decrees of the populacy (*a*).

Cæcilia Didia Lex, the authors Q. Cæcilius Metellus and T. Didius, Consuls, *A* 655, for the regulating the proceedings in enacting laws; ordaining, That in one question (*uná rogatione*) but one single matter should be proposed to the people, lest, while they gave their suffrage in one word, they should be forced to assent to a whole bill, if they liked the greatest part of it, tho' they disliked the rest; or throw out a bill for several clauses which they did not approve of, though perhaps they would have been willing to pass some part of it. Requiring also, That, before any law was preferred at the comitia, it should be exposed to the public view three market-days (*tribus nundinis*) before-hand (*b*).

P. *Manutius* makes the Cæcilian and Didian two distinct laws; the first part composing the former, and the other the latter.

Junia Licinia Lex, the authors D. Junius Silanus, and L. Licinius Muræna, Consuls, *A.* 691, ordaining, That such as did not observe the former law, relating to the publishing the draughts of new bills for three Nundinæ, should incur a greater penalty than the said law enjoined (*c*).

Licinia Æbutia Lex, the authors Licinius and Æbutius, Tribunes of the Commons; ordaining, That when any law was preferred relating to any charge or power, not only the person who brought in the bill, but likewise his colleagues in any office which he already enjoyed, and all his relations, should be incapable of being invested with the said charge or power (*d*).

Cornelia

(*a*) *Flor. Epit. Liv.* lib. **11**. (*b*) *A. Gell.* lib. 15. cap. 27. *Cic. Philip.* 5. pro *Domo, ad Attic.* Epist. 9. lib. 1. (*c*) *Cic. Philip.* 3. ad *Attic.* Epist. 5. lib. 2. Epist. 15. lib. 4. (*d*) *Cic. in Orat.* 2. *contra Rull.* & in *Orat. pro Domo sua.*

Cornelia Lex, the author C. Cornelius, Tribune of the Commons, *A*. 686, ordaining, That no perſon ſhould, by the votes of the Senate, be exempted from any law, (as uſed to be allowed upon extraordinary occaſions) unleſs two hundred Senators were preſent in the houſe ; and that no perſon, thus excuſed by the Senate, ſhould hinder the bill of his exemption from being carried afterwards to the Commons for their approbation (*a*).

Ampia Labiena Lex, the authors T. Ampius and T. Labienus, Tribunes of the Commons, *A*. 693, conferring an honourable privilege on Pompey the Great, that, at the Circenſian games, he ſhould wear a golden crown, and be habited in the triumphal robes ; and that at the ſtage-plays he ſhould have the liberty of wearing the Prætexta and a golden crown (*b*).

(*a*) *Aſcon. in Cornel.* (*b*) *Vell. Paterc.* lib. 2.

CHAP. XXVIII.

Laws *relating to the Provinces, and the Governors of them.*

Sempronia Lex, the author C. Sempronius Gracchus, Tribune of the Commons, *A*. 630, ordaining, That, before the annual Comitia for chuſing Conſuls, the Senate ſhould, at their pleaſure, determine the particular conſular provinces, which the new Conſuls, when deſigned, ſhould divide by lot. As alſo, that whereas heretofore the Tribunes had been allowed the privilege of interpoſing againſt a decree of Senate, they ſhould be deprived of that liberty for the future (*a*).

Cornelia Lex, the author L. Cornelius Sylla, Dictator, *A*. 673, ordaining, That whoever was ſent with any command into a province ſhould hold that command till he returned to Rome ; whereas, heretofore, their office was to continue no longer than a ſet time ; upon the expiration of which, if no ſucceſſor was ſent in their room, they were put to the trouble and inconvenience of getting a new commiſſion from the Senate.

(*a*) *Cic. pro domo ſua, in Vatin. de Provinciis Conſul. Salluſt. in Bell. Jugurth.*

It was a clause in this law, that every governor of a province, when another was sent to succeed him, should have thirty days allowed him in order to his removal (*a*).

Julia Lex Prima, the author C. Julius Cæsar, Consul with M. Calpurnius Bibulus, *A.* 691, comprised under several heads, as that Achaia, Thessaly, and all Greece, should be entirely free; and that the Roman magistrate should sit as judge in those provinces (*b*): That the towns and villages, thro' which the Roman magistrates pass towards the provinces, should be obliged to supply them and their retinue with hay and other conveniences on the road (*c*): That the governors, when their office was expired, should leave a scheme of their accounts in two cities of their provinces, and, at their arrival at Rome, should deliver in a copy of the said accompts at the public treasury (*d*): That the governors of provinces should, upon no account, accept of a golden coronet, unless a triumph had been decreed them by the Senate (*e*): That no chief commander should go beyond the bounds of his province, or enter on any other dominions, or lead the army out, or engage in any war, without the express order of the Senate or people (*f*).

Julia Lex Secunda, the author the same Julius Cæsar, in his dictatorship, ordaining, That no Prætorian province should be held above a year, and no consular province more than two years (*g*).

Clodia Lex, the author P. Clodius, Tribune of the Commons, *A.* 695, ordaining, That all Syria, Babylon, and Persia, should be committed to Gabinius the Consul; and Macedon, Achaia, Thessaly, Greece, and Bœtia, to his colleague Piso, with the proconsular power; and that a sum should be paid them out of the treasury, to defray the charges of their march thither with an army (*h*).

Vatinia Lex, the author P. Vatinius, Tribune of the Commons, *A.* 694, ordaining, That the command of all Gallia Cisalpina and Illyricum should be conferred on Cæsar for five years together without a decree of Senate, and without the formality of casting lots; that the particular persons mentioned in the bill should go with him in the quality of Legati without the deputation of the Senate: That the army to be sent with him
should

(*a*) *Cicero, Ep.* 9. *and Lentul. & lib* 3. *ad Attic. Ep.* 6. (*b*) *Cic. pro domo, in Pisonem, & de Provinc. Consul.* (*c*) *Cicero in Pisonem.* (*d*) *Ib.* (*e*) *Ib.* (*f*) *Ibid. & pro Posthum.* (*g*) *Cicero Philip.* 3. (*h*) *Cicero pro domo, & pro Sextio.*

should be paid out of the treasury ; and that he should transplant a colony into the town of Novocomum in Gallia (a).

Clodia Lex de Cypro, the author P. Clodius, Tribune of the Commons, *A.* 695, ordaining, That the island Cyprus should be reduced into a Roman province : That Ptolemy King of Cyprus should be publicly exposed to sale, habited in all regal ornaments, and his goods in like manner sold by auction : That M. Cato should be sent with the Prætorian power into Cyprus, to take care of the selling the King's effects, and conveying the money to Rome (b).

Trebonia Lex, the author L. Trebonius, Tribune of the Commons, *A.* 698, decreeing the chief command in Gallia to Cæsar, five years longer than had been ordered by the Vatinian law; and so depriving the Senate of the power of recalling him and substituting another general in his room (c).

Titia Lex, barely mentioned by Cicero (d), and not explained by Manutius or Rosinus. The purport of it seems to have been, that the provincial Quæstors should take their places by lot, in the same manner as the Consuls and Prætors; as may be gathered from the scope of the passage in which we find it.

(a) *Cicero in Vatinium, & pro Balbo, Sueton. in Julio. Sallust in Jugurth.* (b) *Cicero pro Domo, pro Sextio, de Provin. Consular.* (c) *Cicero* lib. 8, 9, 10. *Epist. ad Attic. Florus, Epist. Liv.* lib. 105. (d) In *Orat. pro Muræna.*

CHAP. XXIX.

LEGES AGRARIÆ, *or Laws relating to the Division of Lands among the People.*

Cassia Lex, the author Sp. Cassius Viscellinus, Consul with Proculus Virginius, *A.* 267, ordaining, That the land taken from the Hernici should be divided, half among the Latins, and half among the Roman Commons (a). This law did not hold.

Licinia Lex, the author C. Licinius Stolo, Tribune of the Commons, *A.* 277, ordaining, That no person should possess above five hundred acres of land ; or keep more than an hundred head of great, or five hundred head of small cattle (b).

Flaminia

(a) *Liv.* lib. 2. *Valer. Max.* lib. 5. cap. 8. (b) *Liv.* lib. 6. *Appian. A. Gellius,* Plin. *Patercul. Plutarch,* &c.

Flaminia Lex, the author C. Flaminius, Tribune of the Commons, *A*. 525, ordaining, That Picenum, a part of Gallia, whence the Senones had been expelled, should be divided among the Roman soldiers (*a*).

Sempronia Lex prima, the author T. Sempronius Gracchus, Tribune of the Commons, *A*. 620, confirming the Licinian law, and requiring all persons who held more land than that law allowed, immediately to resign it into the Commons, to be divided among the poorer citizens, constituting three officers to take care of the business (*b*).

This law being levelled directly against the interest of the richer men of the city, who had by degrees contrived to engross almost all the land to themselves, after great heats and tumults, at last cost the author his life.

Sempronia Lex altera, preferred by the same person, upon the death of King Attalus, who left the Roman State his heir: It ordained, That all ready money found in the King's treasury should be bestowed on the poorer citizens, to supply them with instruments and other conveniencies required for agriculture: And that the King's lands should be farmed at an annual rent by the Censors; which rent should be divided among the people (*c*).

Thoria Lex, the author Sp. Thorius, Tribune of the Commons, ordaining, That no person should pay any rent to the people, of the lands which he possessed; and regulating the affair of grazing, and pasture (*d*). Two large fragments of this law, which was of a great length, are copied from two old brazen tables, by Sigonius (*e*).

Cornelia Lex, the author L. Cornelius Sylla, Dictator, and Consul with Q. Metellus, *A*. 673, ordaining, That the lands of proscribed persons should be common. This is chiefly to be understood of the lands in Tuscany, about Volaterræ and Fesulæ, which Sylla divided amongst his soldiers (*f*).

Servilia Lex, the author P. Servilius Rullus, Tribune of the Commons, *A*. 690, in the consulship of Cicero and Antony, containing many particulars, about selling several houses, fields, &c. that belonged to the public, for the purchasing land in other parts of Italy; about creating ten men to be supervisors of the business, and abundance of other heads, several of which are

---

(*a*) *Cic.* in *Cat. Major.*   (*b*) *Cic. pro Sextio, Plut.* &c.   (*c*) *Cic. Verr.* 5. *Plut.* &c.   (*d*) *Cic. de Orat.* lib. 2. & *in Bruto.*   (*e*) *De Antiq. Jur. Ital.* lib. 2.   (*f*) *Cic. in Rullum, pro Roscio, Sallust in Cat.*

are repeated by Cicero in his three orations extant against this law, by which he hindered it from passing.

Flavia Lex, the author L. Flavius, Tribune of the Commons, *A.* 693, about dividing a sufficient quantity of land among Pompey's soldiers and the Commons (*a*).

Julia Lex, the author Julius Cæsar, Consul with Bibulus, *A.* 691, ordaining, That all the land in Campania, which used formerly to be farmed at a set rent of the State, should be divided among the Commons: As also, That all members of the Senate should swear to confirm this law, and to defend it against all opposers. Cicero calls this *Lex Campania* (*b*).

Manilia Lex, the author C. Manilius, Tribune of the Commons, in the time of the Jugurthine war, ordaining, That in the bounds of the lands there should be left five or six feet of ground, which no person should convert to his private use, and that commissioners should be appointed to regulate this affair (*c*). From this law *de Limitibus* the author took the surname of *Limentanus*, as he is called by Sallust (*d*).

(*a*) *Cicero ad Attic.* lib. 1. (*b*) *Velleius Paterc.* lib. 2. *Plut. in Pomp. Cæs. & Cat. Uticens. ad Attic.* lib. 2. epist. 18. (*c*) *Cicero, lib.* 2. *de Leg.* (*d*) *In Bell. Jugurth.*

C H A P. XXX.

L A W s *relating to* C O R N.

SEMPRONIA Lex, the author C. Sempronius Gracchus, (not T. Sempronius Gracchus, as Rosinus has it) ordaining, That a certain quantity of corn should be distributed every month among the Commons, so much to every man; for which they were only to pay the small consideration of a semissis and a triens (*a*).

Terentia Cassia Lex, the authors M. Terentius Varro Lucullus and C. Cassius, Consuls, *A.* 680, ordaining, That the same set price should be given for all corn bought up in the provinces, to hinder the exactions of the Quæstors (*b*).

Clodia Lex, the author P. Clodius, Tribune of the Commons, *A.* 695, ordaining, That those quantities of corn, which were

(*a*) *Flor. Epit.* l. 6o. *Vell. Pat.* l. 2. &c. (*b*) *Cic. in Verrin.* 5.

were formerly sold to the poor people at six asses and a triens the bushel, should be distributed among them *gratis* (a).

Hieronica Lex, the author Hiero, tyrant of Sicily, regulating the affair between the farmers and the Decumani, (or gatherers of the corn-tax, which, because it consisted of a tenth part, they called *Decumæ*) ordaining the quantity of corn, the price, and the time of receiving it; which, for the justice of it, the Romans still continued in force, after they had possessed themselves of that island (b).

(a) *Cicero pro Sextio, in Pison.* &c.   (b) *Cicero in Ver.* 4.

CHAP. XXXI.

Laws *for the Regulating of* Expences.

ORCHIA Lex, the author C. Orchius, Tribune of the Commons *A.* 566, defining the number of guests which were allowed to be present at any entertainment (a).

Fannia Lex, the author C. Fannius, Consul, *A.* 588, ordaining, That upon the higher festivals no person should expend more than a hundred asses in a day; on ten other days in every month thirty asses; and at all other times ten (b).

Didia Lex, enacted about eighteen years after the former, ordaining, That the laws for regulating expences should reach all the Italians as well as the inhabitants of Rome; and that not only the masters of extravagant treats, but the guests too, should incur a penalty for their offence (c).

Lex Licinia, the author P. Licinius Crassus the Rich, agreeing in most particulars with the Fannian law; and further prescribing, That on the kalends, nones, and nundinæ, thirty asses should be the most that was spent at any table; and that on ordinary days, which were not particularly excepted, there should be spent only three pounds of *dry* flesh, and one pound of salt meat; but allowing as much as every body pleased of any fruits of the ground.

Caro arida opponitur salsamento, Casaubon. in A. Gell. Notæ MSS. in Bib. C. C. C. Oxon.

Cornelia Lex, the author L. Cornelius Sylla, enacted, not so much for the retrenching of extravagant

(a) *Macrobii Saturn.* lib. 2. cap. 14.   (b) *Ibid. & A. Gell.* lib. 2. cap. 24.   (c) *Ibid. & A. Gell.* lib. 2. cap. 24.

extravagant treats, as for the lowering the price of provisions (*a*).

Æmilia Lex, the author M. Æmilius Lepidus, Conful, about *A*. 675, refpecting the feveral forts of meats in ufe at that time, and ftating the juft quantities allowable of every kind (*b*).

Antia Lex, the author Antius Reftio: a further effay toward the fuppreffing of luxury, the particulars of which we are not acquainted with. But Macrobius gives us this remarkable ftory of the author, that finding his conftitution to be of very little force, by reafon of the great head that prodigality and extravagance had gained in the city, he never afterwards fupped abroad as long as he lived, for fear he fhould be forced to be a witnefs of the contempt of his own injunctions, without being in a condition to punifh it (*c*).

Julia Lex, preferred in the time of Auguftus, allowing two hundred feftertii for the provifions on the Dies Profefti, three hundred on the common feftivals in the kalendar, and a thoufand at marriage-feafts, and fuch extraordinary entertainments (*d*).

A. Gellius further adds, that he finds in an old author an edict, either of Auguftus or Tiberius, (he is uncertain which) raifing the allowance according to the difference of the feftivals, from three hundred to two thoufand feftertii (*e*).

Hither may be referred the *Lex Oppia*, the author C. Oppius Tribune of the Commons, *A*. 540, in the heat of the fecond Punic war, ordaining, That no woman fhould have above half an ounce of gold, wear a party-coloured garment, or be carried in a chariot in any city, town, or to any place within a mile's diftance, unlefs upon the account of celebrating fome facred folemnity (*f*).

(*a*) *A. Gell.* lib. 2. cap. 24.   (*b*) *Ibid.*   (*c*) *Macrob.* & *A. Gell.*
(*d*) *A. Gell.*   (*e*) *Ibid.*   (*f*) *Liv.* lib. 34. *Tac. Ann.* 3.

CHAP.

CHAP. XXXII.

LAWS relating to MARTIAL AFFAIRS.

SACRATA Lex, Militaris, the author, probably, M. Valerius Corvus, Dictator, A. 411, ordaining, That no soldier's name which had been entered in the muster-roll, should be struck out, unless by the party's consent: And that no person who had been military Tribune, should execute the office of *Ductor Ordinum* (*a*).

Sempronia Lex, the author C. Sempronius Gracchus, Tribune of the Commons, A. 630, ordaining, That the soldiers should receive their clothes *gratis* at the public charge, without any diminution of their ordinary pay: And that none should be obliged to serve in the army, who was not full seventeen years old (*b*).

Maria Porcia Lex, the authors L. Marius and Porcius Cato, Tribunes of the Commons, A. 691, ordaining, That a penalty should be inflicted on such commanders as writ falsely to the Senate, about the number of the slain on the enemies side, and of their own party: And that they should be obliged, when they first entered the city, to take a solemn oath before the Quæstors, that the number which they returned was true, according to the best computation (*c*).

Sulpicia Lex, the author P. Sulpicius, Tribune of the Commons, A. 665, ordaining, That the chief command in the Mithridatic war, which was then enjoined by L. Sylla, should be taken from him and conferred on C. Marius (*d*).

Gabinia Lex, the author A. Gabinius, Tribune of the Commons, A. 685, ordaining, That a commission should be granted to Cn. Pompey, for the management of the war against the pirates for three years, with this particular clause, that upon all the sea on this side Hercules's pillars, and in the maritime provinces as far as 400 stadia from the sea, he should be impowered to command Kings, Governors, and States, to supply him with all the necessaries in expedition (*e*).

Manilia

(*a*) Liv. lib. 7. (*b*) Plut. in C. Gracch. (*c*) Valer. Max. l. 2. c. 8.
(*d*) Vell. Paterc. lib. 2. Flor. Epit. 77. Plutarch in Sylla & Mario, &c.
(*e*) Asconius in Cornelian Vell. Paterc. lib. 2. Plutarch in Pomp. Cicero de Lege Manilia. & post Reditum in Senat.

Manilia Lex, the author C. Manilius, Tribune of the Commons, *A.* 687, ordaining, That all the forces of Lucullus, and the province under his government, should be given to Pompey; together with Bithynia, which was under the command of Glabrio; and that he should forthwith make war upon Mithridates, retaining still the same naval forces, and the sovereignty of the seas, as before (*a*).

(*a*) *Cicero de Lege Manilia, Plutarch. in Pomp. Flor. Epitom.* 100.

CHAP. XXXIII.

De Tutelis, *or Laws concerning* WARDSHIPS.

ATILIA Lex, the author and time unknown, prescribing, That the Prætor, and the major part of the Tribunes, should appoint guardians to all such minors to whom none had been otherwise assigned (*a*).

The Emperor Claudius seems to have abrogated this law, when, as Suetonius informs us, he ordered, that the assignment of guardians should be in the power of the Consuls (*b*).

Lætoria Lex, ordaining, That such persons as were distracted, or prodigally squandered away their estates, should be committed to the care of some proper persons, for the security of themselves and their possessions; and that whoever was convicted of defrauding any in those circumstances should be deemed guilty of a high misdemeanor (*c*).

(*a*) *Liv.* lib. 39. (*b*) *Sueton. in Claud.* cap. 23. (*c*) *Cicero de Offic.* lib. 3. *de Nat. Deor.* lib. 3.

CHAP. XXXIV.

Laws *concerning Wills, Heirs, and Legacies.*

FURIA Lex, the author C. Furius, Tribune of the Commons, ordaining, That no perſon ſhould give, by way of legacy, above a thouſand aſſes, unleſs to the relations of the maſter who manumized him, and to ſome other parties there excepted (*a*).

Voconia Lex, the author Q. Voconius Saxa, Tribune of the Commons, *A.* 584, ordaining, That no woman ſhould be left heireſs to an eſtate; and that no *Cenſus* ſhould, by his will, give above a fourth part of what he was worth to a woman. This ſeems to have been enacted to prevent the decay and extinction of noble families (*b*).

By the word *Cenſus* is meant any rich perſon, who was rated high in the Cenſor's books.

(*a*) *Cicer. pro Balbo.*   (*b*) *Cicero in Ver.* 3. *Seneſt. de Finib.*

CHAP. XXXV.

Laws *concerning Money, Uſury,* &c.

SEMPRONIA Lex, the author M. Sempronius, Tribune of the Commons, *A.* 560, ordaining, That, in lending money to the allies of Rome and the Latins, the tenor of the Roman laws ſhould be ſtill obſerved, as well as among the citizens (*a*).

Valeria Lex, the author Valerius Flaccus, Conſul with L. Cornelius Cinna, ordaining, (to oblige the poorer part of the city) That all creditors ſhould diſcharge their debtors upon the receipt of a fourth part for the whole ſum. This law, as moſt unreaſonable, is cenſured by Paterculus (*b*).

Gabinia

(*a*) *Liv.* lib. 35. *Cicero de offic.* 2.   (*b*) Lib. 2. cap. 23.

Gabinia Lex, the author Aul. Gabinius, Tribune of the Commons, *A.* 685, ordaining, That no action should be granted for the recovery of any money taken up, *verfura factú*, i. e. first borrowed upon a small use, and then lent out again upon a greater; which practice was highly unreasonable (*a*).

Claudia Lex, the author Claudius Cæsar, commanding, That no usurer should lend money to any person in his nonage, to be paid after the death of his parents (*b*).

Vespasian added a great strength to this law, when he ordained, That those usurers who lent money to any *Filius Familiæ*, or son under his father's tuition, should have no right ever to claim it again, not even after the death of his parents (*c*).

(*a*) *Cicero ad Attic*. lib. 5. Epist. *ult*. lib. 6. Epist. 2.   (*b*) *Tacit*. Annal. 11.   (*c*) *Sueton*. *in Vesp*. cap. 11.

CHAP. XXXVI.

Laws *concerning the* Judges.

Sempronia Lex, the author C. Sempronius Gracchus, Tribune of the Commons, *A.* 630, ordaining, That the right of judging, which had been assigned to the Senatorian order by Romulus, should be transferred from them to the Equites (*a*).

Servilia Lex, the author Q. Servilius Cœpio, Consul, with C. Atilius Serranus, *A.* 647, abrogating in part the former law, and commanding, That the privilege therein mentioned should be divided between both the orders of Knights and Senators (*b*).

Plutarch and Florus make C. Sempronius Gracchus to have appointed 300 Senators, and 600 Equites, for the management of judgments; but this seems rather to belong to the Servilian law, if not totally a mistake (*c*). This law was soon after repealed.

Livia Lex, the author M. Livius Drusus, Tribune of the Commons, *A.* 662, ordaining, That the judiciary power should be

(*a*) *Asconius in Divin. Tacit*. Ann. 12. *Vell. Paterc*. l. 2.   (*b*) *Cic. de Art. Rhet*. lib. 2. *de Oratore in Bruto, in Orat. pro Scauro*. (*c*) *Cic. de Orator*. 3. *Flor*. Epit. 71.

be placed in the hands of an equal number of Senators and Knights (*a*).

But this, among other conſtitutions of that author, was abrogated the very ſame year, under pretence of being made inauſpiciouſly.

Plautia Lex, the author M. Plautius Silvanus, Tribune of the Commons, *A* 664, ordaining, That every tribe ſhould chuſe out of their own body fifteen perſons to ſerve as judges every year ; by this means making the honour common to all three orders, according as the votes carried it in every tribe (*b*).

Cornelia Lex, the author L. Cornelius Sylla, Dictator, *A*. 673, taking away the right of judging entirely from the Knights, and reſtoring it fully to the Senators (*c*).

Aurelia Lex, the author L. Aurelius Cotta, Prætor, *A*. 653, ordaining, That the Senatorian and Equeſtrian orders, together with the Tribuni Ærarii, ſhould ſhare the judicial power between them (*d*).

Pompeia Lex, the author Pompey the Great, Conſul with Craſſus, *A*. 698, ordaining, That the judges ſhould be choſen otherwiſe than formerly, out of the richeſt in every century ; yet, notwithſtanding, ſhould be confined to the perſons mentioned in the Aurelian law (*e*).

Julia Lex, the author Julius Cæſar, confirming the aforeſaid privilege to the Senators and Knights, but excluding the Tribuni Ærarii (*f*).

Roſinus ſets this law before that of Pompey, but it is very plain, it was not made till afterwards.

Antonia Lex, the author M. Antony, Conſul with Julius Cæſar, *A*. 709, ordaining, That a third decury of judges ſhould be added to the two former, to be choſen out of the centurions (*g*).

(*a*) *Aſconius* in *Cornelian.*   (*b*) *Cicero pro Cornel. & ad Att.* 4.
(*c*) *Flor.* Epit. 89. *Aſcon.* in *Divinat.*   (*d*) *Cicero* in *Verrinis, Vell.* l. 2.
(*e*) *Cicero* in *Piſonem.*   (*f*) *Suet.* in *Julio.* cap. 41.   (*g*) *Cicero* in *Philipp.* 1. & 5.

CHAP.

CHAP. XXXVII.

Laws *relating to* Judgments.

*P*OMPEIA *Lex*, the author Pompey the Great, sole Consul, *A.* 701, forbidding the use of the Laudatores in trials (*a*).

Memmia Lex, ordaining, That no person's name should be received into the roll of criminals, who was absent upon the public account (*b*).

Remmia Lex, ordaining, That persons convicted of calumny should be stigmatized (*c*).

Both these laws sometimes go under the name of *Memmiæ*, and sometimes of *Remmiæ;* the distinction here observed is owing to P. Manutius.

Cincia Lex, the author M. Cincius, Tribune of the Commons, *A.* 549, forbidding any person to accept of a gift upon account of judging a cause. This is commonly called *Lex Muneralis* (*d*).

(*a*) *Plutarch. in Pomp. & in Catone Uticens. Valer. Max.* l. 6. c. 2.
(*b*) *Cicero in Vatin. Val. Max.* l. 3. c. 7. (*c*) *Cicero pro Sext. Roscio.*
(*d*) *Liv.* lib. 34. *Tacit.* Ann. 14. *Cicero ad Attic.* lib. 1. *de Oratore.* 2. *de Senect.*

CHAP. XXXVIII.

Laws *relating to* Crimes.

THE crimes or actions, that tended to the prejudice of the State, have been already reckoned up, and briefly explained. The laws on this subject are very numerous, and by reason of their great usefulness, have been preserved at large in the labours of the Civilians, with the particular heads of which they consisted. It will be sufficient to the present design,

design, to mention such as are hinted at in the ordinary classics, and to speak of those only in general.

DE MAJESTATE.

Gabinia Lex, already described among the laws relating to assemblies.

Apuleia Lex, the author L. Apuleius, Tribune of the Commons, *A.* 652. It seems to have been enacted for the restraint of public force and sedition in the city (*a*). Sigonius thinks, that it was this law which made the question de Majestate perpetual.

Varia Lex, the author L. Varius, Tribune of the Commons, *A.* 662, ordaining, That all such persons should be brought to a public trial who had any way encouraged or assisted the confederates in the late war against Rome (*b*).

Cornelia Lex, the author L. Cornelius Sylla, Dictator, *A.* 670, making it treason to lead an army out of a province, or to engage in a war without special orders; to endeavour the ingratiating one's self so with the army as to make them ready to serve his particular interest; or to spare, or ransom a commander of the enemy when taken prisoner; or to pardon the captains of robbers and pirates; or for a Roman citizen to reside without orders at a foreign court; and assigning the punishment of *Aquæ & Ignis Interdictio* to all that should be convicted of any of these crimes (*c*).

Julia Lex, the author Julius Cæsar, either in his first consulship, or after the Pharsalian victory, ordaining the punishment mentioned in Sylla's law, to be inflicted on all that were found guilty *de Majestate*; whereas Sylla intended it only for the particulars which he there specifies (*d*).

Antonia Lex, the author Mark Antony, allowing those who were condemned *de Majestate* an appeal to the people; which before was allowed only in the crime which they called *Perduellio*, one part of the *Crimen Majestatis*, of the most heinous nature; which the lawyers define, *Hostili animo adversus Rempublicam esse*. This law was repealed by Augustus (*e*).

De

(*a*) *Cicero de Orator*. lib. 2.   (*b*) *Cicero pro Scauro, pro Cornel. Tusculan*. 2. in *Bruto. Valerius Maximus*, lib. 8. cap 6.   (*c*) *Cicero* in *Pison. pro Cluent. &c.*   (*d*) *Cicero, Philipp*. 1.   (*e*) P. *Manut*. lib. *de Legibus*.

De Adulterio & Pudicitia.

Julia Lex, the author Auguſtus Cæſar, as Suetonius informs us (*a*). Juvenal mentions this law in his ſecond ſatyr, and ſeems to intimate, that it was afterwards confirmed, and put in full force by the Emperor Domitian; the rigour of it is there very handſomely expreſſed:

————*Leges revocabat amaras* (*b*)
Omnibus, atque ipſis Veneri Martique, timendas.

Scatinia Lex, the author C. Scatinius Aricinus, Tribune of the Commons; though ſome think it was called *Lex Scantinia*, from one Scantinius, Tribune of the Commons, againſt whom it was put in execution. It was particularly levelled againſt the keepers of catamites, and againſt ſuch as proſtituted themſelves for this vile ſervice (*c*). The penalty enjoined by the author was only pecuniary; but Auguſtus Cæſar made it afterwards capital (*d*).

Cornelia Lex inter ſicarios, & veneficos;

The author Cornelius Sylla, Dictator. It was directed againſt ſuch as killed another perſon with weapons or poiſon, or fired houſes, or took away any perſon's life by falſe accuſation; with ſeveral other heads.

It was a clauſe in this law, That the perſon who ſtood accuſed of the crimes therein mentioned, might have his choice of letting the jury give their verdict *clam, vel palam*, by voices or by tablets (*e*).

De Parricidis.

The old law which proſcribed the odd ſort of puniſhment proper to this crime was reſtored and confirmed by Pompey the Great, with the title of *Lex Pompeia* (*f*).

Cornelia Lex falſi.

Sylla the Dictator, as he appointed a proper Prætor to make inquiſition into what they called *Crimen falſi*, ſo he enacted this law

---

(*a*) *In Aug.* c. 34.   (*b*) *Juv. Sat.* 2. v. 30.   (*c*) *Quintil.* l. 4. cap. 2. lib. 7. cap. 4. *Cicero Philip.* 3. *Juv. &c.*   (*d*) *Juſt. Inſtit.* lib. 4.   (*e*) *Cic. pro Cluent.*   (*f*) *Juſt. Inſt.* lib. 4. *& alii.*

law as the rule and standard in such judgment (a). It takes in all forgers, concealers, interliners, &c. of wills; counterfeiters of writs and edicts; false accusers, and corrupters of the jury; together with those that any ways debased the public coin, by shaving or filing the gold, or adulterating the silver, or publishing any new pieces of tin, lead, &c. and making those incur the same penalty (which was *aquæ & ignis interdictio*) who voluntarily connived at the offenders in these particulars.

Leges de vi.

Plautia, or *Plotia Lex*, the author P. Plautius, Tribune of the Commons, *A.* 675, against those that attempted any force against the State or Senate; or used any violence to the magistrates, or appeared armed in public upon any ill design, or forcibly expelled any person from his lawful possession. The punishment assigned to the convicted was *aquæ & ignis interdictio* (b).

Clodia Lex, the author P. Clodius, Tribune of the Commons, *A.* 695, ordaining, That all those should be brought to their trial, who had executed any citizen of Rome without the judgment of the people, and the formality of a trial (c).

The author, being a mortal enemy of Cicero's, levelled this law particularly against him; who in the time of the Catilinarian conspiracy, for the greater expedition and security, having taken several of the chief parties concerned, first imprisoned, and afterwards executed them, only upon a decree of the Senate. Clodius having highly ingratiated himself with the people by several popular laws, easily got this act to pass, and so obliged Cicero to go into exile.

Pompeia Lex, the author Pompey the Great, in his third consulship, *A.* 701. It was directed especially against the authors of the late riot, upon the account of Clodius and Milo; in which one of the Curiæ had been set on fire, and the palace of Lepidus the Interrex, assaulted by force. This law introduced a much shorter form of judgment than had been formerly used, ordaining, That the first three days in every trial should be spent in hearing and examining witnesses, and then allowing only one day for the two parties to make their formal accusation and defence; the first being confined to two hours, and the other

to

(a) *Cic. de Nat. Deor.* lib 3. *Suet. in Aug.* cap. 33.   (b) *Sueton. in Julio*, c. 3. *Dio*, l. 39. *Cicero pro Sextio, pro Milone.*   (c) *Vell. Paterc.* lib. 2. *Cic. ad Attic.* lib. 3. *Dio*, lib. 38.

to three. Hence the author of the dialogue concerning famous orators, attributed to Quintilian or Tacitus, observes, That Pompey was the first who deprived eloquence of its old liberty, and confined it to bounds and limits (a).

Leges de Ambitu.

Fabia Lex, prescribing the number of Sectatores allowed to any candidate (b). This did not pass.

Acilia Calpurnia Lex, the authors M. Acilius Glabrio and C. Calpurnius Piso, Consuls, A. 686, ordaining, That, besides the fine imposed, no person convicted of this crime should bear an office, or come into the Senate (c).

Tullia Lex, the author M. Tullius Cicero, Consul with C. Antonius, A. 690, ordaining, That no person, for two years before he sued for an office, should exhibit a show of gladiators to the people, unless the care of such a solemnity had been left to him by will: That Senators, convicted of the *crimen ambitus*, should suffer *aquæ & ignis interdictio* for ten years; and that the Commons should incur a severer penalty than had been denounced by the Calpurnian law (d).

Aufidia Lex, the author Aufidius Lurco, Tribune of the Commons, A. 692, more severe than that of Tully; having this remarkable clause, that if any candidate promised money to the Tribunes, and did not pay it, he should be excused; but, in case he actually gave it, should be obliged to pay to every tribe a yearly fine of 3000 sestertii (e).

Lex Licinia de Sodalitiis, the author M Licinius Crassus, Consul with Cn. Pompey, A. 691, appointing a greater penalty than formerly to offenders of this kind (f). By Sodalitia, they understood an unlawful making of parties at elections; which was interpreted as a sort of violence offered to the freedom of the people. It is strange, that this sense of the word should have escaped Cooper and Littleton.

Asconius seems to imply, that the *Sodalitia* and *Ambitus* were two different crimes, when he tells us, that Milo was arraigned on those two accounts at two several times, and not before the same Quæstor (g).

F f *Pompeia*

(a) *Ascon. in Milon. Cic. de finib.* 4. *Cæs. de Bell. Civ.* lib. 3. &c.
(b) *Cic. pro Muræna.* (c) *Cic. pro Muræna, pro Cornel, &c.*
(d) *Cic. in Vatin. pro Sextio, pro Muræna. Dio,* lib. 37. (e) *Cic. ad Attic.* l. 1. ep. 11. (f) *Cic. pro Planc.* (g) *In Argument. Milon.*

Pompeia Lex, the author Pompey the Great, sole Consul, *A*. 701. By this it was enacted, That whoever, having been convicted of a crime of this nature, should afterwards impeach two others of the same crime, so that one of them was condemned, should himself, upon that score, be pardoned. The short form of judgment, mentioned in *Pompeia Lex de vi*, was ordered too by this law (*a*).

Julius Cæsar quite ruined the freedom and fair proceedings in elections, when he divided the right of chusing magistrates between himself and the people, or rather disposed of all offices at his pleasure (*b*). Hence Lucan :

——*Nam quo melius Pharsalicus annus* (*c*)
Consule notus erit ? fingit solemnia campus,
Et non admissæ dirimit suffragia Plebis ;
Decantatque Tribus, & vana versat in Urna.
Nec cœlum servare licet ; tonat Augure surdo :
Et lætæ jurantur aves, bubone sinistro.

From what brave Consul could the year receive
A surer mark, than death and wars shall leave ?
Assemblies are a jest ; and, when they meet,
The gaping croud is bubbled with a cheat.
The lots are shook, and sorted tribes advance ;
But Cæsar, not blind fortune, rules the chance.
Nor impious Rome heav'n's sacred signs obeys,
While Jove still thunders, as the augurs please :
And when left owls some dire disaster bode,
The staring miscreants, at their master's nod,
Look to the right, and swear the omen's good.

But Augustus restored the old privilege to the Comitia, and restrained unlawful courses used in the canvassing at elections by several penalties (*d*) ; and published, for this purpose, the *Lex Julia de ambitu*, mentioned in the Pandects.

Leges de Pecuniis repetundis.

Calpurnia Lex, the author L. Calpurnius Piso Frugi, *A*. 605, ordaining a certain Prætor for the inquisition of this crime, and laying a great penalty on offenders (*e*).

Cæciliæ

(*a*) *In Argument. Milonian.* (*b*) *Sueton. in Julio*, cap. 41.
(*c*) Lib. 5. ver. 391.   (*d*) *Sueton. in August.* cap. 40.   (*e*) *Cicero in Bruto, de offic.* lib. 2. *Orat.* 3. *in Verrem.*

Cæcilia Lex, mentioned by Valerius Maximus (*a*). Sigonius believes this law to be the very same with the former, and that either the two Tribunes, Cæcilius and Calpurnius, joined in the making of it; and so it came to be called either Calpurnia, or Cæcilia, at pleasure; or that in this place we ought to read Calpurnia, instead of Cæcilia.

Junia Lex, the author probably M. Junius Pennus, Tribune of the Commons, *A*. 627, ordaining, That, besides the *Litis Æstimatio*, or rating of the damages, the person convicted of this crime should suffer banishment (*b*).

Servilia Lex, the author C. Servilius Glaucia, Prætor, A. 653, several fragments of which are collected from authors, and transcribed from brazen tablets by Sigonius (*c*).

Acilia Lex, the author *M*. Acilius Glabrio; in which was this remarkable clause, That the convicted person should be allowed neither *Ampliatio*, nor *Comperhendinatio*; neither a new hearing at a set time prefixed by the Prætor, nor an adjournment of the trial, till the third day after the first appearing of the parties in the court (*d*).

Cornelia Lex, the author L. Cornelius Sylla, Dictator; ordaining, That, besides the *Litis Æstimatio*, the person convicted of this crime should be interdicted the use of fire and water (*e*).

Julia Lex, the author L. Julius Cæsar; this kept its authority through the whole series of the Emperors, and is still celebrated in the Pandects: A great part of it was levelled against the misdemeanors of provincial governors; many of which, according to this law, are alledged against Piso, who had been Proconsul in Macedonia, by Cicero, in his 37th oration.

(*a*) Lib. 6. cap. 9. Sect. 10. (*b*) *Cic. in Verrem. & pro Balbo Vell. Paterc.* lib. 2. (*c*) *Cic. pro Posthum. pro Balbo, in Verrem. Sigon. de judiciis*, lib. 2. cap. 27. (*d*) *Cic. in Verrem. Ascon. in easdem.* (*e*) *Cic. pro Cluentio; in Verrem, Ascon. Pædian. in Verrinas.*

C H A P. XXXIX.

Miscellany Laws not spoken of under the general Heads.

CLODIA Lex de Collegiis, the author P. Clodius, Tribune of the Commons, *A.* 695, ordaining, That the *Collegia,* or companies of artificers instituted by Numa, which had in a great measure been laid down, should be all revived, and observed as formerly, with the addition of several new companies *(a).*

Cæcilia Lex de Jure Italiæ, & tributis tollendis ; the author Q. Cæcilius Metellus Nepos, Prætor, *A.* 693, ordaining, That the tax called *Portoria* should be taken off from all the Italian States *(b).*

Portoria, according to Sigonius's explication, was a sort of toll paid always at the carrying of any exportable goods to the haven ; whence the collectors of it were called *Portitores.*

Lex Julia de maritandis ordinibus.

The Romans, consulting the grandeur of their republic, had always a particular honour for a married state ; and nothing was more usual than for the Censors to impose a fine upon old batchelors. Dionysius Halicarnasseus *(c)* mentions an old constitution, by which all persons of full age were obliged to marry : But the first law, of which we have any certainty, was this of Augustus Cæsar, preferred *A.* 736. It did not pass before it had received several amendments, being at first rejected for its extreme severity. This is the subject of Propertius's seventh elegy of the third book :

Gavisa est certe sublatam Cynthia legem, &c.

My Cynthia laugh'd to see the bill thrown out, *&c.*

Horace calls it *Lex Marita (d).*

A. 672, this law, being improved and enlarged, was preferred in a new bill by Papius and Poppæus, the Consuls at that

---

(a) Cic. pro Sextio ; in Pison. pro Domo. Ascon. in Cornel. (b) Dio, l. 37. *Cic. in Epist. ad Attic. (c)* Lib. 9. *(d)* In *Carmine Sæculari.*

that time: whence it is sometimes called *Papia Poppæa Lex*, and generally *Julia Papia*.

A great part of the general heads are collected by Lipsius, in his comment on Tacitus (a); among which, the most remarkable are those which contain the sanctions of rewards and punishments.

As to the first of these, it was hereby ordained, That all the magistrates should take precedence according to their number of children; or a married man before a batchelor: That in elections, those candidates should be preferred who had the most numerous offspring; and that any person might stand sooner than ordinary for any office, if he had as many children as he wanted years to be capable of bearing such a dignity (b): That whoever in the city had three children, in the other parts of Italy four, and in the provinces five (or as some say, seven) should be excused from all troublesome offices in the place where he lived. Hence came the famous *jus trium liberorum*, so frequently to be met with in Pliny, Martial, &c. by which the Emperor often obliged such persons with this privilege to whom nature had denied it.

Of the penalties incurred by such as in spite of this law lived a single life, the chief was, That unmarried persons should be incapable of receiving any legacy or inheritance by will, unless from their near relations; and such as were married, and yet had no children, above half an estate. Hence, Plutarch has a severe reflection on the covetous humour of the age: " That several of the Romans did not marry for the " sake of heirs to their own fortunes; but that they themselves " might, upon this account, be capable of inheriting the es-" tates of other men (c)."

And Juvenal alludes to the same custom.

Jam Pater es; dedimus quod famæ opponere possis (d).
Jura Parentis habes; propter me scriberis Hæres;
Legatum omne capis, nec non & dulce caducum.

Now by my toil thou gain'st a father's fame;
No more shall pointing crowds attest thy shame,
Nor hooting boys thy impotence proclaim.
Thine is the privilege our laws afford
To him that stands a father on record:

In

(a) *Excurs. ad Tacit. Ann.* l. 3. *Liter. C. Vid. Suet. in Octavio.* c. 34.
(b) *Plin. Epist.* l. 7.   (c) *Plut.* περὶ φιλοστοργίας.   (d) *Sat.* 9. v. 86.

In misers wills you stand unquestion'd now,
And reap the harvest which you could not sow.

Claudia Lex de scribarum nogotiatione.

This law is barely mentioned by Suetonius (*a*); and seems a part of the *Lex Claudia*, or *Clodia*, about the trading of the Senators, already explained. It appears therefore, that not only the Senators, but the Scribes too, or at least those Scribes who assisted the Quæstors, were forbid to make use of a vessel of above three hundred amphoræ: We may reasonably suppose, that this prohibition was not laid upon them, in respect of their order and degree, which were not by any means eminent, but rather upon account of their particular place or office; because it looked very improper, that persons who were concerned in the public accounts, should at the same time, by dealing in traffic and merchandize, endeavour rather the filling their own coffers, than improving the revenues of the State (*b*).

Manilia Lex; this law, as well as the former, depends upon a single authority, being just named by Sallust (*c*), and not explained by Manutius or Rosinus. It seems to have been to this purpose, that since affairs had been very often ill managed by the nobility; those persons, whose ancestors had bore no magistracy in the State, such as they called *Homines navi*, should, for the future, be allowed the privilege of holding public offices (*d*).

Atinia Lex de Furtis, ordaining, That no prescription should secure the possession of stolen goods; but that the proper owner should have an eternal right to them (*e*).

(*a*) *In Domit.* cap. 9.   (*b*) *V. Torrent. in not. ad locum.*   (*c*) *In Bell. Jugurthin.*   (*d*) *V. Rivium. in not. ad locum.*   (*e*) *Cicero Verr.* 3. *A. Gell.* cap. 7.

PART II. BOOK IV.

Of the ROMAN *Art of* WAR.

CHAP. I.

The Levies of the ROMAN *Foot.*

AT the same time of the year as the Consuls were declared *elect* or *designed,* they chose the military Tribunes, fourteen out of the body of the Equites, who had served in the army five years; and ten out of the commonalty, such as had made ten campaigns. The former they called *Tribuni Juniores,* and the latter *Seniores.*

The Consuls having agreed on a levy, (as, in the time of the commonwealth, they usually did every year) they issued out an edict, commanding all persons who had reached the military age (about seventeen years) to appear (commonly) in the capitol, or in the area before the capitol, as the most sacred and august place on such a day. The people being come together, and the Consuls who presided in the assembly having taken their seat, in the first place, the four-

and-

and-twenty Tribunes were difpofed of, according to the number of legions they defigned to make up, which was generally four. The *junior* Tribunes were affigned, four to the firft legion, three to the fecond, four to the third, and three to the laft. The *fenior* Tribunes, two to the firft legion and the third, three to the fecond and laft. After this, every tribe, being called out by lot, was ordered to divide into their proper centuries; one of each century were foldiers cited by name, with refpect had to their eftate and clafs; for which purpofe, there were tables ready at hand, in which the name, age, and wealth of every perfon was exactly defcribed. Four men, as much alike in all circumftances as could be pitched upon, being prefented out of the century, firft the Tribunes of the firft legion chofe one, then the Tribunes of the fecond another, the Tribunes of the third legion a third man, and the remaining perfon fell to the Tribunes of the fourth. Then four more were drawn out; and now the right of chufing firft belonged to the Tribunes of the fecond legion; in the next four to the Tribunes of the third legion; then to the Tribunes of the fourth legion, and fo round, thofe Tribunes chufing laft the next time, who chofe firft the time before; the moft equal and regular method imaginable.

Cicero has remarked a fuperftitious cuftom obferved in thefe proceedings; that the firft foldiers pitched upon fhould, for the omen's fake, be fuch as had fortunate names, as Salvius, Valerius, and the like (*a*).

There were many legal excufes which might keep perfons from the lift; as, in cafe they were fifty years old, for then they could not be obliged to ferve; or if they enjoyed any civil or facred office, which they could not conveniently relinquifh; or if they had already made twenty campaigns, which was the time required for every foot-foldier; or if, upon account of extraordinary merit, they had been, by public authority, releafed from the trouble of ferving for fuch a time; or if they were maimed in any part, and fo ought not to be admitted into the legions; as Suetonius tells us of a father who cut off the thumbs of his two fons, on purpofe to keep them out of the army (*b*). And Valerius Maximus gives a relation of the like nature (*c*).

Otherwife

(*a*) Cic. de Divinat. lib. 1.   (*b*) Sueton. Auguft. cap. 24.   (*c*) Val. Max. lib. 6. cap. 3.

Otherwise they were necessitated to submit; and, in case of a refusal, were usually punished either with imprisonment, fine, or stripes, according to the lenity or severity of the Consul. And therefore it seems strange that Machiavel should particularly condemn the Roman discipline, upon account of forcing no one to the wars, when we have, in all parts of history, such large intimations of a contrary practice. Nay, we read too of the conquisitores, or impress-masters, who were commissioned, upon some occasions, to go about, and compel men to the service of the State.

Valerius Maximus (*a*) gives us one example of changing this custom of taking out every particular soldier by the Tribunes, for that of chusing them by lot. And Appianus Alexandrinus (*b*) acquaints us, That in the Spanish war, managed by Lucullus, upon complaint to the Senate of several unjust practices in the levies, the Fathers thought fit to chuse all the soldiers by lot. Yet the same author assures us, That within five years time the old custom returned, of making the levies in the manner already described.

However, upon any extraordinary occasion of immediate service, they omitted the common formalities, and, without much distinction, listed such as they met with, and led them out on an expedition. These they termed *Militis Subitarii.*

(*a*) Lib. 6. cap. 3.   (*b*) *In Iberic.*

CHAP. II.

The Levy and Review of the CAVALRY.

ROMULUS, having established the Senate, chose three hundred of the stoutest young men out of the most noble families to serve on horseback; but after the institution of the Census by Servius Tullius, all those persons had the honour of being admitted into the order of the Equites who were worth four hundred sestertia; yet no man was thus enrolled by the Kings or Consuls, or afterwards by the Censors, unless, besides the estate required, no exception could be taken against his person or morals. If these were unquestionable, his name was entered among the Knights, and a horse and ring given him at the public charge; he being obliged to appear for the future on horseback, as often as the State should have occasion for his service.

So that there being always a sufficient number of Equites in the city, there needed only a review in order to fit them for service. Learned men have very little agreement in this point; yet we may venture to take notice of three several sorts of reviews, *Probatio*, *Transvectio*, and what they termed properly *Recensio*; though they are usually confounded, and seldom understood.

The *Probatio* we may conceive to have been a diligent search into the lives and manners of the Equites, and a strict observation of their plights of body, arms, horses, &c. This is supposed to have been commonly made once a-year.

Transvectio Lipsius makes the same as *Probatio*, but he is certainly mistaken, since all the hints we meet with concerning it in authors argue it to have been rather a pompous ceremony and procession, than an examination. The most learned Grævius observes it to have been always made in the forum (*a*). Dionysius describes it in the following manner: "The sacrifices being finished, all those who are allowed horses at the expence of the State, ride along in order, as if returning from a battle, being habited in the togæ palmatæ, or the trabeæ, and crowned with wreaths of olive. The procession begins at the temple of Mars, without the walls, and is carried on through all the eminent parts of the city, particularly the forum, and the temple of Castor and Pollux. The number sometimes reaches to five thousand; every man bearing the gifts and ornaments received, as a reward of his valour, from the General. A most glorious sight, and worthy of the Roman grandeur (*b*)."

This solemnity was instituted to the honour of Castor and Pollux, who, in the battle with the Latins, about the year of the city 257, appeared in the field personally assisting the Romans, and, presently after the fight, were seen at Rome (just by the fountain where their temple was afterwards built) upon horses all foaming with white frothy sweat, as if they had rode post to bring tidings of the victory (*c*).

The proper *recensio* was the account taken by the Censors every lustrum, when all the people, as well as the Equites, were

---

(*a*) *Præfat. ad* I. *Vol. Thesaur. Ant. Rom.*   (*b*) *Dionys. Halic.* lib. 6.   (*c*) *Plut. in Coriolan.*

were to appear at the general survey: So that it was only a more solemn and accurate sort of probation, with the addition of enrolling new names, cancelling old ones, and other circumstances of that nature.

Besides all this, it was an usual custom for the Equites, when they had served out their legal time in the wars, to lead their horse solemnly into the forum, to the seat of the two Censors, and there having given an account of the commanders under whom they had served, as also of the time, places, and actions relating to their service, they were discharged every man with honour or disgrace, according as he deserved. For this account we are beholden to Plutarch, who gives a particular relation how this ceremony was performed with universal applause by Pompey the Great.

It might be brought as a very good argument of the obscurity and confusion of these matters, that, of two very learned men, one makes this *Equi redditio* the same as the *Probatio* (a), the other the same as the *Transvectio* (b).

————*Non nostrum tantas componere lites.*

The Emperors often took a review of the cavalry; and Augustus particularly restored the old custom of the Transvectio, which had before been discontinued for some time.

It is hard to conceive that all the Roman horse in the army should consist of Knights; and for that reason Sigonius, and many other learned men, make a distinction in the cavalry, between those who served *Equo publico*, and those that served *Equo privato*; the former they allow to have been of the order of Knights, the latter not. But Grævius, and his noble countryman Schelius, have proved this opinion to be a groundless conjecture. They demonstrate, from the course of history, that from the beginning of the Roman State till the time of Marius, no other horse entered the legions but the true and proper Knights, except in the midst of public confusion, when order and discipline were neglected.

After that period, the military affairs being new-modelled, the Knights thought not fit to expose themselves abroad in the legions, as they had formerly done, but generally kept at home to enjoy their estates, and to have a hand in the transactions

---

(a) *Herman. Hugo de Militia Equestri,* lib. 2. cap. 5.   (b) *Sigon. Annot. ad Liv.* lib. 9. cap. 46.

tranfactions of the city; and their places in the army were filled by foreign horfe; or if they ever made campaigns themfelves, they held fome poft of honour and command. Hence under the Emperors a man might be a Knight, and have the honour of a *public horfe*, without ever engaging in the public caufe, or fo much as touching arms; which confideration made fome princes lay afide the cuftom of allowing the Knights a horfe, and leave them only their gold ring to diftinguifh their order, as Pliny (a) *fenior* affirms to have been done in his time.

(a) Lib. 33. cap. 1. vid. Grævr. Præf. ad Vol. I. Th. Rom.

CHAP. III.

The MILITARY OATH, *and the Levies of the* CONFEDERATES.

THE levies being finifhed, the Tribunes of every legion chofe out one whom they thought the fitteft perfon, and gave him a folemn oath at large, the fubftance of which was, that he fhould oblige himfelf to obey the commanders in all things to the utmoft of his power, be ready to attend whenever they ordered his appearance, and never to leave the army but by their confent. After he had ended, the whole legion, paffing one by one, every man, in fhort, fwore to the fame effect, crying, as he went by, *Idem in me.*

This, and fome other oaths, were fo effential to the military ftate, that Juvenal ufed the word *Sacramenta* for *Milites,* or *Militiæ*. Sat. xvi. 35.

Præmia nunc alia, atque alia emolumenta notemus Sacramentorum.——

As to the raifing the confederate troops, Polybius informs us, that at the fame time as the levies were made in Rome, the Confuls gave notice to the cities of the allies in Italy, intimating the number of forces they fhould have occafion to borrow of them, together with the time and place, when and

and where they should have them make their rendezvous. The states accordingly convened their men, and choosing out their desired number, gave them an oath, and assigned them a commander in chief, and a pay-master General. We may observe, that in the time of Polybius all Italy was indeed subject to the Romans; yet no state or people in it had been reduced into the form of a province; retaining, for the generality, their old governors and laws, and being termed *Socii*, or confederates.

But, after all, the Italians were not only divided into separate provinces, but afterwards honoured with the *Jus Civitatis;* the name of *Socii* ceased, all the natives of Italy being accounted Romans; and therefore, instead of the Social troops, the Auxilia were afterwards procured, which are carefully to be distinguished from the former. They were sent by foreign states and Princes, at the desire of the Roman Senate, or Generals, and were allowed a set pay from the Republic; whereas the Socii received no consideration for their service, but a distribution of corn.

CHAP. IV.

Of the EVOCATI.

THE most eminent degree of soldiers were the *Evocati*, taken as well out of allies as citizens, out of horse as foot, not by force, but at the request and intreaty of the Consuls, or other officers: For which purpose letters were commonly dispatched to every particular man whom they designed thus to invite into their service. These were old experienced soldiers, and generally such as had served out their legal time, or had received particular marks of favour as a reward of their valour, on which accounts they were styled *Emeriti*, and *Beneficiarii:* Scarce any war was undertaken, but a great number of those were invited into the army, therefore they had the honour to be reckoned almost equal with the Centurions. In the field they usually guarded the chief standard, being excused from all the military drudgery, of standing on the watch, labouring in the works, and other servile employments.

The

The Emperor Galba gave the fame name of *Evocati* to a felect band of young gentlemen of the Equeftrian rank, whom he kept as a guard in his palace (*a*).

(*a*) Sueton. *in Galb.* cap. 10.

CHAP. V.

The feveral Kinds of the Roman *Foot, and their Divifion into* Manipuli, Cohorts, *and* Legions.

THE whole Roman infantry was divided into four forts, *Velites, Haftati, Principes,* and *Triarii.*

The *Velites* were commonly fome of the Tiros, or young foldiers, of mean condition, and lightly armed. They had their name *a volando,* or *a velocitate,* from their fwiftnefs and expedition. They feem not to have been divided into diftinct bodies or companies, but to have hovered in loofe order before the army.

The *Haftati* were fo called, becaufe they ufed in ancient times to fight with fpears, which were afterwards laid afide, as incommodious; thefe were taken out the next in age to the Velites.

The *Principes* were generally men of middle age, and of greateft vigour; it is probable that, before the inftitution of the Haftati, they ufed to begin the fight, whence they borrowed their name.

The *Triarii* were commonly veterans, or hardy old foldiers, of long experience, and approved valour. They had their name from their pofition, being marfhalled in the third place, as the main ftrength and hopes of their party. They are fometimes called *Pilarii,* from their weapons the *pila.*

Every one of thefe grand divifions, except the Velites, compofed thirty Manipuli, or Companies; every Manipulus made two Centuries, or Ordines.

Three Manipuli, one of the Haftati, another of the Principes, and a third of the Triarii, compofed a *Cohors.* Among thefe, one was filled with fome of the choiceft foldiers and officers, obtaining the honourable title of *Prima Cohors.* We meet

meet too with the *Prætoria Cohors*, inſtituted by Scipio Numantius; ſelected for the moſt part out of the Evocati or Reformades, and obliged only to attend on the Prætor or General: And this gave original to the *Prætoriani*, the life-guard of the Emperors.

Ten cohorts made up a legion; the exact number of foot, in ſuch a battalion, Romulus fixed at three thouſand; though Plutarch aſſures us, that, after the reception of the Sabines into Rome, he increaſed it to ſix thouſand. The common number afterwards, in the firſt times of the free State, were four thouſand: In the war with Hannibal, it aroſe to five thouſand. After this, it is probable they ſunk to about four thouſand, or four thouſand two hundred again; which was the number in the time of Polybius.

In the age of Julius Cæſar, we do not find any legions exceeding the Polybian number of men; and he himſelf expreſsly ſpeaks of two legions, that did not make above ſeven thouſand between them (*a*).

The number of legions kept in pay together was different, according to the various times and occaſions. During the free State, four legions were commonly fitted up every year, and divided between the Conſuls: Yet, in caſes of neceſſity, we ſometimes meet with no leſs than ſixteen or eighteen in Livy.

Auguſtus maintained a ſtanding army of twenty-three, or (as ſome will have it) of twenty-five legions; but in after-times we ſeldom find ſo many.

They borrowed their names from the order in which they were raiſed, as *Prima, Secunda, Tertia;* but becauſe it uſually happened, that there were ſeveral *Prima, Secunda*, &c. in ſeveral places, upon that account they took a ſort of ſurname beſides, either from the Emperors who firſt conſtituted them, as Auguſta, Claudiana, Galbiana, Flavia, Ulpia, Trajana, Antoniana; or from the provinces which had been conquered chiefly by their valour, as Parthica, Scythica, Gallica, Arabica, &c.; or from the names of the particular deities for whom their commanders had an eſpecial honour, as Minervia, and Apollinaris: Or from the region where they had their quarters; as Cretenſis, Cyrenaica, Britannica, &c. Or ſometimes upon account of the leſſer accidents; as *Adjutrix, Martia, Fulminatrix, Rapax*, &c.

CHAP.

(*a*) *Commentar.* lib. 5.

CHAP. VI.

The Division of the CAVALRY, *and of the* ALLIES.

THE horse required to every legion was three hundred, divided into ten turmæ, or troops, thirty to a troop, every turmæ making three decuriæ, or bodies of men.

This number of three hundred they termed *Justus Equitatus*, and is understood as often as we meet wth *Legio cum suo Equitatu*, or *Legio cum justo Equitatu*. And though we now and then find a different number, as two hundred, in a place or two of Livy and Cæsar, yet we must suppose this alteration to have proceeded from some extraordinary cause, and consequently to be of no authority against the common current of history.

The foreign troops under which we may now comprise the Socii and auxiliaries were not divided, as the citizens, into legions, but first into two great bodies, termed *Alæ*, or *Cornuæ*, and those again into companies, usually of the same nature with those of the Romans; though, as to this, we have little light in history, as being a matter of small importance.

We may further remark, That the forces which the Romans borrowed of the confederate states were equal to their own in foot, and double in horse; though by disposing and dividing them with great policy and caution, they prevented any design that they might possibly entertain against the natural forces; for about a third part of the foreign horse, and a fifth of the foot, was separated from the rest, under the name of *Extraordinarii*, and a more choice part of those with the title of *Ablecti*.

In the time of the Emperors, the auxiliary troops were commonly honoured with the name and constitution of Legions, though the more ancient appellation of *Alæ* frequently occurs.

They were called *Alæ* from their position in the army; and therefore we must expect sometimes to find the same name applied to the Roman soldiers, when they happened to have the same stations.

CHAP.

CHAP. VII.

The Officers in the ROMAN *Army; and, first, of the Centurions and Tribunes; with the Commanders of the Horse, and of the Confederate Forces.*

THE military officers may be divided, according to Lipsius, into proper and common; the first presiding over some particular part, as the Centurions and Tribunes, the other using an equal authority over the whole force, as the Legati and the General.

We cannot have a tolerable notion of the Centurions, without remembering what has been already delivered: That every one of the thirty manipuli in a legion was divided into two *ordines*, or ranks; and, consequently the three bodies of the *Hastati, Principes*, and *Triarii*, into twenty orders a-piece, as into ten manipuli. Now every manipulus was allowed two Centurions, or Captains; one to each order or century: And to determine the point of priority between them, they were created at two different elections. The thirty, who were made first, always took the precedency of their fellows, and therefore commanded the right-hand orders, as the others did the left.

The *Triarii*, or *Pilani*, being esteemed the most honourable, had their Centurions elected first; next to them the *Principes*, and afterwards the *Hastati*; whence they were called *Primus & secundus Pilus, primus & secundus Princeps, primus & secundus Hastatus*, and so on.

Here it may be observed, That *primi Ordines* is used sometimes in historians for the Centurions of those orders; and the same Centurions are sometimes styled *Principes Ordinum*, and *Principes Centurionum*.

We make take notice too, what a large field there lay for promotion; first, through all the orders of the Hastati, then quite through the Principes; and afterwards from the last order of the Triarii to the Primipilus, the most honourable of the Centurions, and who deserves to be particularly described.

This officer, besides his name of *Primipilus*, went under the several titles of *Dux Legionis, Præfectus Legionis, Primus*

Centurionum, and *Primus Centurio;* and was the Centurion of the right hand order of the first manipulus of the Triarians or Pilani, in every legion. He presided over all the other Centurions; and, generally, gave the word of command in exercises and engagements, by order of the Tribunes. Besides this, he had the care of the eagle, or chief standard of the legion: Hence, *Aquilæ præesse* is to bear the dignity of Primipilus; and, hence, *Aquila* is taken by Pliny for the said office; and Juvenal seems to intimate the same:

> *Ut locupletum Aquilam tibi Sexagesimus annus*
> *Adferat.* Sat xiv. 197.

Nor was this station only honourable, but very profitable too; for he had a special stipend allowed him, probably as much as a Knight's estate; and, when he left that charge, was reputed equal to the members of the Equestrian order, bearing the title of *Primipilarius;* in the same manner as those who had discharged the greatest civil offices were stiled ever after *Consulares, Censorii, Prætorii, Quæstorii,* and *Ædilitii.*

The badge of the Centurion's office was the *vitis,* or rod, which they bore in their hand, whence *vitem poscere* imports the same as to sue for a Centurion's place. The Evocati too had the privilege of using the vitis, as being in all respects rather superior to the Centurions.

As to the reason why this rod should be made of a vine-branch, an old scholiast upon Juvenal has a merry fancy, that Bacchus made use of such a scepter in his martial expedition, and recommended the use of it to posterity.

Besides the Centurions, every manipulus had two *vexillarii,* or ensigns; and every Centurion chose two *Optiones,* or *Succenturiones,* to be his deputies or lieutenants.

The Tribunes owe their name and original to Romulus's institution, when he chose three officers in chief of that nature, out of the three tribes into which he divided his city. The number afterwards increased to six in every legion. They were created, as at first by the Kings, so afterwards by the Consuls for some time, till about *A. U. C.* 393, when the people assumed this right to themselves: And though in the war with Perseus King of Macedon this privilege was regained by the Consuls (*a*), yet we find that, in the very same war, it quickly after

---

(*a*) *Liv.* l. 42.

after returned to the people (a). It is probable, that soon after they divided this power between them; one half of the Tribunes being assigned by the Consuls, the other half elected by the people. The former sort were termed *Rufuli*, or *Rutuli*, because one Rutilius Rufus preferred a law in their behalf. The others *Comitiati*, because they obtained their command by the public votes in the Comitia (b). They were sometimes taken out of the Equestrian and Senatorian orders: And in the time of the Cæsars, most, (if not all) of the Tribunes seem to have been either Senators or Knights. Upon which account, they were divided into the *Laticlavii* and the *Augusticlavii;* the *latus clavus* properly belonging to the former, and the *augustus clavus* to the latter.

The business of the Tribunes was to decide all controversies in the army; to give the word to the watch; besides the care of the works and camp, and several other particulars, which will fall under our notice upon some other occasion.

They had the honour of wearing a gold ring, in the same manner as the Equites; and, because their office was extremely desired, to encourage and promote as many as possible, their command lasted but six months. For the knowledge of both these customs, we are beholden to one verse of Juvenal, Sat. vii. 89.

Semestri vatum digitos circumligat auro.

Every *turma*, or troop of horse, had three *decurions*, or captains of ten; but he that was first elected commanded the troop, and the others were but his lieutenants; though every one of the decurions had an *optio*, or deputy under him.

As to the confederate, or foreign force, we are not certain how the smaller bodies of them were commanded; but it seems most probable, that the Romans generally marshalled them according to their own discipline, and assigned them officers of the same nature with those of the legions. But the two *alæ*, or great divisions of the allies, we are assured, had each a præfect appointed them by the Roman Consul, who governed in the same manner as the legionary Tribunes.

CHAP.

(a) *Liv.* lib. 43.   (b) *Ascon. Pædian. in Verrin.*

CHAP. VIII.

The Legati, *and the* Imperator, *or General.*

THE design of the Legati, at their first institution, was not so much to command as to advise: The Senate selecting some of the oldest and most prudent members to assist the General in his councils. Dionysius calls this " the most honour-
" able and sacred office among the Romans, bearing not only
" the authority of a commander, but, withal, the sanctity and
" veneration of a priest (a)." And he and Polybius give them no other name than Πρεσβύται, Πρεσβύται καὶ σύμβουλοι, *elders*, or *elders* and *counsellors*.

They were chosen commonly by the Consuls; the authority of the Senate concurring with their nomination: Though this was sometimes slighted, or contradicted, as appears from Cicero, in his orations for Sextus, and against Vatinius.

They commanded in chief under the General, and managed all affairs by his permission, whence Cæsar calls this power *Opera fiduciaria* (b). And when the Consul or Proconsul was absent, they had the honour to use the fasces, and were intrusted with the same charge as the officer whom they represented.

As to the number of the Legati we have no certainty; but we may suppose this to have depended upon the pleasure of the General, and upon the nature and consequence of the affair in which they were engaged: However, we have tolerable ground to assign one to every legion.

Under the Emperors there were two sorts of Legati, *Consulares* and *Prætorii*, the first of which commanded whole armies, as the Emperors Lieutenant-Generals, and the other only particular legions.

The General excelled all other officers, not only because he had the chief command of the whole army, horse and foot, legions, and auxiliaries; but especially as he was allowed the *auspicia*, or the honour of taking omens, by help of the divines, which made a very solemn ceremony in all martial expeditions. Hence they were said, *gerere rem suis auspiciis*, and
suis

(a) *Dionys. Halicarn.* lib. 11.   (b) *Bello Civil.* lib. 2.

suis divis: This was most properly applied, when they did not act in person: As Suetonius, when he reckons up the conquests of Augustus, expresses himself, *Domuit autem partim ductu, partim auspiciis suis*, &c. (*a*).

Machiavel (*b*) highly extolls the wisdom of the Romans in allowing their Generals unlimited commissions, by which they were impowered to fight or not to fight; to assault such a town, or to march another way, without controul; the Senate reserving to themselves only the power of making peace, and decreeing war, unless upon extraordinary occasions. This was several times the cause of remarkable victories, that in all probability had been otherwise prevented. Thus when Fabius Maximus had given the Tuscans a considerable defeat at Sutrium, and entered on a resolution to pass the Ciminian forest, a very dangerous and difficult adventure; he never staid to expect farther orders from Rome, but immediately marched his forces into the enemy's country, and, at the other side of the forest, gave them a total overthrow. In the mean time, the Senate, fearing he might venture on such a hazardous attempt, sent the Tribunes of the Commons, with other officers, to desire Fabius, that he would not by any means think of such an enterprize; but not arriving till he had effected his design, instead of hindering his resolution, they returned home with the joyful news of his success (*c*).

The setting out of the General was attended with great pomp and superstition. The public prayers and sacrifices for his success being finished, he, habited in a rich paludamentum, a robe of purple or scarlet, interwoven with gold, begun his march out of the city, accompanied with a vast retinue of all sexes and ages; especially, if the expedition were undertaken against any potent or renowned adversary; all persons being desirous to see, and follow with their wishes, him on whom all their hopes and fortunes depended.

If it would not be too minute, we might add a description of the General's led horses, with their rich trappings of purple and cloth of gold; such as Dionysius tells us they brought to honest Quintius the Dictator, in lieu of those he had left with his plough; Or, as that of Pompey the Great, which Plutarch mentions to have been taken by the enemy in the war with Sertorius.

The

(*a*) *Sueton. in Aug.* cap. 21. (*b*) Machiavel's *Discourse on Liv.*
(*c*) *Liv.* lib. 9.

The old Romans had one very superstitious fancy in reference to the General, that if he would consent to be *devoted* or sacrificed to Jupiter, Mars, the Earth, and the Infernal Gods, all the misfortunes which otherwise might have happened to his party, would, by virtue of that pious act, be transferred on their enemies. This opinion was confirmed by several successful instances, and particularly in the most renowned family of the Decii; of whom, the father, son, and grandson, all devoted themselves for the safety of their armies: The first being Consul with Manlius, in the war against the Latins; and perceiving the left wing, which he commanded, to give back, he called out to Valerius the high priest, to perform on him the ceremony of consecration (which we find described by Livy in his eighth book) and immediately spurred his horse into the thickest of the enemy's forces, where he was killed, and the Roman army gained the battle. His son died in the same manner in the Tuscan war, and his grandson in the war with Pyrrhus; in both which, the Romans were successful. Juvenal has left them this deserved encomium in his eighth satyr, 254.

Plebeiæ Deciorum animæ, plebeia fuerunt
Nomina: pro totis Legionibus hi tamen, & pro
Omnibus auxiliis, atque omni pube Latina
Sufficiunt Diis Infernis Terræque Parenti:
Pluris enim Decii quam qui servantur ab illis.

From a mean stock the pious Decii came,
Small their estates, and vulgar was their name;
Yet such their virtue, that their loss alone
For Rome and all our legions could atone:
Their country's doom they by their own retriev'd,
Themselves more worth than all the host they sav'd.

[MR STEPNEY.

CHAP.

CHAP. IX.

Of the ROMAN *Arms and Weapons.*

FOR the knowledge of this subject, we need not take up with the common division into offensive and defensive, but rather rank them both together, as they belonged to the several sorts of soldiers already distinguished.

As to the Velites, their arms were the Spanish swords, which the Romans thought of the best shape and temper, and fittest for execution, being something like the Turkish scymetars, but more sharp at the point.

Hostæ, or javelins, seven in number to every man, very light and slender.

Parma, a kind of round buckler, three feet in diameter, of wood covered with leather.

Galea or *Galerus,* a light casque for their head, generally made of the skin of some wild beast, to appear the more terrible. Hence Virgil, Æn. vii. 688.

———*Fulvosque lupi de pelle galeros.*

and Propertius, iv. xi. 20.

Et galea hirsuta compta lupina juba.

It seems probable, that after the time when the Socii were admitted into the Roman legions, the particular order of the Velites was discontinued, and some of the youngest soldiers were chosen out upon occasion to skirmish before the main body. Hence we find, among the light forces in the times of the Emperors, the *sagittarii* and *funditores,* the darters and slingers, who never constituted any part of the proper Velites. And so, before the institution of the Velites, we meet with the *Rorarii,* whom Sallust calls *Ferentarii,* who performed the same duty with several sorts of weapons.

Some attribute the like employment to the Accensi; but these were rather supernumerary recruits, or a kind of serjeants, in the more ancient armies.

The armies of the *Hastati, Principes,* and *Triarii,* were in a great measure the same; and therefore Polybius has not divided them in his description, but speaks of them all together.

Their

Their sword was the same as that of the Velites; nor need we observe any thing more about it, only that the Roman soldiers used commonly to wear it on their right side, that it might not hinder their shield, tho' they are often represented otherwise in ancient monuments.

Their other arms, worth our notice, were the *Scutum*, the *Pilum*, the *Galea*, and the *Lorica*.

The *Scutum* was a buckler of wood, the parts being joined together with little plates of iron, and the whole covered with a bull's hide: An iron plate went about it without, to keep off blows, and another within, to hinder it from taking any damage by lying on the ground: In the middle was an iron bofs, or *umbo*, jutting out, very serviceable to glance off stones and darts, and sometimes to press violently upon the enemy, and drive all before them. They are to be distinguished from the *Clypei*, which were less, and quite round, belonging more properly to other nations, though, for some time, used by the Romans. The *Scuta* themselves were of two kinds, the *Ovata* and the *Imbricata*; the former is a plain oval figure, the other oblong, and bending inward like a half cylinder. Polybius makes the *Scuta* four feet long, and Plutarch calls them ποδήρεις, *reaching down to the feet* (a). And it is very probable, that they covered almost the whole body, since in Livy we meet with soldiers who stood on the guard, sometimes sleeping with their head laid on their shield, having fixed the other part of it on the earth (b).

The *Pilum* was a missive weapon, which, in a charge, they darted at the enemy. It was commonly four-square, but sometimes round, composed of a piece of wood about three cubits long, and a slip of iron of the same length, hooked and jagged at the end. They took abundance of care in joining the two parts together, and did it so artificially, that it would sooner break in the iron itself than in the joint. Every man had two of these pila, and this number the poet alludes to,

Bina manu lato crispans hastilia ferro. Vir. Æn. i. 317.

Quæ duo sola manu gestans acclivia monti
Fixerat, intorquet jacula.   Statius, *Thebaid*. ii.

C. Marius

(a) *Plut. in Æmilio.*   (b) *Liv.* lib. 44.

C. Marius, in the Cimbrian war, contrived thefe *pila* after a new fafhion: For before, where the wood-way joined to the iron, it was made faft with two iron pins; now Marius let one of them alone as it was, and pulling out the other, put a weak wooden peg in its place; contriving it fo, that, when it was ftruck in the enemy's fhield, it fhould not ftand outright as formerly; but the wooden peg breaking, the iron fhould bend, and fo the javelin fticking faft by its crooked point, fhould weigh down the fhield (*a*).

The *galea* was a head-piece, or morrion, coming down to the fhoulders, commonly of brafs; though Plutarch tells us, that Camillus ordered thofe of his army to be iron, as the ftronger metal (*b*). The lower part of this they called *buccula*, as we have it in Juvenal:

———*Fracta de caffide buccula pendens.* Sat. x. 134.

A chap-fall'n beaver loofely hanging by
The cloven helm.———

On the top was the *crifta*, or creft, in adorning of which the foldiers took great pride. In the time of Polybius they wore plumes of feathers dyed of various colours, to render themfelves beautiful to their friends, and terrible to their enemies, as the Turks do at prefent. But in moft of the old monuments we find the crefts reprefented otherwife, and not much different from thofe on the top of our modern head-pieces. Virgil mentions the feathers on a particular occafion:

Cujus olorinæ furgunt de vertice pennæ. Æn. x. 187.

And he defcribes Mezentius's creft as made of a horfe's main:

———*Criftaque hirfutus equina.* Æn. x. 869.

But whatever the common foldiers had for their creft, thofe of the officers were more fplendid and curious, being ufually worked in gold or filver, and reaching quite crofs the helmet for diftinction-fake. If we might fpeak of thofe of foreign commanders, the creft of King Pyrrhus, as very fingular, would deferve our remark, which Plutarch defcribes as made of two goats horns (*c*).

The

(*a*) Plutarch. in Mario.   (*b*) Id. in Camill.   (*c*) Id. in Pyrrho.

The *lorica* was a brigantine, or coat of mail, generally made of leather, and worked over with little hooks of iron, and sometimes adorned with small scales of thin gold, as we find in Virgil:

 Loricam concertam hamis.   Æn. iii. 467.

And,

 Nec duplici squama lorica fidelis & auro.   Æn. ix. 707.

Sometimes the *loricæ* were a sort of linen cassocks, such as Suetonius attributes to Galba, and like that of Alexander in Plutarch, or those of the Spanish troops described by Polybius in his account of the battle of Cannæ.

The poorer soldiers, who were rated under a thousand drachms, instead of this brigantine, wore a *pectorale*, or breast-plate of thin brass, about twelve fingers square; and this, with what has already been described, rendered them completely armed; unless we add *ocreæ*, or greaves, which they wore on their legs, which perhaps they borrowed (as many other customs) from the Grecians, so well known by the title of

 ―――――Εὐκνήμιδες Ἀχαιοί.

In the elder times of the Romans, their horse used only a round shield, with a helmet on their head, and a couple of javelins in their hands, great part of their body being left without defence; but as soon as they found the great inconveniencies to which they were hereby exposed, they began to arm themselves like the Grecian horse, or much like their own foot, only their shield was a little shorter and squarer, and their lance, or javelin thicker with spikes at each end, that, if one miscarried, the other might be serviceable.

             CHAP.

CHAP. X.

The Order of the ROMAN *Army drawn up in Battalia.*

WHEN the officers marshalled the army in order to an engagement, the *Hastati* were placed in the front in thick and firm ranks; the *Principes* behind them, but not altogether so close, and after them the *Triarii*, in so wide and loose an order, that, upon occasion, they could receive both the *Principes* and the *Hastati* into their body in any distress. The *Velites*, and in latter times the bowmen and slingers, were not drawn up in this regular manner, but disposed of either before the front of the *Hastati*, or scattered up and down among the void spaces of the same *Hastati*, or sometimes placed in two bodies in the wings; but wherever they were fixed, these light soldiers began the combat, skirmishing in flying parties with the first troops of the enemy. If they prevailed, which very seldom happened, they prosecuted the victory; but upon a repulse they fell back by the flanks of the army, or rallied again in the rear. When they were retired, the *Hastati* advanced against the enemy; and in case they found themselves overpowered, retiring softly toward the *Principes*, fell into the intervals of their ranks, and, together with them, renewed the fight. But if the *Principes* and the *Hastati* thus joined were too weak to sustain the fury of the battle, they all fell back into the wider intervals of the *Triarii;* and then all together being united into a firm mass, they made another effort, much more impetuous than any before: If this assault proved ineffectual, the day was entirely lost as to the foot, there being no further reserves.

This way of marshalling the foot was exactly like the order of trees which gardeners call the *quincunx*, which is admirably compared to it in Virgil (*a*):

> *Ut sæpe ingenti bello cum longa cohortes*
> *Explicuit legio, & campo stetit agmen aperto.*
> *Directæque*

(*a*) *Georg.* ii. 279.

Directæque acies, ac late fluctuat omnis
Ære renidenti tellus, necdum horrida miscent
Prælia, sed dubius mediis Mars errat in armis:
Omnia sunt paribus numeris dimensa viarum.
Non animum modo uti pascat prospectus inanem;
Sed quia non aliter vires dabit omnibus æquas
Terra, neque in vacuum poterunt se extendere rami.

As legions in the field their front display,
To try the fortune of some doubtful day,
And move to meet their foes with sober pace,
Strict to their figure, tho' in wider space,
Before the battle joins, while from afar
The field yet glitters with the pomp of war;
And equal Mars, like an impartial lord,
Leaves all to fortune, and the dint of sword;
So let thy vines in intervals be set,
But not their rural discipline forget;
Indulge their width, and add a roomy space,
That their extremest lines may scarce embrace.
Nor this alone t' indulge a vast delight,
And make a pleasing prospect for the sight:
But for the ground itself, this only way
Can equal vigour to the plants convey,
Which crowded, want the room their branches to display.
                                                    Mr DRYDEN.

 And as the reason of that position of the trees is not only for beauty and figure, but that every particular tree may have room to spread its roots and boughs, without entangling and hindering the rest, so in this ranking of the men, the army was not only set out to the best advantage, and made the greatest show, but every particular soldier had free room to use his weapons, and to withdraw himself between the void spaces behind him, without occasioning any confusion or disturbance.
 The stratagem of rallying thus three times has been reckoned almost the whole art and secret of the Roman discipline; and it was almost impossible it should prove unsuccessful, if duly observed: For fortune, in every engagement, must have failed them three several times before they could be routed; and the enemy must have had the strength and resolution to overcome

ICONISMUS ACIEI VULGATÆ

overcome them in three several encounters, for the decision of one battle; whereas most other nations, and even the Græcians themselves, drew up their whole army, as it were, in one front, trusting themselves and fortunes to the success of a single charge.

The Roman cavalry was posted at the two corners of the army, like the wings on a body, and fought sometimes on foot, sometimes on horseback, as occasion required, in the same manner as our dragoons: The confederate, or auxiliary forces, composed the two points of the battle, and covered the whole body of the Romans.

As to the stations of the commanders, the General commonly took up his post near the middle of the army, between the *Principes* and the *Triarii*, as the fittest place to give orders equally to all the troops. Thus Virgil disposes of Turnus:

———*Medio Dux agmine Turnus*
Vertitur Arma tenens——————*Æn.* ix. 28.

The *Legati* and Tribunes were usually posted by him; unless the former were ordered to command the wings, or the others some particular part of the army.

The *Centurions* stood every man at the head of his century to lead them up; though sometimes, out of courage and honour, they exposed themselves in the van of the army: As Sallust reports of Cataline, that he posted all his choice Centurions, with the *Evocati*, and the flower of the common soldiers, in the front of the battle. But the *Primipili*, or chief Centurions, had the honour to stand, with the Tribunes, near the General's person.

The common soldiers were placed in several ranks, at the discretion of the Centurions, according to their age, strength, and experience, every man having three feet square allowed him to manage his arms in: And it was most religiously observed in their discipline, never to abandon their ranks, or break their order upon any account.

But besides the common methods of drawing up this army, which are sufficiently explained by every historian of any note, there were several other very singular methods of forming their battle into odd shapes, according to the nature of the enemy's body.

Such

Such as the *Cuneus;* when an army was ranged in the figure of a wedge, the moſt proper to pierce and break the order of the enemy. This was otherwiſe called *Caput porcinum,* which, in ſome meaſure, it reſembled.

The *Globus;* when the ſoldiers caſt themſelves into a firm, round body, practiſed uſually in caſes of extremity.

The *Forfex,* an army drawn up, as it were, into the form of a pair of ſheers. It ſeems to have been invented on pur‑ poſe to receive the *Cuneus,* in caſe the enemy ſhould make uſe of that figure. For while he endeavoured to open, and, as it were, to cleave their ſquadrons with his wedge, by keeping their troops open like their ſheers, and receiving him in the middle, they not only hindered the damage deſigned to their own men, but commonly cut the adverſe body in pieces.

The *Pyrgus,* an oblong ſquare figure, after the faſhion of a tower, with very few men in a file, and the files extended to a great length. This ſeems of very ancient original, as be‑ ing mentioned in Homer:

Οἱ δέ τε πυρηδὸν σφίας αὐτοὺς ἀρτύναντες. Iliad. μ. 43.

The *ſerra,* or ſaw, when the firſt companies in the front of the army, beginning the engagement, ſometimes proceed‑ ed, and ſometimes drew back; ſo that, by the help of a large fancy, one might find ſome reſemblance between them and the teeth of that inſtrument.

CHAP.

CHAP. XI.

The Ensigns and Colours; the Music; the Word *in Engagements; the Harangues of the General.*

THERE are several things still behind, relating to the army, very observable, before we come to the camp and discipline; such as the ensigns, the music, the word or sign in engagements, and the harangues of the General.

As to the ensigns, they were either proper to the foot or to the horse. Ensigns belonging to the foot were either the common one of the whole legion, or the particular ones of the several manipuli.

The common ensign of the whole legion was an eagle of gold or silver, fixed on the top of a spear, holding a thunderbolt in her talons, as ready to deliver it. That this was not peculiar to the Romans, is evident from the testimony of Xenophon; who informs us, That the royal ensign of Cyrus was a golden eagle spread over a shield, and fastened on a spear; and that the same was still used by the Persian Kings (*a*).

What the ensigns of the manipuli formerly were, the very words point out to us; for as Ovid expresses it,

> *Pertica suspensos portabat longa Maniplos,*
> *Unde Maniplaris nomina miles habet.*

Manipulus properly signifies a whisp of hay, such as in ruder times the soldiers carried on a pole for an ensign.

But this was in the rustic age of Rome; afterwards they made use of a spear with a transverse piece on the top, almost like a cross; and sometimes with a hand on the top, in allusion to manipulus: Below the transverse part was fastened one little orbicular shield, or more, in which they sometimes placed the smaller images of the Gods, and in latter times, of the Emperors.

Augustus

(*a*) *De instit. Cyri. lib.* 7.

Augustus ordered a globe fastened on the head of a spear to serve for this use, in token of the conquest of the whole world.

The ensign of the horse was not solid as the others, but a cloth, almost like our colours, spread on a staff. On these were commonly the names of the Emperors, in golden or purple letters.

The religious care the soldiers took of the ensigns was extraordinary; they worshipped them, swore by them, and incurred certain death if they lost them. Hence it was an usual stratagem in a dubious engagement, for the commanders to snatch the ensigns out of the bearer's hands, and throw them among the troops of the enemy, knowing, that their men would venture the extremest danger to recover them.

As for the several kinds of standards and banners, introduced by the later Emperors, just before Christianity, and afterwards, they do not fall under the present enquiry, which is confined to the more flourishing and vigorous ages of the commonwealth.

The Romans used only wind-music in their army; the instruments, which served for that purpose, may be distinguished into the *Tubæ*, the *Cornua*, the *Buccinæ*, and the *Litui*.

The *Tuba* is supposed to have been exactly like our trumpet, running on wider and wider in a direct line to the orifice.

The *Cornua* was bent almost round; they owe their name and original to the horns of beasts, put to the same use in the ruder ages.

The *Buccinæ* seem to have had the same rise, and may derive their name from *Bos* and *Cano*. It is very hard to distinguish these from the *Cornua*, unless they were something less, and not quite so crooked: Yet it is most certain, that they were of a different species; because we never read of the *Cornua* in use with the watch, or centinels, but only these *Buccinæ*.

The *Litui* were a middle kind between the *Cornua* and the *Tubæ*, being almost straight, only a little turning in at the top, like the *Lituus*, or sacred rod of the Augur, whence they borrowed their name.

These instruments being all made of brass, the players on them went under the name of *Æneatores*, besides the particular terms of *Tubicines*, *Cornicines*, *Buccinatores*, &c.; and there seems to have been a set number assigned to every manipulus and turma, besides several of a higher order, and common to the whole legion. In a battle, the

the former took their station by the ensign, or colours of their particular company or troop; the others stood near the chief eagle in a ring, hard by the General and prime officers; and when the alarm was to be given, at the word of the General, these latter began it, and were followed by the common sound of the rest, dispersed through the several parts of the army.

Besides this *classicum*, or alarm, the soldiers gave a general shout at the first encounter (a), which in latter ages they called *barritus*, from a German original.

This custom seems to have risen from an instinct of nature, and is attributed almost to all nations that engaged in any martial action; as by Homer to the Trojans; by Tacitus to the Germans; by Livy to the Gauls; by Quintus Curtius to the Macedonians and Persians; by Thucydides, Plutarch, and other authors, to the Grecians. Polyænus honours Pan with the invention of the device, when he was Lieutenant-General to Bacchus in the Indian expedition; and if so, we have a very good original for the *terrores panici*, or panic fears, which might well be the consequence of such a dismal and surprising clamour. The Romans made one addition to this custom, at the same time clashing their arms with great violence, to improve the strength and terror of the noise. This they called *concussio armorum*.

Our famous Milton has given a noble description of it, as used by the rebel angels after their leader's speech for the renewing of the war:

> He spake: And, to confirm his words, out flew
> Millions of flaming swords, drawn from the thighs
> Of mighty cherubims; the sudden blaze
> Far round illumin'd hell: Highly they rag'd
> Against the Highest, and fierce with grasped arms
> Clash'd on their sounding shields the din of war,
> Hurling defiance tow'rd the gate of heav'n.
> *Par. Lost.* B. I.

The signs of battle, besides the *classicum*, were either a flag or standard, erected for that purpose, which Plutarch, in two several places, calls a *purple robe;* or more properly some word

---

(a) *Gell. Noct. Attic.* lib. 1. cap. 11.

word or sentence communicated by the General to the chief officers, and by them to the whole army. This commonly contained some good omen; as, *Felicitas, Libertas, Victoria, Fortuna Cæsaris,* and the like; or else the name of some deity, as Julius Cæsar used *Venus Genetrix,* and Augustus *Apollo.* The old *tessera,* put to this use, seems to have been a sort of tally delivered to every soldier, to distinguish him from the enemy; and, perhaps, on that they used to inscribe some particular word or sentence, which afterwards they made use of without the tally.

One great encouragement, which the soldiers received in their entrance on any adventure, was from the harangue of the General; who, upon the undertaking an enterprize, had a throne erected with green turf, surrounded with the *fasces,* ensigns, and other military ornaments; from whence he addressed himself to the army, put them in mind of the noble atchievements of their ancestors, told them their own strength, and explained to them the order and force of the enemy; raising their hopes with the glorious rewards of honour and victory, and dissipating their fears by all the arguments that a natural courage and eloquence could suggest: This was termed *allocutio.* Which custom, though now laid aside as antiquated and useless, yet is highly commended in the ancient discipline, and, without doubt, has been often the cause of extraordinary successes, and the means of stifling sedition, hindering rash action, and preventing many unfortunate disorders in the field.

CHAP. XII.

The Form and Division of the ROMAN *Camp.*

THE Romans were more exact in nothing than in forming their camp: And two very great commanders, Philip of Macedon, and King Pyrrhus, upon view of their admirable order and contrivance herein, are reported to have expressed the greatest admiration imaginable of the Roman art, and to have thought them more than Barbarians, as the Grecians termed all people besides themselves.

Before

Before we take a particular prospect of the camp, we had best distinguish between the *Castra Æstiva*, and *Castra Hyberna:* The former were sometimes light and moveable, so that they might be set up or taken down in a night, and then they called them simply *Castra*. At other times, when they designed to continue long in their encampments, they took more pains to fortify and regulate them for the convenience and defence of their men, and then they termed them *Castra Stativa*.

As for the *Hyberna*, or winter-quarters, they were commonly taken up in some city or town, or else so built and contrived as to make almost a town of themselves. And hence the Antiquarians observe, that the modern towns, whose names end in *cester*, were originally these *Castra Hyberna* of the Romans.

The figure of the Roman camp was four-square, divided into two chief partitions, the upper and the lower. In the upper partition were the pavilion of the General, and the lodgments of the chief officers: In the lower were disposed the tents of the common soldiers, horse and foot.

The General's apartment, which they called *Prætorium* (because the ancient Latins stiled all their commanders *Prætores*) seems to have been of a round figure: The chief parts of it were the tribunal, or General's pavilion; the augurale, set aside for prayers, sacrifices, and other religious uses; the apartments of the young noblemen, who came under the care of the General, to inform themselves in the nature of the countries, and to gain some experience in military affairs: These gentlemen had the honourable title of *Imperatoris Contubernales*.

On the right side of the Prætorium stood the *Quæstorium;* assigned to the Quæstor, or Treasurer of the army, and hard by the forum; serving not only for the sale of commodities, but also for the meeting of councils, and giving audience to ambassadors: This is sometimes called *Quintana*.

On the other side of the Prætorium were lodged the *Legati*, or Lieutenant-Generals: And below the Prætorium the Tribunes took up their quarters, by six and six, opposite to their proper legions, to the end they might the better govern and inspect them.

The *Præfecti* of the foreign troops were lodged at the sides of the Tribunes, over-against their respective wings: Behind these were the lodgments of the *Evocati*, and then those of the *Extraordinarii* and *Ablecti Equites*, which concluded the higher part of the camp.

Between the two partitions was included a spot of ground, about an hundred feet in length, which they called *Principia*, where the altars and statues of the gods, and (perhaps) the chief ensigns were fixed altogether.

The middle of the lower partition, as the most honourable place, was assigned to the Roman horse; and next to them were quartered the *Triarii*, then the *Principes*; close by them the *Hastati*, afterwards the foreign horse; and, in the last place, the foreign foot.

But the form and dimensions of the camp cannot be so well described any other way as in a table, where they are exposed to view. However, we may remark two great pieces of policy in the way of disposing the confederates; for, in the first place, they divided the whole body of foreigners, placing part in the highest partition of the camp, and part in the lower; and then the matter was ordered so that they should be spread in thin ranks round the troops of the State; so that the latter, possessing the middle space, remained firm and solid, while the others were masters of very little strength, being separated at so vast a distance from one another, and lying just on the skirts of the army.

The Romans fortified their camp with a ditch and parapet, which they termed *fossa* and *vallum*: In the last, some distinguish two parts, the *agger* and the *sudes*. The *agger* was no more than the earth cast up from the *vallum*; and the *sudes* were a sort of wooden stakes to secure and strengthen it. (α)

C H A P. XIII.

Of the Duties, Works, and Exercises of the Soldiers.

THE duties and works of the soldiers consisted chiefly in their watches and guards, and their diligence in casting up intrenchments and ramparts, and such other laborious services.

The

(a) ———— βαθυαν ταφρον ορυξαν

The watches and guards were divided into the *Excubiæ*, and the *Vigiliæ:* The firſt kept by day, and the other by night.

As to the *Excubiæ*, they were kept either in the camp or at the gates and intrenchments. For the former, there was allowed a whole manipulus to attend before the Prætorium, and four ſoldiers to the tent of every Tribune.

The *Triarii*, as the moſt honourable order, were excuſed from the ordinary watches, yet being placed exactly oppoſite to the *Equites*, they were obliged to have an eye over their horſes.

The *Excubiæ*, at the gates of the camp, and at the intrenchments, they properly called *Stationes*. There ſeems to have been aſſigned one company of foot, and one troop of horſe to each of the four gates every day; and it was a moſt unpardonable crime to deſert their poſt, or abandon their corps of guards. The excellency of the Roman diſcipline, in this particular, has appeared on many occaſions to their great honour, and to the benefit of their affairs. To give one inſtance: At the ſiege of Agrigentum in Sicily, in the firſt Punic war, when the Roman guards had diſperſed themſelves abroad a little farther than they ought into the fields for forage; and the Carthaginians, laying hold on the opportunity, made a vigorous ſally from the town, and in all probability would have forced the camp; the ſoldiers, who had careleſsly neglected their duty, being ſenſible of the extreme penalty they had incurred, reſolved to repair the fault by ſome remarkable behaviour; and accordingly rallying together, they not only ſuſtained the ſhock of the enemy, to whom they were far inferior in number, but in the end made ſo great a ſlaughter among them, as compelled them to retreat to their works, when they had well nigh forced the Roman lines (a).

The night-guards, aſſigned to the General and Tribunes, were of the ſame nature as thoſe in the day. But the proper *vigiles* were four in every manipulus, keeping guard three hours, and then relieved by fours; ſo that there were four ſets in a night, according to the four watches, which took their name from this cuſtom.

The way of ſetting this nightly guard was by a tally or *teſſera*, with a particular inſcription given from one Centurion to another, quite through the army, till it came again to the Tribune who at firſt delivered it. Upon the receipt of this, the

(a) *Poly.* lib. 1.

the guard was immediately set. The person deputed to carry the *tessera* from the Tribunes to the Centurions was called *Tesserarius*.

But because this was not a sufficient regulation of the business, they had the *circutio vigilum*, or a visiting the watch, performed commonly about four times in the night, by some of the horse. Upon extraordinary occasions, the Tribunes and Lieutenant-Generals, and sometimes the General himself, made these circuits in person, and took a strict view of the watch in every part of the camp.

Livy (*a*), when he takes an occasion to compare the Macedonians with the Roman soldiers, gives the latter particularly the preference, for their unwearied labour and patience in carrying on their works. But that this was no mean encomium, appears from the character Polybius (*b*) has bestowed on the Macedonians, that scarce any people endured hardships better, or were more patient of labour; whether in their fortifications or encampments, or in any other painful and hardy employment incident to the life of a soldier. There is no way of showing the excellency of the Romans in this affair, but by giving some remarkable instances of the military works; and we may be satisfied with an account of some of them, which occur under the conduct of Julius Cæsar.

When he besieged a town of the Atuatici in Gallia, he begirt it with a rampart of twelve feet high, and as many broad, strengthening it with a vast number of wooden forts; the whole compass included fifteen miles: And all this he finished with such wonderful expedition, that the enemy were obliged to confess, they thought the Romans were assisted in these attempts by some supernatural or divine power (*c*).

At another time, in an expedition against the Helvetii in the same country, with the assistance only of one legion, and some provincial soldiers, he raised a wall nineteen miles long, and sixteen feet high, with a ditch proportionable to defend it (*d*).

More remarkable than either of these were his fortifications before Alesia, or Alexia in Burgundy, described by himself at large in his seventh book; by which he protected his army against fourscore thousand men that were in the town; and two hundred and forty thousand foot, and eight thousand horse that were arrived to the assistance of the enemy (*e*).

But

(*a*) Lib. 9.   (*b*) Lib. 9.   (*c*) *Cæsar de Bell. Gall.* lib. 2. cap. 8.
(*d*) *Idem, Bell. Gall.*   (*e*) *Idem,* lib. 7.

But his most wonderful performance, of this nature, were the works with which he shut up Pompey and his army in Dyrrachium, reaching from sea to sea; which are thus elegantly described by Lucan, lib. vi.

> *Franguntur montes, planumque per ardua Cæsar*
> *Ducit opus: pandit fossas, turritaque summis*
> *Disponit Castella jugis, magnoque recessu*
> *Amplexus fines, saltus, nemorosaque tesqua,*
> *Et silvas, vastaque feras indagine claudit:*
> *Non desunt campi, non desunt pabula magno,*
> *Castraque Cæsareo circumdatus aggere mutat,* &c.

> Vast cliffs, beat down, no more o'erlook the main,
> And levell'd mountains form a wond'rous plain:
> Unbounded trenches with high forts secure
> The stately works, and scorn a rival power.
> Woods, forests, parks, in endless circuits join'd,
> With strange inclosures cheat the savage kind.
> Still Pompey's foragers secure may range;
> Still he his camp, without confinement, change, *&c.*

The exercises of their body were walking, running, vaulting, leaping, and swimming. The first was very serviceable upon account of tedious marches, which were sometimes of necessity to be undertaken; the next to make them give a more violent charge to the enemy; and the two last for climbing the ramparts, and passing the ditches. The vaulting belonged properly to the cavalry, and is still owned as useful as ever.

The exercises of their arms Lipsius divides into *palaria* and *armatura*.

The *Exercitia ad Palum*, or *Palaria*, were performed in this manner: They set up a great post about six feet high, suitable to the stature of a man; and this the soldiers were wont to assail with all instruments of war, as if it were indeed a real enemy; learning upon this, by the assistance of the *campidoctores*, how to place their blows aright. Juvenal brings in the very women affecting this exercise:

> ————*Vel quis non vidit vulnera Pali*
> *Quem cavat assiduis sudibus, scutoque lacessit?* Sat. vi. 246.

Who

> Who has not seen them when without a blush,
> Against the post their wicker-shields they crush,
> Flourish the sword, and at the plastron push?
> > [MR DRYDEN.

Armatura consisted chiefly in the exercises performed with all manner of missive weapons; as throwing of the spear or javelin, shooting of arrows, and the like; in which the *tyrones*, or new listed men, were trained with great care, and with the severest discipline: Juvenal may, perhaps, allude to this custom in his fifth Satyr, 153.

> *Tu scabie frueris mali, quod in aggere rodit*
> *Qui tegitur parma & galea, metuensque flagelli*
> *Discit ab hirsuto jaculum toquere Capella.*

> To you such scabb'd harsh fruit is given, as raw
> Young soldiers at their exercising gnaw,
> Who trembling learn to throw the fatal dart,
> And under rods of rough Centurions smart.
> > MR DRYDEN.

Nor did the common soldiers only practise these feats, but the commanders themselves often set them an example of industry, and were very eminent for their dexterity in performances of this nature. Thus the famous Scipio is described by Italicus:

> *Ipse inter medios venturæ ingentia laudis*
> *Signa dabat, vibrare sudem, transmittere saltu*
> *Murales fossas, undosum frangere nando*
> *Indutus thoraca vadum, spectacula tantæ*
> *Ante acies virtutis erant; sæpe alite planta*
> *Illa perfossum, & campi per aperta volantem*
> *Ipse pedes prævertit equum; sæpe arduus idem*
> *Castrorum spateum & saxo transfinsit & hasta.*   Lib. viii.

> Among the rest the noble Chief came forth,
> And show'd glad omens of his future worth;
> High o'er his head, admir'd by all the brave,
> He brandish'd in the air his threat'ning stave;
> Or leap'd the ditch, or swam the spacious moat,
> Heavy with arms, and his embroider'd coat,
> Now fiery steeds, though spurr'd with fury on,
> On foot he challeng'd, and on foot out-run.

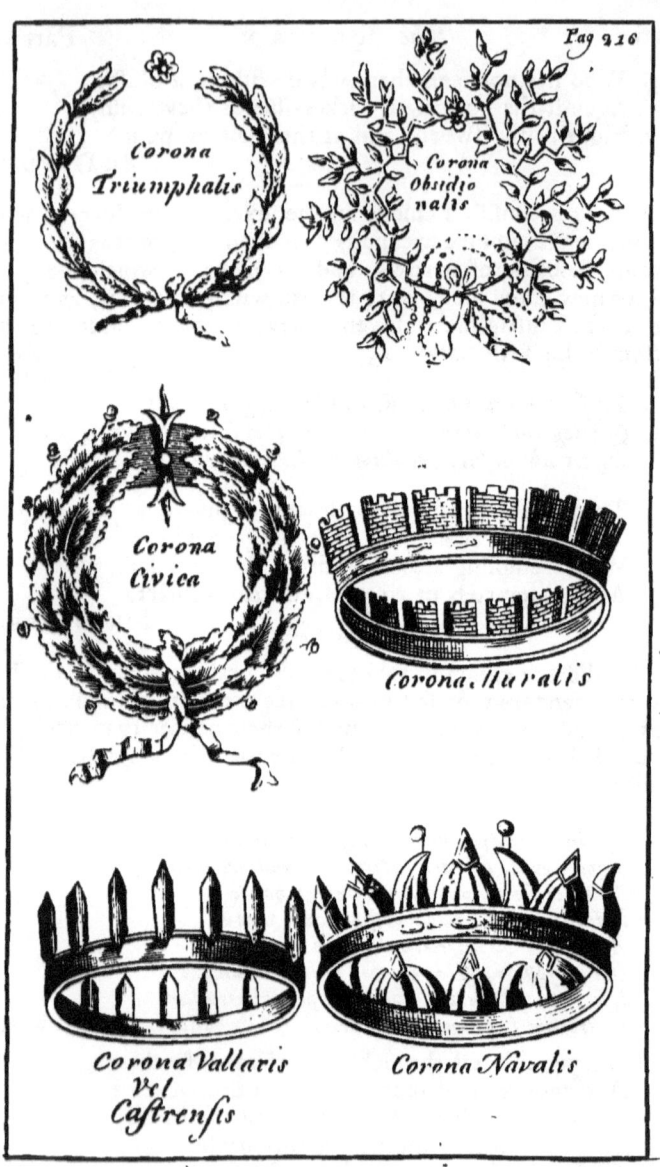

While cross the plain he shap'd his airy course,
Flew to the goal, and sham'd the gen'rous horse.
Now pond'rous stones, well pois'd, with both his hands,
Above the wond'ring crowd unmov'd he sends;
Now cross the camp aims his long ashen spear,
Which o'er ten thousand heads flies singing thro' the air.

Thus have we taken a short view of the chief duties, works, and exercises of the soldiers; but we must not forget their constant labour and trouble of carrying their baggage on their shoulders in a march; this was commonly so heavy a burden, and so extremely tiresome, that Virgil calls it *injustus fascis*. Geor. iii. 346.

Non secus ac patriis acer Romanus in armis
Injusto sub fasce viam dum carpit, & hosti
Ante exspectatum positis stat in ordine castris.

Thus under heavy arms the youth of Rome
Their long laborious marches overcome;
Bending with unjust loads they chearly go,
And pitch their sudden camp before the foe.
Mr DRYDEN.

CHAP. XIV.

Of the SOLDIERS PAY.

THE Roman pay consisted of three parts, money, corn, and cloathes.

As to the money, it is very certain, that for above three hundred years together the army served *gratis*, and at their own charge; and when afterwards a certain pay came to be established, it was no more than two *oboli* a-day to the common foot, to the horse a *drachma* a-piece. It is probable, that the Tribunes received what was counted very considerable (though Polybius is silent in this matter) since, in several authors, we find a large salary expressed by a metaphor taken from a Tribune's stipend: Thus Juvenal particularly;

———*Alter enim, quantum in legione Tribuni*
Accipiunt, donat Calvinæ vel Catienæ.   Sat. iii. 132.

For t' other wealthy rogue can throw away,
Upon a fingle girl, a Tribune's pay.

Yet Lipfius has conjectured, from very good authority, that it could not be more than four times the ordinary ftipend, or a *drachma*, and two *oboli*.

And thefe were all fuch mean confiderations, that Livy had very good reafon for his remark: *Nulla unquam refpublica fuit, in quam tam feræ avaritia luxuriaque immigraverint, nec ubi tantus ac tam diu paupertati ac parcimoniæ honos fuit* (a). "Never was there any ftate or kingdom in which avarice and "luxury fo late gained a head, or where honeft poverty and "frugality continued longer in efteem and veneration."

Julius Cæfar was the firft that made any confiderable alteration in this affair, who, Suetonius affirms, doubled the legionary pay for ever.

Auguftus fettled a new ftipend raifed to ten *affes* a-day; and the following Emperors made fuch large additions, that, in the time of Domitian, the ordinary ftipend was twenty-five *affes per diem*.

The officers whom they received the money from were the *Quæftores*, or rather the *Tribuni Ærarii*, who were a diftinct fociety from the former, and who, (as Voffus (b) has fettled the point) were commiffioned to take up money of the Quæftors to pay off the army. But it is probable, that, being many in number, as they are conftantly reprefented in hiftory, they had fome other bufinefs befides this given in charge. Calvin the Civilian fays, That they had the fupervifal of all the money coined in the city, as the Quæftor took care of the taxes coming in from the provinces (c).

Befides the pay received in money, we read of corn and cloathes as often given to the foldiers: But Polybius affures us, that the Quæftor always fubtracted fome part of their pay on that account: And Plutarch, among the popular laws of C. Gracchus, makes him the author of one, ordaining, That the foldiers fhould be clothed at the expence of the State, without the leaft diminution of their ftipend. The wheat allowed to the foot was every man four *modii* a-month; to the horfe two *modii*, and feven of barley.

It was common for the foldiers, efpecially in the time of the ftrict difcipline, to prepare the corn themfelves for their own

---

(a) *Liv.* lib. 1. (b) *In Etym Lat. in Voc. Trib.* (c) *Calv. Jur in Voc. Trib. Ærarii.*

own use; and therefore some carried hand-mills about with them, to grind it with; others pounded it with stones; and this, hastily baked upon the coals, very often furnished them with a meal, which they made upon tables of turf, with no other drink than bare water, or what they called *posca*, water sharpened with a mixture of vinegar.

CHAP. XV.

Of the MILITARY PUNISHMENTS.

THE punishments used in the camp, were such as reached either the offenders bodies, credit, or goods. The corporal punishments were usually beating with the *vites* or rods, or bastinading with the *fustes:* The last, tho' already reckoned up among the civil punishments which did not touch the life of the malefactors; yet in the camp it was for the most part capital, and was performed after this manner: The convicted person being brought before the Tribune, was by him gently struck over the shoulders with a staff: After this, the criminal had liberty to run, but, at the same time, the rest of the soldiers had liberty to kill him if they could: So that being prosecuted with swords, darts, stones, and all manner of weapons on every hand, he was presently dispatched. This penalty was incurred by stealing any thing out of the camp; by giving false evidence; by abandoning their post in battle; by pretending falsely to have done some great exploit, out of hopes of a reward; or by fighting without the General's order; by losing their weapons; or aggravating a misdemeanour less than either of these, by repeating it three times.

If a great number had offended, as running from their colours, mutinying, or other general crimes, the common way of proceeding to justice was by *decimation,* or putting all the criminals names together in a shield or vessel, and drawing them out by lot; every tenth man being to die without reprieve, commonly in the manner just now described; so that by this means, though all were not alike sensible of the punishment, yet all were frighted into obedience. In later authors we meet sometimes with *vicesimatio,* and *centesimatio,* which words sufficiently explain themselves.

The punishments which reached no farther than their credit, by exposing them to public shame, were such as these; degrading them from a higher station to a lower; giving them a set quantity of barley instead of wheat; ungirding them, and taking away their belt; making them stand all supper-time, while the rest sat down, and such other little marks of disgrace.

Besides these, A. Gellius has recorded a very singular punishment, by letting the delinquent blood. His judgment concerning the original of this custom is to this purpose: He fancies that, in elder times, this used to be prescribed to the drowsy and sluggish soldiers rather as a medicinal remedy than a punishment; and that in after-ages it might have been applied in most other faults, upon this consideration, That all those who did not observe the rules of their discipline were to be looked upon as stupid or mad. And for persons in those conditions, blood-letting is commonly succesful (*a*); but because this reason is hardly satisfactory, the great critic Muretus has obliged us with another, believing the design of this custom to have been, That those mean-spirited wretches might lose that blood with shame and disgrace which they dared not spend nobly and honourably in the service of their country (*b*).

As for the punishments relating to their goods and money, the Tribunes might for several faults impose a fine on the delinquents, and force them to give a pledge, in case they could not pay. Sometimes too they stopped the stipend; whence they were called by way of reproach, *Ære diruti*.

(*a*) *A. Gell.* l. 10. c. 8.   (*b*) *Muret. Varior. Lect.* l. 13. c. 20.

CHAP. XVI.

Of the MILITARY REWARDS.

BUT the encouragements of valour and industry were much more considerable than the proceedings against the contrary vices. The most considerable (not to speak of the promotion from one station to the other, nor of the occasional *donatives* in money, distinguished by this name from the largesses bestowed on the common people, and termed *congiaria*, were first the *dona imperatoria*, such as

The *hasta pura*, a fine spear of wood without any iron on it: such an one as Virgil has given Sylvius in the sixth of the Æneids: 760.

Illa

Ille (vides?) pura juvenis qui nititur hasta.

This present was usually bestowed on him who in some little skirmish had killed an enemy, engaging him hand to hand. They were reckoned very honourable gifts, and the gods are commonly represented with such spears on the old coins. Mr Walker derives hence the custom of our great officers carrying white rods or staves, as ensigns of their places.

The *armillæ*, a sort of bracelets, given upon account of some eminent service, only to such as were born Romans.

The *torques*, golden and silver collars, wreathed with curious art and beauty. Pliny attributes the golden collars to the auxiliaries, and the silver to the Roman soldiers; but this is supposed to be a mistake.

The *phaleræ*, commonly thought to be a suit of rich trappings for a horse; but because we find them bestowed on the foot as well as the cavalry, we may rather suppose them to have been golden chains of a like nature with the *torques*, only that they seem to have hung down to the breast, whereas the other went only round the neck. The hopes of these two last are particularly urged, among the advantages of a military life, by Juvenal, Sat. xvi. 60.

Ut læti phaleris omnes, & torquibus omnes.

The *vexilla*, a sort of banners of different colours, worked in silk, or other curious materials, such as Augustus bestowed on Agrippa, after he had won the sea-fight at Actium.

Next to these were the several coronets, received on various occasions. As,

Corona civica, given to any soldier that had saved the life of a Roman citizen in an engagement. This was reckoned more honourable than any other crown, tho' composed of no better materials than oaken boughs. Virgil calls it *civilis quercus*, Æn. vi. 772.

Atque umbrata gerunt civili tempora quercu.

Plutarch has guessed very happily at the reason why the branches of this tree should be made use of before all others: For the oaken wreath, says he, being otherwise sacred to Jupiter, the great guardian of their city, they might therefore think it the most proper ornament for him who had preserved a citizen. Besides, the oak may very well claim the preference in this case; because in the primitive times that tree alone was thought almost sufficient for the preserving of man's life: Its acorns were the principal diet of the old mortals, and the honey,

ney, which was commonly found there, presented them with a very pleasant liquor (*a*).

It was a particular honour conferred on the persons who had merited this crown, that, when they came to any of the public shows, the whole company, as well Senate as people, should signify their respect, by rising up when they saw them enter; and that they should take their seat on these occasions among the Senators; being also excused from all troublesome duties and services in their own persons, and procuring the same immunity for their father and grandfather by his side (*b*).

Corona muralis, given to him who first scaled the walls of a city in a general assault; and therefore in the shape of it there was some allusion made to the figure of a wall.

Corona castrensis, or *vallaris*, the reward of him who had first forced the enemy's entrenchments.

Corona navalis, bestowed on such as had signalized their valour in an engagement at sea; being set round with figures like the beaks of ships.

———*Cui belli insigne superbum*
Tempora navali fulgent rostrata corona. Vir. Æn. viii. 684.

Lipsius fancies the *corona navalis* and the *rostrata* to have been distinct species, though they are generally believed to be the same kind of crown.

Coronæ obsidionalis: This was not, like the rest, given by the General to the soldiers, but presented by the common consent of the soldiers to the General, when he had delivered the Romans or their allies from a siege. It was composed of the grass growing in the besieged place.

Corona triumphalis, made with wreaths of laurel, and proper only to such Generals as had the honour of a triumph. In after-ages this was changed for gold *, and not restrained only to those that actually triumphed, but presented on several other accounts, as commonly by the foreign states and provinces to their patrons and benefactors. Several of the other crowns too are thought to have been of gold; as the *castrensis*, the *mural*, and the *naval*.

* *Aureum coronarium.*

Besides these, we meet with the *corona aurea*, often bestowed on soldiers without any other additional term.

And

(*a*) Plutarch. *in Coriolan.*   (*b*) Plin. lib. 16., cap. 4.

And Dion Cassius mentions a particular sort of coronet made of olive boughs, and bestowed, like the rest, in consideration of some signal act of valour.

Lipsius believes these to have succeeded in the room of the golden crowns, after they were laid aside.

The most remarkable person upon record in history for obtaining a great number of these rewards was one C. Siccius (or Sicinus) Dentatus; who had received, in the time of his military service, eight crowns of gold, fourteen civic crowns, three mural, eighty-three golden *torques*, sixty golden *armillæ*, eighteen *hastæ puræ*, and seventy-five *phaleræ* (a).

But far greater honours were conferred on the victorious Generals, some of which were usually decreed them in their absence, others at their arrival in the city.

Of the former kind were the *salutatio imperatoris*, and the *supplication*; of the latter, the *ovation* and the *triumph*.

The first of these was no more than the saluting the Commander in Chief with the title of *Imperator*, upon account of any remarkable success; which title was decreed him by the Senate at Rome, after it had been given him by joint acclamations of the soldiers in the camp.

The *supplicatio* was a solemn procession to the temple of the gods, to return thanks for any victory.

After obtaining any such remarkable advantage, the General commonly gave the Senate an account of the exploit by letters wreathed about with laurel *, in which, after the account of his success, he desired the favour of a *supplication*, or public thanksgiving.

* *Literæ Laureatæ.*

This being granted for a set number of days, the Senate went in a solemn manner to the chief temples, and assisted at the sacrifices proper to the occasion; holding a feast in the temples to the honour of the respective deities. Hence Servius explains that of Virgil,

———*Simul Divûm Templis indicit Honorem*; Æn. i. 636.

as alluding to a solemn supplication.

In the mean time the whole body of the commonalty kept holy-day, and frequented the religious assemblies; giving thanks for the late success, and imploring a long continuance of the divine favour and assistance.

Octavius

(a) *A. Gell.* lib. 2, cap. 11. *Valer. Max.* &c.

Octavius Cæsar, together with the Consuls, Hirtius and Panſa, upon their raiſing the ſiege of Mutina, were honoured with a ſupplication fifty days long.

At laſt this ceremony became ridiculous; as appears from the *ſupplications* decreed Nero for the murder of his mother, and for the fruitfulneſs of Poppæa, of which we read in Tacitus.

The ovation ſome fancy to have derived its name from ſhouting *evion!* to Bacchus; but the true original is *ovis*, the ſheep which was uſually offered in this proceſſion, as an ox in the triumph. The ſhow generally began at the Albanian mountain, whence the General, with his retinue, made his entry into the city: He went on foot with many flutes, or pipes, ſounding in concert as he paſſed along, wearing a garment of myrtle as a token of peace, with an aſpect rather raiſing love and reſpect than fear. A. Gellius informs us, that this honour was then conferred on the victor, when either the war had not been proclaimed in due method, or not undertaken againſt a lawful enemy, and on a juſt account; or when the enemy was but mean and inconſiderable (*a*). But Plutarch has delivered his judgment in a different manner: He believes, that heretofore the difference betwixt the *ovation* and the *triumph* was not taken from the greatneſs of the atchievments, but from the manner of performing them: For they who, having fought a ſet battle, and ſlain a great number of the enemy, returned victors, led that martial, and (as it were) cruel proceſſion of the triumph. But thoſe who without force, by benevolence and civil behaviour, had done the buſineſs, and prevented the ſhedding of human blood; to theſe commanders cuſtom gave the honour of this peaceable ovation. For a pipe is the enſign or badge of peace, and myrtle, the tree of Venus, who, beyond any other deities, has an extreme averſion to violence and war (*b*).

But whatever other difference there lay between theſe two ſolemnities, we are aſſured the triumph was much the more noble and ſplendid proceſſion. None were capable of this honour but Dictators, Conſuls, or Prætors; tho' we find ſome examples of different practice; as particularly in Pompey the Great, who had a triumph decreed him, while he was only a Roman Knight, and had not reached the Senatorian age (*c*).

A regular account of the proceedings, at one of theſe ſolemnities, will give us a better knowledge of the matter, than a
larger

(*a*) *Noct. Att.* l. 5. c. 6.   (*b*) *Plut. in Marcell.*   (*c*) *Plut. in Pomp.*

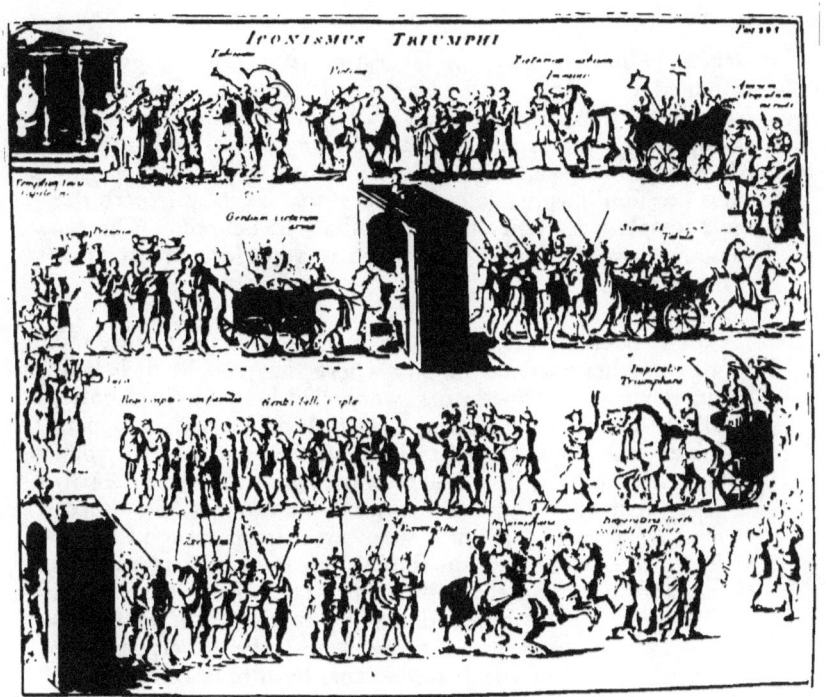

larger difquifition about the feveral parts and appendages that belonged to it. And this the excellent Plutarch has favoured us with, in his defcription of Paulus Æmilius's triumph after the taking King Perfeus prifoner, and putting a final period to the Macedonian empire. This muft be owned to be the moft glorious occafion imaginable; and therefore we may expect the moft complete relation that can poffibly be defired. The ceremony then of Æmilius's triumph was performed after this manner:

"The people erected fcaffolds in the forum and circus, and all the other parts of the city where they could beft behold the pomp. The fpectators were clad in white garments; all the temples were open, and full of garlands and perfumes; the ways cleared and cleanfed by a great many officers and tipftaffs, that drove away fuch as thronged the paffage, or ftraggled up and down. This triumph lafted three days: On the firft, which was fcarce long enough for the fight, were to be feen the ftatues, pictures, and images of an extraordinary bignefs, which were taken from the enemy, drawn upon feven hundred and fifty chariots. On the fecond was carried, in a great many wains, the faireft and the richeft armour of the Macedonians, both of brafs and fteel, all newly furbifhed and glittering; which, although piled up with the greateft art and order, yet feemed to be tumbled on heaps carelefsly and by chance; helmets were thrown on fhields, coats of mail upon greaves, Cretan targets, and Thracian bucklers and quivers of arrows lay huddled among the horfes bitts; and through thefe appeared the points of naked fwords, intermixed with long fpears. All thefe arms were tied together with fuch a juft liberty, that they knocked againft one another as they were drawn along, and made a harfh and terrible noife; fo that the very fpoils of the conquered could not be held without dread. After thefe waggons loaded with armour, there followed three thoufand men, who carried the filver that was coined in feven hundred and fifty veffels, each of which weighed three talents, and was carried by four men. Others brought filver bowls, and goblets, and cups, all difpofed in fuch order, as to make the beft fhow, and all valuable, as well for their bignefs as the thicknefs of their engraved work. On the third day, early in the morning, firft came the trumpeters, who did not found as they were wont in a proceffion or fo-

" lemn entry, but such a charge as the Romans use when they
" encourage their soldiers to fight. Next followed young
" men girt about with girdles curiously wrought, who led
" to the sacrifice 120 stalled oxen, with their horns gilded,
" and their heads adorned with ribbands and garlands; and
" with these were boys that carried platters of silver and
" gold. After this was brought the gold coin, which was
" divided into vessels that weighed three talents, like to those
" that contained the silver; they were in number fourscore,
" wanting three. These were followed by those that brought
" the consecrated bowl, which Æmilius caused to be made, that
" weighed ten talents, and was all beset with precious stones:
" Then were exposed to view the cups of Antigonus and Se-
" leucus, and such as were made after the fashion invented by
" Thericles, and all the gold plate that was used at Perseus's
" table. Next to these came Perseus's chariot, in the which
" his armour was placed, and on that his diadem: And after
" a little intermission, the King's children were led captives,
" and with them a train of nurses, masters, and governors;
" who all wept, and stretched forth their hands to the specta-
" tors, and taught the little infants to beg and intreat their
" compassion. There were two sons and a daughter, who,
" by reason of their tender age, were altogether insensible of
" the greatness of their misery; which insensibility of their
" condition rendered it much more deplorable, insomuch that
" Perseus himself was scarce regarded as he went along, whilst
" pity had fixed the eyes of the Romans upon the infants, and
" many of them could not forbear tears: All beheld the sight
" with a mixture of sorrow and joy, until the children were
" past. After his children and their attendants came Perseus
" himself, clad all in black, and wearing slippers, after the
" fashion of his country: He looked like one altogether asto-
" nished and deprived of reason, through the greatness of his
" misfortunes. Next followed a great company of his friends
" and familiars, whose countenances were disfigured with
" grief, and who testified to all that beheld them by their
" tears, and their continual looking upon Perseus, that it was
" his hard fortune they so much lamented, and that they were
" regardless of their own.—After these were carried four hun-
" dred crowns, all made of gold, and sent from the cities by
" their respective ambassadors to Æmilius, as a reward due to
" his valour. Then he himself came, seated on a chariot mag-
" nificently adorned, (a man worthy to be beheld, even with-

" out

" out thefe enfigns of power;) he was clad in a garment of
" purple interwoven with gold, and held out a laurel branch
" in his right-hand. All the army, in like manner, with boughs
" of laurel in their hands, and divided into bands and compa-
" nies, followed the chariot of their commander; some singing
" odes (according to the usual custom) mingled with raillery;
" others, songs of triumph, and the praises of Æmilius's deeds,
" who was admired and accounted happy by all men, yet un-
" envied by every one that was good."

There was one remarkable addition to this solemnity, which, though it seldom happened, yet ought not to escape our notice: This was when the Roman General had, in any engagement, killed the chief commander of the enemy with his own hands: For then, in the triumphal pomp, the arms of the slain Captain were carried before the victor, decently hanging on the stock of an oak, and so composing a trophy. In this manner the procession went on to the temple of Jupiter Feretrius (so called *a feriendo*) and the General making a formal dedication of his spoils (the *spolia opima*, as they termed them) hung them up in the temple. The first, who performed this gallant piece of religion was Romulus, when he had slain A-cron King of the Cæninenses; the second Cornelius Cossus, with the arms of Tolumnius, a General of the Veientes; the third and last M. Marcellus, with those taken from Viridomarus, King of the Gauls; whence Virgil says of him, Æn. vi. 859:

Tertiaque arma patri suspendet capta quirino.

Where quirino must be understood only as an epithet applied to Jupiter, as denoting his authority and power in war; as the same word is attributed to Janus, by Horace and Suetonius. Therefore Servius is most certainly guilty of a mistake, when he tells us, that the first spoils of this nature were, according to Numa's laws, to be presented to Jupiter; the second to Mars; and the third to Quirinus, or Romulus; for that decree of Numa only took place, if the same person had the good fortune to take these spoils three times; but we are assured, that not only Romulus, but Cossus and Marcellus too, all made the dedication to Jupiter.

The admirers of the Roman magnificence will be infinitely pleased with the relation already given from Plutarch of the triumphal pomp; while others, who fancy that people to have been possess'd with a strange measure of vain-glory, and attribute all their military state and grandeur to ambitious ostentation, will be much better satisfied with the satirical account which Juvenal furnishes us with in his tenth Satyr. He is saying, that Democritus found subject enough for a continual fit of laughter, in places where there was no such formal pageantry, as is commonly to be seen in Rome: And then he goes on, 36.

> *Quid, si vidisset Prætorem curribus altis*
> *Extantem, & medio sublimem in pulvere Circi.*
> *In tunica Jovis, & pictæ Sarrana ferentem*
> *Ex humeris aulæa togæ, magnæque coronæ*
> *Tantum orbem, quanto cervix non sufficit ulla?*
> *Quippa tenet sudans hanc publicus, & sibi Consul*
> *Ne placeat, curru servus portatur eodem.*
> *Da nunc & volucrem, Sceptro quæ surgit eburno,*
> *Illinc cornicines, hinc præcedentia longi*
> *Agminis officia, & niveos ad fræna Quirites,*
> *Defossa in loculis, quos sportula fecit amicos.*

What had he done, had he beheld on high
Our Consul seated in mock-majesty:
His chariot rolling o'er the dusty place,
While with dumb pride, and a set formal face,
He moves in the dull ceremonial track,
With Jove's embroider'd coat upon his back:
A suit of hangings had not more opprest
His shoulders, than a long laborious vest.
A heavy gewgaw (call'd a crown) that spread
About his temples, drown'd his narrow head;
And would have crush'd it with the massy freight,
But that a sweating slave sustain'd the weight;
A slave in the same chariot seen to ride,
To mortify the mighty madman's pride.
And now the imperial eagle rais'd on high,
With golden beak (the mark of majesty)
Trumpets before, and on the left and right
A cavalcade of nobles all in white:
In their own natures false and flattering tribes;
But made his friends by places and by bribes.

[MR DRYDEN.

CHAP. XVII.

The ROMAN *Way of declaring War, and of making Leagues.*

THE Romans used abundance of superstition in entering upon any hostility, or closing in any league or confederacy: The public ministers, who performed the ceremonial part of both these, were the Feciales, or heralds, already described among the priests; nothing remains but the ceremonies themselves, which were of this nature. When any neighbouring State had given sufficient reason for the Senate to suspect a design of breaking with them; or had offered any violence or injustice to the subjects of Rome, which was enough to give them the repute of enemies; one of the Feciales, chosen out of the college upon this occasion, and habited in the vest belonging to his order, together with his other ensigns and habiliments, set forward for the enemy's country. As soon as he reached the confines, he pronounced a formal declaration of the cause of his arrival, calling all the gods to witness, and imprecating the divine vengeance on himself and his country, if his reasons were not just. When he came to the chief city of the enemy, he again repeated the same declaration, with some addition, and withal desired satisfaction. If they delivered into his power the authors of the injury, or gave hostages for security, he returned satisfied to Rome; if otherwise, they desired time to consider; he went away for ten days, and then came again to hear their resolution. And this he did, in some cases, three times: But, if nothing was done toward an accommodation in about thirty days, he declared that the Romans would endeavour to assert their right by their arms. After this the herald was obliged to return, and to make a true report of his embassy before the Senate, assuring them of the legality of the war which they were now consulting to undertake; and was then again dispatched to perform the last part of the ceremony, which was to throw a spear into, (or towards the enemy's country) in token of defiance, and, as a summons to war, pronouncing at the same time a set form of words to the like purpose.

As to the making of leagues, Polybius acquaints us, that the ratification of the articles of an agreement, between the Romans and the Carthaginians, was performed in this manner: The Carthaginians swore by the god of their country; and the Romans, after their ancient custom, swore by *a stone*, and then by Mars. They swore by a stone thus: The herald who took the oath, having sworn in behalf of the public, takes up a stone, and then pronounces these words:

"If I keep my faith, may the gods vouchsafe their assistance, and give me success; if, on the contrary, I violate it, then may the other party be entirely safe, and preserved in their country, in their laws, in their possessions, and, in a word, in all their rights and liberties; and may I perish and fall alone, as now this stone does;" and then he lets the stone fall out of his hands (a).

Livy's account of the like ceremony is something more particular, yet differs little in substance; only that he says the herald's concluding clause was, "otherwise may Jove strike the Roman people as I do this hog;" and accordingly he killed a hog that stood ready by with the stone which he held in his hand. This last opinion is confirmed by the authority of Virgil, when, speaking of the Romans and Albanians, he says, Æn. viii. 641:

———*Et cæsa jungebant fœdera porca.*

And perhaps both these customs might be in use in different times.

(*a*) *Polyb.* lib. 3.

CHAP.

CHAP. XVIII.

The Roman *Method of treating the People they conquered; with the Constitution of the* Coloniæ, Municipia, Præfecturæ, *and* Provinces.

THE civil usage and extraordinary favours, with which the Romans obliged the poor conquered nations, has been reasonably esteemed one of the prime causes of the extent of their dominions, and the establishment of their command: Yet when they saw occasion, they were not to seek in severer methods, such as the seizing on the greatest part of the enemy's land, or removing the natives to another soil. If a State or people had been necessitated to surrender themselves into the Roman power, they used *sub jugum mitti*, to be made pass under a yoke, in token of subjection: For this purpose they set up two spears, and laying a third cross them at the top, ordered those who had surrendered their persons to go under them without arms or belts. Those who could not be brought to deliver themselves up, but were taken by force, as they suffered several penalties, so very often *sub corona venibant*, they were publicly sold for slaves. Where by *corona* some understand a sort of chaplets which they put about the captives heads for distinction; others would have it mean the ring of the Roman soldiers, who stood round the captives while they were exposed to sale. A. Gellius prefers the former reason (*a*).

The several forms of government, which the Romans established in their conquests, are very well worth our knowledge, and are seldom rightly distinguished; we may take notice of these four: Colonies, Municipia, Præfecturæ, and Provinces.

Colonies (properly speaking) were states, or communities, where the chief part of the inhabitants had been transplanted from Rome: And tho' mingled with the natives who had been left in the conquered place, yet obtained the whole power and authority in the administration of affairs. One great advantage of this institution was, that by this means the veteran
soldiers,

(*a*) Lib. 7. cap. 4.

soldiers, who had served out their legal time, and had spent their vigour in the honour and defence of their country, might be favoured with a very agreeable reward, by forming them into a colony, and sending them where they might be masters of large possessions, and so lead the remainder of their days in ease and plenty.

Municipia were commonly corporations, or enfranchised places, where the natives were allowed the use of their old laws and constitutions, and at the same time honoured with the privilege of Roman citizens. But then this privilege, in some of the municipia, reached no farther than the bare title, without the proper rights of citizens; such as voting in the assemblies, bearing offices in the city, and the like. The former honour gave them the name of *Cives Romani*, the other only of *Romani*, as P. Manutius with his usual exactness has distinguished (*a*). Of this latter sort, the first example were the Cærites, a people of Tuscany, who, preserving the sacred relics of the Romans when the Gauls had taken the city, were afterwards dignified with the name of *Roman* citizens; but not admitted into any part of the public administration. Hence the Censors tables, where they entered the names of such persons as for some misdemeanour were to lose their right of suffrage, had the name of *Cærites Tabulæ* (*b*).

The *Præfecturæ* were certain towns in Italy, whose inhabitants had the name of the *Roman* citizens; but were neither allowed to enjoy their own laws nor magistrates, being governed by annual Præfects sent from Rome. These were generally such places as were either suspected, or had some way or other incurred the displeasure of the Roman state; this being accounted the hardest condition that was imposed on any people of Italy (*c*).

The differences between the proper citizens of Rome and the inhabitants of municipia, colonies, and præfecturæ, may be thus in short summed up: The first and highest order were registered in the *census*, had the right of suffrage, and of bearing honours; were assessed in the poll-tax, served in the legions, used the Roman laws and religion, and were called *Quirites* and *Populus Romanus*. The *Municipes* were allowed the four first of these marks, and were denied the four last. The *Coloni* were in these three respects like the true citizens, that

(*a*) *De Civitat.* Rom. p. 29.   (*b*) *A. Gell.* lib. 16. cap. 13.
(*c*) *Calv. Lexicon. Juridic. in voce.*

that they used the Roman laws and religion, and served in the legions; but they were debarred the other five conditions. The people in the Præfecturæ had the hardest measure of all; being obliged to submit to the Roman laws, and yet enjoying no farther privilege of citizens (*a*).

All other cities and states in Italy, which were neither Colonies, Municipia, nor Præfecturæ, had the name of *Fœderatæ Civitates*, enjoying entirely their own customs, and forms of government, without the least alteration, and only joined in confederacy with the Romans, upon such terms as had been adjusted between them (*b*).

The provinces were foreign countries, of larger extent, which, upon the entire reducing them under the Roman dominions, were new-modelled according to the pleasure of the conquerors, and subjected to the command of annual governors sent from Rome, being commonly assigned such taxes and contributions as the Senate thought fit to demand. But because the several towns and communities in every country did not behave themselves in the same manner toward the Romans, some professing more friendship, and a desire of union and agreement; while others were more obstinate and refractory, and unwilling to part with their own liberty upon any terms; therefore, to reward those people who deserved well at their hands, they allowed some places the use of their own constitutions in many respects, and sometimes excused the inhabitants from paying tribute; whence they were termed *Immunes*, in opposition to the *Vectigales*.

The tribute exacted from the provinces was of two sorts, either certain or uncertain. The certain tribute, or *stipendium*, was either a set sum of money to be collected by the provincial Quæstor, which they called *pecunia ordinaria*, or else a subsidy raised on the provincials for particular occasions; such as the maintaining of so many soldiers, the rigging out and paying such a number of vessels, and the like, termed *pecunia extraordinaria*.

The uncertain tribute consisted of what they called, *portorium, scriptura*, and *decuma*. The *portorium* was a duty imposed upon all goods and wares imported and exported.

The *scriptura* was a tax laid upon pastures and cattle.

(*a*) P. Manut. de Civ. Rom. p. 30. (*b*) Ibid.

The *decuma* was the quantity of corn which the farmers were obliged to pay to the Roman State commonly the tenth part of their crop. But besides this, which they properly termed *frumentum decumanum*, and which was farmed by the publicans, hence called *decumani*, there was the *frumantum emptum*, and *frumentum æstimatum*, both taken up in the provinces. The *frumentum emptum* was of two sorts, either *decumanum*, or *imperatum ;* the former was another tenth, paid upon the consideration of such a sum as the Senate had determined to be the price of it, who rated it so much a bushel at their pleasure. The *frumentum imperatum* was a quantity of corn equally exacted of the provincial farmers after the two tenths, at such a price as the two magistrates pleased to give. *Frumentum æstimatum,* was a corn tax required of the chief magistrate of the province for his private use, and the occasions of his family. This was commonly compounded for in money, and on that account, took its name *ab æstimando,* from rating it at such a sum of money.

Besides all these, Sigonius mentions *frumentum honorarium,* upon the authority of Cicero, in his oration against Piso : But perhaps Cicero, in that place, does not restrain the *honorarium* to corn, but may mean, in general, the present usually made to provincial governors, soon after their entrance on their office.

After Augustus had made a division of the provinces between himself and the people, the annual taxes, paid by the provinces under the Emperor, were called *stipendia,* and those that were gathered in the people's provinces, *tributa* (*a*).

(*a*) *Calvin.* Lexicon. Jurid. *in Tributa.*

CHAP.

CHAP. XIX.

The ROMAN *Way of taking Towns; with the most remarkable Inventions and Engines made use of in their Sieges.*

BEFORE we inquire into this subject, a very memorable custom presents itself to our notice, which was practised almost as soon as the Roman army invested any town; and that was the *evocatio deorum tutelarium,* or inviting out the guardian deities: The reason of which seems to have been, either because they thought it impossible to force any place, while it enjoyed such powerful defenders; or else, because they accounted it a most heinous act of impiety to act in hostility against the persons of the gods. This custom is described at large by Macrobius in his Saturnalia, lib. 3. cap. 9.

The Romans were seldom desirous of attempting any town by way of siege, because they thought it would scarce answer the expence and incommodity of the method; so that this was generally their last hopes; and in all their great wars there are very few examples of any long leaguers undertook by them. The means by which they possessed themselves of any important places, were commonly either by storm, or immediate surrendery. If they took a town by storm, it was either by open force, or by stratagem. In the former, they made their attacks without battering the walls, and were only said, *aggredi urbem cum corona,* " to begirt a town;" because they drew their whole army round the walls, and fell on all the quarters at once. If this way was ineffectual, they battered down the walls with their rams and other engines. Sometimes they mined, and entered the town under-ground: Sometimes, that they might engage with the enemy upon equal terms, they built wooden towers, or raised mounts to the height of the walls, from whence they might gall and molest them within their works. The besieged were in most danger in the first case upon a general assault; for their walls were to be made good in all places at once; and it fell out many times, that there were not men enough to supply and relieve all the parts; and if they had a sufficient number of men, yet all perhaps were not of equal courage; and if any gave ground, the whole

whole town was in a great hazard of being lost: So that the Romans oftentimes carried very confiderable places at one ftorm. But if they battered the walls with engines, they were under fome difadvantage, their quarters being of neceffity to be extended, fo that they muft be thinner and weaker in fome places than in others, and unable to make a ftout oppofition againft any confiderable fally. Befides, the befieged were not at a lofs for ways of defeating their ftratagems; as, they eluded the force of their mines by countermining, or by difturbing them in their works; particularly putting oil and feathers, with other ftinking ftuff, into barrels of wood; then fetting them on fire, they tumbled them among the Romans, that the noifomnefs of the ftench might force them to quit their ftations. Their towers of wood, their rams, and other engines, they commonly fet on fire, and deftroyed; and then for the mounts which were raifed againft the walls, they ufed, by digging underneath, to fteal away the earth, and loofen the foundations of the mount till it fell to the ground.

Upon this account, the Romans (as was before obferved) much preferred the fudden and brifk way of attacking a place; and if they did not carry it in a little time, they frequently raifed the fiege, and profecuted the war by other means. As Scipio, in his African expedition, having affaulted Utica without fuccefs, changed his refolution, drew off his men from the place, and addreffed himfelf wholly to bring the Carthaginian army to an engagement. And therefore, though fometimes they continued a tedious fiege, as at Veii, Carthage, and Jerufalem, yet generally they were much more defirous of drawing the enemy to a battle; for by defeating an army they many times got a whole kingdom in a day, whereas an obftinate town has coft them feveral years.

See Machiavel's Art of WAR, Book II.

The inventions and engines, which the Romans made ufe of in their fieges, were very numerous, and the knowledge of them is but of little fervice at prefent; however, we may take a fhort view of the moft confiderable of them, which moft frequently occur in Cæfar, and other hiftorians: Thefe are the *turres mobiles*, the *teftudines*, the *mufculus*, the *vineæ*, and the *plutei*, together with the *aries*, the *balifta*, the *catapulta*, and the *fcorpio*.

The

The *turres mobiles*, or moveable turrets, were of two sorts, the lesser and the greater: The lesser sort were about sixty cubits high, and the square sides seventeen cubits broad; they had five or six, and sometimes ten stories, or divisions, every division being made open on all sides. The greater turret was 120 cubits high, 23 cubits square; containing sometimes fifteen, sometimes twenty divisions. They were of very great use in making approaches to the walls, the divisions being able to carry soldiers with engines, ladders, casting-bridges, and other necessaries. The wheels, on which they went, were contrived to be within the planks, to defend them from the enemy, and the men, who were to drive them forward, stood behind, where they were most secure; the soldiers in the inside were protected by raw hides, which were thrown over the turret in such places as were most exposed.

The *testudo* was properly a figure which the soldiers cast themselves into, so that their targets should close all together above their heads, and defend them from the missive weapons of the enemy; as if we suppose the first rank to have stood upright on their feet, and the rest to have stooped lower and lower by degrees, till the last rank kneeled down upon their knees; so that every rank covering with their target the heads of all in the rank before them, they represented a tortoise-shell, or a sort of pent-house. This was used as well in field-battles as in sieges. But besides this, the Romans called, in general, all their covered defensive engines *testudines*: Among which, those, which most properly obtained the name, seem to have been almost of an oval figure, composed of boards, and wattled up at the sides with wickers, serving for the conveyance of the soldiers near the walls, on several occasions; they run upon wheels, and so were distinguished from the *vineæ*, with which they are sometimes confounded.

The *musculus* is conceived to have been much of the same nature as the *testudines*; but it seems to have been of a smaller size, and composed of stronger materials, being exposed a much longer time to the force of the enemy; for in these *musculi* the pioneers were sent to the very walls, where they were to continue, while with their *dolabræ*, or pick-axes, and other instruments, they endeavoured to undermine the foundations. Cæsar has described the *musculus* at large in his second book of the civil wars.

The *vineæ* were composed of wicker hurdles laid for a roof on the top of posts, which the soldiers, who went under it for shelter, bore up with their hands. Some will have them to have been contrived with a double roof; the first and lower roof of planks, and the upper roof of hurdles, to break the force of any blow without disordering the machine.

The *plutei* consisted of the same materials as the former, but were of a much different figure, being shaped like an arched sort of waggon; and having three wheels, so conveniently placed, that the machine would move either way with equal ease. They were put much to the same use as the *musculi*.

The engines hitherto described were primarily intended for the defence of the soldiers; the offensive are yet behind. Of these the most celebrated, and which only deserves a particular description, was the *aries*, or ram : This was of two sorts, the one rude and plain, the other artificial and compound. The former seems to have been no more than a great beam which the soldiers bore on their arms and shoulders, and with one end of it by main force assailed the wall. The compound ram is thus described by Josephus : " The ram," says he, " is a
" vast long beam, like the mast of a ship, strengthened at one
" end with a head of iron, something resembling that of a
" ram, whence it took its name. This is hung by the midst
" with ropes to another beam, which lies cross a couple of
" posts, and hanging thus equally balanced, it is by a great
" number of men violently thrust forward and drawn back-
" ward, and so shakes the wall with its iron head. Nor is
" there any tower or wall so thick or strong, that, after the
" first assault of the ram, can afterwards resist its force in the
" repeated assaults (*a*)."

Plutarch informs us, that Mark Antony, in the Parthian war, made use of a ram of fourscore feet long : And Vitruvius tells us, that they were sometimes 106, sometimes 120 feet in length; and to this perhaps the force and strength of the engine was in a great measure owing. The ram was managed at one time by a whole century, or order of soldiers; and they, being spent, were seconded by another century; so that it played continually without any intermission, being usually covered with a *vinea*, to protect it from the attempts of the enemy.

As

(*a*) *Flav. Joseph. de Excidio Hierosolym.* lib. 3.

As for the other engines, which served not for such great uses, and are not so celebrated in authors, a mechanical description of them would be vexatious as well as needless: only it may in short be observed, that the *balista* was always employed in throwing great stones, the *catapulta* in casting the larger sort of darts and spears, and the *scorpio* in sending the lesser darts and arrows.

CHAP. XX.

The Naval Affairs of the ROMANS.

THE Romans, though their city was seated very conveniently for maritime affairs, not being above fifteen miles distant from the Tyrrhenian sea, and having the river Tyber running through it, capable of receiving the smaller vessels, yet seem to have wholly neglected all naval concerns for many years after the building of Rome. And some are willing to assign this as one of the main causes which preserved that State so long in its primitive innocence and integrity, free from all those corruptionns which an intercourse with foreigners might probably have brought into fashion. However Dionysius assures us, that Ancus Martius built Ostia at the mouth of the Tyber for a port, that the city might by this means be supplied with the commodities of the neighbouring nations (*a*). And it appears from the reasons of the Tarentine war agreed upon by all historians, that the Romans in that age had a fleet at sea. Yet Polybius expressly maintains, that the first time they ever adventured to sea was in the first Punic war (*b*); but he must either mean this only ships of war, or else contradict himself: For in another part of his works, giving up a transcript of some articles agreed on between the Romans and the Carthaginians in the consulship of M. Brutus and Horatius, soon after the expulsion of the royal family, one of the articles is to this effect, " That the *Romans*, and the allies " of the *Romans* shall not navigate beyond the *Fair Promon-* " *tory*, unless constrained by weather, or an enemy, &c." And after this, in two other treaties which he has presented us with, there are several clauses to the same purpose (*c*).

But

(*a*) *Dionys. Halic.* lib. 3.   (*b*) Lib. 1.   (*c*) *Polyb.* lib. 3.

But howsoever these matters are to be adjusted, we are assured, that about the year of the city 492 (*a*), the Romans observing that the coast of Italy lay exposed to the depredations of the Carthaginian fleet, which often made descents upon them, and considering withal that the war was likely to last, they determined to render themselves masters of a naval army. So wonderful was the bravery and resolution of that people in enterprizes of the greatest hazard and moment; that having hitherto scarce dreamed of navigation, they should, at one heat, resolve on so adventurous an expedition, and make the first proof of their skill in a naval battle with the Carthaginians, who had held the dominion of the sea uncontested, derived down to them from their ancestors. Nay, so utterly ignorant were the Romans in the art of ship-building, that it would have been almost impossible for them to have put their design in effect, had not fortune, who always espoused their cause, by a mere accident instructed them in the method. For a Carthaginian galley, which was out a-cruising, venturing too near the shore, chanced to be stranded, and before they could get her off, the Romans, intercepting them, took her; and by the model of this galley they built their first fleet. But their way of instructing their seamen in the use of the oar is no less remarkable, wherein they proceeded after this manner: They caused banks to be contrived on the shore in the same fashion and order as they were to be in their gallies, and placing their men with their oars upon the banks, there they exercised them: An officer, for that purpose, being seated in the midst, who, by signs with his hand, instructed them how at once and altogether they were to dip their oars, and how in like manner to recover them out of the water; and by this means they became acquainted with the management of the oar. But in a little time, finding their vessels were not built with extraordinary art, and consequently proved somewhat unweildy in working, it came into their heads to remedy this defect, by contriving some new invention, which might be of use to them in fight. And then it was that they devised the famous machine called the *corvus*; which was framed after the following manner: They erected on the prow of their vessels a round piece of timber, of about a foot and a half diameter, and about twelve feet long; on

the

(*a*) *Casaubon.* Chronolog. ad *Polyb.*

the top whereof they had a block or pulley. Round this piece of timber they laid a stage, or platform of boards, four feet broad, and about eighteen feet long; which was well framed, and fastened with iron. The entrance was longways, and it moved about the aforesaid upright piece of timber, as on a spindle, and could be hoisted up within six feet of the top: About this a sort of parapet, knee high, which was defended with upright bars of iron, sharpened at the end; towards the top whereof there was a ring: Through this ring, fastening a rope, by the help of the pulley, they hoisted or lowered the engine at pleasure; and so with it attacked the enemy's vessels, sometimes on their bow, and sometimes on their broad-side, as occasion best served. When they had grappled the enemy with those iron spikes, if they happened to swing broad-side to broad-side, then they entered from all parts; but in case they attacked them on the bow, they entered two and two by the help of this machine, the foremost defending the fore-part, and those that followed the flanks, keeping the boss of their bucklers level with the top of the parapet.

To this purpose Polybius (according to the late most excellent version) gives us an account of the first warlike preparations which the Romans made by sea. We may add, in short, the order which they observed in drawing up their fleet for battle, taken from the same author: The two Consuls were in the two admiral gallies in the front of their two distinct squadrons, each of them just a-head of their divisions, and a-breast of each other; the first fleet being posted on the right, the second on the left, making two long files or lines of battle. And whereas it was necessary to give a due space between each galley, to ply their oars, and keep clear one of another, and to have their heads or prows looking somewhat outwards, this manner of drawing up did therefore naturally form an angle, the point whereof was at the two admiral-gallies, which were near together; and as their two lines were prolonged, so the distance grew consequently wider and wider towards the rear. But because the naval as well as the land army, consisted of four legions, and accordingly the ships made four divisions, two of these are yet behind: Of which the third fleet, or third legion, was drawn up frontways in the rear of the first and second, and so stretching along from point to point composed a triangle, whereof the third line was the base. Their vessels of burthen, that carried their horses and baggage, were in the rear of these; and were, by the help of small boats provided for that purpose, towed or drawn after them. In the rear of all was the fourth fleet, called the *Triarians*, drawn up likewise in rank or frontways, parallel to the third: But these made a longer line, by which means the extremities stretched out, and extended beyond the two angles at the base. The several divisions of the army, being thus disposed, formed, as is said, a triangle; the area within was void, but the base was thick and solid, and the whole body quick, active, and very difficult to be broken.

If we descend to a particular description of the several sorts of ships, we meet commonly with three kinds, ships of war, ships of burthen, and ships of passage: The first for the most part rowed with oars; the second steered with sails; and the last often towed with ropes. Ships of passage were either for the transportation of men, such as the ὁπλιταγωγοί, or ςρατιώτιδες; or of horses, as the *Hippagines*. The ships of burthen, which the Roman authors call *naves onerariæ*, and the Græcian φορτικοί, and ὁλκάδες, (whence the name of *hulks* may properly be derived) served for the conveyance of victuals and other provisions, and sometimes too for the carrying over soldiers, as we find in Cæsar. Of the ships of war, the most considerable were the *naves longæ*, or gallies, so named from their form, which was the most convenient to wield round, or to cut their way; whereas the ships of burthen were generally built rounder and more hollow, that they might be the more easy to load, and might hold the more goods. The most remarkable of the *naves longæ* were the *triremis*, the *quadriremis*, and the *quinqueremis*. Τριήρης, Τετρήρης, and Πεντήρης; exceeding one another by one bank of oars; which banks were raised slopingly one above another; and consequently those which had most banks were built highest, and rowed with the greatest strength. Some indeed fancy a different original of these names, as that in the *triremis*, for example, either there were three banks one after the other on a level, or three rowers sat upon one bank; or else three men tugged all together at one oar: But this is contrary, not only to the authority of the classics, but to the figures of the *triremes* still appearing in ancient monuments. Besides these, there were two other rates, one higher, and the other lower. The higher rates we meet with are the *hexeres*, the *hepteres*, the *octeres*, and so on to the δεκακαιδεκήρης; nay, Polybius relates, that Philip of Macedon,

father

father to Perseus, had an ἑκκαιδεκήρης (a); which Livy translates, *navis quam sexdecim versus remorum agebant* (b), a ship with sixteen banks: Yet this was much inferior to the ship built by Philopater, which Plutarch tells us had forty banks (c). The lower rates were the *biremis* and the *moneres*. The *biremis*, in Greek διήρης, or δίκροτος, consisted of two banks of oars: Of these, the fittest for service, by reason of their lightness and swiftness, were called *liburnicæ*, from the Liburni, a people in Dalmatia, who first invented that sort of building; for, being *corsairs*, they rowed up and down in these light vessels, and maintained themselves by the prizes they took (d). Yet, in latter times, all the smaller, and more expedite ships, whether they had more or less than two banks, were termed in general *liburnæ*, or *liburnicæ*. Thus Horace and Propertius call the ships which Augustus made use of in the sea-engagement at Actium: And Florus informs us, that his fleet was made up of vessels from three to six banks (e). Suetonius mentions an extravagant sort of *liburnicæ*, invented by the Emperor Caligula, adorned with jewels in the poop, with sails of many colours, and furnished with large porticoes, bagnios, and dining-rooms, besides the curious rows of vines and fruit-trees of all sorts (f).

The *moneres*, mentioned by Livy, was a gallery, having but one single bank of oars, of which we find five sorts in authors, the εἰκόβορος, or *actuari*, the τριακόντορος, the τισσαρακόντορος, the πεντηκόντορος, and the ἑκατόντορος, of twenty, thirty, forty, fifty, and a hundred oars.

It may be observed, that though these under-rates are supposed to have been built in the form of the *naves longæ*, yet they are not so generally honoured with that name; and sometimes in authors of credit we find them directly opposed to the *naves longæ*, and at other times to the μάχιμοι, or war-ships.

But the ships of war occur under several other different denominations, as the *tectæ*, or *constratæ*, or the *apertæ*. The *tectæ*, or κατάφρακτοι, were so called, because they had καταστρώματα, or hatches, whereas the *apertæ*, or ἄφρακτοι, had none. The greater ships, as the *quadriremis*, and upwards, seem

---

(a) *Polyb. in Fragment.*   (b) Lib. 53.   (c) *In Demetrio.*
(d) *Dacier on Horace*, Epod. 1.   (e) Lib. 4. cap. 11.   (f) *Suet. in Calig.* cap. 37.

seem always to have had hatches; the *triremes* and *biremes* are sometimes described otherwise; and all below these were *apertæ*. Cicero and other authors sometimes use the word *aphractum* for a particular sort of ship; and Polybius κατάφρακτος, for a *quinqueremis*. Besides these, we meet with the *naves rostratæ* and *naves turritæ*: The first were such as had beaks, or rostra, necessary to all ships which were to engage in a battle. The others were such as had turrets erected on their decks, from whence the soldiers used all manner of weapons and engines, as if it had been on land, and so engaged with the greatest fury imaginable; as Virgil describes the fight at Actium:

>———*Pelago credas innare revulsas*
>*Cycladas, aut montes concurrere montibus altos;*
>*Tanta mole viri turritis puppibus instant.* Æn. viii. 691.

The officers in the navy were, *Præfectus, Classis*, or Admiral, and sometimes the *Duumviri*, when two were joined in commission together with the *Trierarchus*, or Captain of a particular ship, most properly of the *Triremis;* the *Gubernator*, or Master; the *Celeustes*, or Boatswain, and others of inferior note.

Under the Emperors, as there were legions established in most part of the Roman dominions, so they had constantly fleets in those seas, which lay conveniently for the defence of neighbouring countries. As Augustus kept one navy at Misenum, in the *Mare Inferum*, to protect and keep in obedience France, Spain, Mauritania, Egypt, Sardinia, and Sicily: Another at Ravenna, in the *Mare Superum*, to defend and bridle Epirus, Macedon, Achaia, Crete, Cyprus, together with all Asia. Nor were their navies only maintained on the seas, but several too on principal rivers, as the *Germanica Classis* on the Rhine, the *Danubiana*, the *Euphratensis*, &c. to be met with in Tacitus, and other historians.

[See Sir Henry Savil's *Dissertation* at the end of his translation *of Tacitus*.]

To this subject of the Roman shipping we may add a very remarkable custom of such as had escaped a wreck at sea,

sea, which we find hinted at in almost every place of the poets, and often alluded to by other authors; on which a great modern critic delivers himself to this purpose :

It was a custom for those who had been saved from a shipwreck, to have all the circumstances of their adventure represented on a tablet. Some persons made use of their tablet to move the compassion of those that they met, as they travelled up and down ; and by their charity to repair their fortunes, which had suffered so much at sea. These Juvenal describes, Sat. xiv. 301.

> ———*Mersa rate naufragus assem*
> *Dum rogat, & picta se tempestate tuetur.*

His vessel sunk, the wretch at some lane's end
A painted storm for farthings does extend,
And lives upon the picture of his loss.

For this purpose they hung the tablet about their necks, and kept singing a sort of canting verses, expressing the manner of their misfortunes ; almost like the modern pilgrims, Persius, Sat. i. 88.

> ———*Cantet si naufragus, assem*
> *Protulerim? Cantas cum fracta te in trabe pictum*
> *Ex humero portes ?*

Say, should a shipwreck'd sailor sing his woe,
Would I be mov'd to pity ; or bestow
An alms ? Is this your season for a song,
When your despairing phiz you bear along,
Daub'd on a plank, and o'er your shoulders hung ?

Others hung up such a tablet in the temple of the particular deity, to whom they had addressed themselves in their exigence, and whose assistance had, as they thought, effected their safety. This they termed properly *votiva tabella*." Juvenal has a fling at the Roman superstition in this point, when he informs us, that is was the business of a company of painters to draw pictures on these accounts for the temple of Isis.

———*Quam*

—*Quam votiva testantur fana tabella*
Plurima, pictores quis nescit ab Iside pasci? xii. 27.

Such as in Isis' dome may be survey'd,
On votive tablets to the life pourtray'd,
Where painters are employ'd and earn their bread.

But the custom went much farther; for the lawyers at the bar used to have the case of the client expressed in a picture, that by showing his hard fortune, and the cruelty and injustice of the adverse party, they might move the compassion of the judge. This Quintilian declares himself against in his sixth book. Nor was this all; for such persons as had escaped in any fit of sickness, used to dedicate a picture of the deity whom they fancied to have relieved them. And this gives us a light into the meaning of Tibulus, lib. 1. eleg. 3.

Nunc Dea, nunc succurre mihi; nam posse mederi
 Picta docet Templis multa tabella tuis.

Now Goddess, now thy tortur'd suppliant heal;
For votive paints attest thy sacred skill.

Thus some Christians, in ancient times (*a*), upon a signal recovery of their health, used to offer a sort of medal in gold or silver, on which their own effigies were expressed, in honour of the saint whom they thought themselves obliged to for their deliverance. And this custom still obtains in the popish countries (*b*).

(*a*) *Causabon. in Persium,* Sat 1. v. 88. (*b*) *Dacier. on Horace.* lib. 1. Od. 5.

PART

PART II. BOOK V.

Miscellany Customs of the ROMANS.

CHAP. I.

Of the Private SPORTS *and* GAMES.

A Great part of the Roman pomp and superstition was taken up in their games and shows, and therefore very many of their customs have a dependence on those solemnities. But, in our way, we should not pass by the private sports and diversions; not that they are worth our notice in themselves, but because many passages and allusions in authors would otherwise be very difficult to comprehend.

The private games, particularly worth our remark, are the *Latrunculi*, the *Tali*, the *Tesseræ*, the *Pilæ*, the *Par impar*, and the *Trochus*.

The game at *Latrunculi* seems to have been much of the same nature as the modern chess; the original of it is generally referred to Palamedes's invention at the siege of Troy; though Seneca attributes it to Chilon, one of the seven Grecian sages; and some fancy that Pyrrhus, King of Epirus, contrived this sport, to instruct the soldiers, after a diverting manner,

in

in the military art. However, it is certain it expresses the chance and order of war so very happily, that no place can lay so just a claim to the invention as the camp. Thus the ingenious Vida begins his poem on this subject:

> *Ludimus effigiem belli, simulataque veris*
> *Prælia, buxo acies fictas, & ludicra regna :*
> *Ut gemini inter se reges, albusque, nigerque,*
> *Pro laude oppositi, certant bicoloribus armis.*

> War's harmless shape we sing, and boxen trains
> Of youth, encount'ring on the Cedar plains :
> How two tall kings, by diff'rent armour known,
> Traverse the field, and combat for renown.

The chess-men, which the Romans used, were generally of wax or glass; their common name was *Calculi*, or *Latrunculi :* The poets sometimes term them *Latrones*, whence *Latrunculus* was at first derived : For *latro*, among the ancients, signified at first a servant, (as the word *knave* in English) and afterwards a soldier.

Seneca has mentioned this play oftener, perhaps, than any other Roman author; particularly in one place he has a very remarkable story, in which he designs to give us an example of wonderful resolution and contempt of death; though some will be more apt to interpret it as an instance of insensible stupidity. The story is this : One Canius Julius (whom he extols very much on other accounts) had been sentenced to death by Caligula : The Centurions coming by with a tribe of malefactors, and ordering him to bear them company to execution, happened to find him engaged at this game. Canius, upon his first summons, presently fell to counting his men, and bidding his antagonist be sure not to brag falsely of the victory after his death; he only desired the Centurion to bear witness, that he had one man upon the board more than his companion, and so very readily joined himself to the poor wretches that were going to suffer (*a*).

But the largest and the most accurate account of the *Latrunculi*, given us by the ancients, is to be met with in the poem to Piso; which some will have to be Ovid's, others Lucan's, and many the work of an unknown author.

The

(*a*) *Seneca de Tranquil. Animi*, cap. 14.

The *tali* and *tesseræ*, by reason of so many passages in authors equally applicable to both, have oftentimes been confounded with one another, and by some distinguished as a separate game from the *lusus aleæ*, or dice: Whereas, properly speaking, the Greeks and Romans had two sorts of games at dice, the *ludus talorum*, or play at cock-all, and the *ludus tesserarum*, or what we call dice. They played at the first with four *tali*, and at the other with three *tesseræ*. The *tali* had but four sides, marked with four opposite numbers; one side with a *tres*, and the opposite with a *quatre*; one with an *ace*, and the contrary with the *sice*. The dice had six faces, four marked with the same number as the *tali*, and the two others with a *deux* and a *cinque*, always one against the other; so that in both plays the upper number and the lower, either on the *talus* or *tessera*, constantly made seven.

There were very severe laws in force against these plays, forbidding the use of them at all seasons, only during the *Saturnalia*; though they gamed ordinarily at other times, notwithstanding the prohibition. But there was one use made of them at feasts and entertainments, which perhaps did not fall under the extent of the laws, and that was, to throw dice who should command in chief, and have the power of prescribing rules at a drinking-bout, who in Horace is called *arbiter bibendi*.

They threw both the *tali* and the *tesseræ* out of a long box, for which they had several names, as *fritillum*, *pyrgus*, *turricula*, *orca*, &c.

There are many odd terms scattered up and down in authors, by which they signified their fortunate and unfortunate cast; we may take notice of the best and the worst. The best cast with the *tali* was, when there came up four different numbers, as *tres*, *quatre*, *sice*, *ace*: The best with the dice was three *sices*; the common term for both was *Venus* or *Basilicus*; the poorest cast in both having the name of *canis*. Persius opposes the *senio* and the *canicula* as the best and worst chances:

——*Quid dexter senio ferret,*
Scire erat in votis; damnosa canicula quantum
Raderet, angustæ collo non fallier orcæ.   Sat. iii. 48.

But then my study was to cog the dice,
And dext'rously to throw the lucky sice;

> To shun *ames-ace*, that swept my stakes away,
> And watch the box, for fear they should convey
> False bones, and put upon me in the play.
>
> Mr DRYDEN.

The wiser and severer Romans thought this sedentary diversion fit only for aged men, who could not so well employ themselves in any stirring recreation. "Let them," says old Cato in Tully, "have their armour, their horses, and their "spears; let them take their club and their javelin; let them "have their swimming matches and their races, so they do "but leave us, among the numerous sports, the *tali* and "the *tessera*." But the general corruption of manners made the case quite otherwise. Juvenal, xiv. 4:

> *Si damnosa senem juvat alea, ludit & heres*
> *Bullatus, parvoque eadem movet arma fritillo.*

> If gaming does an aged sire entice,
> Then my young master swiftly learns the vice,
> And shakes, in hanging-sleeves, the little box and dice.
>
> Mr DRYDEN.

Nor was it probable that this game should be practised with any moderation in the city, when the Emperors were commonly professed admirers of it. Augustus himself played unreasonably, without any regard to the time of the year (a). But the great master of this art was the Emperor Claudius, who by his constant practice (even as he rode about in his chariot) gained so much experience as to compose a book on the subject. Hence Seneca, in his sarcastical relation of the Emperor's Apotheosis, when, after a great many adventures, he has at last brought him to hell, makes the infernal judges condemn him (as the most proper punishment in the world) to play continually at dice with a box that had the bottom out; which kept him always in hopes, and yet always baulked his expectations:

> *Nam quoties missurus erat resonante fritillo,*
> *Utraque subducto fugiebat tessera fundo;*
> *Cumque recollectos auderet mittere talos,*
> *Lusuro similis semper, semperque petenti,*
>
> *Decepere*

(a) *Sueton. Aug.* cap. 71.

Decepere fidem: refugit, digitosque per ipsos
Fallax assiduo dilabitur alea furto.
Sic cum jam summi tanguntur culmina montis,
Irrita Sisyphio volvuntur pondera collo.

For whensoe'er he shook the box to cast,
The rattling dice delude his eager haste:
And if he try'd again, the waggish bone
Insensibly was thro' his fingers gone;
Still he was throwing, yet he ne'er had thrown.
So weary Sisyphus, when now he sees
The welcome top, and feeds his joyful eyes,
Straight the rude stone, as cruel fate commands,
Falls sadly down, and meets his restless hands.

The ancients had four sorts of *pilæ*, or balls, used for exercise and diversion. The *follis* or baloon, which they struck about with their arm, guarded for that purpose with a wooden bracer: Or, if the baloon was little, they used only their fists. The *pilo trigonalis*, the same as our common balls; to play with this, there used to stand three persons in a triangle, striking it round from one to another; he who first let it come to the ground was the loser (*a*). *Paganica*, a ball stuffed with feathers, which Martial thus describes, xiv. 45.

Hæc quæ difficili turget paganica pluma,
Folle minus laxa est, & minus arcta pila.

The last sort was the *harpastum*, a harder kind of ball, which they played with dividing into two companies, and striving to throw it into one another's goals, which was the conquering cast.

The game at *par impar*, or even and odd, is not worth taking notice of any farther than to observe, that it was not only proper to the children, as it is generally fancied: For we may gather from Suetonius, that it was sometimes used at feasts and entertainments, in the same manner as the dice and chess (*b*).

The *trochus* has been often thought the same as the *turbo*, or top; or else of like nature with our billiards: But both these

---

(*a*) *Dacier ou Horace.* Book 2. Sat. 2.   (*b*) *Sueton. in Aug.* cap. 71.

opinions are now exploded by the curious. The *trochus* therefore was properly a hoop of iron five or six feet diameter, set all over in the inside with iron rings. The boys and young men used to whirl this along, as our children do wooden hoops, directing it with a rod of iron, having a wooden handle; which rod the Græcians called ἱλαρίη, and the Romans *radius*. There was need of great dexterity to guide the hoop right. In the mean time, the rings, by the clattering which they made, not only gave the people notice to keep out of the way, but contributed very much to the boys diversion (*a*). We must take care not to think this only a childish exercise, (since we find Horace (*b*) ranking it with other manly sports.

> *Ludere qui nescit, compestribus abstinet armis,*
> *Indoctusque pilæ, discive, trochive quiescit.*

(*a*) Dacier. *on Horace*, Book 3. Od. 24.   (*b*) De Art. Poet.

CHAP. II.

Of the Circensian *Shows, and first of the* Pentathlum, *the Chariot Races, the* Ludus Trojæ, *and the* Pyrrhica Saltatio.

IT is hard to light on any tolerable division which would take in all the public sports and shows; but the most accurate seems to be that which ranks them under two heads, *Ludi Circenses*, and *Ludi Scenici*; But because this division is made only in respect of the form and manner of the solemnities, and of the place of action, there is need of another to express the end and design of their institution; and this may be *Ludi Sacri, Votivi*, and *Funebres*.

The Circensian plays may very well include the representations of sea-fights, and sports performed in the amphitheatres: For the former were commonly exhibited in the Circo's fitted for that use; and when we meet with the *Naumachiæ*, as places distinct from the Circo's, we suppose the structure to have been of the same nature. And, as to the amphitheatres, they

they were erected for the more convenient celebration of some particular shows, which used before to be presented in the Circo's, so that, in this extent of the head, we may inform ourselves of the *Pentathlum*, of the chariot races, of the *Ludus Trojæ*, of the shows of wild beasts, of the combats of the gladiators, and of the *Naumachiæ*.

The *Pentathlum*, or *Quinquertium*, as most of their other sports, was borrowed from the Græcian games; the five exercises that composed it were running, wrestling, leaping, throwing, and boxing. The two last have something particularly worth our notice; the former of them being sometimes performed with the *discus*, and the other with the *cestus*: The *discus*, or quoit made of stone, iron, or copper, five or six fingers broad, and more than a foot long, inclining to an oval five: They sent this to a vast distance, by the help of a leathern thong tied round the person's hand that threw. Several learned men have fancied, that, instead of the aforesaid thong, they made use of a twist or brede of hair; but it is possible they might be deceived, by that passage of Claudian:

> *Quis melius vibrata puer vertigine molli*
> *Membra rotet ? vertat quis marmora crine supino ?*

> What youth could wind his limbs with happier care ?
> Or fling the marble-quoit with toss'd back hair ?

Where the poet by *crine supino* intends only to express the extreme motion of the person throwing; it being very natural on that account to cast back his head, and so make the hair fly out behind him (*a*).

Homer has made Ajax and Ulysses both great artists at this sport: And Ovid, when he brings in Apollo and Hyacinth playing at it, gives an elegant description of the exercise:

> *Corpora veste levant, & succo pinguis olivæ*
> *Splendescunt, latique ineunt certamina disci;*
> *Quem prius aerias libratum Phœbus in auras*
> *Misit, & oppositas disjecit pondere nubes.*
> *Decidit in solidam longo post tempore terram*
> *Pondus, & exhibuit junctam cum viribus artem* (*b*).

They

(*a*) Dacier. on Horace, Book I. Od. 8.   (*b*) Metamorphos. 10.

> They strip, and wash their naked limbs with oil,
> To whirl the quoit, and urge the sportive toil.
> And first the god his well-pois'd marble flung,
> Cut the weak air, and bore the clouds along:
> Sounding at last, the massy circle fell,
> And show'd his strength a rival to his skill.

Scaliger, who attributes the invention of the whole *Pentathlum* to the rude country people, is of opinion, That the throwing the *discus* is but an improvement of their old sport of casting their sheep-hooks: This conjecture seems very likely to have been borrowed from a passage of Homer: II. Ψ. 845.

> Ὅσσον τίς τ' ἔρριψε καλαύροπα βυκόλος ἀνὴρ.
> Ἡ δέ θ' ἑλισσομένη πέταται διὰ βῦς ἀγελαίας,
> Τόσσον παντὸς ἀγῶνος ὑπέρβαλε.

> As when some sturdy hind his sheep-hook throws,
> Which, whirling, lights among the distant cows;
> So far the hero casts o'er all the marks.

And indeed the judgment of the same critic, that these exercises owe their original to the life of shepherds, is no more than what his admired Virgil has admirably taught him in the second Georgic, 527.

> *Ipse dies agitat Festos; subitusque per herbam*
> *Ignis ubi in medio, & Socii cratera coronant,*
> *Te libans Lenæe vocat, pecorisque magistris*
> *Velocis jaculi certamina ponit in ulmo;*
> *Corporaque agresti nudat prædura palæstra.*

> When any rural holydays invite
> His genius forth to innocent delight;
> On earth's fair bed, beneath some sacred shade,
> Amidst his equal friends carelessly laid,
> He sings thee, Bacchus, patron of the vine.
> The beechen bowl foams with a flood of wine;
> Not to the loss of reason, or of strength,
> To active games, and manly sports at length.

Their mirth afcends; and with full veins they fee
Who can the beft at better trials be.
Mr COWLEY.

The *ceſtus* were either a fort of leathern guards for the hands, compofed of thongs, and commonly filled with lead or iron to add force and weight to the blow; or, according to others, a kind of whirl-bats, or bludgeons of wood, with lead at one end: Though Scaliger cenfures the laſt opinion as ridiculous; and therefore he derives the word from κἰσον, a girdle or belt (a). This exercife is moſt admirably defcribed by Virgil in the combat of Dares and Entellus, Æneid 5. The famous artiſt, at the *ceſtus*, was Eryx of Sicily, overcome at laſt at his own weapons by Hercules. Pollux too was as great a maſter of this art as his brother Caſtor at encounters on horfeback. The fight of Pollux and Amytus, with the *ceſtus*, is excellently related by Theocritus, Idyllium 30.

The CHARIOT-RACES occur as frequently as any of the Circenſian fports. The moſt remarkable thing belonging to them was the factions, or companies of the charioteers; according to which the whole town was divided, fome favouring one company, and fome another. The four ancient companies were the *Praſina*, the *Ruſſata*, the *Alba*, or *Albata*, and the *Veneta*; the green, the red, the white, and the ſky-coloured, or fea-coloured. This diſtinction was taken from the colour of their liveries, and is thought to have borne fome allufion to the four feafons of the year; the firſt refembling the fpring, when all things are green; the next, the fiery colour of the fun in fummer; the third, the hoar of autumn; and the laſt, the clouds of winter. The *Praſina* and the *Veneta* are not fo eafy names as the other two; the former is derived from πράσον, a leek, and the other from *veneti*, or the Venetians, a people that particularly affect that colour. The moſt taking company were commonly the green, efpecially under Caligula, Nero, and the following Emperors; and in the time of Juvenal, as he hints in his eleventh fatyr, and with a fine ſtroke of his pen handfomely cenfures the ſtrange pleafure which the Romans took in the fights, 139.

————————*Mihi pace*
Immenſæ nimiæque licet ſi dicere plebis.
Totam

(a) *De Re Poetica*, lib. 1. cap. 22.

Totam hodie Romam circus capit, & fragor aurem
Percutit, eventum viridis quo colligo panni :
Nam si deficeret, mæstam attonitamque videres
Hanc urbem, veluti Cannarum in pulvere victis
Consulibus. ─────

This day all Rome (if I may be allow'd,
Without offence to such a numerous crowd,
To say all Rome) will in the circus sweat,
Echoes already to their shouts repeat.
Methinks I hear the cry──"Away, away,
"The green have won the honour of the day."
Oh! should the sports be but one year forborn,
Rome would in tears her lov'd diversion mourn ;
And that would now a cause of sorrow yield,
Great as the loss of Cannæ's fatal field.

Mr CONGREVE.

The Emperor Domitian, as Suetonius informs us, added two new companies to the former, the *Golden* and the *Purple* (a). Xiphilin calls them the *Golden* and the *Silver ;* but this seems to be a mistake, because the silver liveries would not have been enough to distinguish from the white. But these new companies were soon after laid down again by the following Emperors (b).

In ordinary reading, we meet only with the *bigæ* and the *quadrigæ;* but they had sometimes their *sejuges, septemjuges,* &c. And Suetonius assures us, that Nero, when he was a performer in the Olympic games, made use of a *decemjugis,* a chariot drawn with ten horses coupled together (c). The same Emperor sometimes brought in pairs of camels to run the circo instead of horses (d) And Heliogabalus obliged elephants to the same service (e).

The races were commonly ended at seven turns round the *meta,* tho', upon extraordinary occasions, we now and then meet with fewer heats. In the like manner, the usual number of *missus,* or matches, were twenty-four, though sometimes a far greater number were exhibited. For Suetonius tells us, that the Emperor Domitian presented an hundred matches in one day (f). De la Cerda will have us believe

it

───────

(a) *Domitian,* cap 7.   (b) *Lipsf. Com. in locum.*   (c) *Suet. Ner.* cap. 24.   (d) *Idem,* cap. 12.   (e) *Lamprid. in Heliogab.*
(f) *Domitian,* cap. 4.

it is not meant of the number of the matches, but only of the chariots, so as to make no more than twenty-five *missus's*: But his opinion is not taken notice of by the critics who have commented on Suetonius. Servius (*a*), on that verse of Virgil, Geor. iii. 18.

Centum quadrijugos agitabo ad flumina currus,

takes occasion to inform us, that anciently there were always twenty-five matches of chariots, four in every match, so as to make a hundred in all. The last *missus* was set out at the charge of the people, who made a gathering for that purpose, and was therefore called *ærarius*; but when this custom of a supernumerary *missus* was laid aside, the matches were no more than twenty-four at a time, yet the last four chariots still kept the name of *missus ærarius*.

The time when the races should begin was anciently given notice of by sound of trumpet; but afterwards the common sign was the *mappa*, or napkin, hung out at the Prætor's, or the chief magistrate's seat. Hence Juvenal calls the Megalensian games,

——*Megalesiacæ spectacula mappæ.*   Sat. xi. 191.

The common reason given for this custom is, that Nero being once at dinner, and the people making a great noise, desiring that the sports might begin, the Emperor threw the napkin he had in his hand out of the window, as a token that he had granted their request (*b*).

The victors in these sports were honoured with garlands, coronets, and other ornaments, after the Grecian manner; and, very often, with considerable rewards in money; insomuch that Juvenal makes one eminent charioteer able to buy a hundred lawyers:

——*Hinc centum patrimonia causidicorum,*
Parte alia solum russati pone Lacerta.   Sat. vii. 118.

It has been already hinted, that they reckoned the conclusion of the race from the passing by the *meta* the seventh time; and this Propertius expressly confirms, Book 2. Eleg. 24.

(*a*) *Ad Georg.* 3.   (*b*) *Cassiodor.* lib. Epist. 5.

Aut prius infecto depofcit præmia curfu,
Septima quam metam triverit arte rota.

What charioteer would with the crown be grac'd,
Ere his feventh wheel the mark has lightly pafs'd?

So that the greateft fpecimen of art and flight appears to have been to avoid the *meta* handfomely, when they made their turns; otherwife the chariot and the driver would come into great danger as well as difgrace :

————*Metaque fervidis*
Evitata rotis.   Hor. Od. 1.

On this account it is that Theocritus, when he gives a relation of the exercifes in which they inftructed young Hercules, affigns him in this point, as a matter of the greateft confequence, his own father for his tutor :

Ἵππους δ᾽ ἐξελάσασθαι ὑφ᾽ ἅρματι καὶ περὶ νύσσαν
Ἀσφαλέως κάμπτοντα τροχῷ σύριγγα φυλάξαι,
Ἀμφιτρύων ὃν παῖδα φίλα φρονέων ἐδίδασκεν
Αὐτὸς, ἐπεὶ μάλα πολλὰ θοῶν ἐξύρατ᾽ ἀγώνων
Ἄρεῖ ἐν ἱπποβότῳ κειμήλια· καὶ οἱ ἀαγεῖς
Δίφροι ἐφ᾽ ὧν ἐπέβαινε, χρόνῳ διέλυσαν ἱμάντας.   Εἰδύλ. κδ. 117.

To drive the chariot, and with fteady fkill
To turn, and yet not break the bending wheel,
Amphytrio kindly did inftruct his fon :
Great in that art ; for he himfelf had won
Vaft precious prizes on the Argive plains :   ⎫
And ftill the chariot which he drove remains, [reins. ⎬
Ne'er hurt i' th' courfe, tho' time had broke the falling ⎭
                                                   Mr CREECH.

They who defire to be informed of the exact manner of thefe races, which certainly were very noble and diverting, may poffibly receive as much pleafure and fatisfaction from the defcription which Virgil has left us of them in fhort, as they could expect from the fight itfelf. Georg. iii. 103.

Nonne

Nonne vides ? cum præcipiti certamine campum
Corripuere, ruuntque effusi carcere currus ;
Cum spes arrectæ juvenum, exultantiaque haurit
Corda pavor pulsans : illi instant verbere torto,
Et proni dant lora : volat vi fervidus axis.
Jamque humiles, jamque elati sublime videntur
Aera per vacuum ferri, atque assurgere in auras.
Nec mora nec requies : at fulvæ nimbus arenæ
Tollitur ; humescunt spumis flatuque sequentum :
Tantus amor laudum, tantæ est victoria curæ.

Hast thou beheld, when from the goal they start,
The youthful charioteers with beating heart
Rush to the race ; and panting scarcely bear
Th' extremes of fev'rish hopes and chilling fear ;
Stoop to the reins, and lash with all their force ;
The flying chariot kindles in the course.
And now a-low, and now a-loft they fly,
As borne thro' air, and seem to touch the sky :
No stop, no stay, but clouds of sand arise,
Spurn'd and cast backward on the follower's eyes :
The hindmost blows the foam upon the first :
Such is the love of praise, and honourable thirst.
Mr Dryden.

The *Troja*, or *Ludus Trojæ*, is generally referred to the invention of Ascanius. It was celebrated by companies of boys neatly dressed, and furnished with little arms and weapons, who mustered in the public circus. They were taken, for the most part, out of the noblest families ; and the captain of them had the honourable title of *Princeps Juventutis ;* being sometimes next heir to the empire, and seldom less than the son of a principal Senator. This custom is so very remarkable, that it would be an unpardonable omission, not to give the whole account of it in Virgil's own words ; especially, because the poet, using all his art and beauties on this subject, as a compliment to Augustus (a great admirer of the sport) has left us a most inimitable description.

Æneid

Æneid 5. Ver. 545.

At pater Æneas, nondum certamine missi,
Custodem ad sese comitemque impubis Iuli
Epytidem vocat, & fidam sic fatur ad aurem:
Vade age, & Ascanio, si jam puerile paratum
Agmen habet secum, cursusque instruxit equorum,
Ducat avo turmas, & sese ostendat in armis,
Dic, ait. Ipse omnem longo decedere circo
Infusum populum, & campos jubet esse patentes.
Incedunt pueri, pariterque ante ora parentum
Frænatis lucent in equis : quos omnis euntes
Trinacriæ mirata fremit Trojæque juventus.
Omnibus in morem tonsa coma pressa corona:
Cornea bina ferunt præfixa hastilia ferro ;
Pars leves humero pharetras : It pectore summo
Flexilis obtorti per collum circulus auri.
Tres equitum numero turmæ, ternique vagantur
Ductores : Pueri bis seni quemque secuti,
Agmine partito fulgent paribusque Magistris.
Una acies juvenum, ducit quam parvus ovantem
(Nomen avi referens) Priamus, tua clara, Polite,
Progenies, auctura Italos : quem Thracius albis
Portat equus bicolor maculus : vestigia primi
Alba pedis, frontemque ostentans arduus albam.
Alter Atys, genus unde Atti duxere Latini :
Parvus Atys, pueroque puer dilectus Iulo.
Extremus, formaque ante omnes pulcher Iulus
Sidonio est invectus equo ; quem candida Dido
Esse sui dederat monimentum & pignus amoris.
Cætera Trinacriis pubes senioris Acestæ
Fertur equis.
Excipiunt plausu pavidos, gaudentque tuentes
Dardanidæ, veterumque agnoscunt ora parentum.
Postquam omnem læti concessum oculosque suorum
Lustravere in equis : signum clamore paratis
Epytides longe dedit, insonuitque flagello.
Olli discurrere pares, atque agmina terni
Diductis solvere choris : rursusque vocati
Convertere vias, infestaque tela tulere.
Inde alios ineunt cursus, aliosque recursus,

Adversis

Adversis spatiis, alternosque orbibus orbes
Impediunt, pugnæque cient simulachra sub armis:
Et nunc terga fugæ nudant, nunc spicula vertunt
Infensi, facta pariter nunc pace feruntur:
Ut quondam Creta fertur labyrinthus in alta
Parietibus textum cæsis iter, ancipitemque
Mille viis habuisse dolum, qua signa sequendi
Falleret indeprensus & irremeabilis error.
Haud alitur Teucrûm nati vestigia cursu
Impediunt, texuntque fugas & prælia ludo:
Delphinum similes, qui per maria humida nando
Carpathium Libycumque secant, luduntque per undas,
Hunc morem, hos cursus, atque hæc certamina primus
Ascanius, longam muris cum cingeret Albam,
Rettulit, & priscos docuit celebrare Latinos;
Quo puer ipse modo, secum quo Troia pubes,
Albani docuere suos: hinc maxima porro
Accepit Roma, & patrium servavit honorem:
Trojaque nunc pueri, Trojanum dicitur agmen.

But Prince Æneas, e'er the games were done,
Now call'd the wise instructor of his son,
The good Epytides, whose faithful hand
In noble arts the blooming hero train'd:
To whom the royal chief his will declar'd;
Go, bid Ascanius, if he stands prepar'd
To march his youthful troops, begin the course,
And let his grandsire's shade commend his growing force.
Thus he; and order'd straight the swarming tide
To clear the circus; when from ev'ry side
Crowds bear back crowds, and leave an open space,
Where the new pomp in all its pride might pass.
The boys move on, all glitt'ring lovely bright,
On well-rein'd steeds, in their glad parents sight.
Wond'ring, the Trojan and Sicilian youth
Crown with applause their virtue's early growth;
Their flowing hair close flow'ry chaplets grace,
And two fair spears their eager fingers press.
Part bear gay quivers, on their shoulders hung,
And twists of bending gold lie wreath'd along
Their purple vest, which at the neck begun,
And down their breasts in shining circles run.

Three

Three lovely troops three beauteous captains led,
And twice six boys each hopeful chief obey'd.
The first gay troop young Priam marshals on,
Thy seed, Polites, not to fame unkown,
That with Italian blood shall join his own:
Whose kinder genius, rip'ning with his years,
His wretched grandsire's name to better fortune bears.
A Thracian steed, with spots of spreading white,
He rode, that paw'd, and crav'd the promis'd fight.
A lovely white his hither fetlock stains,
And white his high-erected forehead shines.
And next with stately pace young Atys mov'd,
Young Atys, by the young Ascanius lov'd.
From this great line the noble Attian stem,
In Latium nurs'd, derive their ancient name.
The third with his command Ascanius grac'd,
Whose godlike looks his heav'nly race confess'd;
So beautiful, so brave, he shone above the rest.
His sprightly steed from Sidon's pasture came,
The noble gift of the fair Tyrian dame,
And fruitless pledge of her unhappy flame.
The rest Sicilian coursers all bestrode,
Which old Acestes on his guests bestow'd.
Them, hot with beating hearts, the Trojan crew
Receive with shouts, and with fresh pleasure view;
Discov'ring in the lines of ev'ry face
Some venerable founder of their race.
And now the youthful troop their round had made,
Panting with joy, and all the crowd survey'd;
When sage Epytides, to give the sign,
Crack'd his long whip, and made the course begin.
At once they start, and spur with artful speed,
Till in the troops the little chiefs divide
The close battalion: then at once they turn,
Commended back; while from their fingers borne,
Their hostile darts aloft upon the wind
Fly shiv'ring: then in circling numbers join'd,
The manag'd coursers with due measures bound,
And run the rapid ring, and trace the mazy round.
Files facing files, their bold companions dare.
And wheel, and charge, and urge the sportive war.
Now flight they feign, and naked backs expose;
Now with turn'd spears drive headlong on the foes;
And now, confed'rate grown, in peaceful ranks they close.

As

As Crete's fam'd labyrinth to a thousand ways,
And thousand darken'd walls the guest conveys;
Endless, inextricable rounds amuse,
And no kind track the doubtful passage shews.
So the glad Trojan youth their winding course
Sporting pursue : and charge the rival force.
As sprightly dolphins in some calmer road
Play round the silent waves, and shoot along the flood.
Ascanius, when (the rougher storms o'erblown,)
With happier fates he rais'd fair Alba's town ;
This youthful sport, this solemn race renew'd,
And with new rites made the plain Latins proud.
From Alban sires, th' hereditary game
To matchless Rome by long succession came :
And the fair youth in this diversion train'd.
Troy they still call, and the brave Trojan band.

Lazius in his commentaries *de Repub. Romana* fancies the justs and tournaments, so much in fashion about two or three hundred years ago, to have owed their original to this *Ludus Trojæ*, and that *tournamenta* is but a corruption of *trojamenta*. And the learned and noble Du Fresne acquaints us that many are of the same opinion. However, though the word may perhaps be derived with more probability from the French *tourner*, to turn round with agility, yet the exercises have so much resemblance as to prove the one an imitation of the other.

The *Pyrrhice*, or *Saltatio Pyrrhica*, is commonly believed to be the same with the sport already described. But, besides, that none of the ancients have left any tolerable grounds for such a conjecture, it will appear a different game, if we look a little into its original, and on the manner of the performance. The original is, by some, referred to Minerva, who led up a dance in her amour, after the conquest of the Titans: By others, to the Curetes, or Corybantes, Jupiter's guard in his cradle ; who leaped up and down, clashing their weapons, to keep old Saturn from hearing the cries of his infant son. Pliny attributes the invention to Pyrrhus, son to Achilles, who instituted such a company of dancers at the funeral of his father (a). However, that it was very ancient is plain from Homer ;

(a) *Nat. Hist.* lib. 57.

Homer; who, as he hints at it in several descriptions, so particularly he makes the exact form and manner of it to be engraved on the shield of Achilles, given him by Vulcan. The manner of the performance seems to have consisted chiefly in the nimble turning of the body, and shifting every part, as if it were done to avoid the stroke of an enemy: And therefore this was one of the exercises in which they trained the young soldiers. Apuleius describes a Pyrrhic dance, performed by young men and maids together (a): which alone would be enough to distinguish it from the *Ludus Trojæ*. The best account we meet with of the Pyrrhic dance is in Claudian's poem on the sixth consulship of Honorius:

Armatos hic sæpe choros, certaque vagandi
Textûs lege fugas, inconfusosque recursus,
Et pulchras errorum artes, jucundaque Martis
Cernimus: insonuit cum verbere signa magister;
Mutatosque edant pariter tot pectora motus,
In latus allisis clypeis, aut rursus in altum
Vibratis: grave parma sonat mucronis acuti.
Verbere, & umbonum pulsu modulante resultans
Ferreus alterno concentus clauditur ense.

Here too the warlike dancers bless our sight,
Their artful wand'ring, and their laws of flight,
And unconfus'd return, and inoffensive fight.
Soon as the master's *crack* proclaims the prize,
Their moving breasts in tuneful changes rise;
The shields salute their sides, or straight are shown
In air high waving; deep the targets groan
Struck with alternate swords, which thence rebound,
And end the concert and the sacred sound.

The most ingenious Mr Cartwright, author of the *Royal Slave*, having occasion to present a warlike dance in that piece, took the measures of it from this passage of Claudian, as the most exact pattern antiquity had left. And in the printed play, he has given no other description of that dance, than by setting down the verses whence it is copied.

Julius.

(a) *Milesiar.* lib. 10.

Julius Scaliger tells us of himself, that, while a youth, he had often danced the Pyrrhic before the Emperor Maximilian, to the amazement of all Germany; and that the Emperor was once so surprized at his warlike activity, as to cry out, "This boy either was born in a coat of mail, instead of a skin, "or else has been rocked in one instead of a cradle (*a*)."

(*a*) Poet. lib. 1. cap. 18.

CHAP. III.

Of the Shows of Wild Beasts, and of the Naumachiæ.

THE shows of beasts were in general designed for the honour of Diana, the patroness of hunting. For this purpose, no cost was spared to fetch the most different creatures from the farthest parts of the world: Hence Claudian,

———*ratibus pars ibat onustis*
Per freta, vel fluvios; exsanguis dextera torpet
Remigis, & proprium metuebat navita mercem.

———Part in laden vessels came,
Borne on the rougher waves, or gentler stream;
The fainting slave let fall his trembling oar;
And the pale master fear'd the freight he bore.

And presently after,

———*Quodcunque tremendum est*
Dentibus, aut insigne jubis, aut nobile cornu,
Aut rigidum setis capitur, decus omne timorque
Sylvarum, non caute latent, non mole resistunt.

All that with potent teeth command the plain,
All that run horrid with erected mane,
Or proud of stately horns, or bristling hair,
At once the forest's ornament and fear;

Torn

Torn from their deſarts by the Roman pow'r,
Nor ſtrength can ſave, nor craggy dens ſecure.

Some creatures were preſented merely as ſtrange ſights and rarities, as the crocodiles, and ſeveral outlandiſh birds and beaſts; others for the combat, as lions, tygers, leopards, &c. other creatures, either purely for delight, or elſe for the uſe of the people, at ſuch times as they were allowed liberty of catching what they could for themſelves, as hares, deer, and the like. We may reckon up three ſorts of diverſions with the beaſts, which all went under the common name of *venatio*; the firſt, when the people were permitted to run after the beaſts, and catch what they could for their own uſe; the ſecond, when the beaſts fought with one another; and the laſt, when they were brought out to engage with men.

When the people were allowed to lay hold on what they could get, and carry it off for their own uſe, they called it *venatio direptionis*: This ſeems to have been an inſtitution of the Emperors. It was many times preſented with extraordinary charge, and great variety of contrivances. The middle part of the circus being ſet all over with trees, removed thither by main force, and faſtened to huge planks, which were laid on the ground; theſe, being covered with earth and turf, repreſented a natural foreſt, into which the beaſts being let from the *caveæ*, or dens under ground, the people, at a ſign given by the Emperor, fell to hunting them, and carried away what they killed to regale upon at home. The beaſts uſually given were boars, deer, oxen, and ſheep. Sometimes all kinds of birds were preſented after the ſame manner. The uſual way of letting the people know what they ſhould ſeize, was by ſcattering among them little tablets, or tickets, (*teſſeras*) which entitled thoſe who caught them to the contents of their inſcription. Sometimes every ticket was marked with ſuch a ſum of money, payable to the firſt taker. Theſe largeſſes were in general termed *miſſilia*, from their being thrown and diſperſed among the multitude (*a*).

The fights between beaſts were exhibited with great variety; ſometimes we find a tyger matched with a lion, ſometimes a lion with a bull, a bull with an elephant, a rhinoceros with a bear, &c. Sometimes we meet with a deer hunted

on

(*a*) Bullenger de Ven. Circi, cap. 23.

on the area by a pack of dogs. But the most wonderful sight was, when by bringing the water into the amphitheatre, huge sea-monsters were introduced to combat with wild beasts:

> *Nec nobis tantum sylvestria cernere monstra*
> *Contigit, æquorcos ego cum certantibus ursis*
> *Spectavi vitulos.* Calphurn. Eclog. 7.

Nor Sylvan monsters we alone have view'd,
But huge sea-calves, dy'd red with hostile blood
Of bears, lie flound'ring in the wond'rous flood.

The men that engaged with wild beasts had the common name of *bestiarii*. Some of these were condemned persons, and have been taken notice of in other places (*a*): Others hired themselves at a set pay, like the Gladiators; and, like them too, had their schools where they were instructed and initiated in such combats. We find several of the nobility and gentry many times voluntarily undertaking a part in these encounters. And Juvenal acquaints us, that the very women were ambitious of showing their courage on the like occasions, though with the forfeiture of their modesty:

> *Cum——————Mævia Tuscum*
> *Figat aprum, & nuda teneat venabula mamma.* Sat. i. 22.

Or when with naked breast the mannish whore
Shakes the broad spear against the Tuscan boar.

And Martial compliments the Emperor Domitian very handsomely on the same account, Spectac. vi.

> *Belliger invictis quod Mars tibi sævit in armis,*
> *Non satis est, Cæsar, sævit & ipsa Venus.*
> *Prostratum vasta Nemees in valle leonem*
> *Nobile & Herculeum fama canebat opus.*
> *Prisca fides taceat: Nam post tua munera, Cæsar,*
> *Hæc jam fœminea vidimus acta manu.*

Not Mars alone his bloody arms shall weild;
Venus, when Cæsar bids, shall take the field,
Nor only wear the breeches, but the shield.
The savage tyrant of the woods and plain,
By Hercules in doubtful combat slain,

(*a*) Book 3. chap. 20.

Still fills our ears within the Nemean vale,
And mufty rolls the mighty wonder tell :
No wonder now ; for Cæfar's reign has fhewn
A woman's equal power ; the fame renown
Gain'd by the diftaff which the club had won.

Thofe who coped on the plain ground with beafts commonly met with a very unequal match ; and therefore, for the moſt part, their fafety confifted in the nimble turning of their body, and leaping up and down to elude the force of their adverfary. Therefore Martial may very well make a hero of the man who flew twenty beafts, all let in upon him at once, though we fuppofe them to have been of the inferior kind :

Herculeæ laudis numeretur gloria : plus eſt
  Bis denas pariter perdomuiſſe feras.

Count the twelve feats that Hercules has done ;
Yet twenty make a greater, join'd in one.

But becaufe this way of engaging commonly proved fuccefsful to the beaſt, they had other ways of dealing with them, as by affailing them with darts, fpears, and other miffive weapons, from the higher parts of the amphitheatre, where they were fecure from their reach ; fo as by fome means or other they commonly contrived to difpatch three or four hundred beafts in one fhow.

In the fhow of wild beafts exhibited by Julius Cæfar in his third confulfhip, twenty elephants were oppofed to five hundred footmen ; and twenty more with turrets on their backs, fixty men being allowed to defend each turret, engaged with five hundred foot, and as many horfe (*a*).

The NAUMACHIÆ owe their original to the time of the firſt Punic war, when the Romans firſt initiated their men in the knowledge of fea-affairs. After the improvement of many years, they were defigned as well for the gratifying the fight as for increafing their naval experience and difcipline ; and therefore compofed one of the folemn fhows, by which the Magiftrates or Emperors, or any affecters of popularity, fo often made their court to the people.

The ufual accounts we have of thefe exercifes feem to reprefent them as nothing elfe but the image of a naval fight ; but

(*a*) Plin. *Nat. Hiſt.* lib. 8. cap. 7.

but it is probable that sometimes they did not engage in any hostile manner, but only rowed fairly for the victory. This conjecture may be confirmed by the authority of Virgil, who is acknowledged by all the critics, in his descriptions of the games and exercises, to have had an eye always to his own country, and to have drawn them after the manner of the Roman sports. Now the sea-contention, which he presents us with, is barely a trial of swiftness in the vessels, and of skill in managing the oars, as is most admirably delivered in his fifth book: 114.

> *Prima pares ineunt gravibus certamina remis*
> *Quatuor ex omni delecta classe carinæ*, &c.

The *Naumachiæ* of Claudius, which he presented on the Fucine lake before he drained it, deserve to be particularly mentioned, not more for the greatness of the show, than for the behaviour of the Emperor; who, when the combatants passed before him with so melancholy a greeting as, *Ave imperator, morituri te salutant*, returned in answer, *Avete vos*; which when they would gladly have interpreted as an act of favour, and a grant of their lives, he soon gave them to understand that it proceeded from the contrary principle of barbarous cruelty and insensibility (*a*).

The most celebrated *Naumachiæ* were those of the Emperor Domitian; in which were engaged such a vast number of vessels as would have almost formed two complete navies (*b*) for a proper fight, together with a proportionable channel of water, equalling the dimensions of a natural river. Martial has a very genteel turn on this subject, Spectac. 24.

> *Si quis ades longis serus spectator ab oris,*
>   *Cui lux prima sacri muneris ista dies,*
> *Ne te decipiat ratibus navalis Enyo,*
>   *Et par unda fretis: hic modo terra fuit.*
> *Non credis? spectes dum laxent æquora Martem;*
>   *Parva mora est, dices, hic modo pontus erat.*

> Stranger, whoe'er from distant parts arriv'd,
> But this one sacred day in Rome hast liv'd;
> Mistake not the wide flood, and pompous show
> Of naval combats: Here was land but now.

(*a*) *Suet. Claud.* c. 43. *Tacit. An.* XIII.   (*b*) *Suet. in Domit.* c. 4.

Is this beyond your credit ? Only stay
'Till from the fight the vessels bear away ;
You'll cry with wonder, Here but now was sea !

It is related of the Emperor Heliogabalus, that, in a representation of a naval fight, he filled the channel where the vessels were to ride, with wine instead of water (*a*). A story scarce credible, though we have the highest conceptions of his prodigious luxury and extravagance.

(*a*) *Lampridius in Heliogab.*

C H A P. IV.

Of the GLADIATORS.

THE first rise of the Gladiators is referred to the ancient custom of killing persons at the funerals of great men. For the old heathens fancying the ghosts of the deceased to be satisfied, and rendered propitious by human blood, at first they used to buy captives, or untoward slaves, and offered them at the obsequies : Afterwards they contrived to veil over their impious barbarity with the specious show of pleasure, and voluntary combat ; and therefore training up such persons as they had procured in some tolerable knowledge of weapons ; upon the day appointed for the sacrifices to the departed ghosts, they obliged them to maintain a mortal encounter at the tombs of their friends. The first show of Gladiators *, exhibited at Rome, was that of M. and D. Brutus, upon the death of their father, *A. U. C.* 490, in the consulship of Ap. Claudius and M. Fulvius (*a*).

* *Munus Gladiatorum.*

Within a little time, when they found the people exceedingly pleased with such bloody entertainments, they resolved to give them the like diversion as soon as possible ; and therefore it soon grew into a custom, that not only the heir of any great or rich citizen newly deceased, but that all the principal magistrates should take occasions to present the people with these shows, in order to procure their esteem and affection. Nay, the very priests were sometimes the exhibitors of such impious pomps ; for we meet with the *Ludi Pontificales*

(*a*) *Val. Max.* lib. 2. cap. 4.

Book V.   *The* GLADIATORS.   271

Pontificales in Suetonius *(a)*, and with the *Ludi Sacerdotales* in Pliny *(b)*.

As for the Emperors, it was so much their interest to ingratiate themselves with the commonalty, that they obliged them with these shows almost upon all occasions: As on their birthday; at the time of a triumph, or after any signal victory; at the consecration of any public edifices; at the games which several of them instituted to return in such a term of years; with many others, which occur in every historian.

And as the occasions of these solemnities were so prodigiously increased, in the same manner was the length of them, and the number of the combatants. At the first show exhibited by the Bruti, it is probable there were only three pair of Gladiators, as may be gathered from that of Ausonius:

Tres primas Thracum pugnas, tribus ordine bellis,
Juniadæ patrio inferias misere sepulchro.

Yet Julius Cæsar, in his ædileship, presented three hundred and twenty pair *(c)*. The excellent Titus exhibited a show of Gladiators, wild beasts, and representations of sea-fights, a hundred days together *(d)*: And Trajan, as averse from cruelty as the former, continued the solemnity of this nature a hundred and twenty-three days, during which he brought out a thousand pair of Gladiators *(e)*. Two thousand men of the same profession were listed by the Emperor Otho to serve against Vitellius. Nay, long before this, they were so very numerous, that, in the time of Catilinarian conspiracy, an order passed to send all the Gladiators up and down into the garrisons, for fear they should raise any disturbance in the city *(f)*, by joining with the disaffected party. And Plutarch informs us, that the famous Spartacus, who at last gathered such a numerous force as to put Rome under some unusual apprehensions, was no more than a Gladiator, who, breaking out from a show at Verona, with the rest of his gang, dared to proclaim war against the Roman State *(g)*.

In the mean time, the wise and the better Romans were very sensible of the dangerous consequences which a corruption of this nature might produce; and therefore Cicero preferred a law, that no person should exhibit a show of Gladiators within two years before he appeared candidate for an office

(a) August, cap. 44.   *(b) Epist.* lib. 7.   *(c) Plutarch. in Cæs.*
(d) Dio, lib. 68.   *(e) Tacitus.*   *(f) Sallust. Catalin.*   *(g) Plutarch. in Crass.*

office (*a*). Julius Cæsar ordered, that only such a number of men of this profession should be in Rome at a time (*b*). Augustus decreed, that only two shows of Gladiators should be presented in a year, and never above sixty pair of combatants in a show (*c*). Tiberius provided, by an order of the Senate, that no person should have the privilege of gratifying the people with such a solemnity, unless he was worth four hundred thousand sesterces (*d*).

Nerva in a great measure regulated this affair, after the many abuses of the former Emperors; but the honour of entirely removing this barbarity out of the Roman world was reserved for Constantine the Great, which he performed about the year of the city 1067, nigh six hundred years after their first institution. Yet under Constantius, Theodosius, and Valentinian, the same cruel humour began to revive, till a final stop was put to it by the Emperor Honorius; the occasion of which is given at large by the authors of ecclesiastical history.

Thus much may be proper to observe in general concerning the origin, increase, and restraint of this custom. For our farther information, it will be necessary to take particular notice of the condition of the Gladiators, of their several orders, or kinds, and of their manner of duelling.

As for their condition, they were commonly slaves, or captives; for it was an ordinary custom to sell a disobedient servant to the *Lanistæ*, or the instructors of the Gladiators, who, after they had taught them some part of their skill, let them out for money at a show. Yet the freemen soon put in for a share of this privilege to be killed in jest; and accordingly many times offered themselves to hire for the amphitheatre, whence they had the name of *Auctorati*. Nay, the Knights and noblemen, and even the Senators themselves, at last were not ashamed to take up the same profession, some to keep themselves from starving, after they had squandered away their estates, and others to curry favour with the Emperors; so that Augustus was forced to command, by a public edict, that none of the senatorian order should turn Gladiators (*e*); and soon after he laid the same restraint on the Knights (*f*). Yet these prohibitions were so little regarded by the following Princes, that Nero presented at one show (if the numbers of Suetonius are not corrupted) 400 Senators, and 600 of the Equestrian rank (*g*).

But

(*a*) *Cicero in Vatin.*   (*b*) *Suet. Cæs.* cap. 10.   (*c*) *Dio.*
(*d*) *Tacit. An.* 4.   (*e*) *Dio, lib.* 48.   (*f*) *Sueton Aug.* cap. 43.
Dio, lib. 54.   (*g*) *Idem, Ner.* cap. 12.

But all this will look like no wonder, when, upon a farther search, we meet with the very women engaging in these public encounters, particularly under Nero and Domitian. Juvenal has exposed them very handsomely for this mannish humour in his sixth Satire, 254:

> *Quale decus rerum, si conjugis auctio fiat,*
> *Balteus & manicæ, & cristæ, crurisque sinistri*
> *Dimidium tegmen? vel si diversa movebit*
> *Prælia, tu felix, ocreas vendente puella.*
> *Hæ sunt quæ tenui sudant in cyclade: quarum*
> *Delicias & panniculus bombycinus urit.*
> *Adspice quo fremitu monstratos perferat ictus,*
> *Et quanto galeæ curvetur pondere; quanta*
> *Poplitibus sedeat quam densa fascia libro!*

> Oh! what a decent sight 'tis to behold
> All thy wife's magazine by auction sold!
> The belt, the crested plume, the several suits
> Of armour, and the Spanish-leather boots!
> Yet these are they that cannot bear the heat
> Of figur'd silks, and under sarsenet sweat.
> Behold the strutting Amazonian whore,
> She stands in guard, with her right foot before;
> Her coats tuck'd up, and all her motions just,
> She stamps, and then cries Hah! at every thrust.
>   [MR DRYDEN.

Yet the women were not the most inconsiderable performers, for a more ridiculous set of combatants are still behind; and these were the dwarfs, who, encountering one another, or the women, at these public diversions, gave a very pleasant entertainment. Statius has left us this elegant description of them: Syl. I. vi. 57.

> *Hic audax subit ordo pumilorum,*
> *Quos natura brevi statu peractos,*
> *Nodosum semel in globum ligavit.*
> *Edunt vulnera, conferuntque dextras,*
> *Et mortem sibi, qua manu, minentur,*
> *Ridet Mars pater, & cruenta Virtus;*
> *Casuræque vagis grues rapinis,*
> *Mirantur pumilos ferociores.*

To mortal combat next succeed
Bold fencers of the Pigmy breed,
Whom nature, when she half had wrought,
Not worth her farther labour thought,
But clos'd the rest in one hard knot.
With what a grace they drive their blow,
And ward their jolt-head from their foe?
Old Mars and rigid Virtue smile
At their redoubted champion's toil.
And cranes, to please the mob, let fly,
Admir'd to see their enemy
So often by themselves o'ercome,
Inspir'd with nobler hearts at Rome.

The several kinds of Gladiators worth observing were the *Retiarii*, the *Secutores*, the *Myrmillones*, the *Thracians*, the *Samnites*, the *Pinnirapi*, the *Essedarii*, and the *Andabatæ*. But before we inquire particularly into the distinct orders, we may take notice of several names attributed in common to some of every kind upon various occasions. Thus we meet with the *Gladiatores Meridiani*, who engaged in the afternoon, the chief part of the show being finished in the morning. *Gladiatores Fiscales*, those who were maintained out of the Emperor's fiscus, or private treasury, such as Arrian calls Καισαρος μονομάχυς, *Cæsar's Gladiators*: *Gladiatores Postulatitii*, commonly men of great art and experience, whom the people particularly desired the Emperor to produce: *Gladiatores Catervarii*, such as did not fight by pairs, but in small companies: Suetonius uses *Catervarii Pugiles* in the same sense (*a*). *Gladiatores Ordinarii*, such as were presented according to the common manner, and at the usual time, and fought the ordinary way; on which account they were distinguished from the *Catervarii*, and the *Postulatitii*.

As for the several kinds already reckoned up, they owed their distinction to their country, their arms, their way of fighting, and such circumstances, and may be thus, in short, described:

The *Retiarius* was dressed in a short coat, having a *fuscina* or trident in his left-hand, and a net in his right, with which he endeavoured to entangle his adversary, and then with his trident might easily dispatch him; on his head he wore only a hat

---

(*a*) *Aug.* cap. 45.

a hat tied under his chin with a broad ribbon. The *Secutor* was armed with a buckler and a helmet, wherein was the picture of a fish, in allusion to the net. His weapon was a scymetar, or *falx supina*. He was called *Secutor*, because, if the *Retiarius*, against whom he was always matched, should happen to fail in casting his net, his only safety lay in flight; so that in this case he plyed his heels as fast as he could about the place of combat, till he had got his net in order for a second throw: In the mean time this Secutor or follower pursued him, and endeaved to prevent his design. Juvenal is very happy in the account he gives us of a young nobleman that scandalously turned Retiarius in the reign of Nero: Nor is there any relation of this sort of combat so exact in any other author.

―――――*Et illic*
Dedecus urbis habes: nec myrmillonis in armis,
Nec clypeo Gracchum pugnantem aut falce supina,
(Damnat enim tales habitus, sed damnat & odit:)
Nec galea faciem abscondit, movet ecce tridentem,
Postquam librata pendentia retia dextra
Nequicquam effudit, nudum ad spectacula vultum
Erigit, & tota fugit agnoscendus arena.
Credamus tunicæ, de faucibus aurea cum se
Porrigat, & longo jactetur spira galero:
Ergo ignominiam graviorem pertulit omni
Vulnere, cum Graccho jussus pugnare secutor. Sat. viii. 199.

Go to the lists where feats of arms are shewn,
There you'll find Gracchus from Patrician grown
A fencer, and the scandal of the town.
Nor will he the Myrmillo's weapons bear,
The *modest helmet* he disdains to wear.
As Retiarius he attacks his foe:
First waves his *trident* ready for the throw,
Next casts his *net*, but neither levell'd right,
He stares about, expos'd to public sight,
Then places all his safety in his flight.
Room for the noble Gladiator! see
His coat and hatband show his quality.
Thus when at last the brave Myrmillo knew
'Twas Gracchus was the wretch he did pursue,

To conquer such a coward griev'd him more.
Than if he many glorious wounds had bore.
[MR STEPNEY.

Here the poet seems to make the *Myrmillo* the same as the *Secutor*, and thus all the comments explain him. Yet Lipsius will have the *Myrmillones* to be a distinct order, who fought completely armed: and therefore he believes them to be the *Crupellarii* of Tacitus (a), so called from some old Gallic word, expressing, that they could only creep along by reason of their heavy armour.

The Thracians made a great part of the choicest Gladiators, that nation having the general repute of fierceness and cruelty beyond the rest of the world. The particular weapon they used was the *Sica*, or faulchion; and the defence consisted in a *parma*, or little round shield, proper to their country.

The original of the Samnite Gladiators is given us by Livy: The Campanians, says he, bearing a great hatred to the Samnites, they armed a part of their Gladiators after the fashion of that country, and called them *Samnites* (b). What these arms were, he tells us in another place; they wore a shield at the top to defend the breasts and shoulders, and growing more narrow towards the bottom, that it might be moved with the greater convenience; they had a sort of belt coming over their breasts, a greave on their left foot, and a crested helmet on their heads; whence it is plain that description of the Amazonian fencer, already given from Juvenal, is expressly meant of assuming the armour and duty of a *Samnite* Gladiator.

> *Balteus & manica & crista, crurisque sinistri*
> *Dimidium tegmen.*

The *Pinna*, which adorned the *Samnite*'s helmet, denominated another sort of Gladiators *Pinnirapi*, because, being matched with the *Samnites*, they used to catch at those *pinnæ*, and bear them off in triumph, as marks of their victory. Dr Holyday takes the *Pinnirapus* to be the same as the *Retiarius* (c).

Lipsius fancies the *procuratores*, mentioned by Cicero in his oration for P. Sextius, to have been a distinct species, and that they were generally matched with the Samnites; tho' perhaps the words of Cicero may be thought not to imply so much.
The

(a) *Annal*. lib. 5.   (b) Lib. 9.   (c) Illustration on *Juvenal*, Sat. 3.

Book V. *The* GLADIATORS.

The *Hoplomachi*, whom we meet with in Seneca (a) and Suetonius (b), may probably be the same either with the Samnites or Myrmillones, called by the Greek name ὁπλομάχοι, because they fought in armour.

The *Essedarii*, mentioned by the same authors (c), and by Tully (d), were such as on some occasions engaged one another out of chariots *, though perhaps at other times they fought on foot like the rest. The *essedum* was a sort of waggon, from which the Gauls and the Britons used to assail the Romans in their engagements with them.

* *Esseda*.

The *Andabatæ*, or Ἀναβάται, fought on horseback, with a sort of helmet that covered all the face and eyes, and therefore *andabatarum more pugnare*, is to combat blindfold.

As to the manner of the Gladiators combats, we cannot apprehend it fully, unless we take in what was done before, and what after the fight, as well as the actual engagement. When any person designed to oblige the people with a show, he set up bills in the public places, giving an account of the time, the number of the Gladiators, and other circumstances. This they called *munus pronunciare*, or *proponere;* and the *libelli*, or bills, were sometimes termed *edicta;* many times, besides these bills, they set up great pictures, on which were described the manner of the fight, and the effigies of some of the most celebrated Gladiators, whom they intended to bring out. This custom is elegantly described by Horace, Book 2. Sat. vii. 95:

> *Vel cum pausiaca torpes, insane, tabella,*
> *Qui peccas minus atque ego, cum fulvi, rutubæque,*
> *Aut placideiani contento poplite miror*
> *Prælia rubrica picta aut carbone, velut si*
> *Revera pugnent, feriant, vitentque moventes*
> *Arma viri?*

Or when on some rare piece you wond'ring stand,
And praise the colour and the master's hand,
Are you less vain than I, when in the street
The painted canvas holds my ravish'd sight;
Where with bent knees the skilful fencers strive
To speed their pass, as if they mov'd alive;
And with new flights so well express'd engage,
That I amaz'd stare up, and think them on the stage.

At

(a) *Controvers.* lib. 3.   (b) *In Calig.* 3.   (c) *Senec* Ep. 39.
Sueton. Calig. 35. *Claud.* 21.   (d) *In Epistolis.*

At the appointed day for the show, in the first place the Gladiators were brought out all together, and obliged to take a circuit round the *arena* in a very solemn and pompous manner. After this they proceeded, *paria componere,* to match them by pairs, in which care was used to make the matches equal. Before the combatants fell to it in earnest, they tried their skill against one another with more harmless weapons, as the *rudes,* spears without heads, the blunted swords, the foils, and such like. This Cicero admirably observes: *Si in illo ipso Gladiatorio vitæ certamine, quo ferro decernitur, tamen ante congressum multa fiunt, quæ non ad vulnus, sed ad speciem valere videantur; quanto magis hoc in oratione expectandum est?* "If in the "mortal combats of the Gladiators, where the victory is de- "cided by arms before they actually engage, there are seve- "ral flourishes given, more for a show of art than a design of "hurting; how much more proper would this look in the "contention of an orator?" This flourishing before the fight was called in common *prælusio,* or in respect to the swords, only *ventilatio.* This exercise was continued, till the trumpets sounding gave them notice to enter on more desperate encounters, and then they were said *vertere arma:*

———*Ita rem natam esse intelligio,*
Necessum est versis armis depugnarier. Plaut.

The terms of striking were *petere* and *repetere;* of avoiding a blow, *exire.* Virg. Æn. v. 438.

Corpore tela modo, atque oculis vigilantibus exit.

When any person received a remarkable wound, either his adversary or the people used to cry out, *habet,* or *hoc habet.* This Virgil alludes to, Æn. xii. 294:

———*Teloque orantem multa trabali*
Desuper altus equo gravitur ferit, atque ita fatur:
Hoc habet; hæc magnis melior data victima divis.

———Him, as much he pray'd,
With his huge spear Messapus deeply struck
From his high courser's back, and chasing spoke,
He has it; and to this auspicious blow
A nobler victim the great gods shall owe.

The party who was worsted *submitted his arms*, and acknowledged himself conquered; yet this would not save his life, unless the people pleased, and therefore he made his application to them for pity. The two signs of favour and dislike given by the people were, *premere pollicem*, and *vertera pollicem*, phrases which the critics have quarrelled much about to little purpose. But M. Dacier seems to have been more happy in his explanation than his predecessors. The former he takes to be a clenching of the fingers of both hands between one another, and so holding the two thumbs upright close together. This was done to express their admiration of the art and courage showed by both combatants, and a sign to the conqueror to spare the life of his antagonist, as having performed his part remarkably well. Hence Horace, to signify the extraordinary commendation that a man could give to one of his own temper and disposition, says, Ep. xviii. 66:

Fautor utroque tuum laudabit pollice ludum.

And Meander has δακτύλους πιέζειν, *to press the fingers*, a custom on the Grecian stage, designed for a mark of approbation, answerable to our clapping.

But the contrary motion, or bending back of the thumbs, signified the dissatisfaction of the spectators, and authorized the victor to kill the other combatant outright for a coward.

———*Verso pollice vulgi*
Quemlibet occidunt populariter.   Juv. Sat. iii. 36.

Where influenc'd by the rabble's bloody will,
With thumbs bent back, they popularly kill.

Besides this privilege of the people, the Emperors seem to have had the liberty of saving whom they thought fit, when they were present at the solemnity; and, perhaps, upon the bare coming in of the Emperor into the place of combat, the Gladiators, who in that instant had the worst of it, were delivered from farther danger:

Cæsaris adventu tuta Gladiator arena
Exit, & auxilium non leve vultus habet.   Martial.

Where Cæsar comes, the worsted fencer lives,
And his bare presence (like the gods) reprieves.

After the engagement there were several marks of favour conferred on the victors, as many times a present of money, perhaps gathered up among the spectators, which Juvenal alludes to, Sat. vii:

Acciepi victori populus quod postulat aurum.

———————Take the gains
A conq'ring fencer from the crowd obtains.

But the most common rewards were the *pileus* and the *rudis:* The former was given only to such Gladiators as were slaves, for a token of their obtaining freedom. The *rudis* seems to have been bestowed both on slaves and freemen, but with this difference, that it procured for the former no more than a discharge from any further performance in public, upon which they commonly turned *lanistæ*, spending their time in training up young fencers. Ovid calls it *tuta rudis:*

Tutaque deposito poscitur ense rudis.

But the *rudis*, when given to such persons as, being free, had hired themselves out for these shows, restored them to a full enjoyment of their liberty. Both these sorts of *rudiarii*, being excused from further service, had a custom to hang up their arms in the temple of Hercules, the patron of their profession, and were never called out again without their consent. Horace has given us a full account of this custom in his first epistle to Mæcenas:

Prima dicte mihi, summa dicende camena,
Spectatum satis & donatum jam rude, quæris,
Mæcenas iterum antiquo me includere ludo.
Non eadem est ætas, non mens. Vejanius, armis
Herculis ad postem fixis, latet abditus agro:
Ne populum extrema toties exoret arena.

Mæcenas,

> Mæcenas, you whose name and title grac'd
> My early labours, and shall crown my last:
> Now, when I've long engag'd with wish'd success,
> And full of fame, obtain'd my writ of ease;
> While sprightly fancy sits with heavy age,
> Again you'd bring me on the doubtful stage.
> Yet wise Vejanius, hanging up his arms
> To Hercules, yon little cottage farms:
> Lest he be forc'd, if giddy fortune turns,
> To cringe to the vile rabble, whom he scorns.

The learned Dacier, in his observation on this place, acquaints us, That it was a custom for all persons, when they laid down any art or employment, to consecrate the proper instruments of their calling to the particular deity who was acknowledged for the president of that profession. And therefore the Gladiators, when thus discharged, hung up their arms to Hercules, who had a chapel by every amphitheatre, and where there were no amphitheatres, in circo; and over every place assigned to such manly performances there stood a Hercules, with his club.

We may take our leave of the Gladiators with the excellent passage of Cicero, which may serve in some measure as an apology for the custom: *Crudele Gladiatorum spectaculum & inhumanum nonnullis videri solet: & haud scio an non ita sit, ut nunc fit: tum vero sontes ferro depugnabant, auribus fortasse multæ, oculis quidem nulla poterat esse fortior contra dolorem & mortem disciplina (a).* "The shows of Gladiators may possibly, to "some persons, seem barbarous and inhuman; and indeed, as "the case now stands, I cannot say that the censure is unjust: "But in those times, when only guilty persons composed the "number of combatants, the ear perhaps might receive many "better instructions; but it is impossible that any thing which "affects our eyes, should fortify us with more success against "the assaults of grief and death."

(a) *Tuscul. Quæst.* 2.

CHAP. V.

Of the LUDI SCENICI, *or Stage-Plays: And first of the Satires and the Mimick-Pieces, with the Rise and Advances of such Entertainments among the* ROMANS.

THE LUDI SCENICI, or stage-plays, have been commonly divided into four species, Satire, Mimic, Tragedy, and Comedy. The elder Scaliger will have satire to have proceeded from tragedy, in the same manner as the mimus from comedy: But we are assured this was in use at Rome long before the more perfect dramas had gained a place on the stage. Nor has the same excellent critic been more happy in tracing the original of this sort of poetry as far as Greece: For we cannot suppose it to bear any resemblance to the chorus, or dance of satires, which used to appear in the theatres at Athens, as an appendage to some of their tragedies, thence called *Satyrique*. This kind of Greek farce was taken up purely in the characters of mirth and wantonness, not admitting those sarcastical reflections, which were the very essence of the Roman satire. Therefore Casaubon and Dacier, without casting an eye towards Greece, make no question but the name is to be derived from *satura*, a Roman word, signifying *full*: The [*u*] being changed into an [*i*], after the same manner as *optumus* and *maxumus* were afterwards spelled *optimus* and *maximus*. *Satura*, being an adjective, must be supposed to relate to the substantive *lanx*, a platter or charger; such as they filled yearly with all sorts of fruit, and offered to their gods at their festivals, as the *primitiæ*, or first gatherings of the season. Such an expression might be well applied to this kind of poem, which was full of various matter, and written on different subjects. Nor are there wanting other instances of the same way of speaking: as particularly *per Saturam Sententias exquirere*, is used by Salluft, to signify the way of voting in the Senate, when neither the members were told, nor the voices counted, but all gave their suffrages promiscuously, and without observing any order. And the *historiæ Saturæ*, or *per Saturam* of Festus, were nothing else but miscellaneous tracts of history. The original of the Roman satire will lead us into the knowledge of the first representations of persons, and the rude essays towards dramatic poetry, in the rustic ages of Rome; for which we are beholden to the accurate research of Dacier, and the improvement of him by Mr Dryden.

During the space of almost four hundred years from the building of the city, the Romans had never known any entertainments of the stage. Chance and jollity first found out those verses which they called *Saturnian*, because they supposed such to have been in use under Saturn, and *Fescennine*, from Fescennia, a town in Tuscany, where they were first practised. The actors, upon occasion of merriment, with a gross and rustic kind of raillery, reproached one another *ex tempore* with their failings; and at the same time were nothing sparing of it to the audience. Somewhat of this custom was afterwards retained in their *Saturnalia*, or feast of Saturn, celebrated in December; at least all kind of freedom of speech was then allowed to slaves, even against their masters: And we are not without some imitation of it on our Christmas-gambols. We cannot have a better notion of this rude and unpolished kind of farce, than by imagining a company of clowns on a holiday dancing lubberly, and upbraiding one another in *ex tempore* doggrel, with their defects and vices, and the stories that were told of them in bake-houses and barbers-shops.

This rough-cast unhewn poetry was instead of stage-plays for the space of a hundred and twenty years together; but then, when they began to be somewhat better bred and entered, as one may say, into the first rudiments of civil conversation, they left their hedge-notes for another sort of poem a little more polished, which was also full of pleasant raillery, but without any mixture of obscenity. This new species of poetry appeared under the name of *Satire*, because of its variety, and was adorned with compositions of music, and with dances.

When Livius Andronicus, about the year of Rome 514, had introduced the new entertainments of tragedy and comedy, the people neglected and abandoned their old diversion of satires: But, not long after, they took them up again, and then they joined them to their comedies, playing them at the end of the drama; as the French continue at this day to act their farces in the nature of a separate representation from their tragedies.

A year after Andronicus had opened the Roman stage with his new dramas Ennius was born; who, when he was grown to man's estate, having seriously considered the genius of the people, and how eagerly they followed the first satires, thought it would be worth his while to refine upon the project, and to write satires, not to be acted upon the theatre, but read. The event was answerable to his expectation, and his design being improved by Pacuvius, adorned with a more graceful turn by Lucilius, and advanced to its full height by Horace, Juvenal, and Persius, grew into a distinct species of poetry, and has ever met with a kind reception in the world. To the same original we owe the other sort of satire, called *Varronian*, from the learned Varro, who first composed it. This was written freely, without any restraint to verse or prose, but consisted of an intermixture of both; of which nature are the Satyricon of Petronius, Seneca's mock Deification of the Emperor Claudius, and Boethius's Consolations.

As for the Mimus, from Μιμεῖσθαι, *to imitate*, Scaliger defines it to be, a " poem imitating any sort of actions, so as to make " them appear ridiculous (*a*)." The original of it he refers to the comedies, in which, when the chorus went off the stage, they were succeeded by a sort of actors, who diverted the audience for some time with apish postures and antic dances. They were not masked, but had their faces smeared over with soot, and dressed themselves in lamb-skins, which are called *Pescia* in the old verses of the Salii.

These wore garlands of ivy, and carried baskets full of herbs and flowers to the honour of Bacchus, as had been observed in the first institution of the custom at Athens. They acted always barefoot, and were thence called *Planipedes*.

These diversions being received with universal applause by the people, the actors took assurance to model them into a distinct entertainment from the other plays, and present them by themselves. And perhaps it was not till now, that they undertook to write several pieces of poetry with the name of *Mimi*, representing an imperfect sort of drama, not divided into acts, and performed only by a single person. These were a very frequent entertainment of the Roman stage long after tragedy and comedy had been advanced to their full height, and seemed to have always maintained a very great esteem in the town.

The

(*a*) *De Re Poet.* lib. 1. cap. 10.

The two famous mimics, or pantomimi, as they called them, were Laberius and Publius, both co-temporary to Julius Cæsar. Laberius was a person of the Equestrian rank, and, at threescore years of age, acted the mimic pieces of his own composing, in the games which Cæsar presented to the people; for which he received a reward of five hundred sestertia, and a gold ring, and so recovered the honour which he had forfeited by performing on the stage (*a*). Macrobius has given us part of a prologue of this author, wherein he seems to complain of the obligations which Cæsar laid on him to appear in the quality of an actor, so contrary to his own inclination, and to the former course of his life. Some of them, which may serve for a taste of his wit and style, are as follow:

> *Fortuna immoderata in bono æque atque in malo,*
> *Si tibi erat libitum literarum laudibus*
> *Floris cacumen nostræ famæ frangere,*
> *Cur, cum vigebam membris præviridantibus,*
> *Satisfacere populo & tali cum poteram viro,*
> *Non flexibilem me concurvasti ut carperes?*
> *Nunc me quo dejicis? Quid ad scenam affero?*
> *Decorem formæ, an dignitatem corporis?*
> *Animi virtutem, an vocis jucundæ sonum?*
> *Ut hedera serpens vires arboreas necat;*
> *Ita me vetustas amplexu annorum enecat.*
> *Sepulchri similis, nihil nisi nomen retineo.*

Horace indeed expressly taxes his composures with want of elegance (*b*): But Scaliger (*c*) thinks the censure to be very unjust; and that the verses cited by Macrobius are much better than those of Horace, in which this reflection is to be found.

There goes a sharp repartee of the same Laberius upon Tully, when, upon receiving the golden ring of Cæsar, he went to resume his seat among the Knights; they, out of a principle of honour, seemed very unwilling to receive him; Cicero particularly told him, as he passed by, That indeed he would make room for him with all his heart, but that he was squeezed up already himself. No wonder (says Laberius) that you, who commonly make use of two seats at once, fancy yourself squeezed up, when you sit like other people.

In

(*a*) *Suet.* in *Jul.* c. 39. *Macrob. Saturn.* l. 2. c. 7.   (*b*) *Lib.* 1. *Sat.* 10.   (*c*) *De Re Poet.* lib. 1. cap. 19.

In which he gave a very severe wipe on the double-dealing of the Orator (a).

Publius was a Syrian by birth, but received his education at Rome in the condition of a slave. Having by several specimens of wit obtained his freedom, he set to write mimic pieces, and acted them with wonderful applause about the towns in Italy. At last, being brought to Rome, to bear a part in Cæsar's plays, he challenged all the dramatic writers and actors, and won the prize from every man of them, one by one, even from Laberius himself (b). A collection of sentences taken out of his works is still extant. Joseph Scaliger gave them a very high encomium, and thought it worth his while to turn them into Greek.

(a) *Macrob. Saturn.* lib. 2. cap. 7.   (b) *Idem*, lib. 2. cap. 7.

CHAP. VI.

Of the ROMAN *Tragedy and Comedy.*

THE Roman tragedy and comedy were wholly borrowed from the Græcians, and therefore do not so properly fall under the present design : Yet, in order to a right understanding of these pieces, there is scope enough for a very useful inquiry, without roaming so far as Athens, unless upon a necessary errand. The parts of a play, agreed on by ancient and modern writers, are these four : First, The *protasis*, or entrance, which gives a light only to the characters of the persons, and proceeds very little to any part of the action. Secondly, The *epitasis*, or working up of the plot, where the play grows warmer ; the design or action of it is drawing on, and you see something promising that will come to pass. Thirdly, The *catastasis*, or, in a Roman word, the *status*, the height and full growth of the play : This may properly be called the counter-turn, which destroys that expectation, embroils the action in new difficulties, and leaves us far distant from that hope in which it found us. Lastly, The *catastrophe*, or Δύσις, the discovery, or unravelling of the plot. Here we see all things settled again on their first foundation, and, the obstacles which hindered the design or action of the play at once removed ; it ends with that resemblance of truth and nature,

nature, that the audience are satisfied with the conduct of it (a). It is a question whether the first Roman drama's were divided into acts; or at least it seems probable, that they were not admitted into comedy, till after it had lost its chorus, and so stood in need of some more necessary divisions than could be made by the music only. Yet the five acts were so established in the time of Horace, that he gives it for a rule, Art. Poet. 189.

> *Neve minor, neu sit quinto productior actu*
> *Fabula.*

The distinction of the scenes seems to have been an invention of the grammarians, and is not to be found in the old copies of Plautus and Terence; and therefore these are wholly left out in the excellent French and English translations.

The dramas, presented at Rome, were divided in general into *Palliatæ* and *Togatæ*, Græcian, and properly Roman. In the former, the plot being laid in Greece, the actors were habited according to the fashion of that country; in the other, the persons were supposed to be Romans. But then the comedies properly Roman were of several sorts: *Prætextatæ*, when the actors were supposed to be persons of quality, such as had the liberty of wearing the *prætexta*, or purple gown: *Tabernariæ*, when the *tabernæ*, low ordinary buildings, were expressed in the scenes, the persons being of the lower ranks. Suetonius (b) informs us, That C. Melissus, in the time of Augustus, introduced a new sort of *togatæ*, which he called *Trabeatæ*. Monsieur Dacier is of opinion, that they were wholly taken up in matters relating to the camp, and that the persons represented were some of the chief officers (c): For the *trabea* was the proper habit of the Consul, when he set forward on any warlike design. There was a species of comedy different from both these, and more inclining to farce, which they called *Atellana*, from Atella, a town of the Oscians in Campania, where it was first invented. The chief design of it was mirth and jesting, (though sometimes with a mixture of debauchery, and lascivious postures) and therefore the actors were not reckoned among the *histriones*, or common players, but kept the benefit of their tribe, and might be listed for soldiers, a privilege allowed only to freemen. Sometimes perhaps

---

(a) Mr Dryden's *Dramat. Essay.*   (b) *De Claris Grammat.* 21.
(c) *Not. on Horace's Art. Poet.*

haps the *Atellanæ* were presented between the acts of other comedies, by way of exodium or interlude : As we meet with *exodium atellanicum* in Suetonius (*a*).

Though all the rules by which the drama is practised at this day, either such as relate to the justness and symmetry of the plot, or the episodical ornaments, such as descriptions, narrations, and other beauties not essential to the play, were delivered to us by the ancients, and the judgments which we make, of all performances of this kind, are guided by their examples and directions ; yet there are several things belonging to the old dramatic pieces, which we cannot at all understand by the modern, since, not being essential to these works, they have been long disused. Of this sort we may reckon up, as particularly worth our observation, the buskin and the sock, the masques, the chorus, and the flutes.

The *cothurnus* and the *soccus* were such eminent marks of distinction between the old tragedy and comedy, that they were brought not only to signify those distinct species of dramatic poetry, but to express the sublime and the humble style in any other composition : As Martial calls Virgil *cothurnatus*, though he never meddled with tragedy :

Grande Cothurnati pone Maronis opus.

This *cothurnus* is thought to have been a square high sort of boot, which made the actors appear above the ordinary size of mortals, such as they supposed the old heroes to have generally been ; and at the same time, giving them leave to move but slowly, were well accommodated to the state and gravity which subjects of that nature required. Yet it is plain they were not in use only on the stage ; for Virgil brings in the Goddess Venus in the habit of a Tyrian maid, telling Æneas, i. 340.

Virginibus Tyriis mos est gestare pharetram,
Purpureoque alte suras vincire cothurno.

From which it appears, that the hunters sometimes wore buskins to secure their legs : But then we must suppose them to be much lighter and better contrived than the other, for fear they should prove a hindrance to the swiftness and agility

(*a*) *Tiber.* 45.

lity required in that sport. The women in some parts of Italy still wear a sort of shoes, or rather stilts, somewhat like these buskins which they call *cioppini*; Lassels informs us, that he had seen them at Venice a full half-yard high.

The *soccus* was a slight kind of covering for the feet, whence the fashion and the name of our socks are derived. The comedians wore these, to represent the vility of the person they represented, as debauched young sparks, old crazy misers, pimps, parasites, strumpets, and the rest of that gang; for the sock being proper to the women, as it was very light and thin, was always counted scandalous when worn by men. Thus Seneca (*a*) exclaims against Caligula for sitting to judge upon life and death in a rich pair of socks, adorned with gold and silver.

Another reason why they were taken up by the actors of comedy might be, because they were the fittest that could be imagined for dancing. Thus Catullus invokes Hymen, the patron of weddings, lib. 9:

> *Huc veni niveo gerens*
> *Luteum pede soccum,*
> *Excitusque hilari die,*
> *Nuptialia concinens*
> *Voce carmina tinnula,*
> *Pelle humum pedibus*———

The *persona*, or mask, A. Gellius (*b*) derives (according to an old author) from *persono*, to sound thoroughly; because these vizards, being put over the face, and left open at the mouth, rendered the voice much clearer and fuller, by contracting it into a lesser compass. But Scaliger will not allow of this conjecture. However the reason of it (which is all that concerns us at present) appears from all the old figures of the masks, in which we find always a very large wide hole designed for the mouth. Madam Dacier, who met with the draughts of the comic vizards in a very old manuscript of Terence, informs us, that they were not like ours, which cover only the face, but that they came over the whole head, and had always a sort of peruke of hair fastened on them, proper to the person whom they were to represent.

The original of the mask is referred by Horace to Æschylus, whereas before the actors had no other disguise, but to smear

(*a*) *Benefic.* lib. 2. cap. 12.   (*b*) *Noct.* lib. 5. cap. 7.

smear over their faces with odd colours; and yet this was well enough, when their stage was no better than a cart.

> *Ignotum tragicæ genus invenisse camenæ*
> *Dicitur, & plaustris vexisse poemata Thespis:*
> *Quæ canerent agerentque peruncti fæcibus ora.*
> *Post hunc personæ pallæque repertor honestæ*
> *Æschylus, & modicis implevit pulpita tignis;*
> *Et docuit magnumque loqui, nitique Cothurno.* Ars Poet. 275.

> When Thespis first expos'd the tragic muse,
> Rude were the actors, and a cart the scene;
> Where ghastly faces, stain'd with lees of wine,
> Frighted the children, and amus'd the crowd.
> This Æschylus (with indignation) saw,
> And built a stage, found out a decent dress,
> Brought vizards in, (a civiler disguise)
> And taught men how to speak, and how to act.
> My Lord ROSCOMMON.

The *Chorus* Hedelin defines to be a company of actors, representing the assembly or body of those persons, who either were present, or, probably might be so, upon that place or scene where the business was supposed to be transacted. This is exactly observed in the four Grecian dramatic poets, Æschylus, Sophocles, Euripides, and Aristophanes; but the only Latin tragedies which remain, those under the name of *Seneca*, as they are faulty in many respects, so particularly are they in the choruses; for sometimes they hear all that is said upon the stage, see all that is done, and speak very properly to all; at other times one would think they were blind, deaf, or dumb. In many of these dramas, one can hardly tell whom they represent, how they were dressed, what reason brings them on the stage, or why they are of one sex more than of another. Indeed the verses are fine, full of thought, and over-loaded with conceit, but may in most places be very well spared, without spoiling any thing either in the sense or the reputation of the poem. Besides, the Thebais has no chorus at all, which may give us occasion to doubt of what Scaliger affirms so positively, that tragedy was never without choruses. For it seems probable enough, that in the time of the debauched and loose Emperors, when mimicks and buffoons came in for interludes to tragedy as well as comedy, the chorus ceased by degrees to be a part of the dramatic poem, and dwindled into a troop of muficians and dancers, who marked the intervals of the acts.

The office of the chorus is thus excellently delivered by Horace, De Art. Poet. 193:

Actoris partes chorus officiumque virile
Defendat: neu quid medios intercinat actus,
Quod non propofito conducat & hæreat apte.
Ille bonis faveatque & concilietur amicis,
Et regat iratos, & amet peccare timentes;
Ille dapes laudet menfæ brevis; ille falubrem
Juftitiam, legefque & apertis otia portis.
Ille tegat commiffa; deofque precetur & orec,
Ut redeat miferis, abeat fortuna fuperbis.

A chorus fhould fupply what action wants,
And has a generous and manly part,
Bridles wild rage, loves rigid honefty,
And ftrict obfervance of impartial laws,
Sobriety, fecurity, and peace,
And begs the gods to turn bright fortune's wheel,
To raife the wretched, and pull down the proud;
But nothing muft be fung between the acts,
But what fome way conduces to the plot.
My Lord ROSCOMMON.

This account is chiefly to be underftood of the chorus of tragedies; yet the old comedies, we are affured, had their chorufes too, as yet appears in Ariftophanes; where, befides thofe compofed of the ordinary fort of perfons, we meet with one of clouds, another of frogs, and a third of wafps, but all very conformable to the nature of the fubject, and extremely comical.

It would be foreign to our prefent purpofe to trace the original of the chorus, and to fhow how it was regulated by Thefpis (generally honoured with the title of the firft tragedian;) whereas before it was nothing elfe but a company of muficians finging and dancing in honour of Bacchus. It may be more proper to obferve how it came, after fome time, to be left out in comedy, as it is in that of the Romans. Horace's reafon is, that the malignity and fatyrical humours of the poets was the caufe of it; for they made the chorufes abufe people fo severely, and with so bare a face, that the magistrates at last forbade them to use any at all : De Art. Poet. 283.

> ———————*Chorusque*
> *Turpiter obticuit, sublato jure nocendi.*

But, perhaps, if the rules of probability had not likewise seconded this prohibition, the poets would have preserved their chorus still, bating the satyrical edge of it. Therefore a farther reason may be offered for this alteration. Comedy took its model and constitution from tragedy ; and, when the downright abusing of living persons was prohibited, they invented new subjects, which they governed by the rules of tragedy ; but as they were necessitated to paint the actions of the vulgar, and consequently confined to mean events, they generally chose the place of their scene in some street, before the houses of those whom they supposed concerned in the plot : Now it was not very likely that there should be such a company in those places, managing an intrigue of inconsiderable persons from morning till night. Thus comedy of itself let fall the chorus, which it could not preserve with any probability.

The *tibiæ*, or flutes, are as little understood as any particular subject of antiquity, and yet without the knowledge of them we can make nothing of the titles prefixed to Terence's comedies. Horace gives us no further light into this matter, than by observing the difference between the small rural pipe, and the larger and louder flute, afterwards brought into fashion ; however his account is not to be passed by, Ars Poet. 202.

> *Tibia non ut nunc orichalco vincta, tubæque*
> *Æmula ; sed tenuis simplexque foramine pauco,*
> *Adspirare & adesse choris erat utilis, atque*
> *Nondum spissa nimis complere sedilia flatu :*
> *Quo sane populus numerabilis, utpote parvus,*
> *Et frugi castusque verecundusque coibat.*
> *Postquam cœpit agros extendere victor, & urbem*
> *Latior amplecti murus, vinoque diurno*
> *Placari genius festis impune diebus ;*
> *Accessit numerisque modisque licentia major.*
> *Indoctus quid enim saperet, liberque laborum*
> *Rusticus urbano confusus, turpis honesto ?*

Sic

Sic priscæ motumque & luxuriam addidit arti
Tibicen, traxitque vagus per pulpita vestem.

First the shrill sound of a small rural pipe
(Not loud like trumpets, nor adorn'd as now)
Was entertainment for the infant stage,
And pleas'd the thin and bashful audience
Of our well-meaning frugal ancestors.
But when our walls and limits were enlarg'd,
And men (grown wanton by prosperity)
Studied new arts of luxury and ease,
The verse, the music, and the scenes improv'd;
For how should ignorance be judge of wit?
Or men of sense applaud the jests of fools?
Then came rich cloathes and graceful action in,
And instruments were taught more moving notes.
[My Lord ROSCOMMON.

This relation, though very excellent, cannot salve the main difficulty; and that is, to give the proper distinction of the flutes, according to the several names under which we find them, as the *Pares* and *Impares*, the *Dextræ* and *Sinistræ*, the *Lydiæ*, the *Sarranæ*, and the *Phrygiæ*. Most of the eminent critics have made some essays towards the clearing of this subject, particularly Scaliger, Aldus Manutius, Salmasius, and Tanaquillus Faber: from whose collections, and her own admirable judgment, Madam Dacier has lately given us a very rational account of the matter. The performers of the music (says she) played always on two flutes the whole time of the comedy; that which they stopped with their right-hand, was on that account called right-handed; and that which they stopped with their left, left-handed: The first had but a few holes, and sounded a deep base; the other had a great number of holes, and gave a shriller and sharper note. When the musicians played on two flutes of a different sound, they used to say the piece was played *Tibiis imparibus*, with *unequal flutes*: or, *Tibiis dextris & sinistris*, with *right* and *left-handed flutes*. When they played on two flutes of the same sound, they used to say the music was performed *Tibiis paribus dextris*, on *equal right-handed flutes*, if they were of the deeper sort; or else *Tibiis paribus sinistris*, on *equal left handed flutes*, if they were those of the shriller note.

Two equal right-handed flutes they called *Lydian*, two equal left-handed ones *Sarranæ*, or *Tyrian*; two unequal flutes *Phrygian*, as imitations of the music of those countries. The last sort Virgil expressly attributes to the Phrygians, Æneid. ȹ. 618:

O vere Phrygiæ, neque enim Phryges! ite per alta
Dindyma, ubi assuetis biforem dat Tibia cantum.

Where, by *biforem cantum*, the commentators understand an equal sound, such as was made by two different pipes, one flat, and the other sharp.

The title of Terence's *Andria* cannot be made out according to this explanation, unless we suppose (as there is very good reason) that the music sometimes changed in the acting of a play, and at the proper intervals two right-handed and two left-handed flutes might be used.

Our late ingenious translators of Terence are of a different opinion from the French Lady, when they render *Tibiis paribus dextris & sinistris*, "two equal flutes, the one right-handed, and the other left-handed;" whereas the music should seem rather to have been performed all along on two equal flutes, sometimes on two right-handed, and sometimes on two left-handed.

Old Donatus would have us believe that the right-handed, or *Lydian* flutes, denoted the more serious matter and language of the comedy; that the left-handed, or *Sarranæ*, were proper to express the lightness of a more jocose style; and that when a right-handed flute was joined with a left-handed, it gave us to understand the mixture of gravity and mirth in the same play. But since the title of the *heautontimoroumenos*, or *self-tormentor*, informs us, that the music was performed the first time of acting on unequal flutes, and the second time on right-handed flutes, we cannot agree with the old scholiast, without supposing the same play at one time to be partly serious, and partly merry, and at another time to be wholly of the graver sort, which would be ridiculous to imagine; therefore the ingenious Lady happily advanceth a very fair opinion, that the music was not guided by the subject of the play, but by the occasion on which it was presented. Thus in the pieces which were acted at funeral solemnities, the music was performed on two right-handed flutes, as the most grave and melancholy. In those acted on any joyful account, the music

Book V.   *of the* ROMANS.   295

fic confifted of two left-handed flutes, as the brifkeft and moft airy. But in the great feftivals of the gods, which participated of an equal fhare of mirth and religion, the mufic in the comedies was performed with unequal flutes, the one right-handed, and the other left-handed; or elfe by turns, fometimes on two right-handed flutes, and fometimes on two left-handed, as may be judged of Terence's *Andria*.

If any thing farther deferves our notice in relation to the Roman dramas, it is the remarkable difference between their actors and thofe of Greece; for at Athens the actors were generally perfons of good birth and education, for the moft part orators or poets of the firft rank. Sometimes we find Kings themfelves performing on the theatres; and Cornelius Nepos affures us, that to appear on the public ftage was not in the leaft injurious to any man's character or honour (a).

But in Rome we meet with a quite contrary practice; for the *Hiftriones* (fo called from *Hifter*, fignifying a player in the language of the Tufcans, from whom they were firft brought to Rome to appeafe the gods in time of a plague) were the moft fcandalous company imaginable, none of that profeffion being allowed the privilege to belong to any tribe, or ranked any higher than the flaves; however, if any of them happened at the fame time to be excellent artifts, and men of good morals, they feldom failed of the efteem and refpect of the chiefeft perfons in the commonwealth. This is evident from the account we have in hiftory of the admirable Rofcius, of whom Tully, his familiar friend, has left this lafting commendation: *Cum artifex ejufmodi fit, ut folus dignus videatur effe, qui in Scena fpectetur tum vir ejufmodi eft, ut folus dignus videator qui eo non accidat* (b). So compleat an artift, that he feemed the only perfon who deferved to tread the ftage; and yet at the fame time fo excellent a man in all other refpects, that he feemed the only perfon who of all men fhould not take up that profeffion.

(a) *In Præfat. Vit.*   (b) *Pro* Quinct.

CHAP.

CHAP. VII.

Of the Sacred, Votive, and Funeral Games.

THE sacred games, being instituted on several occasions to the honour of several deities, are divided into many species, all which very frequently occur in authors, and may be thus in short described.

The *LUDI MEGALENSES* were instituted to the honour of the great goddess, or the mother of the gods, when her statue was brought with so much pomp from Pessinum to Rome; they consisted only of scenical sports, and were a solemn time of invitation to entertainments among friends. In the solemn procession the women danced before the image of the goddess, and the magistrates appeared in all their robes, whence came the phrase of *purpura megalensis:* They lasted six days, from the day before the nones of April, to the ides. At first they seem to have been called the *megalensia*, from μίγας, great, and afterwards to have lost the *n*; since we find them more frequently under the name of *megalesia*. It is particularly remarkable in these games, that no servant was allowed to bear a part in the celebration.

The *LUDI CEREALES* were designed to the honour of Ceres, and borrowed from Eleusine in Greece. In these games the matrons represented the grief of Ceres, after she had lost her daughter Proserpine, and her travels to find her again. They were held from the day before the ides of April, eight days together in the Circus; where, besides the combats of horsemen, and other diversions, was led up the *pompa circensis*, or *cerealis*, consisting of a solemn procession of the persons that were to engage in the exercises, accompanied with the magistrates and ladies of quality, the statues of the gods, and of the famous men, being carried along in state, on waggons, which they called *thensæ*.

LUDI FLORALES, sacred to Flora, and celebrated (upon advice of the Sibylline oracles) every spring, to beg a blessing on the grass, trees, and flowers. Most have been of opinion that they owed their original to a famous whore, who, having gained a great estate by her trade, left the commonwealth

commonwealth her heir, with this condition, that every year they should celebrate her birth-day with public sports; the magistrates, to avoid such a public scandal, and at the same time to keep their promise, held the games on the day appointed, but pretended that it was done in the honour of a new goddess, the Patroness of flowers. Whether this conjecture be true or not, we are certain that the main part of the solemnity was managed by a company of lewd strumpets, who ran up and down naked, sometimes dancing, sometimes fighting, or acting the mimic. However, it came to pass, the wisest and gravest Romans were not for discontinuing this custom, though the most indecent imaginable; for Portius Cato, when he was present at these games, and saw the people ashamed to let the women strip while he was there, immediately went out of the theatre, to let the ceremony have its course (*a*). Learned men are now agreed, that the vulgar notion of *Flora*, the Strumpet, is purely a fiction of Lactantius, from whom it was taken. Flora appears to have been a Sabine goddess; and the *ludi florales* to have been instituted A. U. C. 613, with the fines of many persons then convicted of the *crimen peculatus*, for appropriating to themselves the public land of the State (*b*).

LUDI MARTIALES, instituted to the honour of *Mars*, and held twice in the year, on the 4th of the ides of May, and again on the kalends of August, the day on which his temple was consecrated. They had no particular ceremonies that we can meet with, besides the ordinary sports in the circus and amphitheatre.

LUDI APOLLINARES, celebrated to the honour of *Apollo*. They owe their original to an old prophetical sort of a poem casually found, in which the Romans were advised, that, if they desired to drive out the troops of their enemies which infested their borders, they should institute yearly games to Apollo, and at the time of their celebration make a collection out of the public and private stocks, for a present to the god, appointing ten men to take care they were held with the same ceremonies as in Greece (*c*). Macrobius relates, that, the first time these games were kept, an alarm being given by the enemy, the people immediately marched out against them, and, during the fight, saw a cloud of arrows discharged

---

(*a*) *Valer. Maxim.* lib. 2. cap. 10. (*b*) Græv. *Præfat. ad 1 Tom. Thesaur. A. R.* (*c*) *Liv.* lib. xxv.

discharged from the sky on the adverse troops, so as to put them to a very disorderly flight, and secure the victory to the Romans (a). The people sat to see the Circensian plays, all crowned with laurel; the gates were set open, and the day kept sacred with all manner of ceremonies. These games at first were not fixed, but kept every year upon what day the Prætor thought fit, till about the year of the city 545, a law passed to settle them for ever on a constant day, which was near the nones of July: This alteration was occasioned by a grievous plague then raging in Rome, which they thought might, in some measure, be allayed by that act of religion (b).

LUDI CAPITOLINI, instituted to the honour of *Jupiter Capitolinus*, upon the account of preserving his temple from the Gauls. A more famous sort of Capitoline games were brought up by Domitian, to be held every five years, with the name of *Agones Capitolini*, in imitation of the Græcians. In these the professors of all sorts had a public contention, and the victors were crowned and presented with collars, and other marks of honour.

LUDI ROMANI, the most ancient games instituted at the first building of the circus by *Tarquinius Priscus*. Hence in a strict sense, *ludi circenses*, are often used to signify the same solemnity. They were designed to the honour of the three great deities, Jupiter, Juno, and Minerva. It is worth observing, that though they were usually called *circenses*, yet in Livy we meet with the *ludi Romani scenici* (c), intimating that they were celebrated with new sports. The old *fasti* make them to be kept nine days together, from the day before the nones, to the day before the ides of September: In which too we find another sort of *Ludi Romani*, celebrated five days together, within two days after these. P. Manutius thinks the first to have been instituted very late, not till after the prosecution of Verres by Cicero (d).

LUDI CONSUALES, instituted by *Romulus*, with design to surprize the Sabine virgins; the account of which is thus given us by Plutarch: " He gave out as if he had found
" an altar of a certain god hid under ground; the god they
" called *Consus*, the god of counsel: This is properly Neptune,
" the inventor of horse-riding; for the altar is kept covered
" in the great circus; only at horse-races, then it appears to
" public view; and some say, it was not without reason,
" that

(*a*) *Saturn.* lib. 1. cap. 17.   (*b*) *Liv.* lib. 25.   (*c*) *Liv.* 3.
(*d*) *Manut. in Verrin.*

" that this god had his altar hid under ground, becaufe all
" counfels ought to be fecret and concealed. Upon difcovery
" of this altar, Romulus, by proclamation, appointed a day
" for a fplendid facrifice, and for public games and fhows, to
" entertain all forts of people, and many flocked thither ; he
" himfelf fat uppermoft among his nobles, clad in purple. Now
" the fign of their falling on was to be, whenever he arofe
" and gathered up his robe, and threw it over his body, his
" men ftood all ready armed, with their eyes intent upon him ;
" and when the fign was given, drawing their fwords, and
" falling on with a great fhout, bore away the daughters of
" the Sabines, they themfelves flying without any let or hind-
" rance." Thefe games were celebrated yearly on the
twelfth of the kalends of September, confifting for the moft
part of horfe-races, and encounters in the Circus.

LUDI COMPITALITII, fo called from the *compita*, or
crofs-lanes, where they were inftituted and celebrated by the
rude multitude that was got together, before the building of
Rome. They feem to have been laid down for many years,
till Servius Tullius revived them. They were held during the
compitalia, or feaft of the *Lares*, who prefided as well over
ftreets as houfes. Suetonius tells us, that Auguftus ordered the
lares to be crowned twice a-year, at the Compitalitian games,
with fpring-flowers (a). This crowning the houfehold-gods,
and offering facrifices up and down in the ftreets, made the
greateft part of the folemnity of the feaft.

LUDI AUGUSTALES and *PALATINI*, both inftituted
to the honour of Auguftus, after he had been enrolled in the
number of the gods; the former by the common confent of
the people, and the other by his wife Livia, which were always celebrated in the palace (b). They were both continued
by the fucceeding Emperors.

LUDI SÆCULARES, the moft remarkable games that
we meet with in the Roman ftory. The common opinion
makes them to have had a very odd original, of which we
have a tedious relation in Valerius Maximus (c) of the ancients, and Angelus Palitianus (d) of the moderns. Monfieur
Dacier, in his excellent remarks on the fecular poem of Horace, paffes by this old conceit as trivial and fabulous, and
affures

(a) *Aug.* cap. 32.   (b) *Dio.* lib. 56. *Sueton Calig.* 56.   (c) Lib.
2. cap. 4.   (d) *Mifcellan.* cap. 58.

assures us, that we need go no farther for the rise of the custom than to the Sibylline oracles, for which the Romans had so great an esteem and veneration.

In these sacred writings there was one famous prophecy to this effect, that if the Romans, at the beginning of every age, should hold solemn games in the Campus Martius to the honour of Pluto, Proserpine, Juno, Apollo, Diana, Ceres, and the Parcæ, or three fatal sisters, their city should ever flourish, and all nations be subjected to their dominion. They were very ready to obey the oracle, and, in all the ceremonies used on that occasion, conformed themselves to its directions. The whole manner of the solemnity was as follows: In the first place, the heralds received orders to make an invitation of the whole world to come to " a feast which they had never seen " already, and should never see again." Some few days before the beginning of the games, the *Quindecimviri*, taking their seats in the capitol, and in the Palatine temple, distributed among the people purifying compositions, as flambeaus, brimstone, and sulphur. From hence the people passed on to Diana's temple on the Aventine mountain, carrying wheat, barley, and beans, as an offering; and after this they spent whole nights in devotion to the Destinies. At length, when the time of the games was actually come, which continued three days and three nights, the people assembled in the Campus Martius, and sacrificed to Jupiter, Juno, Apollo, Latona, Diana, the Parcæ, Ceres, Pluto, and Proserpine: On the first night of the feast, the Emperor, accompanied by the *Quindecimviri*, commanded three altars to be raised on the bank of the Tyber, which they sprinkled with the blood of three lambs, and then proceeded to burn the offerings and the victims. After this they marked out a space which served for a theatre, being illuminated by an innumerable multitude of flambeaus and fires: Here they sung some certain hymns composed on this occasion, and celebrated all kinds of sports. On the day after, when they had been at the capitol to offer the victims, they returned to the Campus Martius, and held sports to the honour of Apollo and Diana. These lasted till the next day, when the noble matrons, at the hour appointed by the oracle, went to the capitol to sing hymns to Jupiter. On the third day, which concluded the feast, twenty-seven young boys, and as many girls, sung, in the temple of Palatine Apollo, hymns and verses in Greek and Latin, to recommend the city to the

protection

protection of those deities whom they designed particularly to honour by their sacrifices.

The famous secular poem of Horace was composed for this last day, in the secular game held by Augustus. Dacier has given his judgment on this poem, as the masterpiece of Horace, and believes that all antiquity cannot furnish us with any thing more happily complete.

There has been much controversy, whether these games were celebrated every hundred, or every hundred and ten years. For the former opinion, Censorinus (a) alledges the testimony of Valerius, Antias, Varro, and Livy; and this was certainly the space of time which the Romans called *sæculum*, or an age. For the latter, he produceth the authority of the registers, or commentaries of the *Quindecimviri*, and the edicts of Augustus, besides the plain evidence of Horace in his secular poem, 21:

Certus undenos decies per annos, &c.

This last space is expressly enjoined by the Sibylline oracle itself; the verses of which, relating to this purpose, are transcribed by Zosimus, in the second book of his history:

'Αλλ' ὅπυ ἄν μήκιστος ἴκη χρόνος ἀνθρώποισι
Ζωῆς, τίς ἐτίων καλὸν δίκα κύκλον ὁδεύων, &c.

Yet, according to the ancient accounts we have of their celebration in these several ages, neither of these periods are much regarded.

The first were held, *A. U. C.* 245, or 298.
The second, *A.* 330, or 408.
The third, *A.* 518.
The fourth, either *A.* 605, or 608, or 628.
The fifth, by Augustus, *A.* 736.
The sixth, by Claudius, *A.* 800.
The seventh, by Domitian, *A.* 841.
The eighth, by Severus, *A.* 957.
The ninth, by Philip, *A.* 1000.
The tenth, by Honorius, *A.* 1157.

The disorder, without question, was owing to the ambition of the Emperors, who were extremely desirous to have the honour of celebrating these games in their reign; and therefore, upon the slightest pretence, many times made them

(a) *De Die Natali*, cap. 17.

them return before their ordinary courfe. Thus Claudius pretended that Auguftus had held the games before their due time, that he might have the leaft excufe to keep them within fixty-four years afterwards. On which account, Suetonius tells us, that the people fcoffed his criers, when they went about proclaiming games that no body had ever feen, nor would fee again; whereas there were not only many perfons alive who remembered the games of Auguftus, but feveral players who had acted in thofe games were now again brought on the ftage by Claudius (*a*).

What part of the year the fecular games were celebrated in is uncertain; probably in the times of the commonwealth on the days of the nativity of the city, *i. e.* the 9. 10. 11. *Kal. Maii*, but, under the Emperors, on the day when they came to their power (*b*).

We may conclude our inquiry into this celebrated fubject with two excellent remarks of the French critic. The firft is, that in the number three, fo much regarded in thefe games, they had probably an allufion to the triplicity of Phœbus, of Diana, and of the Deftinies.

The other obfervation which he obliges us with is, that they thought the girls, who had the honour to bear a part in finging the fecular poem, fhould be the fooneft married. This fuperftition they borrowed from the theology of the Grecians, who imagined, that the children who did not fing and dance at the coming of Apollo fhould never be married, and fhould certainly die young. To this purpofe Callimachus in his hymn to Apollo:

Μήτε σιωπηλὴν κίθαριν, μήδ' ἄψοφον ἴχνος
Τῦ Φοίβυ τυς παῖδας ἔχειν ἐπιδημήσαντος,
Εἰ τελείες μέλλυσι γάμος, πολιήν τε κερεῖσθαι.

And Horace, encouraging the chorus of girls to do their beft in finging the fecular poem, tells them how proud they would be of it when they were well married:

Nupta jam dices: Ego diis amicum,
Sæculo feftas referente luces,
Reddidi carmen, docilis modorum.

Vatis Horati. Lib. iv. Od. 6.

All

(*a*) Sueton. Claud. 21.   (*b*) *Mr Walker of Coins*, p. 168.

Book V. *The Votive Games*, &c.

All those games, of what sort soever, had the common name of *Votivi*, which were the effect of any vow made by the Magistrates or Generals, when they set forward on any expedition, to be performed in case they returned successful. These were sometimes occasioned by advice of the Sibylline oracles, or of the soothsayers: and many times proceeded purely from a principle of devotion and piety in the Generals. Such particularly were the *Ludi Magni*, often mentioned in historians, especially by Livy. Thus he informs us, That in the year of the city 536, Fabius Maximus the Dictator, to appease the anger of the gods, and to obtain success against the Carthaginian power, upon the direction of the Sibylline oracles vowed the *Great Games* to Jupiter, with a prodigious sum to be expended at them; besides three hundred oxen to be sacrificed to Jupiter, and several others to the rest of the deities (a). M. Acilius the Consul did the same in the war against Antiochus (b). And we have some examples of these games being made *quinquennial*, or to return every five years (c). They were celebrated with Circensian sports four days together (d).

To this head we may refer the

Ludi Victoriæ, mentioned by Vell. Paterculus (e), and Asconius (f): They were instituted by Sylla, upon his concluding the civil war. It seems probable, that there were many other games with the same title, celebrated on account of some remarkable success, by several of the Emperors.

The *Ludi Quinquennales*, instituted by Augustus Cæsar after his victory against Anthony: which resolving to deliver famous to succeeding ages, he built the city Nicopolis, near Actium, the place of battle, on purpose to hold these games; whence they are often called *Ludi Actiaci*. They consisted of shows of Gladiators, wrestlers, and other exercises, and were kept as well at Rome as at Nicopolis. The proper curators of them were the four colleges of priests, the *Pontifices*, the *Augurs*, the *Septemviri* and *Quindecimviri*.

Virgil, in allusion to this custom, when he brings his hero to the promontory of Actium, makes him hold solemn games, with the lustrations and sacrifices used on that occasion by the Romans:

Lustramurque Jovi, votisque incendimus aras;
Actiaque Iliacis celebramus littora Ludis. Æn. 3. 279.

(a) *Liv.* lib. 22. (b) *Idem*, lib. 36. (c) *Liv.* lib. 27, & lib. 30. (d) *Ibid.* (e) *Lib.* cap. 27. (f) *In Verrin*, 2.

Nero, after the manner of the Græcians, instituted *quinquennial* games, at which the most celebrated masters of music, horse-racing, wrestling, &c. disputed for the prize (*a*).

The same exercises were performed in the *quinquennial* games of Domitian, dedicated to Jupiter Capitolinus, together with the contentions of orators and poets (*b*), at which the famous Statius had once the ill fortune to lose the prize; as he complains of several times in his miscellany poems.

Ludi decennales, or games to return every tenth year, were instituted by Augustus, with this political design, to secure the whole command to himself, without incurring the envy or jealousy of the people. For every tenth year proclaiming solemn sports, and so gathering together a numerous company of spectators, he there made proffer of resigning his imperial office to the people, though he immediately resumed it, as if continued to him by the common consent of the nation (*c*). Hence a custom was derived for the succeeding Emperors, every tenth year of their reign, to keep a magnificent feast, with the celebration of all sorts of public sports and exercises (*d*).

The *Ludi Triumphales* were such games as made a part of the triumphal solemnity.

Ludi Natalitii, instituted by every particular Emperor to commemorate his own birth-day.

Ludi Juvenales, instituted by Nero at the shaving of his beard, and at first privately celebrated in his palace or gardens; but they soon became public, and were kept in great state and magnificence. Hence the games held by the following Emperors in the palace, yearly on the first of January, took the name of *Juvenalia* (*e*).

Cicero speaks of the *Ludi Juventutis*, instituted by Salinator in the Senensian war, for the health and safety of the youth, a plague then reigning in the city (*f*).

The *Ludi Miscelli*, which Suetonius makes Caligula to have instituted at Lyons in France, seem to have been a miscellany of sports, consisting of several exercises joined together in a new and unusual manner (*g*).

The *LUDI FUNEBRES*, assigned for one species of the Roman public games, as to their original and manner, have

---

(*a*) *Sueton. Ner.* 12. (*b*) *Idem Domit.* 4. (*c*) *Dio.* l. 35. (*d*) *Ibid.*
(*e*) *Sueton. Ner.* 11. *Casaubon. ad loc.* (*f*) *In Bruto.* (*g*) *Sueton. Cal.* 20. *Torrent. ad loc.*

have been already described in the chapter of the Gladiators. It may be proper to observe farther, that Tertullian, in his particular tract *De Spectaculis*, as he derives the custom of the gladiatorian combats from the funeral rites, so he takes notice, that the word *munus*, applied originally to these shows, is no more than *officium*, a kind office to the dead. We must remember, that tho' the shows of Gladiators, which took their rise from hence, were afterwards exhibited on many other occasions, yet the primitive custom of presenting them at the funerals of great men all along prevailed in the city and Roman provinces; nor was it confined only to persons of quality, but almost every rich man was honoured with this solemnity after his death; and this they very commonly provided for in their wills, defining the number of Gladiators who should be hired to engage, insomuch, that when any wealthy person deceased, the people used to claim a show of Gladiators, as their due, by long custom. Suetonius to this purpose tells us of a funeral, in which the common people extorted money by force from the deceased person's heirs, to be expended on this account (*a*).

Julius Cæsar brought up a new custom of allowing this honour to the women, when he obliged the people with a feast and a public show in memory of his daughter (*b*).

It is very memorable, that though the exhibitors of these shows were private persons, yet, during the time of the celebration, they were considered as of the highest rank and quality; having the honour to wear the *prætexta*, and to be waited on by the lictors and beadles, who were necessary to keep the people in order, and to assist the *designatores*, or marshallers of the procession (*c*).

(*a*) *Suet. Tit.* 37.   (*b*) *Idem Jul.* 26.   (*c*) *Kirchman. de Funer. Rom.* lib. 4. cap. 8.

CHAP. VIII.

Of the ROMAN *Habit.*

THE Roman habit has given as much trouble to the critics as any other part of antiquity; and though the most learned men have been so kind as to leave us their thoughts on this subject, yet the matter is not fully explained, and the controversies about it admit of no decision. However, without inquiring into the several fashions of the Romans, or defining the exact time when they first changed their leathern jerkins, or primitive hides of wild beasts, for the more decent and graceful attires, it will be sufficient to the present design to observe the several sorts of garments in use with both sexes, and to give the best distinction of them that can be found out at this distance.

The two common and celebrated garments of the Romans were the *toga* and the *tunica*.

The *toga*, or gown, seems to have been of a semi-circular form, without sleeves, different in largeness, according to the wealth or poverty of the wearer, and used only upon occasion of appearing in public, whence it is often called *vestis forensis* (*a*).

The colour of the gown is generally believed to have been white. The common objections against this opinion are, how it could then be distinguished from the *toga candida*, used by competitors for offices? or how it comes to pass, that we read particularly of their wearing white gowns on holidays and public festivals, as in Horace,

> *Ille repotia, natales, aliosque dierum*
> *Festos albatus celebret* (*b*).————

if their ordinary gown were of the same coulour? But both these scruples are easily solved; for between the *toga alba* and *candida*, we may apprehend this difference, that the former was the natural colour of the wool, and the other an artificial white, which appeared with a greater advantage of lustre; and

---

(*a*) Ferrar. de Re Vestiar. l. 1. c. 28.   (*b*) Lib. 2. Sat. 2. 60.

p. 306

1 Palliatulus. 2 Patricius Puer Prætextatus.
4 Servus Lacernatus.

1 Palliatus 2 Togatus — 3 Cucutus 4 Stolata —   1 Imperator Chlamydatus 2 Patricius Puer Prætextatus
3 Mercurius Tæmulatus — 4 Servus Lacernatus —

and therefore Polybius chuseth rather to call the candidate's gown λαμπρά, than λευκή; not of a bare white, but of a bright shining colour; for this purpose, they made use of a fine kind of chalk, whence Persius took the hint of *cretata ambitio* (*a*). As to the holidays, or solemn festivals, on which we find the Romans always attired in white, it is reasonable to believe, that all persons of any fashion constantly put on new gowns, which were of the purest white, on these occasions, and those of meaner condition might perhaps chalk over their old gowns, which were now grown rusty, and had almost lost their colour (*b*).

The dispute between Manutius and Sigonius, whether the Roman gown was tied about with a girdle or not, is commonly decided in favour of Manutius; yet it must be acknowledged, that the best authors allow some kind of *cincture* to the gown; but then it must be understood to be performed only by the help of the gown itself, or by that part of it which, coming under the right arm, was drawn over to the left shoulder, and so covering the *umbo*, or knot of plaits which rested there, kept the gown close together. This lappet Quintilian calls the *belt*, in his advice to the orators about this matter: *Ille qui sub humero dextro ad sinistrum oblique ducitur, velut balteus, nec strangulet, nec fluat* (*c*).

The *belt* being loosed, and the left arm drawn in, the gown flowed out, and the *sinus*, or main lappet, hung about the wearer's feet; this was particularly observed in Cæsar, who commonly let his gown hang dragging after him; whence Sylla used to advise the noblemen, *ut puerum male præcinctum caverent* (*d*).

The accurate Ferrarius is certainly in a mistake as to this point, for maintaining, that the gown had no kind of *cinctus* but what they called *gabinus*, he will have this meant only of the *tunica*; but the plain words of Macrobius make such a supposition impossible, and *laciniam trahere* expressly points out the gown; for the tunick, being only a short vest, cannot by any means be conceived to have a lappet dragging on the ground (*e*).

The same fault, which Sylla objected to Cæsar, was commonly observed in Mæcenas, and is a mark of that effeminate softness which makes an unhappy part of his character in history. The

(*a*) *Sat.* 5. *ver.* 177. (*b*) *Lipſ. Elect.* l. 1. c. 13. (*c*) *Inſtitut.* lib. 11. cap. 3. (*d*) *Sueton. Jul.* cap. 45. *Macrob. Saturnal.* lib. 2. cap. 3. (*e*) *Grævius ad Sueton. Jul.* 45.

The learned Grævius obferves, that the word *præcingi* was proper to the gown, becaufe the lappet did not clofe about the whole gown, but only the fore-part of it (*a*).

The *cinctus gabinus* is moft happily defcribed by Ferrarius: *Cinctus gabinus non aliud fuit quam cum togæ lacinia lævo brachio fubducta in tergum ita rejiciebatur, ut contracta retraheretur ad pectus, atque ita in nodum necteretur; qui nodus five cinctus togam contrahebat, brevioremque & ftrictiorem reddidit* (*b*). " The cinctus gabinus was nothing elfe, but when the lappet " of the gown, which ufed to be brought up to the left fhoul- " der, being drawn thence, was caft off in fuch a manner up- " on the back, as to come round fhort to the breaft, and there " faften in a knot, which knot or cincture tucked up the gown, " and made it fhorter and ftraiter." This *cinctus* was proper only to the Confuls or Generals upon fome extraordinary occafions, as the denouncing war, burning the fpoils of the enemy, devoting themfelves to death for the fafety of their army, and the like; it was borrowed from the inhabitants of Gabii, a city of Campania, who, at the time of a public facrifice, happening to be fet upon fuddenly by their enemies, were obliged through hafte to gather up their gowns in this manner, and fo march out to oppofe them (*c*).

In the ordinary wear, the upper part of the gown ufed to lye over the right fhoulder, yet upon occafion it was an eafy matter to draw back that part again, and make it cover the head; and learned men are of opinion, that the Romans, while they continued in the city, made ufe of this fort of covering only for the head, never appearing in any kind of caps or hats, unlefs they were on a journey out of town. Thus Plutarch informs us of the deference paid to the great men as they paffed the ftreets : Οἱ Ῥωμαῖοι τῶν ἀνθρώπων τοῖς ἀξίοις τιμῆς ἀπαντῶντες, κἂν τυχῶσιν ἐπὶ τῆς κεφαλῆς τὸ ἱμάτιον ἔχοντες, ἀποκαλύπτονται. " The Romans, when they meet any perfon who deferves a " particular refpect, if they chance to have their gown on " their head, prefently uncover." And the fame author, reckoning up the marks of honour which Sylla fhowed Pompey, adds, καὶ τῆς κεφαλῆς ἀπάγοντος τὸ ἱμάτιον, " and pulling off his gown " from his head."

The feveral forts of the Roman gowns, were the *toga prætexta*, the *pulla*, the *fordida*, the *picta*, *purpurea*, *palmata*, &c. or the *trabea*.

Every

(*a*) Ibid.   (*b*) *De Re Veftiar.* lib. 1. cap. 14.   (*e*) *Servius ad Virgil,* Æn. 7. v. 612.

Every one knows that the gown was the diftinguifhing mark of the Romans from the Greeks, who wore the *pallium*, or cloak, as their common garment, whence *togatus* and *palliatus* are often ufed for Roman and Græcian; as alfo that the gown was the proper badge of peace, being generally laid afide upon engaging in any martial defign; yet it appears, from feveral paffages of Livy and Plutarch, that it was fometimes worn in the camp; if fo, perhaps the Equites and Centurions had this peculiar privilege, and that only when they lay in the camp without any thoughts of fudden action, as Manutius learnedly conjectures (a).

The *toga prætexta* had a border of purple round the edges, whence it took its name, and in allufion to which, the Græcian writers call it περιπόρφυρον. It feems originally to have been appropriated to the magiftrates and fome of the priefts, when at firft introduced by Tullus Hoftilius. How it came to be beftowed on the young men is differently related. Some fancy that Tarquinius Prifcus, in a triumph for a victory againft the Sabines, firft honoured his own fon with the *prætexta* and the *bulla aurea*, as rewards for his valour, for killing one of his enemies with his own hands; for as the former was the robe of the magiftrates, fo the *bulla aurea* was till then only ufed by Generals in their triumphal proceffion, being a fort of hollow golden ball hanging about their necks, in which was enclofed fome fecret amulet or prefervative againft envy. Others, without regarding this firft ftory, tell us, that the fame Tarquin, among other wife conftitutions, took particular care in affigning the proper habit to the boys, and accordingly ordained that the fons of noblemen fhould make ufe of the *prætexta* and the *bulla aurea*, provided their father had borne any curule office, and that the reft fhould wear the *prætexta* only, as low as the fons of thofe who had ferved on horfeback in the army the full time that the law required. A third party refer the original of this cuftom to Romulus himfelf, as the confequence of a promife made to the Sabine virgins, that he would beftow a very confiderable mark of honour on the firft child that was born to any of them by a Roman father. Many believe that the reafon of giving them the *bulla* and the *prætexta* was, that the former, being fhaped like a heart, might, as often as they looked on it, be no inconfiderable incitement to courage; and that the purple of the gown might remind

---

(a) *De Quæfitis per Epift.* lib. 1. Ep. 1.

remind them of the modesty which became them at that age (a).

But on what account soever this institution took its rise, it was constantly observed by all the sons of the *ingenui* or free-born. The *libertini* too in some time obtained the same privilege, only instead of the golden *bulla* they wore a leathern one, as Juvenal intimates, Sat. 5. 164:

——Etruscum puero si contigit aurum,
Vel nodus tantum & signum, de paupere loro.

It is commonly believed that the boys changed this gown at the age of 14 years for the *toga virilis;* but Monsieur Dacier makes this a great mistake ; for, till they were 13 years old, he says, they wore a sort of vest with sleeves, which they called *alicata chlamys*, and then left off that to put on the *prætexta*, which they did not change till they had reached the age of puberty, or the 17th year (b).

It is a very pertinent remark, that this *prætexta* was not only a token of the youth and quality of the wearer, but besides this they had the repute of a sacred habit; and therefore, when they assigned it for the use of the boys, they had this especial consideration, that it might be a kind of guard or defence to them against the injuries to which that age was exposed (c). Thus the poor boy in Horace cries out to the witch *canidia* that was tormenting him,

Per hoc inane purpuræ decus precor. Epod. 5.

And Persius calls it *custus purpura* in his fifth Satyr. But Quintilian most expressly, *Ego vobis allego etiam illud sacrum prætextarum, quo sacerdotes velantur, quo Magistratus, quo infirmitatem pueritiæ sacrum facimus ac venerabilem (d).* "I acknowledge too the sacred habit of the *prætexta*, the robe of priests and magistrates, and that by which we derive an holy reverence and veneration to the helpless condition of childhood."

We find further, that the citizens daughters were allowed a sort of *prætexta*, which they wore till the day of marriage. Thus Cicero against Verres, *Eripies pupillæ togam prætextam.* And Propertius, *Mox ubi jam facibus cessit prætexta maritis.* The *prætorii* and *consulares* too (if not all the Senators) at the *Ludi Romani* made use of the *prætexta* (e). And the matrons on the *caprotine nones* celebrated the festival in this sort of gown (f). The

(a) *Macrob. Saturnal.* lib. 1. cap. 6. (b) *Dacier on Horace*, lib. 5. Ode 5. ((c) *Dacier.* ibid. (d) *In Declamat.* (e) *Cicero Philip.* 2. (f) *Varro de Ling. Lat.* lib. 5.

The *toga pura* was the ordinary garment of private persons when they appeared abroad, so called because it had not the least addition of purple to the white; we meet with the same gown under the name of *virilis* and *libera*: It was called *toga virilis*, or the *manly* gown; because when the youths came to man's estate, or to the age of seventeen years, they changed the *prætexta* for this habit, as was before observed; on which occasion the friends of the youngster carried him into the forum (or sometimes into the capitol) and attired him in the new gown with abundance of ceremony; this they called *dies tirocinii*, the day on which he commenced a *tiro*, in relation to the army, wherein he was now capacitated to serve.

It had the name of *toga libera*, because at this time the young men entered on a state of freedom, and were delivered from the power of their tutors and instructors. Thus the young gentleman intimates in Persius:

Cum primum pavido custos mihi purpura cessit,
Bullaque succinctus laribus donata pependit;
Cum blandi comites, totaque impune suburra
Permisit sparsisse oculos jam candidus umbo. Sat. 5. 30.

When first my childish robe resign'd its charge,
And left me unconfin'd to live at large;
When now my golden bulla (hung on high
To household-gods) declar'd me past a boy;
And my white plaits proclaim'd my liberty;
When with my wild companions I could rowl
From street to street, and sin without controul.
[Mr Dryden.

But, for all this liberty, they had one remarkable restraint, being obliged for the first whole year to keep their arms within their gown, as an argument of modesty. This Cicero observes, *Nobis quidem olim annus erat unus ad cohibendum bracchium toga constitutus* (a).

The *toga pulla* and *sordida* are very commonly confounded; yet, upon a strict inquiry, it will appear that the first sort was proper to persons in mourning, being made of black cloth, whence the persons were called *atrati*. The *toga sordida* was black as well as the other, but from a different cause, having grown so by the long wearing and sullying of it; and this (as has been already observed) was worn by the prisoners at their trial

(a) Cicero pro Cælio.

trial, as well as by the ordinary people. It may here be remarked, that the *pullati*, whom we meet with in the classics, were not only those who wore the *toga pulla*, or the *toga sordida*, but such too as were attired in the *penulæ* or *lacernæ*, which were usually black. Thus the learned Casaubon interprets *pullatorum turba* in Suetonius (*a*); and Quintilian calls the rabble *pullatus circulus* (*b*), and *pullata turba* (*c*). Hence it may reasonably be conjectured, that when the Roman state was turned into a monarchy, the gowns began to be laid aside by men of the lower rank; the *penulæ* and *lacernæ* being introduced in their room, and commonly worn without them, or sometimes over them: this irregularity had gained a great head, even in Augustus's time, who, to rectify it in some measure, commanded the Ædiles that they should suffer no person in the forum or circus to wear the *lacerna* over his gown, as was then an ordinary practice. The same excellent prince, taking notice at a public meeting of an innumerable company of rabble in these indecent habits, cried out with indignation, *En*

Romanos rerum dominos gentemque togatam (*d*)*!*

The *toga picta, purpurea, palmata*, the consular *trabea*, the *paludamentum*, and the *chlamys*, had very little difference. (except that the last but one is often given to military officers in general, and sometimes passes for the common soldier's coat) (*e*), and are promiscuously used one for the other, being the robes of state proper to the Kings, Consuls, Emperors, and all Generals during their triumph. This sort of gown was called *picta*, from the rich embroidery, with figures in Phrygian work; and *purpurea*, because the ground-work was purple. The *toga palmata* indeed very seldom occurs, but may probably be supposed the same with the former, called so on the same account as the *tunica palmata*, which will be described hereafter. That it was a part of the triumphal habit, Martial intimates,

I comes, & magnos illæsa merere triumphos,
Palmataque ducem (sed cito) redde togæ. vii. 1.

Antiquaries are very little agreed in reference to the *trabea*. Paulus Manutius was certainly out, when he fancied it to be the same as the *toga picta*, and he is accordingly corrected

(*a*) *August.* cap. 40.   (*b*) Lib. 2. cap. 12.   (*c*) Lib 6. cap. 4.
(*d*) *Sueton. August.* cap. 40.   (*e*) *Bayf. de Re Vest.* cap. II.

corrected by Grævius (a). The vulgar opinion follows the distinction of Servius and Scaliger into three sorts; one proper to the Kings, another to the Consuls, and a third to the Augurs. But Lipsius (b) and Rubenius (c) acknowledge only one proper sort of *trabea* belonging to the Kings; being a white gown bordered with purple, and adorned with *clavi* or *trabes* of scarlet; whereas the vests of the Consuls, and the Augurs, and the Emperors, were called by the same name, only because they were made in the same form: For the old *paludamentum* of the Generals was all scarlet, only bordered with purple; and the *chlamydes* of the Emperors were all purple, commonly beautified with a golden or embroidered border.

Sidoniam picto chlamydem circumdata limbo. Virg. Æn. 4.

When the Emperors were themselves Consuls, they wore a *trabea* adorned with gems, which were allowed to none else. Claudian, in his poems of the third, fourth, and sixth consulship of Honorius, alludes expressly to this custom:

———*Cinctus mutata Gabinos*
Dives Hydaspæis augescat purpura gemmis.

And again,
—————————*Asperat Indus*
Velamenta lapis, pretiosaque fila smaragdis
Ducta virent———————

And in the last,
Membraque gemmato trabeæ viridantia cinctu.

There are several other names under which we sometimes find the gown, which have not yet been explained, nor would be of much use, if thoroughly understood; such as the *toga undulata, sericulata, rasa, paverata, phryxiana, scutulata,* &c. See Ferrar. de Re Vest. lib. 2. cap. 10.

The *tunica*, or close coat, was the common garment worn within doors by itself, and abroad under the gown: The *protelarii*, the *capite censi*, and the rest of the dregs of the city, could not afford to wear the *toga*, and so went in their *tunics*; whence Horace calls the rabble *tunicatus popellus*, and the author of the Dialogue de Claris Oratoribus, *populus tunicatus*. The old Romans, as Gellius informs us (d), at first were cloathed

(a) *Præfat. ad 1 Vol. Thes. Rom.* (b) *Ad Tacit. Ann.* 3.
(c) *De Re Vestiar. & præcipue de Laticlav.* l. 1. c. 5. (d) Lib. 1. cap. 12.

ed only in the gown. In a little time they found the convenience of a short strait *tunic*, that did not cover the arms, like the Græcian ἐξωμίδες; afterwards they had sleeves coming down to the elbow, but no further. Hence Suetonius tells us, that Cæsar was remarkable in his habit, because he wore the *laticlavian tunic*, closed with gatherings about his wrist (*a*). Rubenius thinks he might use this piece of singularity to show himself descended from the Trojans, to whom Romulus objects, in Virgil, as an argument of their effeminacy.

Et tunicæ manicas, & habent redimicula mitræ (*b*).

And Iulus, or Ascanius, is still to be seen dressed after the same fashion in some old gems (*c*).

Yet in the declension of the empire, the *tunics* did not only reach down to the ankles, whence they are called *talares*, but had sleeves too coming down to the hands, which gave them the name of *chirodotæ*. And now it was counted scandalous to appear without sleeves, as it had been hitherto to be seen in them. And therefore, in the writers of that age, we commonly find the accused persons at a trial habited in the *tunic* without sleeves, as a mark of infamy and disgrace (*d*).

The several sorts of the *tunic* were the *palmata*, the *angusticlavia*, and the *laticlavia*.

The *tunica palmata* was worn by Generals in a triumph, and perhaps always under the *toga picta*. It had its name either from the great breadth of the *clavi*, equal to the palm of the hand, or else from the figures of palms embroidered on it (*e*).

The whole body of the critics are strangely divided about the *clavi*. Some fancy them to have been a kind of flowers interwoven in the cloth; others will have them to be the buttons or clasps by which the *tunic* was held together. A third sort contend, that the *latus clavus* was nothing else but a *tunic* bordered with purple. Scaliger thinks the *clavi* did not belong properly to the vest, but hung down from the neck, like chains and ornaments of that nature; but the most general opinion makes them to have been studs or pearls, something like heads of nails, of purple or gold, worked into the *tunic*.

All the former conjectures are learnedly confuted by the accurate Rubenius, who endeavours to prove, that the *clavi* were

no

(*a*) Sueton. *Jul.* c. 55.   (*b*) Æneid. xi. 616.   (*c*) Rubenius de Laticlav. l. 1. c. 12.   (*d*) Ibidem.   (*e*) Festus in voce.

no more than purple lines or streaks coming along the middle of the garments, which were afterwards improved to golden and embroidered lines of the same nature. We must not therefore suppose them to have received their name as an immediate allusion to the heads of nails, to which they bore no resemblance; but may remember, that the ancients used to inlay their cups and other precious utensils with studs of gold, or other ornamental materials. These, from their likeness to nail-heads, they called in general *clavi:* So that it was very natural to bring the same word to signify these lines of purple, or other colours which were of a different kind from all the rest of the garment, as those ancient *clavi* were of a different colour and figure from the vessels which they adorned.

These streaks were either transverse or straight down the vest; the former were used only in the liveries of the *popæ* and other public servants, by the musicians, and some companies of artificers, and now and then by women, being termed *paragaudæ.* The proper *clavi* came straight down the vest, one of them making the *tunic*, which they called the *angusticlave*, and two the *laticlave*.

However this opinion has been applauded by the learned, monsieur Dacier's judgment of the matter cannot fail to meet with as kind a reception.

He tells us, that the *clavi* were no more than purple galoons, with which they bordered the fore-part of the *tunic* on both sides, and the place where it came together. The broad galoons made the *laticlave*, and the narrow the *angusticlave;* therefore they are strangely mistaken, who make the only difference between the two vests to consist in this, that the one had but a single *clavus*, the other two; and that the senatorian *clavus*, being in the middle of the vest, could possibly be but one. For it is very plain they had each of them two galoons, binding the two sides of the coat where it opened before; so that, joining together with the sides, they appeared just in the middle; whence the Greeks called such a vest μεσοπόρφυρον. That the galoons were sewed on both sides of the coat, is evident beyond dispute, from the following passage of Varro: *Nam si quis tunicam ita consuit, ut altera plagula sit angustis clavis, altera latis, utraque pars in suo genere caret analogia.* "For if any one should sew a coat in this manner, that one "side should have a broad galoon and the other a narrow one, "neither part has any thing properly answering to it." As to the name of the *clavi*, he thinks there needs no further reason to be given, than that the ancients called any thing, which was made with design to be put upon another thing, *clavus* (*a*).

It has been a received opinion, that the *angusticlave* distinguished the Knight from the common people, in the same manner as the *laticlave* did the Senators from those of the Equestrian rank ; but Rubenius avers, that there was no manner of difference between the *tunics* of the Knights and those of the Commons. This conjecture seems to be favoured by Appian, in the second book of his history, where he tells us, ὁ δυλεύων ἐςὶ, τὸ σχῆμα τοῖς δεσπόταις ὅμοιος, χωρὶς γὰρ τῆς βουλευτικῆς ἡ ἄλλη ςολὴ τοῖς θεράπουσιν ἐπίκοινος. "The slave in habits goes like his "master, and, excepting only the Senator's robe, all other "garments are common to the servants." And Pliny, when he says, that the rings distinguished the Equestrian order from the common people, as their *tunic* did the Senate from those that wore the rings, would not probably have omitted the other distinction, had it been real. Besides both these authorities, Lampridius, in the life of Alexander Severus, confirms the present assertion. He acquaints us, that the aforesaid Emperor had some thoughts of assigning a proper habit to servants different from that of their masters ; but his great lawyers, Ulpian and Paulus, dissuaded him from the project, as what would infallibly give occasion to much quarrelling and dissention ; so that, upon the whole, he was contented only to distinguish the Senators from the Knights by their *clavus*.

But all this argument will come to nothing, unless we can clear the point about the use of the purple among the Romans, which the Civilians tell us was strictly forbid the common people under the Emperors. It may therefore be observed, that all the prohibitions of this nature were restrained to some particular species of purple. Thus Julius Cæsar forbade the use of the *conchylian* garments, or the ἀλουργίδες (*b*) ; and Nero afterwards prohibited the ordinary use of the amethystine, or Tyrian purple (*c*). These conjectures of Rubenius need no better confirmation, than that they are repeated and approved by the most judicious Grævius (*d*).

According to this opinion, it is an easy matter to reconcile the contest between Manutius and Lipsius, and the inferior critics

---

(*a*) *Dacier on Horace*, lib. 2. Sat. 5.   (*b*) *Sueton. Jul.* cap. 45.
(*c*) *Idem Nerone*, cap. 32.   (*d*) *Sueton. Jul.* 43. *Otho* 10. *Domitian* 10.

critics of both parties, about the colour of the *tunic*, the former afserting it to be purple, and the other white: For it is evident, it might be called either, if we fuppofe the groundwork to have been white, with the addition of thefe purple lifts or galoons.

As to the perfons who had the honour of wearing the *laticlave*, it may be maintained, that the fons of thofe Senators, who were Patricians, had the privilege of ufing this veft in their childhood, together with the *prætexta;* but the fons of thofe Senators, who were not Patricians, did not put on the *laticlave* till they applied themfelves to the fervice of the commonwealth, and to bear offices (*a*). Yet Auguftus changed this cuftom, and gave the fons of any Senators leave to affume the *laticlave* prefently after the time of their putting on the *toga virilis*, though they were not yet capable of honours (*b*). And, by the particular favour of the Emperors, the fame privilege was allowed to the more fplendid families of the Knights. Thus Ovid fpeaks of himfelf and brother, who are known to have been of the Equeftrian order:

> *Interea, tacito paffu, labentibus annis,*
> *Liberior fratri fumpta mihique toga;*
> *Induiturque humeris cum lato purpura clavo,* &c. (*c*).

And Statius of Metius Celer, whom in another place he terms Spendidiffimus (*d*), (the proper ftyle of the Knights:)

> ———*Puer hic fudavit in armis*
> *Notus adhuc tantum majoris munere clavi* (*e*).

Befides the gown and *tunic*, we hardly meet with any garments of the Roman original, or that deferve the *labour* of an inquiry into their difference. Yet, among thefe, the *lacerna* and the *penula* occur more frequently than any other. In the old glofs upon Perfius, Sat. 1. ver. 68. they are both called *pallia;* which identity of names might probably arife from the near refemblance they bore one to the other, and both to the Græcian *pallium*. The *lacerna* was firft ufed in the camp, but afterwards admitted into the city, and worn upon their gowns, to defend them from the weather. The *penula* was fometimes ufed with the fame defign, but, being fhorter and fitter for expedition, it was chiefly worn upon a journey (*f*).

Rubenius

(*a*) *Pliny*, lib. 8. *Epift.* 23. (*b*) *Sueton. Aug.* cap. 37. (*c*)*Triftium*, lib. 4. *Eleg.* 10. (*d*) *Præfat. ad* i. 3. *Sylv.* (*e*) *Sylv.* l. 3. *carm.* 2. (*f*) *Lipf. Elect.* l. 1. c. 13, & *Dr Holiday on Juvenal*, Sat. 1.

Rubenius will have the *lacerna* and the *penula* to be both a close-bodied kind of frocks, girt about in the middle, the only difference between them being, that the *penulæ* were always brown, the *lacernæ* of no certain colour; and that the *cucullus*, the cowl or hood, was sewed on the former, but worn as a distinct thing from the other (*a*). But Ferrarius, who has spent a whole book in animadverting on that author, wonders that any body should be so ignorant as not to know these two garments to have been quite distinct species (*b*).

It will be expected that the habits of the Roman priests should be particularly described; but we have no certain intelligence, only what concerned the chief of them, the augurs, the flamens, and the pontifices. The augurs wore the *trabea* first dyed with scarlet, and afterwards with purple. Rubenius takes the robe which Herod in derision put on our Saviour to have been of this nature; because St Matthew calls it *scarlet*, and St Luke *purple*. Cicero useth *dibaphus* ("a garment twice dyed") for the augural robe (*c*).

The proper robe of the flamens was the *læna*, a sort of purple *chlamys*, or almost a double gown, fastened about the neck with a buckle or clasp. It was interwoven curiously with gold, so as to appear very splendid and magnificent. Thus Virgil describes his hero in this habit,

   ——*Tyrioque ardebat murice læna*
Demissa ex humeris: dives quæ munera Dido
Fecerat, & tenui telas discreverat auro. Æn. 4. 262.

The pontiffs had the honour of using the *prætexta*; and so had the *epulones*, as we learn from Livy, lib. 43.

The priests were remarkable for their modesty in apparel, and therefore they made use only of the common purple, never affecting the more chargeable and splendid. Thus Cicero, *Vestitus asper nostra hac purpura plebeia ac pene fusca* (*d*). He calls it *our purple*, because he himself was a member of the college of augurs.

There are two farther remarks which may be made in reference to the habits in general. First, that in the time of any public calamity, it was an usual custom to change their apparel, as an argument of humility and contrition; of which we meet with many instances in history. On such occasions the

(*a*) *Le Laticlav.* lib. 1. cap. 6.   (*b*) *Analect. de Re Vest.* cap. ult.
(*c*) *Epist. Famil.* lib. 2. *Epist.* 16.   (*d*) *Pro Sextio.*

the Senators laid by the *laticlave*, and appeared only in the habit of Knights: The Magistrates threw aside the *prætexta*, and came abroad in the senatorian garb: The Knights left off their rings, and the Commons changed their gowns for the *sagum* or military coat (*a*).

The other remark is the observation of the great Casaubon, that the habit of the ancients, and particularly of the Romans, in no respect differed more from the modern dress, than in that they had nothing answering to our breeches and stockings, which, if we were to express in Latin, we should call *femoralia* and *tibialia*. Yet, instead of these, under their lower tunics or waistcoats, they sometimes bound their thighs and legs round with silken scarfs or *fasciæ*; though these had now and then the name of *fœminalia* or *femoralia* and *tibialia* from the parts to which they were applied (*b*).

As to the habit of the other sex, in the ancient times of the commonwealth, the gown was used alike by men and women (*c*). Afterwards the women took up the *stola* and the *palla* for their separate dress. The *stola* was their ordinary vest, worn within doors, coming down to their ankles: When they went abroad they slung over it the *palla* or *pallium*, a long open manteau (*d*), which covered the *stola* and their whole body. Thus Horace,

Ad talos stola demissa & circumdata palla (*e*).

And Virgil, describing the habit of Camilla,

Pro crinali auro, pro longa tegmine pallæ,
Tigridis exuviæ per dorsum a vertice pendent (*f*).

They dressed their heads with what they called *vittæ* and *fasciæ*, ribbons and thin sashes; and the last sort they twisted round their whole body, next to the skin, to make them slender; to which Terence alludes in his eunuch (*g*):

Rubenius has found this difference in the *stolæ*, that those of the ordinary women were white trimmed with golden purls (*h*).

Haud similis virgo est virginum nostrarum; quas matres student
Demissis humeris esse, vincto pectore, ut graciles sient.

The former Ovid makes to be the distinguishing badge of honest matrons and chaste virgins.

Este

(*a*) Ferrar. de Re Vestiar. l. 1. c. 27. (*b*) Sueton. August. c. 82. Casaubon, ad locum. (*c*) Vid. Ferrar. de Re Vest. lib. 2. cap. 17. (*d*) Dacier on Horace. l. 1. Sat. 2. ver. 99. (*e*) Horace, ibid. (*f*) Æn. 11. ver. 576. (*g*) Act. 2. Scen. 3. (*h*) De Laticlav. l. 1. c. 16.

Efte procul vittæ tenues, infigne pudoris (a).
And defcribing the chafte Daphne, he fays,
Vitta coercebat pofitos fine lege capillos (b).

It is very obfervable, that the common courtezans were not allowed to appear in the *ftola*, but obliged to wear a fort of gown, as a mark of infamy, by reafon of its refemblance to the habit of the oppofite fex. Hence in that place of Horace,

———————————*Quid inter*—
Eft, in matrona, ancilla, peccefve togata? L. 1. S. 2. V. 53.

The moft judicious Dacier underftands by *togata* the common ftrumpet, in oppofition both to the matron and the fervant-maid.

Some have thought that the women (on fome account or other) wore the *lacerna* too; but the rife of this fancy is owing to their miftake of that verfe in Juvenal,

Ipfe lacernatæ cum fe jactaret amicæ.

Where it muft be obferved, that the poet does not fpeak of the ordinary Miffes, but of the eunuch Sporus, upon whom Nero made an experiment in order to change his fex. So that Juvenal's *lacernata amica* is no more than if we fhould fay, a *Miftrefs in breeches*.

The attire of the head and feet will take in all that remains of this fubject. As to the firft of thefe, it has been a former remark, that the Romans ordinarily ufed none, except the lappet of their gown; and this was not a conftant cover, but only occafional, to avoid the rain, or fun, or other accidental inconveniencies. Hence it is that we fee none of the old ftatues with any on their heads, befides now and then a wreath, or fomething of that nature. Euftathius, on the firft of the Odyffes, tells us, that the Latins derived this cuftom of going bareheaded from the Greeks; it being notorious, that, in the age of the heroes, no kind of hats or caps were at all in fafhion; nor is there any fuch thing to be met with in Homer. Yet at fome particular times we find the Romans ufing fome fort of covering for the head; as at the facrifices, at the public games, at the feaft of Saturn, upon a journey, or a warlike expedition. Some perfons too were allowed to have their heads always covered; as men who had been lately made free, and were thereupon fhaved clofe on their head, might wear the *pileus*, both as a defence from the cold, and as a badge of their liberty. And the fame privilege was granted to perfons under any indifpofition.

(a) *Metamorph.* lib. 1. Fab. 9.   (b) *Lipfius de Amphitheat.* cap. 19.

As for the several sorts of coverings designed for these uses, many of them have been long confounded beyond any possibility of a distinction; and the learned Salmasius (a) has observed, that the *mitra* and the *pileus*, the *cucullus*, the *galerus*, and the *palliolum*, were all coverings of the head, very little differing from one another, and promiscuously used by authors; however, there are some of them which deserve a more particular inquiry.

The *galerus* Vossius (b) derives from *galea*, the Roman helmet, to which we must suppose it to have borne some resemblance. Servius, when he reckons up the several sorts of the priests caps, makes the *galerus* one of them, being composed of the skin of the beast offered in sacrifice, the other two being the *apex*, a stitched cap in the form of a helmet, with the addition of a little stick fixed on the top, and wound about with white wool, properly belonging to the Flamines; and the *tutulus*, a woollen turban, much like the former, proper to the high-priest. By the *galerus* it is likely he means the *albo-galerus*, made of the skin of a white beast offered in sacrifice, with the addition of some twigs taken from a wild olive-tree, and belonging only to Jupiter's *flamen*; yet we find a sort of *galerus* in use among the ordinary men, and the *galericulum* (which some call *galerus*) common to both sexes: This was a skin so neatly dressed with men or women's hair, that it could not easily be distinguished from the natural; it was particularly used by those who had thin heads of hair, as Suetonius reports of Nero (c); as also by the wrestlers, to keep their own hair from receiving any damage by the nasty oils with which they were rubbed all over before they exercised. This we learn from Martial's distich on the *galericulum*, xiv. 50.

Ne lutet immundum nitidos ceroma capillos,
Hoc poteris madidas condere pelle comas.

The *pileus* was the ordinary cap or hat worn at public shows and sacrifices, and by the freed men; for a journey they had the *petasus*, differing only from the former in that it had broader brims, and bore a nearer resemblance to our hats, as appears from the common pictures of Mercury; and hence it took its name from πετάννυμι, to open or spread out (d).

(a) *In Vopisc. & Græv. in Sueton. Claud.* 2.   (b) Cap. 12.
(c) *Vossius Etymolog. in v. Petasui.*   (d) *Lipsius de Amphitheat.* cap. 19.

The *mitra*, the *tiara*, and the *diadem*, tho' we often meet with them in Roman authors, are none of them beholden to that nation for their original. The mitre seems to owe its invention to the Trojans, being a crooked cap tied under the chin with ribbons; it belonged only to the women among the Romans, and is attributed to the foreign courtesans that set up their trade in that city, such as the

———*picta lupa barbara mitra*

in Juvenal; yet among the Trojans we find it in use among the men. Thus Romulus scouts them in Virgil,

Et tunicæ manicas & habent redimicula mitræ :
O vere Phrygiæ; neque enim Phryges (a) *!*

And even Æneas himself is by Iarbas described in this dress,

Mæonia mentum mitra crinesnque madentem
Subnexus.   Æn. 4. 216.

The *tiara* was the cap of State used by all the eastern Kings and great men, only with this difference, that the princes wore it with a short strait top, and the nobles with the point a little bending downwards (b).

The *diadem* belonged to the Kings of Rome as well as to the foreign Princes; this seems to have been no more than a white scarf, or *fascia*, bound about the head, like that which composeth the Turkish turban. Those who are willing to find some nearer resemblance between the diadem and our modern crowns, may be convinced of their mistake from that passage of Plutarch, where he tells us of a Princess that made use of her diadem to hang herself with (c).

These white *fasciæ* among the Romans were always looked on as the marks of sovereignty; and therefore when Pompey the Great appeared commonly abroad with a white scarf wound about his leg, upon pretence of a bruise or an ulcer; those, who were jealous of his growing power, did not fail to interpret it as an omen of his affecting the supreme command; and one Favonius plainly told him, it made little odds on what part he wore the diadem, the intention being much the same (d).

To descend to the feet, the several sorts of the Roman shoes, slippers, &c. which most frequently occur in reading, are the *perones*, the *calcei lunati*, the *mullei*, the *soleæ* and *crepidæ*, and the *caligæ*, besides the *cothurnus* and *soccus*, which have been already described.

The

(a) Æn. 9. 616. (b) Demster ad Rosin. lib. 5. cap. 35. (c) Plut. in Lucull.   (d) Valer. Max. lib. 6. cap. 2.

The *perones* were a kind of high shoes, rudely formed of raw hides, and reaching up to the middle of the leg; they were not only used by the country people, as some imagine, but in the city too by men of ordinary rank: Nay, Rubenius avers, that in the elder times of the commonwealth, the Senators, as well as others, went in the *peros* (*a*); however, when they came to be a little polished, they left this clumsy wear to the ploughmen and labourers, and we scarce find them applied to any one else by the authors of the flourishing ages. Thus Persius brings in the

―――*Peronatus arator.*   S. 5. V. 102.

And Juvenal,
―――*Quem non pudet alto*
Per glaciem perone tegi―――S. 14. V. 186.

Virgil, indeed, makes some of his soldiers wear the *pero*, but then they were only a company of plain rustics, *legio agrestis*, as he calls them; besides, they wore it but on one foot:

―――*Vestigia nuda sinistri*
Instituere pedis, crudus tegit altera pero.   Æn. 7. 690.

The *calcei lunati* were proper to the Patricians, to distinguish them from the vulgar, so called from an half-moon in ivory worn upon them. Baldwin will have the half-moon to have served instead of a *fibula*, or buckle (*b*); but Rubenius (*c*) refutes this conjecture, by shewing, from Philostratus, that it was worn by way of ornament, not on the fore-part of the shoe, like the buckle, but about the ankle. Plutarch, in his Roman questions, gives abundance of reasons why they used the half-moon rather than any other figure; but none of his fancies have met with any approbation from the learned. The common opinion makes this custom an allusion to the number of Senators at their first institution, which, being a hundred, was signified by the numeral letter C.

Yet the Patricians, before they arrived at the senatorian age, and even before they put on the *prætexta*, had the privilege of using the half-moon on their shoes. Thus Statius, Sylv. v.2.27.

Sic te, clare puer, genitum sibi curia sensit :
Primaque Patricia clausit vestigia luna.

(*a*) *De Laticlav.* l. 2. c. 1.   (*b*) *De Calceo Antiq.* c. 9   (*c*) *De Laticlav.* l. 2. c. 4.

As for the Senators, who were not Patricians, they did not indeed wear the half-moon; but that ornament seems not to have been the only difference between the senatorian and the common shoes; for the former are commonly represented as black, and coming up to the middle of the leg, as in Horace, Book i. Sat. 6. 27.

———*Nigris medium impediit crus*
Pellibus.

Rubenius will have this understood only of the four black straps which he says fastened the Senators shoes, being tied pretty high on the leg (*a*). Dacier tells us the Senators had two sorts of shoes, one for summer, and the other for winter; the summer shoes he describes with such leathern straps crossing one another many times about the leg, and nothing but a sole at the bottom: These he calls *campagi*; though Rubenius attributes this name to a sort of *caligæ* worn by the Senators under the later Emperors (*b*). The winter shoes, he says, were made of an entire black skin, or sometimes a white one, reaching up to cover the greatest part of the leg, without any open place, except on the top (*c*).

It is uncertain whether the *calcei mullei* were so called from the colour of the mullet, or whether they lent a name to that fish from their reddish dye; they were at first the peculiar wear of the Alban Kings, afterwards of the Kings of Rome, and, upon the establishment of the free state, were appropriated to those persons who had borne any Curule office; but perhaps they might be worn only on great days, at the celebration of some public sports, when they were attired in the whole triumphal habit, of which too these shoes made a part. Julius Cæsar, as he was very singular in his whole habit, so was particularly remarkable for wearing the *mullei* on ordinary days, which he did to shew his descent from the Alban Kings (*d*). In colour and fashion they resembled the cothurni, coming up to the middle of the leg, though they did not cover the whole foot, but only the sole, like sandals (*e*). Dacier informs us, that, at such time as the Emperors took up the use of these red shoes, the Curule magistrates changed the fashion for embroidered ones (*f*).

The Roman *soleæ* were a sort of sandals or pontofles, without any upper-leather, so that they covered only the sole of the

---

(*a*) *Dr Re Vest.* l. 2. c. 3.   (*b*) *Ibid.* c. 5.   (*c*) *Dacier on Horace*, Book 1. Sat. 6.   (*d*) *Dio*, l. 49.   (*e*) Lib. 2. c. 2.
(*f*) *Dacier on Horace*, Book 1. Sat. 6.

the foot, being fastened above with straps and buckles; these were the ordinary fashion of the women, and therefore counted scandalous in the other sex: Thus Cicero exposeth Verres (*a*), and Clodius (*b*), for using this indecent wear; and Livy acquaints us, that the great Scipio was censured on the same account (*c*), yet upon all occasions of mirth and recreation, or lawful indulgence, it was customary for the men to go thus loosely shod, as at entertainments, and at the public shows of all sorts in the circos or amphitheatres.

The *crepidæ*, which now and then occur in Roman authors, are generally supposed to be the same as the *soleæ*, under the Greek name κρηπίδες. But Baldwin is so nice as to assign this difference, that the *crepida* had two soles, whereas the *solea* consisted but of one; therefore he is not willing to be beholden to the Greeks for the word, but thinks it may be derived from the *crepitus*, or *creaking* that they made, which could not be so well conceived in those which had but single leather (*d*). That the Grecian κρηπίδες did really make such a kind of noise, which we cannot easily imagine of the *solea*, is plain from the common story of Momus, who being brought to give his censure of Venus, could find no fault, only that her κρηπίς, or slipper, creaked a little too much.

The *caliga* was the soldier's proper shoe, made in the sandal fashion, so as not to cover the upper part of the foot, though it reached to the middle of the leg. The sole was of wood, like our old galoches, or the *chabots* of the French peasants, and stuck full of nails: these nails were usually so very long in the shoes of the scouts and centinels, that Suetonius (*e*) and Tertullian (*f*) call those *caligæ speculatores*, as if, by mounting the wearer to a higher pitch, they gave a greater advantage to the sight.

It was from these *caligæ* that the Emperor Caligula took his name, having been born in the army, and afterwards bred up in the habit of a common soldier (*g*). And hence Juvenal (*h*), and Suetonius (*i*) use *caligati* for the common soldiers, without the addition of a substantive.

(*a*) *Verrin.* 4.   (*b*) *De Harusp. Responf.*   (*c*) Lib. 29.   (*d*) *Baldwin Calc. Antiq.* cap. 13.   (*e*) *Caligul.* cap. 52.   (*f*) *De Coron. Milit.*   (*g*) *Sueton. Caligul.* cap. 9.   (*h*) Sat. 16. v. 24.   (*i*) *August.* 25.

CHAP.

CHAP. IX.

Of the ROMAN Marriages.

THE marriages of the Romans, which have been so learnedly explained by so many eminent hands, as the great lawyers, Tiraguel, Sigonius, Brissonius, and the two Hottomans, will appear very intelligible from a diligent inquiry into the espousals, the persons that might lawfully marry with one another, the proper season for marriage, the several ways of contracting matrimony, the ceremonies of the wedding, and the causes and manner of divorces.

The espousals, or contract before marriage, was performed by an engagement of the friends on both sides, and might be done as well between absent persons as present, as well in private as before witnesses; yet the common way of betrothing was by writing drawn up by common consent, and sealed by both parties. Thus Juvenal, Sat. 6. 199.

> *Si tibi legitimis pactam junctamque tabellis*
> *Non es amaturus.*

And again, Sat. 10. 336.

> ———*Veniet cum Signatoribus auspex.*

Besides this, the man sent a ring as a pledge to the woman, which, in Pliny's time, was used to be of iron, without any stone in it (*a*). Thus the same satyrist,

> *Conventum tamen & pactum & sponsalia, nostra*
> *Tempestate paras, jamque a tonsore magistro*
> *Pecteris, & digito pignus fortasse dedisti.* Sat. 6. 25.

There was no age determined by the laws for espousals, but they might be made at any time, provided that both parties were sensible of the obligations, which they were not supposed to be till their 7th year; yet Augustus afterwards ordered that no espousals should be esteemed valid, except such as were consummated by the nuptials within two years time (*b*).

No Roman might marry with any other than a Roman; but then this was extended to any free denizen of the city, though
born

(*a*) *Plin. Nat. Hist.* lib. 33. cap. 1. (*b*) *Sueton. Aug.* cap. 34.

born in any other parts; for thus Dionysius (*a*) reports of the Latins, Livy (*b*) of the Campanians, and Cicero (*c*) of the inhabitants of Aricia; yet in Rome we meet with one eminent restraint about these matters, and that is a law of the *decemviri*, prohibiting any marriage between the Patrician families and the Plebeians. But within seven or eight years, the Commons had given so many dangerous tokens of their resentment of this injury, that upon the motion of Canuleius, Tribune of the people, the Consuls were even forced to give consent to the enacting of a contrary decree, allowing a free alliance in marriage between persons of all orders and degrees (*d*).

The Romans were very superstitious in reference to the particular time of marriage, fancying several days and seasons very unfortunate to this design; the *kalends, nones*, and *ides* of every month, were strictly avoided; so was the whole feast of the *parentalia* in February, as Ovid observes, Fastor. 2. 561.

Conde tuas, Hymenæ, faces, & ab ignibus atris
  Aufer; habent alias mæsta sepulchra faces.

Go, Hymen, stop the long-expecting dames,
And hide thy torches from the dismal flames;
Thy presence would be fatal while we mourn,
And at sad tombs must other tapers burn.

The whole month of May was looked on as ominous to contracting matrimony, as Plutarch acquaints us in his Roman questions, and Ovid, Fast. 5. 487.

Nec viduæ tædis eadem, nec virginis apta
  Tempora, quæ nupsit non diuturna fuit.
Hac quoque de causa, si te proverbia tangunt,
  Mense malas Maio nubere vulgus ait.

No tapers then should burn, nor ever bride
Link'd at this season long her bliss enjoy'd;
Hence our wise masters of the proverbs say,
" The girls are all stark naught that wed in May."

In short, the most happy season, in all respects, for celebrating the nuptial solemnity, was that which followed the ides of June. Thus Ovid, speaking of his daughter,

Hanc ego cum vellem genero dare, tempora tædis
  Apta requirebam, quæque cavenda forent.

Tunc

(*a*) Lib. 6.   (*b*) Lib. 38.   (*c*) *In Philipp.*   (*d*) *Liv.* lib. 4.

Tunc mihi post sacras monstratur Junius Idus
 Utilis & nuptis utilis esse viris. Fast. vi. 221.

Resolv'd to match the girl, I try'd to find
What days unprosp'rous were, what moons were kind;
After June's sacred ides my fancy stay'd,
Good to the man, and happy to the maid.

The three ways of contracting matrimony were, *farre, coemptione*, and *usu*, which fall properly under the consideration of the civil law; the main difference of them, in short, was this. Confarreatio was, when the matrimonial rites were performed with solemn sacrifices, and offerings of burnt cakes, by the *Pontifex Maximus*, and the *Flamen Dialis*. Pliny says this was the most solemn tie of all (a); yet we are assured, that, after some time, it was almost universally laid aside, as thought to include too many troublesome ceremonies (b). A divorce, after this way of marriage, Festus calls *diffarreatio*. Coemptio was, when the persons solemnly bound themselves to one another by the ceremony of giving and taking a piece of money. The marriage was said to be made *by use*, when, with the consent of her friends, the woman had lived with the man a whole year compleat, without being absent three nights, at which time she was reckoned in all respects a lawful wife, though not near so closely joined as in the former cases.

The nuptial ceremonies were always begun with the taking of omens by the auspices. Hence Tully, *Nubit genero socrus nullis auspicibus, nullis auctoribus, funestis omnibus omnium* (c).

In dressing the bride, they never omitted to divide her locks with the head of a spear, either as a token that their marriages first began by war and acts of hostility upon the rape of the Sabine virgins (d); or as an omen of bearing a valiant and warlike offspring; or to remind the bride, that, being married to one of a martial race, she should use herself to no other than a plain unaffected dress; or because the greatest part of the nuptial care is referred to Juno, to whom the spear is sacred; whence she took the name of *dea quiris, quiris* among the ancients signifying this weapon (e). Ovid alludes to this custom in the second of his *fasti:* 559.

Nec tibi quæ cupidæ matura videbere matri,
 Comat virgineas hasta recurva comas.

Thou

(a) Lib. 18. cap. 2.   (b) Tacit. Annal. 4.   (c) Orat. pro Cluent.
(d) Plutarch in Romul.   (e) Idem, Quæst. Rom. 87.

Book V.   *the* ROMANS.   329

> Thou whom thy mother frets to see a maid,
> Let no bent spear thy virgin-locks divide.

In the next place, they crowned her with a chaplet of flowers, and put on her veil, or *flammeum*, proper to this occasion. Thus Catullus, lix. 6.

> *Cinge tempora floribus*
> *Suaveolentis amaraci :*
> *Flammeum cape.*

And Juvenal, describing Messalina when about to marry Silius :

> ——*Dudum sedet illa parato*
> *Flammneolo.*   Sat. 10.

Instead of her ordinary cloathes, she wore the *tunica recta*, or common *tunick*, called *recta*, from being woven upwards, of the same nature with that which the young men put on with their *manly gown* (a) ; this was tied about with a girdle, which the bridegroom was to unloose.

Being dressed after this manner, in the evening she was led towards the bridegroom's house by three boys habited in the *prætexta*, whose fathers and mothers were alive. Five torches were carried to light her ; for which particular number Plutarch has troubled himself to find out several reasons (b). A distaff and a spindle were likewise borne along with her, in memory of Caia Cecilia, or Tanaquil, wife to Tarquinius Priscus, a famous spinster (c) : And on the same account the bride called herself *Caia*, during the nuptial solemnity, as a fortunate name.

Being come to the door, (which was garnished with flowers and leaves, according to that of Catullus, lxii. 293.

> *Vestibulum ut molli velatum fronde vireret,*)

she bound about the posts with woolen lifts, and washed them over with melted tallow, to keep out infection and sorcery. This custom Virgil alludes to, Æn. 4. 557.

> *Præterea fuit in tectis de marmore templum*
> *Conjugis antiqui, miro quod honore colebat,*
> *Velleribus niveis & festa fronde revinctum.*

Being to go into the house, she was not by any means to touch the threshold, but was lifted over by main strength.

Either because the threshold was sacred to Vesta, a most chaste goddess, and so ought not to be defiled by one in these circumstances ;

3 B

(a) *Pliny*, lib. 8. cap. 48.   (b) *Rom. Quæst.* 2.   (c) *Pliny.* lib. 8. cap. 48.

stances; or else, that it might seem a piece of modesty to be compelled into a place where she should cease to be a virgin (a).

Upon her entrance, she had the keys of the house delivered to her, and was presented by the bridegroom with two vessels, one of fire, the other of water, either as an emblem of purity and chastity, or as a communication of goods, or as an earnest of sticking by one another in the greatest extremities (b).

And now she and her companions were treated by the bridegroom at a splendid feast; on which occasion, the sumptuary laws allowed a little more liberty than ordinary in the expences. This kind of treat was seldom without music, composed commonly of flutes; the company all the while singing *Thalassius*, or *Thalassio*, as the Greeks did *Hymenæus*. There are several reasons given by Plutarch (c) for the use of this word; the common opinion makes it an admonishment to good housewifery; the Greek word ταλασία, signifying *spinning*; and among the conditions which were agreed upon by the Sabines and Romans, after the rape of the virgins, this was one, that the women should be obliged to no servile office for their husbands, any farther than what concerned spinning.

At the same time the bridegroom threw nuts about the room for the boys to scramble: Thus Virgil, Eclog. 8.

Sparge, marite, nuces——

Out of the many reasons given for this custom, the most commonly received makes it a token of their leaving childish divertisements, and entering on a more serious state of life, whence *nucibus relictis* has passed into a proverb. This conjecture is favoured by Catullus, lix. 131:

Da nuces pueris, iners
Concubine: Satis diu
Lusisti nucibus. Lubet
Jam servire Thalassio.
Concubine, nuces da.

In the mean time the genial bed was got ready, and a set of good old wives, that had never been married but to one man, placed the bride on it with a great deal of ceremony. Thus Catullus, lix. 186.

Vos bonæ senibus viris
Cognitæ bene feminæ,
Collocate puellulam.
Jam licet venias, marite, &c.

Nothing

(a) Plut. Rom. Quæst. 1. Serv. ad Virg. Eclog. 8. (b) Plut. Rom. Quæst. 1. (c) Idem in Romul. & Rom. Quæst. 31.

Nothing now remained but for the bridegroom to loose her girdle, a custom that wants no explanation; only it may be observed to have been of great antiquity: Thus Moschus in his story of Jupiter and Europa, 160.

———Ζεὺς δὲ πάλιν ἐτέρηαζετο μορφὴν,
Δῦσι δὲ οἱ πάλιν μίτρην.

Homer, Odyss. 2.

Δῦσιν παρθενικὴν ζώνην.

And Musæus in Hero and Leander, 272.

'Ως ἡ μὲν ταῦτ' ἔπεν. ὁ δ' αὐτίκα λύσατο μίτρην·
Καὶ θεσμῶν ἐπέβησαν ἀριστονόου Κυθερείης.

There seldom wanted a company of boys, and mad sparks got together, to sing a parcel of obscene verses, which were tolerated on this occasion. They consisted of a kind of *fescennine* rhimes. Hence Catullus:

Nec diu taceat procax
Fescennina locutio.

And Claudian:

Permissisque jocis turba licentior
Exultet a tetricis libera legibus.

The day after, the new married man held a stately supper, and invited all his old companions to a drinking-match, which they termed *repotia*.

The whole subject of divorces belongs entirely to the lawyers, and the distinction between *repudium* and *divortium* is owing to their nicety; the first they make the breaking off the contract, or espousal; and the last a separation after actual matrimony. Plutarch mentions a very severe law of Romulus, which suffered not a wife to leave her husband, but gave a man the liberty of turning off his wife, either upon poisoning her children, or counterfeiting his private keys, or for the crime of adultery. But if the husband, on any other occasion, put her away, he ordered one moiety of his estate to be given to his wife, and the other to fall to the Goddess *Ceres*; and that whosoever sent away his wife, should make an atonement to the gods of the earth (*a*). It is very remarkable, that, almost six hundred years after the building of the city, one P. Servilius, or Carvilius Spurius, was the first of the Romans that ever put away his wife (*b*).

(*a*) Plutarch in Romul. (*b*) Valer. Max. lib. 2. cap. 1. Plutarch Compar. Romul. & Thes. & Rom. Qu. 13.

The common way of divorcing was by sending a bill to the woman, containing reasons of the separation, and the tender of all her goods which she brought with her; this they termed *repudium mittere:* Or else it was performed in her presence before sufficient witnesses, with the formalities of tearing the writings, refunding the portion, taking away the keys, and turning the woman out of doors. But however the law of Romulus came to fail, it is certain that in later times the women too, as well as the men, might sue for a divorce, and enter on a separate life. Thus Juvenal, Sat. 9. 74.

———*Fugientem sæpe puellam*
Amplexu rapui; tabulas quoque fregerat, & jam
Signabat.

And Martial, Lib. 10. Epigr. 41.
Mense novo Maii veterem Proculeia maritum
Deseris, atque jubes res sibi habere suas.

We have here a fair opportunity to inquire into the grounds of the common opinion about borrowing and lending of wives among the Romans. He that chargeth them most severely with this practice is the most learned Tertullian, in his Apology, ch. 39. *Omnia indiscreta sunt apud nos*, &c, "All things, (says "he, speaking of the Christians,) are common among us, ex-"cept our wives: We admit no partnership in that one thing, "in which other men are more professedly partners, who not "only make use of their friend's bed, but very patiently ex-"pose their own wives to a new embrace: I suppose, accord-"ing to the institution of the most wise ancients, the Græcian "Socrates, and the Roman Cato, who freely lent out their "wives to their friends!" And presently after, *O sapientia Atticæ & Romanæ gravitatis exemplum! leno est Philosophus & Censor.* "O wondrous example of Attic wisdom, and of Ro-"man gravity! A Philosopher and a Censor turn pimps."

Chiefly on the strength of this authority the Romans have been generally taxed with such a custom; and a very great man of our own country (*a*) expresseth his compliance with the vulgar opinion, though he ingenuously extenuates the fault in a parallel instance. So much indeed must be granted, that though the law made those husbands liable to a penalty, who either hired out their wives for money, or kept them after they had been actually convicted of adultery, yet the bare permission of that crime did not fall under the notice of the

civil

(*a*) *Sir* William Temple's *Introduction to the Hist. of Engl.*

civil power. And Ulpian says expressly, *ei qui patitur uxorem suam delinquere, matrimoniumque suum contemnit; quique contaminatione non indignatur, pœna adulteratorum non infligitur.* "He that suffers his wife to defile his bed, and, contemning "his matrimonial contract, is not displeased at the pollution, "does not incur the penalty of adulterers." But it is almost impossible that this should give occasion to such a fancy, being no more than what is tolerated at present. It may therefore be alledged in favour of the Romans, that this opinion might probably have its rise from the frequent practice of that sort of marriage, according to which a woman was made a wife only by possession and use, without any farther ceremony. This was the most incomplete of all conjugal ties: The wife being so, rather by the law of nature, than according to the Roman constitution; and therefore she was not called *mater-familias*, nor had any right to inherit the goods of her husband, being supposed to be taken purely on the account of procreating issue; so that, after the bearing of three or four children, she might lawfully be given to another man.

As to the example of Cato, (not to urge, that Tertullian has mistook the Censor for him of Utica, and so lost the sting of his sarcasm) the best accounts of that matter may be had from Strabo and Plutarch. The *place* of Strabo is in his 7th Book: Ἱστοροῦσι δὲ περὶ τῶν Ταπύρων ὅτι αὐτοῖς εἴη νόμιμον τὰς γυναῖκας τὰς γαμετὰς ἐκδιδόναι ἑτέροις ἀνδράσιν, ἐπειδὰν ἐξ αὐτῶν ἀνέλωνται δύο ἢ τρία τέκνα, καθάπερ καὶ Κάτων Ὁρτησίῳ δεηθέντι ἐξέδωκε τὴν Μαρκίαν ἐφ' ἡμῶν, κατὰ παλαιὸν Ῥωμαίων ἦδος. "They report of these Tapyrians, that it is counted "lawful among them to give away their wives to other men, "after they have had two or three children by them; as Ca- "to in our time, upon the request of Hortensius, gave him "his wife Marcia, according to the old custom of the Romans." Here by ἐκδιδόναι and ἐξέδωκε we should not understand the lending or letting out of women, but the marrying them to new husbands; as Plato useth ἔκδοσιν θυγατέρων ποιεῖν, "to bestow "daughters in marriage."

Plutarch, before he proceeds to his relation, has premised, that this passage, in the life of Cato, looks like a fable in a play, and is very difficult to be cleared, or made out with any certainty. His narration is taken out of Thraseas, who had it from Munatius, Cato's friend and constant companion, and runs to this effect:

"Quintus Hortensius, a man of signal worth and ap-
"proved virtue, was not content to live in friendship and
"familiarity

" familiarity with Cato, but defired alfo to be united to his
" family, by fome alliance in marriage. Therefore waiting
" upon Cato, he began to make a propofal about taking Cato's
" daughter Porcia from Bibulus, to whom fhe had already
" borne three children, and making her his own wife; of-
" fering to reftore her after fhe had borne him a child, if Bi-
" bulus was not willing to part with her altogether: Adding,
" that though this, in the opinion of men, might feem ftrange,
" yet in nature it would appear honeft and profitable to the
" public, with much more to the fame purpofe. Cato could
" not but exprefs his wonder at the ftrange project, but with-
" al approved very well of uniting their houfes: When Hor-
" tenfius, turning the difcourfe, did not ftick to acknowledge,
" that it was Cato's own wife which he really defired. Ca-
" to, perceiving his earneft inclinations, did not deny his re-
" queft, but faid, that Philip, being the father of Marcia,
" ought alfo to be confulted. Philip, being fent for, came,
" and finding they were all agreed, gave his daughter Mar-
" cia to Hortenfius, in the prefence of Cato, who himfelf alfo
" affifted at the marriage."

So that this was nothing like lending a wife out, but actually marrying her to another while her firft hufband was alive,
to whom fhe might be fuppofed to have come by that kind of
matrimony which is founded on the right of poffeffion. And
upon the whole, the Romans feem to have been hitherto un-
juftly taxed with the allowance of a cuftom not ufually practi-
fed among the moft barbarous and favage part of mankind.

CHAP. X.

Of the ROMAN Funerals.

THE moft ancient and generally received ways of burying
have been interring and burning, and both thefe we find
at the fame time in ufe among the Romans, borrowed in all
probability from the Græcians. That the Græcians interred
their dead bodies may, in fhort, be evinced from the ftory of
the Ephefian matron in Petronius, who is defcribed fitting and
watching her hufband's body laid in a vault; and from the
argument which Solon brought to juftify the right of the Athenians to the ifle of Salamis, taken from the dead bodies that
were buried there, not after the manner of their competitors
the

the Megarenſians, but according to the Athenian faſhion; for the Megarenſians turned the carcaſe to the eaſt, and the Athenians to the weſt; and that the Athenians had a diſtinct ſepulchre for each body, whereas the Megarenſians put two or three into one (a). That the ſame people ſometimes burnt their dead is beyond diſpute, from the teſtimony of Plutarch, who, ſpeaking of the death of Phocion, tells us, that for ſome time none of the Athenians dared light a funeral pile to burn the body after their manner. As alſo from the deſcription of the plague of Athens in Thucidides, ἐπὶ πυρᾶς γὰρ ἀλλοτρίας, &c. with the tranſlation of which paſſage Lucretius concludes his poem:

> *Namque ſuos conſanguineos aliena rogorum*
> *Inſuper exſtructa ingenti clamore locabant,*
> *Subdebantque faces, multo cum ſanguine ſæpe*
> *Rixantes potius quam corpora deſererentur.*

To prove that both theſe ways of burial were uſed by the Romans is almoſt unneceſſary; for burning is known by every one to have been their common practice. And as for interring, their great lawyer Numa particularly forbade the burning of his own body, but commanded it to be laid entire in a ſtone coffin (b). And we learn from Cicero (c), and Pliny (d), that the family of the Cornelii interred their dead all along till the time of Sylla the Dictator, who in his will gave expreſs orders to have his body burnt; probably to avoid the indignities that might have been offered it after burial by the Marian faction, in return for the violence ſhown by Sylla's ſoldiers to the tomb and relics of Marius.

But though burning was the ordinary cuſtom, yet in ſome particular caſes it was poſitively forbid, and looked on as the higheſt impiety. Thus infants, who died before the breeding of teeth, were incloſed unburnt in the ground (e):

> ———*Terra clauditur infans,*
> *Et minor igne rogi.*   Juvenal. Sat. 15.

The place ſet apart for the interment of theſe infants was called *ſuggrundarium*. The ſame ſuperſtition was obſerved in reference to perſons who had been ſtruck dead with lightning or thunder (f). For they were never burnt again, but after a

great

(a) Plutarch. in Solon. (b) Plutarch. in Num. (c) De Leg. l. 2.
(d) N. H. lib. 7. cap. 54. (e) Idem, lib. 7. cap. 16. (f) Idem. lib. 2. cap. 54.

great deal of ceremony performed by the *auspices*, and the sacrifice of a sheep, were either put into the earth, or sometimes let alone to lie upon the ground where they had fallen. In both cases the place was presently inclosed either with a stone wall, or stake, or sometimes only with a rope, having the name of *bidental* from the *bidens* or sheep that were offered. Persius useth *bidental* for the person that had come to this unhappy end, ii. 26.

An quia non fibris ovium, Ergennaque jubente,
Triste jaces lucis, evitandumque bidental.

For they fancied, that, wherever a thunderbolt fell, the gods had a particular desire to have the place sacred to their worship; and therefore, whether the man had been killed or not, they used the same superstition in hallowing the ground (a).

The several sorts of funerals fall under the common heads of *Funus indictivum* and *Funus tacitum*. The Funus indictivum had its name *ab indicendo* from inviting, because on such occasions there was made a general invitation of the people by the mouth of a public crier. This was celebrated with extraordinary splendor and magnificence, the people being presented with public shows, and other common divertisements. The *funus publicum*, which we meet with so often, may be sometimes understood as entirely the same with the *indictive* funeral, and sometimes only as a species of it. It is the same when it denotes all the state and grandeur of the more noble funerals, such as were usually kept for rich and great men. It is only a species of the *indictive* funeral, when either it signifies the proclaiming of a *vacation*, and an injunction of public sorrow, or the defraying the charges of the funeral out of the public stock. For it is probable that, at both these solemnities, a general invitation was made by the crier; yet in this latter it was done by order of the Senate, and in the former by the will of the deceased person, or the pleasure of his heirs. But no one will hence conclude, that the funerals of all such rich men were attended with the formality of a *vacation*, and an order for public grief. For this was accounted the greatest honour that could be showed to the relics of princes themselves: Thus the Senate decreed a public funeral for Syphax, and the once great King of Macedon, who both died in prison under the power of the Romans (b). And
Suetonius

(a) *Dacier on Horace* Art. Poet. ver. 471. (b) *Val. Max.* l. 5. c. 1.

Suetonius informs us, that Tiberius (*a*), and Vitellius (*b*), were buried with the same state: yet, upon account of having performed any signal service to the commonwealth, this honour was often conferred on private men, and sometimes upon women too; as Dio relates of Attia, the mother of Julius Cæsar (*c*); and Xiphilin of Livia (*d*). Nor was this custom peculiar to the Romans, for Laertius reports of Democritus, that deceasing, after he had lived above a hundred years, he was honoured with a *public funeral*. And Justin tells us, that the inhabitants of Marseilles, then a Græcian colony, upon the news of Rome's being taken by the Gauls, kept a *public funeral* to testify their condolence of the calamity (*e*).

There seems to have been different sorts of *public Funerals* in Rome, according to the magistracies, or other honours, which the deceased persons had borne: As the *Prætorium*, the *Consulare*, the *Censorium*, and the *Triumphale*. The two last were by much the more magnificent, which though formerly distinguished, yet in the time of the Emperors were joined in one, with the name of *funus censorium* only, as Tacitus often useth the phrase. Nor was the *censorium* funeral confined to private persons, but the very Emperors themselves were honoured with the like solemnity after their death, as Tacitus reports of Claudius (*f*), and Capitolinus of Pertinax.

The *funus tacitum*, opposed to the *indictive*, or public funeral, was kept in a private manner, without the solemnization of sports, without pomp, without a marshaller or a general invitation. Thus *Seneca de Tranquil. Anim. Marti natus es: minus molestiarum habet funus tacitum.* And Ovid. Trist. 1. Eleg. 3. 259.

Quocunque aspiceres, luctus gemitusque sonabant,
  Formaque non taciti funeris * *instar erat.*   * intus.

This is the same that Capitolinus calls *funus vulgare*, when he reports, that Marcus Antoninus was so extremely kind and municent, as to allow even *vulgar funerals* to be kept at the charge of the public. Propertius calls it *Plebeium funus:*

———————————*Adsint*
  Plebeii parvæ funeris exequiæ. Lib. 2. El. 13.
Ausonius : Funus commune.
  Tu gremio in proavi funus commune locatum.

3 C   And

(*a*) Cap. 75.   (*b*) Cap. 3.   (*c*) Lib. 47.   (*d*) In Tiberio
(*e*) Lib. 43.   (*f*) Annal. 12.

And Suetonius, *funus translatitium*, when he informs us that Britannicus was buried after this manner by Nero (*a*).

To the *silent* funerals may be referred the *funera acerba*, or untimely obsequies of youths and children; which Juvenal speaks of, Sat. 11. 44.

> *Non præmaturi cineres, non funus acerbum*
> *Luxuri., &c.*

And Virgil, Æn. 6. 427.

> *Infantumque animæ flentes in limine primo :*
> *Quos dulcis vitæ exortes & ab ubere raptos*
> *Abstulit atra dies, & funere mersit acerbo.*

The funeral ceremonies may be divided into such as were used to persons when they were dying, and such as were afterwards performed to the dead corpse.

When all hopes of life were now given over, and the soul as it were just ready for its flight, the friends and nearest relations of the dying party were wont to kiss him, and embrace his body till he expired. Thus Suetonius (*b*) relates that Augustus expired *in the kisses of Livia*. Nor need there be any further proof of a custom which every body is acquainted with. The reason of it is not so well known: Most probably, they thought by this pious act to receive into their own bodies the soul of their departing friend. Thus Albinovanus in the Epicede of Livia,

> *Sospite te saltem moriar, Nero ; tu mea condas*
> *Lumina, & accipias hanc animam ore pio.*

For the ancients believed that the soul, when it was about leaving the body, made use of the mouth for its passage; whence *animam in primo ore*, or *in primis labris tenere*, is "to be at death's door." And they might well imagine the soul was thus transfused in the last act of life, who could fancy that it was communicated in an ordinary kiss, as we find they did from these love-verses, recited by Macrobius, the original of which is attributed to Plato:

> *Dum semihulco suavio*
> *Meum pullum suavior,*
>
> *Dulcemquo*

(*a*) *Ner.* 33.   (*b*) *August.* 91.

> *Dulcemque florem spiritus*
> *Duco ex aperto tramite,*
> *Animo tunc ægra & saucia*
> *Cucurrit ad labia mihi,* &c. (*a*).

Nor did they only kiss their friends when just expiring, but afterwards too, when the body was going to be laid on the funeral pile. Thus Tibullus, Lib. 1. Eleg. 1.

> *Flebis & arsuro positum me, Delia, lecto,*
> *Tristibus & lacrymis oscula mixta dabis.*

And Propertius, Lib. 2. Eleg. 12.

> *Osculaque in gelidis pones suprema labellis,*
> *Cum dabitur Syrio munere plenus onyx.*

Another ceremony, used to persons expiring, was the taking off their rings. Thus Suetonius reports, that when the Emperor "Tiberius swooned away, and was reputed dead, his rings "were taken from him, though he afterwards recovered, and "asked for them again (*b*)." They are much mistaken, who fancy him to have done this with design to change his heir; for though it was an usual custom with the ancients to constitute their heir or successor, by giving him their rings on their death-bed, yet this signified nothing, in case a legal will was produced to the contrary (*c*).

But whether they took off the rings to save them from the persons concerned in washing and taking care of the dead body, or on any other account, it is very probable that they were afterwards restored again to the fingers, and burnt in the funeral pile; as may be gathered from that verse of Propertius, where describing the ghost of his mistress in the habit in which she was burned, he says,

> *Et solitum digito beryllon redderat ignis.* Lib. 4. El. 7.

The custom of closing the eyes of a departing friend, common both to the Romans and Græcians, is known by any one that has but looked in a classic author. It may only here be observed, that this ceremony was performed, for the most part, by the nearest

---

(*a*) Macrob. Saturn. lib. 2. cap. 2. (*b*) Cap. 73. (*c*) Val. Max. lib. 7. cap. 8.

nearest relation; as by husbands to their wives, and by wives to their husbands, by parents to their children, and by children to their parents, &c. of all which we have a multitude of instances in the poets. Pliny tells us, that as they closed the eyes of the dying persons, so they opened them too again when the body was laid on the funeral pile: And his reason for both customs is, *ut neque ab homine supremum spectari fas sit, & cœlo non ostendi nefas* (a); "because they counted it equally impious, that the eyes should be seen by men at their last motion, or that they should not be exposed to the view of heaven."

And for the ceremonies used to persons after they were dead, they may be divided into three sorts; such as were performed before the burial, such as concerned the act of the funeral, and such as were done after that solemnity.

Before the burial, we meet with the customs of washing and anointing the corpse, not by any means proper to the Romans, but anciently used by almost all the civilized parts of the world, owing their first rise to the invention of the Ægyptians. These offices in Rome were either performed by the women whom they termed *funereæ*; or else in richer or nobler families by the *libitinarii*, a society of men who got their livelihood by preparing things in order to the solemnization of funerals. They had their names from *Libitina*, the Goddess who presided over obsequies. Hence the word *libitina* is commonly used for death itself; or for every thing in general relating to the funerals, because, in the temple of that Goddess, all necessaries, proper on such occasions, were exposed to sale. Phædrus alludes to this custom, speaking of a covetous miser, Lib. 5. Fab. 77.

Qui circumcides omnem impensam Funeris.
Libitina ne quid de tuo faciat lucrum.

But, to return to the *libitinarii*, they seem to have been the chief persons concerned in ordering funerals, undertaking the whole care and charge of such solemnity at a set price; and therefore they kept a great number of servants to perform the working part, such as the *pollinctores*, the *vespillones*, &c. The first of these were employed to anoint the dead body, and the others we may chance to meet with hereafter. In allusion to this custom of anointing the corpse, Martial (iii. 12.) plays very genteely on the master of an entertainment, where there was much essence to be got, but very little meat.

Unguentum

(a) Lib. 11. cap. 37.

> *Unguentum fateor bonum dedisti*
> *Convivis, here ; sed nihil scidisti.*
> *Res falsa est bene olere & esurire.*
> *Qui non cœnat, & ungitur, Fabulle,*
> *Is vere mihi mortuus videtur.*

When the body had been washed and anointed, they proceeded to wrap it in a garment: The ordinary people for this purpose made use of the common gown; and though in some parts of Italy the inhabitants were so rude as not to wear the gown while they lived, yet Juvenal informs us, that they did not want it at their death:

> *Pars magna Italiæ est, si verum admittimus, in qua*
> *Nemo togam sumit nisi mortuus.*   Sat. 3. 171.

But those who had borne any public office in the State, or acquired any honour in war, were, after their death, wrapped in the particular garment which belonged to their place, or to their triumph; as Livy (*a*) and Polybius (*b*) expressly report. It may here be observed, that the ancients were so very careful and superstitious in reference to their funeral garments, that they often wove them for themselves and their friends during life. Thus Virgil brings in the mother of Euryalus complaining,

> ——— *Nec te, tua funera, mater*
> *Produxi pressive oculos, nec vulnera lavi*
> *Veste tegens, tibi quam noctes festina diesque*
> *Urgebam, & tela curas solator aniles.*   Æn. ix. 426.

If the deceased had by his valour obtained any of the honourable coronets, it was constantly put on his head when the body was dressed for the funeral, that the reward of virtue might in some measure be enjoyed after death, as Cicero observes in his second Book of Laws. Other persons they crowned with chaplets of flowers, and with those too adorned the couch on which the body was laid. The primitive Christians inveighed severely against this custom, as little less than idolatry, as is to be seen particularly in Minutius Felix (*c*) and Tertullian (*d*).

(*a*) Lib. 34.   (*b*) Lib. 6.   (*c*) *Octav.* pag. 109. *Edit Oxon.*
(*d*) *De Corona. Mil.*

The next ceremony that followed was the *collocatio*, or *laying out* of the body, performed always by the nearest relation. Whence Dio censures Tiberius for his neglect of Livia, ὅτι ιτεῦσαν ἐπισκέψατο, ὅτι ἀποθανοῦσαν αὐτὸς ᾠφείλε. "He neither visited her when she was sick, nor laid her out with his own hands, after she was dead."

The place where they laid the body was always near the threshold, at the entrance of the house:

  ―――*recipitque ad limina gressum,*
  Corpus ubi examini positum Pallantis Acœtes
  Servabat senior. Æn. xi. 29.

And they took particular care in placing the body, to turn the feet outward toward the gate, which custom Persius has left us elegantly described in his third Satyr, 103:

  ―――*tandemque beatulus alto*
  Compositus lecto crassisque lutatus amomis,
  In portam rigidos calces extendit―――

The reason of this position was to show all persons whether any violence had been the cause of the party's death, which might be discovered by the outward signs.

We must not forget the *conclamatio*, or general outcry, set up at such intervals before the corpse, by persons who waited there on purpose; this was done, either because they hoped by this means to stop the soul, which was now taking its flight, or else to awaken its powers, which they thought might only lye silent in the body without action. For the first reason we are beholden to Propertius, iv. 7:

  At mihi non oculos quisquam inclamavit euntes,
  Unum impetrassem te revocante diem.

The other is taken from the explication of this custom by Servius, on the sixth of the Æneids, and seems much the more probable design. For the physicians give several instances of persons who, being buried thro' haste in an apoplectic fit, have afterwards come to themselves, and many times miserably perished for want of assistance.

If all this crying out signified nothing, the deceased was said to be *conclamatus*, or past call, to which practice there
               are

are frequent allusions in almost every author. Lucan is very elegant to this purpose:

 ——— *Sic funere primo*
Attonitæ tacuere domus, quum corpora nondum
Conclamata jacent, nec mater crine soluto
Exigit ad sævos famularum brachia planctus.   Lib. 2.

There is scarce any ceremony remaining which was performed before the burial, except the custom of sticking up some sign, by which the house was known to be in mourning. This, among the Romans, was done by fixing branches of cypress, or of the pitch-tree, near the entrance, neither of which trees being once cut down ever revive, and have on that account been thought proper emblems of a funeral (*a*).

Thus much was done before the funeral: In the funeral we may take notice of the *elatio*, or carrying forth, and the act of burial. What concerns the first of these, will be made out in observing the *day*, the *time*, the *persons*, and the *place*. What day after the person's death was appointed for the funeral is not very well agreed on. Servius, on that passage of Virgil, Æn. 5. verse 65.

 Præterea si nona dies mortalibus ægris, &c.

expressly tells us, that "the body lay seven days in the house, "on the eighth day was burned, and on the ninth the relics "were buried." But there are many instances to prove that this set number of days was not always observed. Therefore perhaps this belonged only to the indictive and public funerals, and not to the private and silent, especially not to the *acerba funera*, in which things were always huddled up with wonderful haste. Thus Suetonius reports of the funeral of Britannicus (*b*), and of the Emperor Otho (*c*): And Cicero pro Cluentio, *Eo ipso die puer cum hora undecima in publico & valens visus esset, ante noctem mortuus, & postridie ante lucem combustus.*

As to the *time* of carrying forth the corpse, anciently they made use only of the night; as Servius observes on those words of Virgil,

 ——— *De more vetusto*
Funeras rapuere faces.   Æn. 11. v. 142.

              The

(*a*) Plin. lib. 16. cap. 33.   Serv. ad Æn. 4.   (*q*) Ner. 32.
(*c*) Otho, 81.

The reason he gives for it is, that hereby they might avoid meeting with the magistrates or priests, whose eyes they thought would be defiled by such a spectacle. Hence the funeral had its name *a funalibus*, from the torches; and the *vespillones*, or *vesperones*, were so called from *vesper*, the evening.

Nothing is more evident, than that this custom was not long observed, at least not in the *public* funerals, though it seems to have continued in the *silent* and *private*, as Servius acquaints us in the same place. Hence Nero took a fair excuse for hurrying his brother Britannicus's body into the grave, immediately after he had sent him out of the world. For Tacitus reports, that the Emperor defended the hasty burial which had caused so much talk and suspicion, in a public edict, urging, that it was agreeable to the old institutions, to hide such untimely funerals from mens eyes as soon as possible, and not detain them with the tedious formalities of harangues and pompous processions. It may not be too nice a remark, that, in the more splendid funerals, the former part of the day seems to have been designed for the procession. Thus Plutarch relates of the burial of Sylla, that, the "morning being very "cloudy over head, they deferred carrying forth the corpse "till the ninth hour," or three in the afternoon. But tho' this custom of carrying forth the corpse by night, in a great measure ceased, yet the bearing of torches and tapers still continued in practice. Thus Virgil in the funeral of Pallas, Æn. xi. 144:

———*Lucet via longo*
Ordine flammarum, & late discriminat agros.

And Persius, Sat. 3. 103:

Hinc tuba, candelæ, &c.

And because tapers were likewise used at the nuptial solemnity, the poets did not fail to take the hint for bringing them both into the same fancy. As Propertius, Book 4. Eleg. last:

Viximus insignes inter utramque facem.

And Ovid, in the epistle of Cydippe to Acontius, 172:

Et, face pro thalami, fax mihi mortis erat.

Among

Book V.   *the* ROMANS.   345

Among the persons concerned in carrying forth the corpse we may begin with those that went before the funeral-bed, such as the *Siticines*, the *Præficæ*, the *Ludii*, the *Histriones*, the new freed-men, the bearers of the images, &c The names of *Siticines* A. Gellius (*a*) derives from from *Situs* and *Cano*, from singing to the dead. They were of two sorts, some sounding on the trumpet, others on the flute or pipe. That the trumpets had a share in this solemnity, we learn from Virgil in the funeral of Pallas, Æn. 11. 192.

Exoritur clamorque virum, clangorque tubarum.

And from Propertius, Book 2. Eleg. 7.

Ah! me, tum quales caneret tibi, Cynthia, somnos
Tibia, funesta tristior illa tuba.

And Plutarch tells a notable story of a magpie, that, upon hearing the trumpets at the funeral of a rich man, for some time after quite lost her voice, and could raise no manner of note; when, on a sudden, as if she had been all this while deeply meditating on the matter, she struck up exactly the same tunes that the trumpets had played, and hit all the tunes and changes to admiration (*b*).

For it is likely that the trumpets were used only in the public funerals, to give the people notice to appear at the solemnity, as Lipsius instructs us (*c*).

The *Tibicines* some restrain to the funerals of children and younger persons, as Servius observes on the first of the Æneids, and Statius, Theb. 6. in the funeral of Achemorus:

Tum signum luctus cornu grave mugis adunco
Tibia, cui teneros suetum producere manes.

The learned Dacier has lately declared himself of the same opinion (*d*). But it is certain that this cannot always have held good; for Suetonius mentions the *Tibiæ* in the funeral of Julius Cæsar (*e*), and Seneca in that of Claudius, in his Apocolocynthosis. And Ovid says of himself in plain words,

Interea nostri quid agant nisi triste libelli?
Tibia funeribus convenit ista meis. Trist. v. Eleg. 1.

3 D   Therefore

(*a*) Lib. 20. cap. 2.   (*b*) *Plut. de Animal. Solert.*   (*b*) *De Militia*, lib. 4. cap. 10.   (*d*) *Horace*, Book 1. Sat. 6. v. 44.   (*e*) Cap. 83.

Therefore it seems more probable, that the flutes or pipes were used in all sorts of funerals, as the most accurate Kirchman has given his judgment.

It appears from the figures of trumpets and flutes on the old monuments, that instruments of those kinds, used at funeral solemnities, were longer than the ordinary ones; and so fitted to give a sharper and more mournful sound. Hence Ovid calls the funeral trumpet *longa tuba*.

Pro longa resonent carmina vestra tuba ; Amor. 2. El. 6. 6.

After the musicians went the *præficæ*, or the mourning-women, hired on purpose to sing the *nænia* or *lessus*, the funeral song, filled with the praises of the deceased, but for the most part trifling and mean. Hence the grammarian in Gellius took his flout against the philosophers, *Vos philosophi mera estis (ut M. Cato ait) mortuaria Glossaria. Namque collegistis & lectitastis res tetras & inanes & frivolas, tanquam mulierum vocas præficarum (a) :* " You philosophers (as Cato says) are " mere dealers in trash; for you go and collect a parcel of dry " worthless stuff, just such for the world as old women whine " out, who are hired to sing the mourning-song at a funeral."

That the *ludii* and *histriones*, the mimics and players, went before the funeral bed, and danced after the satyric manner, we have the authority of Dionysius in his ninth book. Suetonius tells a story of the arch-mimic who acted at the funeral of Vespasian (*b*).

The custom for the slaves to go with their caps on before the corpse, and to be thereupon made free, is confirmed by a law of Justinian, and we meet with many examples of it in history.

As to the beds or couches borne before in the funeral solemnity, the design of these was to carry the waxen images of the deceased person's ancestors; which were therefore used only in the funerals of those who had the *jus imaginam*, the right of keeping the effigies of the men of their family, which at home were set up in wooden presses, and taken thence to be publicly shown after this manner, on the death of any of their near relations (*c*). Before the corpse of princes, or some extraordinary persons, not only the effigies of their

---

(*a*) *A. Gell.* lib. 18. cap. 7. (*b*) Cap. 19. (*c*) *Plin. N. H.* lib. 45. cap. 2.

their ancestors, but the statues too of other great men were borne in state. Thus Augustus ordered six hundred beds of images to be carried before, at the funeral of Marcellus; and Sylla the Dictator had no less than six thousand (a).

Besides all this, such as had been eminent for their atchievements in war, and gained any considerable conquest, had the images and representations of the enemies they had subdued, or the cities they had taken, or the spoils won in battle; as Dionysius (b) reports in the funeral of Coriolanus, and Dio (c) in that of Augustus. This custom Virgil alludes to in the funeral of Pallas, xi. 78:

> *Multaque præterea Laurentis præmia pugnæ*
> *Aggerat, & longo prædam jubet ordine duci.*

And a little after,

> *Indutosque jubet truncos hostilibus armis*
> *Ipsos ferre duces, inimicaque nomina figi.*

The Lictors too made a part of the procession, going before the corpse to carry the *fasces*, and other ensigns of honour, which the deceased had a right to in his life-time. It is very remarkable, that the rods were not now carried in the ordinary posture, but turned quite the contrary way, as Tacitus reports in the funeral of Germanicus (d). Hence Albinovanus in the funeral of Drusus:

> *Quos primum vidi fasces, in funere vidi,*
> *Et vidi versos, indiciumque mali.*

We may now go on to the persons who bore the bier, or the funeral-bed; and these were, for the most part, the nearest relations, or the heirs of the deceased. Hence Horace, Book 2. Sat. 5.

> ——————*Cadaver*
> *Unctum oleo largo nudis humeris tulit hæres.*

3 D 2 And

(a) Serv. in Æn. 11.   (b) Lib. 8.   (c) Lib. 56.   (d) Annal. 3.

And Juvenal, Sat. 10. 158:

> *Incolumi Troja, Priamus venisset ad umbras*
> *Assaraci magnis solemnibus, Hectore funus*
> *Portante, & reliquis fratrum cervicibus*——

Thus they report of Metellus, who conquered Macedon, that he was carried to the funeral pile by his four sons; one of which was the Prætor, the other three had been all Consuls, who had triumphed, and one performed the office of Censor (*a*).

Sometimes persons, who had deserved highly of the commonwealth, were borne at their funerals by the magistrates, or the Senators, or the chief of the nobility. This Plutarch relates of Numa, Suetonius of Julius Cæsar (*b*), and Tacitus of Augustus (*c*). And the very strangers and foreigners, that happened to be at Rome at the death of any worthy person, were very desirous of signifying their respects to his memory, by the service of carrying the funeral-bed when he was to be buried; as Plutarch tells us in the funeral of Paulus Æmilius, that as many Spaniards, Ligurians, and Macedonians, as happened to be present at the solemnity, that were young and of vigorous bodies, took up the bed, and bore it to the pile.

Persons of meaner fortunes, and sometimes great men too, if they were hated by the people, were carried to their burial by the Vespillones or by Sandapilones, who lived by this employment. Thus Suetonius (*d*) and Eutropius (*e*) relate of the Emperor Domitian. Therefore, in this last way of bearing out, we may suppose them to have used the *sandapila*, or common *bier*, as in the former the *lecticæ*, or *lecti*, the litters or beds. This bier is what Horace and Lucan call *vilis arca:*

> ——*Angustis ejecta cadavera cellis*
> *Conservus vili portando locabat in arca.* Hor. L. 1. S. 8.

> *Da vilem Magno plebeii funeris arcam,*
> *Qua lacerum corpus siccos effundat in ignes.* Luc. L. 8.

It is worth observing, that sometimes the bier, or bed, was covered, and sometimes not. It was exposed often, if the party

---

(*a*) Plin. lib. 7. cap. 44. Val. Max. lib. 7.   (*b*) Cap. 84.
(*c*) Annal. 1.   (*d*) Cap. 17.   (*e*) Lib. 7.

party had died a natural death, and was not very much deformed by the change; and therefore now and then they used to paint the face, especially of women, to make them appear with more advantage to the sight. Dio tells us in the life of Nero, that he daubed the body of Britannicus over with a sort of white-wash, to hinder the blueness of the flesh, and such other marks of the poison, from being discovered: but a great rain, falling at the time of the procession, washed off the paint, and exposed the fatal tokens to the view of the whole people.

But in case the visage was very much distorted, or upon some other account not fit to be shown, they threw a covering over the bed. Thus Paterculus reports that Scipio Africanus was carried forth to the burial *velato capite* (a). Sometimes too, when the face or the head had been miserably bruised; as if the fall of a house, or some such accident, had occasioned the party's death, they used to enclose the head and face in a masque, to hinder them from appearing; and the funerals in which this was practised they termed *larvata funera*.

But the greatest part of the persons were those that followed the corpse. These in private funerals were seldom many besides the friends and relations of the deceased; and it was very usual in a will, to bestow legacies upon such and such persons, upon condition they should appear at the funeral, and accompany the corpse. But at the *indictive*, or public funerals, the whole city flocked together upon the general invitation and summons. The magistrates and senators were not wanting at the procession, nor even the priests themselves, as we find in the funeral of Numa described by Plutarch.

To give an account of the habit and gesture of the mourners, or of the relations and others that followed the corpse, is in a great measure unnecessary: for the weeping, the bitter complaints against the gods, the letting loose the hair, or sometimes cutting it off, the changing the habit, and the laying aside the usual ornaments, are all too well known to need any explication. Yet there are many things singular in these subjects, which deserve our farther notice. Thus they did not only tear or cut off their hair, but had a custom to lay it on the breast, or sometimes on the tomb of the deceased friend. Hence Ovid of the sisters of Narcissus:

———*Planxere*

(a) Lib. 2.

──────*Planxere sorores*
Naiades, & sectos fratri imposuere capillos.
And Statius, Theb. 7,
──────*Tergoque & pectore fusam*
Cæsariem ferro minuit, sectisque jacentis
Obnubit tenuia ora comis.──────

It is no less observable, that, at the funerals of their parents, the sons were covered on their heads, and the daughters uncovered: Perhaps only to recede as far as possible from their ordinary habit. Yet it is likely that, in ordering the sons to cover their heads at such solemnities, they had regard to the common practice of always wearing something on their heads when they worshipped the gods, and especially when they were present at a sacrifice. The original and grounds of this superstition are most admirably given by Virgil, in the prophet Helenus's instructions to Æneas:

Quin ubi transmissa steterint trans æquora classes,
Et positis aris, jam vota in littore solves,
Purpureo velare comas adopertus amictu:
Nequa inter sanctos ignes in honore deorum
Hostilis facies occurrat, & omina turbet.
Hunc socii morem sacrorum, hunc ipse teneto,
Hac casti maneant in religione nepotes. Æn. 3. 403.

As to the mourning habits, it has been already observed (*a*) that the Senators sometimes on these occasions went attired like Knights, the Magistrates like Senators, &c. and that the common wear for mourning was black. But we may further remark, that though this was the ordinary colour to express their grief, used alike by both sexes, yet after the establishment of the empire, when abundance of party-colours came in fashion, the old primitive white grew so much into contempt, that at last it became proper to the women for their mourning cloathes. Thus Statius in the tears of Hetruscus:

Huc vittata comam niveoque insignis amictu
Mitibus exequiis ades.

And though it may with some reason be thought that the Poet here, directing his speech to the Goddess Piety, gives
her

(*a*) Book. 5. Cap. 7.

her that habit, rather as a mark of purity and innocence than as the proper badge of grief in her fex, yet the matter of fact is ftill evident from the authority of Plutarch, who ftates this as the fubject of one of his problems, and gives feveral reafons for the practice.

After the *PERSONS* follows the *PLACE* whither the proceffion was directed, by which we muft be guided in our next inquiry. In all the funerals of note, efpecially in the public, or *indictive*, the corpfe was brought with a vaft train of followers into the forum. Thus Horace, Book i. Sat. 6.

———*At hic fi plauftra ducenta,*
Concurrantque foro tria funera, magna fonabit
Cornua quod vincatque tubas.

Here one of the neareft relations afcended the roftra, and obliged the audience with an oration in praife of the deceafed. If none of the kindred undertook the office, it was difcharged by fome of the moft eminent perfons in the city for learning and eloquence, as Appian reports of the funeral of Sylla (*a*). And Pliny the Younger reckons it as the laft addition to the happinefs of a very great man, that he had the honour to be praifed at his funeral by the moft eloquent Tacitus, then Conful (*b*); which is agreeable to Quintilian's account of this matter, *Nam & funebres,* &c. " For the funeral orations." fays he, " depend very often on fome public office, and by order of the " Senate are many times given in charge to the magiftrates to " be performed by themfelves in perfon (*c*)."

The invention of this cuftom is generally attributed to Valerius Poplicola, foon after the expulfion of the regal family. Plutarch tells us, that " honouring his colleague's obfequies " with a funeral oration, it fo pleafed the Romans, that it be- " came cuftomary for the beft men to celebrate the funerals of " great perfons with fpeeches in their commendation."

Nor was this honour proper to one fex alone, for Livy reports, that " the matrons, upon account of making a collection " of gold for the deliverance of Rome from the Gauls, were " allowed as a fignal favour to have funeral panegyrics in the " fame manner as the men." Plutarch's relation of this matter differs from Livy only in the reafons of the cuftom: " He " acquaints us, that when it was agreed, after the taking of " Veii, that a bowl of maffy gold fhould be made, and fent to

(*a*) 'Εμφυλ. lib. 1.   (*b*) Lib. 2. Ep. 1.   (*c*) *Inftitut.* l. 3. c. 9.

"to Delphi, there was so great a scarcity of gold, and the
"magistrates so puzzled in considering how to get it, that the
"Roman ladies meeting together, and consulting among them-
"selves, out of the golden ornaments that they wore, contri-
"buted as much as went to the making the offering, which in
"weight came to eight talents of gold. The Senate, to give
"them the honour they had deserved, ordained, that funeral
"orations should be used at the obsequies of women as well
"as of men, which had never been a custom before." But it
seems probable, that this honour was at first only paid to aged
matrons; since we learn, from the same excellent author, that
there was no precedent of any funeral oration on a younger
woman, till Julius Cæsar first made one upon the death of his
own wife.

Cicero (a) and Livy (b) complain very much of this custom
of funeral speeches, as if they had conduced in a great measure to the corruption and falsifying of history. For it being
ordinary on those occasions to be directed more by the precepts of oratory, than by the true matter of fact, it usually
happened, that the deceased party was extolled on the account
of several noble atchievements, to which he had no just pretensions: And especially when they came to inquire into their
stock and original, as was customary at these solemnities, they
seldom failed to clap in three or four of the most renowned
persons of the commonwealth, to illustrate the family of the
deceased; and so by degrees well nigh ruined all proper di-
stinctions of houses and blood.

The next place, to which the corpse was carried, was the
place of burning and burial. It has been a custom amongst
most nations to appoint this without the city, particularly a-
mong the Jews and Greeks; from whom it may be supposed
to have been derived down to the Romans. That the Jews
buried without the city, is evident from several places of the
New Testament. Thus the sepulchre, in which Joseph laid
our Saviour's body, was *in the same place in which he was cru-
cified* (c), which was *near to the city* (d). And we read in St
Matthew, that at our Lord's passion " the graves were open-
" ed, and many bodies of the saints which slept arose, and
" came out of their graves after his resurrection, and went
" into the holy city, and appeared unto many (e)."

As to the Græcians, Servius, in an epistle to Tully (f),
giving an account of the unhappy death of his colleague
Marcellus,

(a) *In Bruto.*   (b) Lib. 8.   (c) John xix. 41.   (d) John xix. 20.   (e) Matth. xxvii. 52, 53.   (f) *Famil.* lib. 4. epist. 12.

Marcellus, which fell out in Greece, tells him, that he could not by any means obtain leave of the Athenians to allow him a burying-place within the city, they urging a religious restraint in that point, and the want of precedents for such a practice.

The Romans followed the same custom from the very first building of the city, which was afterwards settled in a law by the *decemviri*, and often revived and confirmed by several later constitutions. The reason of this ancient practice may be resolved into a sacred and a civil consideration. As to the former, the Romans, and most other people, had a notion, that whatever had been consecrated to the supernal gods was presently defiled upon the touch of a corpse, or even by bringing such a spectacle near it. Thus A. Gellius tells us, that the *Flamen Dialis* might not on any account enter into a place where there was a grave, or so much as touch a dead body (*a*). And if the *Pontifex Maximus* happened to praise any one publicly at a funeral, he had a veil always laid over the corpse to keep it from his sight; as Dio reports of Augustus (*b*), and Seneca of Tiberius (*c*). It is likely that this might be borrowed from the Jewish law, by which the high-priest was forbid to use the ordinary signs of mourning, or to *go in to any dead body* (*d*).

The civil consideration seems to have been, that neither the air might be corrupted by the stench of putrified bodies, nor the buildings endangered by the frequency of funeral fires.

The places then appointed for burial without the city were either private or public; the private places were the fields or gardens belonging to particular families. Hence Martial took the jest in one of his epigrams, on a gentleman that had buried several wives:

Septima jam, Phileros, tibi conditur uxor in agro.
Plus nulli, Phileros, quam tibi reddit ager.

If it were possible, they always buried in that part of the field or garden which lay nearest to the common road, both to put passengers in mind of mortality, and to save the best part of their land. Thus Juvenal, Sat. 1.

—— *Experiar quid concedatur in illos,*
Quorum Flaminia tegitur cinis atque Latina.

(*a*) Lib. 10. cap. 15.   (*b*) Lib. 54.   (*c*) *Consolat. ad Mar.* cap. 51.
(*d*) *Levit.* xxii. 10, 11.

And we have scarce any relation of a burying in authors, but they tell us the urn was laid near such a *way*. Propertius is very earnest in desiring that he may not be buried after this ordinary custom, near a celebrated road, for fear it should disturb his shade:

Di faciant, mea ne terra locet ossa frequenti,
  Qua facit assiduo tramite vulgus iter.
Post mortem tumuli sic infamantur amantum:
  Me tegat arborea devia terra coma.
Aut humer ignotæ cumulis vallatus arenæ;
  Non juvat in media nomen habere via. Lib. 3. El. 16.

The public burying-places were of two sorts; those which were allotted to the poor, and those which were put to this use only at the funerals of great persons. The former were the *puticulæ*, or *puticuli*, without the Esquilian gate; they contained a great quantity of ground, and were put to no other use, than the burying of the bones and ashes of persons of the lowest rank, who had no private place of their own to lay the corpse in. But because the vast number of bones deposited here, infecting the air, rendered the neighbouring parts of the city unhealthy, Augustus gave away a great many acres of this common field to his favourite Mæcenas, who turned it into fine gardens. This Horace tells us at large, Book 1. Sat. 8.

Huc prius angustis ejecta cadavera cellis
Conservus vili portanda locabat in arca:
Hoc miseræ plebi stabat commune sepulchrum, &c.

The public place assigned for the burial of great persons was commonly the *Campus Martius*. This honour could not be procured but by a public decree of Senate, and was never conferred but on men of the highest stations and merits. Thus Plutarch relates of Lucullus and Pompey; Appian of Sylla (*a*) Suetonius of Drusus (*b*), and Virgil of Marcellus:

Quantos ille virum magnam Mavortis ad urbem
Campus aget gemitus? vel quæ, Tiberine, videbis
Funera, cum tumulum præterlabere recentem! Æn. 6.

It

(*a*) Ἐμφυλ. lib. 1.   (*b*) Claud. cap. 1.

It has been said, that the ordinary custom was to bury without the city, but we must except some sepulchres, as those of the *vestal* virgins, whom, Servius tells us, the laws allowed a burying-place within the city (*a*). The same honour was allowed to some extraordinary persons, as to Valerius Poplicola (*b*), and to Fabricius (*c*), being to continue to their heirs. Yet none of the family were afterwards there interred, but the body being carried thither, one placed a burning torch under it, and then immediately took it away, as an attestation of the deceased's privilege, and his receding from his honour; and then the body was removed to another place.

Cicero in his ninth Philippick moves, that Servius Sulpicius, upon account of his many signal services to the commonwealth, may be honoured with a public sepulchre in the *Campus Esquilinus*, or in any other place where the Consul should please, thirty feet in dimension every way, and to remain to his heirs and posterity. But there are not many instances of the like practice.

Having done with the *carrying forth*, we come to the *act of burying*. The corpse being brought in the manner already described without the city, if they designed to burn it, was carried directly to the place appointed for that purpose, (which, if it was joined with the sepulchre, was called *Bustum*, if separate from it, *Ustrina*) and there laid on the *Rogus*, or *Pyra*, a pile of wood prepared to burn it on. This pile was built in the shape of an altar, differing in height according to the quality of the deceased. Thus Virgil, in the funeral of Misenus, Æn. 6.

———*Aramque sepulchri*
Congerere arboribus, cœloque educere certant.

And Ovid against Ibis:

Et dare plebeio corpus inane rogo.

The trees which they made use of were commonly such as had most pitch or rosin in them; and, if they took any other wood, they split it, for the more easy catching fire:

Procumbunt piceæ, sonat icta securibus ilex,   *Fraxineæque*

(*a*) *Ad Æn.* 9.   (*b*) *Plutarch in his life*   (*c*) *Cicero.*

Fraxineaque trabes; cuneis & fiſſile robur
Scinditur.——Virg. Æn. 6.

Round about the pile they uſed to ſet a parcel of cypreſs trees, perhaps to hinder the noiſome ſmell of the corpſe. This obſervation is owing to Virgil in the ſame place:

Ingentem ſtruxere pyram; cui frondibus atris
Intexunt latera, & ferales ante cupreſſos
Conſtituunt.

That the body was placed on the pile, not by itſelf, but together with the couch, or bed, on which it lay, we have the authority of Tibullus, Book 1. El. 1:

Flebis & arſuro poſitum me, Delia, lecto.

This being done, the next of blood performed the ceremony of lighting the pile; which they did with a torch, turning their face all the while the other way, as if it was done out of neceſſity, and not willingly. Thus Virgil, Æn. 6.

———*Subjectam, more parentum,*
Averſi tenuere facem.

As ſoon as the wood took fire, they wiſhed and prayed for a wind to aſſiſt the flames, and haſten the conſuming of the body, which they looked on as a fortunate accident. Thus Cynthia in Propertius:

Cur ventos non ipſe rogis, ingrate, petiſti?

And Plutarch, in the life of Sylla, reports, "That, the day "being cloudy over head, they deferred carrying forth the "corpſe till about three in the afternoon, expecting it would "rain; but a ſtrong wind blowing full againſt the funeral "pile, and ſetting it all on a flame, his body was conſumed "in a moment. As the pile ſhrunk down, and the fire was "upon going out, the clouds ſhowered down, and continued "raining till night. So that his good fortune was firm even "to the laſt, and did, as it were, officiate at his funeral."

At the funerals of the Emperors or renowned Generals, as ſoon as the wood was lighted, the ſoldiers and all the company

company made a solemn course (*decursio*) three times round the pile, to show their affection to the deceased; of which we have numerous examples in history. Virgil has not forgot to express this custom:

> *Ter circum accensos cincti fulgentibus armis*
> *Decurrere rogos; ter mæstum funeris ignem*
> *Lustravere in equis, ululatusque ore dedere.* Æn. 11.

The body never burnt without company; for, because they fancied that the ghosts delighted in blood, it was customary to kill a great number of beasts, and throw them on the pile:

> *Multa boum circa mactantur corpora morti;*
> *Setigerasque sues, raptasque ex omnibus agris*
> *In flammam jugulant pecudes*——Virg. Æn. 11.

In the more ignorant and barbarous ages, they used to murder men, and cast them into the funeral flames of princes and commanders. The poets never burn a hero without this inhuman ceremony. Homer gives Patroclus

Δώδεκα μὲν Τρώων μεγαθύμων υἵας ἐσθλύς.

And Virgil, lib. 10.

> *Quatuor hic juvenes, totidem, quos educat Ufens,*
> *Viventes rapit; inferias quos immolet umbris,*
> *Captivoque rogi perfundat sanguine flammas.*

But, besides those, there were abundance of presents thrown into the fatal flames, of several sorts; these consisted for the most part of costly garments and perfumes thrown on the body as it burned. Thus Virgil, Æn. 6.

> *Purpureasque super vestes, velamina nota,*
> *Conjiciunt.*

And Plutarch makes the extravagant expences of Cato *junior*, at the funeral of his brother Cœpio, to have been taken up in "a vast quantity of costly garments and perfumes."

All the precious gums, essences, and balsams, that the ancients were acquainted with, we find employed in their funerals: Hence

Hence Juvenal describes a fop that used abundance of essence:

> *Et matutino sudans Crispinus amomo,*
> *Quantum vix redolent duo funera*——Sat. 4.

The soldiers and Generals had usually their arms burnt with them on the pile. Thus Virgil in the funeral of Misenus:

> ——*Decorantque super fulgentibus armis.* Æn. 6.

And in another place he adds the spoils taken from the enemy:

> *Hinc alii spolia occisis direpta Latinis*
> *Conjiciunt igni, galeas ensesque decoros,*
> *Frænaque ferventesque rotas: pars, munera nota,*
> *Ipsorum clypeos, & non felicia tela.* Æn. 11.

When the pile was burnt down, they put out the remains of the fire, by sprinkling wine, that they might the more easily gather up the bones and ashes:

> *Postquam collapsi cineres, ac flamma quievit,*
> *Relliquias vino & bibulam lavere favillam.* Virg. Æn. 6.

This gathering up the bones and ashes, and putting them into the urn, was the next office paid to the deceased, which they termed *ossilegium*. The whole custom is most fully and elegantly described by Tibullus in his third Book, Eleg. 2.

> *Ergo ubi cum tenuem,* &c.

How the ashes and bones of the men came to be distinguished from those of the beasts, and wood, and other materials, is not easy to be conceived, unless we suppose the difference to have arose from the artificial placing of the corpse on the pile, so that every thing else should fall away on each side, and leave the human relics in a heap by themselves.

Nothing now remained but to put the urn into the sepulchre, and so sprinkle the company with holy water, and dismiss them, Virg. Æn. 6.

> *Ossaque lecta cado texit Chorinæus aheno:*
> *Idem ter socios pura circumtulit unda,*

Spargens

> *Spargens rore levi, & ramo felicis olivæ,*
> *Lustravitque viros, dixitque novissima verba.*

These *novissima verba* were either directed to the deceased, or to the company. The form of speech, with which they took leave of the deceased was, *Vale, vale, vale, nos te ordine quo natura permiserit, cuncti sequemur*. The form, with which the *Præfica* dismissed the people, was *ILICET*, i. e. *ire licet*. As they went away, they had a custom of wishing for *light earth*, to lie on the relics, which they reckoned a great happiness. Hence it is an usual inscription on ancient funeral monuments *S. T. T. L.* or *Sit tibi terra levis*.

To inquire into the original of sepulchres, their several kinds and forms, the variety of ornaments, the difference of inscriptions, and the many ways of violating the tombs of the dead, would be too nice a disquisition for the present design. Yet we must not pass by the *cœnotaphia* or monuments erected on a very singular account, either to persons buried in another place, or to those who had received no burial, and whose relicks could not be found.

Thus Suetonius tells us, that the soldiers in Germany raised an *honorary tomb* to the memory of Drusus, though his body had been carried to Rome, and deposited in the *campus martius* (a): And we often find the Generals raising tombs to the honour of those soldiers whose bodies could not be found after a fight. These *tumuli inanes* or *honorarii*, when erected to the memory of particular persons, were usually kept as sacred as the true monuments, and had the same ceremonies performed at them. Thus Virgil describes Andromache keeping the anniversary of Hector's death. Æn. 3.

> *Solennes tum forte dapes & tristia dona*
> *Libabat cineri Andromache, manesque vocabat*
> *Hectoreum ad tumulum, viridi quem cespite inanem,*
> *Et geminas, causam lacrymis, sacraverat aras.*

And Æneas tells Deiphobus, that he has paid him such an honour :

> *Tunc egomet tumulum Rhæteo in litore inanem*
> *Constitui, & magna manes ter voce vocavi :*
> *Nomen & arma locum servant.*   Æncid. 6.

AFTER

(a) *Sueton. Claud.* cap. 1.

AFTER the FUNERAL, we are to take notice of the several rites performed in honour of the dead, at the festivals instituted with that design. The chief time of paying these offices was the *Feralia*, or the feast of the ghosts in the month of February; but it was ordinary for particular families to have proper seasons of discharging this duty, as the *Novennalia*, the *Decennalia*, and the like. The ceremonies themselves may be reduced to these three heads, sacrifices, feasts, and games, to which if we subjoin the customs of mourning, and of the consecration, we shall take in all that remains on this subject:

The sacrifices (which they called *Inferiæ*) consisted of liquors, victims, and garlands. The liquors were water, wine, milk, blood, and liquid balsam.

> *Hic duo rite mero libans carchesia Baccho*
> *Fundit humi, duo lacte novo, duo sanguine sacro.* Vir. Æn. 5.

The blood was taken from the victims offered to the *Manes*, which were usually of the smaller cattle, though in ancient times it was customary to use captives or slaves in this inhuman manner.

The balsams and garlands occur every where in the poets. Propert. Lib. 3. Eleg. 16:

> *Afferet huc unguenta mihi, sertisque sepulchrum*
> *Ornabit, custos ad mea busta sedens.*

Tibull. Lib. 2. Eleg. 4.

> *Atque aliquis senior, veteres veneratus amores,*
> *Annua constructo serta dabit tumulo.*

Besides these chaplets, they strowed loose flowers about the monument:

> *Purpureosque jacit flores, actaliafatur.* Æn. 5.

And again, Æn. 6.

> *Tu Marcellus eris. Manibus date lilia plenis:*
> *Purpureos spargam flores; animamque nepotis*
> *His saltem accumulem donis, & fungar inani*
> *Munere.*

The feasts, celebrated to the honour of the deceased, were either private or public. The private feasts were termed *Silicernia*, from *Silex* and *Cœna*, as if we should say Suppers made on a stone. These were prepared both for the dead and the living. The repast designed for the dead, consisting commonly of beans, lettuces, bread and eggs, or the like, was laid on the tomb for the ghosts to come out and eat, as they fancied they would; and what was left they burnt on the stone. Travellers tell us that the Indians at present have a superstitious custom much of this nature, putting a piece of meat always in the grave with the dead body, when they bury in the plantations.

It was from this custom, that, to express the most miserable poverty of creatures almost starved, they used to say, "Such " an one got his victuals from the tombs." Thus Catull. 57.

Uxor Meneni: sæpe quam in sepulchretis
Vidistis ipso rapere rogo cœnam,
Quam devolutum ex igne prosequens panem
A semiraso tunderetur ustore.

And Tibullus's curse is much to the same purpose: i. 5.

Ipsa fame stimulante furens, herbasque sepulchris
Quærat, & a sævis ossa relicta lupis.

The private feasts *for the living* were kept at the tomb of the deceased, by the nearest friends and relations only.

The public feasts were when the heirs or friends of some rich or great person obliged the people with a general treat to his honour and memory; as Cicero reports of the funeral of Scipio Africanus (*a*) and Dio of that of Sylla (*b*). And Suetonius (*c*) relates that Julius Cæsar gave the people a feast in memory of his daughter. There was a custom on these occasions to distribute a parcel of raw meat among the poor people, which they termed *visceratio*; though this was sometimes given without the public feasts.

The funeral games have already been dispatched among the other shows.

As to the custom of mourning, besides what has been before observed by the bye, we may further take notice of the time appointed for that ceremony, and some of the most remarkable ways

(*a*) *In Orat. pro* Murænā.   (*b*) Lib. 37.   (*c*) Cap. 22.

ways of expressing it. "Numa (as Plutarch tells us in his life) prescribed rules for regulating the days of mourning, according to certain times and ages. As for example, a child of three years, and so upwards to ten, was to be mourned for so many months as he was years old. And the longest time of mourning, for any person whatsoever, was not to exceed the term of ten months; which also was the time appointed unto widows to lament the loss of their deceased husbands, before which they could not, without great indecency, pass unto second marriage: But, in case their incontinence was such as could not admit so long an abstinence from the nuptial bed, they were to sacrifice a cow with a calf, for expiation of their fault."

Now Romulus's year consisting but of ten months, when Numa afterwards added two months more, he did not alter the time he had before settled for mourning; and therefore tho' after that time we meet with *luctus annuus*, or a year's mourning, used often upon the death of some eminent person, we must take it only for the old year of Romulus, or the space of ten months.

There were several accidents which often occasioned the concluding of a public or private mourning before the fixed time; such as the dedication of a temple, the solemnity of public games or festivals, the solemn *lustration* performed by the Censor, and the discharging any vow made by a Magistrate or General; which, being times of public rejoicing, would have otherwise implied a contradiction.

As to the tokens of private grief, they had none but what are common to both nations, as the keeping their house for such a time, the avoiding all manner of recreations and entertainments, and the like. But, in public mourning, it was a singular custom to express their concern by making the term and all business immediately to end, and settling a vacation till such a period, of which we have frequent instances.

The last ceremony, designed to be spoken of, was consecration. This belonged properly to the Emperors; yet we meet too with a private consecration, which we may observe in our way. This was, when the friends and relations of the deceased canonized him, and paid him worship in private; a piece of respect commonly paid to parents by their children, as Plutarch observes in his Roman questions; yet the parents too sometimes conferred the same honour on their deceased children, as Cicero promiseth to do for his daughter Tullia, in the

end

end of his Confolation; and though that piece be fufpected, as we now have it, yet the prefent authority lofes nothing of its force, being cited heretofore by Lactantius, according to the copies extant in his time.

The public confecration had its original from the deification of Romulus, but was afterwards difcontinued till the time of the Emperors, on moſt of whom this honour was conferred. The whole ceremony is moſt accurately defcribed by Herodian in his fourth book, the tranflation of which place may conclude this fubject.

"The Romans," fays he, "have a cuſtom to confecrate
" thofe Emperors who leave either fons or defigned fuccef-
" ors at their death; and thofe who received this honour are
" faid to be enrolled among the gods. On this occafion the
" whole city maintains a public grief, mixed as it were with
" the folemnity of a feftival. The true body is buried in a
" very fumptuous funeral, according to the ordinary method.
" But they contrive to have an image of the Emperor in wax
" done to the life; and this they expofe to public view, juſt
" at the entrance of the palace-gate, on a ſtately bed of ivory
" covered with rich garments of embroidered work and cloth
" of gold. So the image lies there all pale, as if under a dan-
" gerous indifpofition. Round the bed there fit, the greateſt
" part of the day, on the left fide, the whole Senate in black;
" on the right the aged matrons, who, either upon account of
" their parents or hufbands, are reputed noble: They wear
" no jewels or gold, or other ufual ornaments, but are attired
" in clofe white veſts, to exprefs their forrow and concern.
" This ceremony continues feven days together; the phyfi-
" cians being admitted every day to the bed, and declaring
" the patient to grow all along worfe and worfe. At laſt,
" when they fuppofe him to be dead, a felect company of
" young gentlemen of the fenatorian order take up the bed
" on their fhoulders, and carry it through the *holy way* into
" the old forum, the place where the Roman magiſtrates u-
" fed to lay down their offices. On both fides there are rai-
" fed galleries with feats one above another, one fide being
" filled with a choir of boys all nobly defcended, and of the
" moſt eminent Patrician families; the other with a like fet
" of ladies of quality, who both together fing hymns and pæ-
" ans, compofed in very mournful and paffionate airs, to the
" praife of the deceafed. When thefe are over, they take up
" the bed again, and carry it into the Campus Martius, where,

" in the widest part of the field, is erected a four-square pile,
" entirely composed of large planks, in shape of a pavilion,
" and exactly regular and equal in the dimensions. This in
" the inside is filled up with dry chips, but without is adorn-
" ed with coverlids of cloth of gold, and beautified with pic-
" tures and curious figures in ivory. Above this is placed
" another frame of wood, much less indeed, but set off with
" ornaments of the same nature, and having little doors or
" gates standing about it. Over this are set a third and fourth
" pile, every one being considerably less than that on which
" it stands; and so others perhaps, till they come to the last
" of all, which forms the top. The figure of this structure,
" altogether, may be compared to those watch-towers which
" are to be seen in harbours of note, and by the fire on their
" top direct the course of the ships into the haven. After
" this, hoisting up the body into the second frame of building,
" they get together a vast quantity of all manner of sweet o-
" dours and perfumes, whether of fruits, herbs, or gums, and
" pour them in heaps all about it; there being no nation or
" city, or indeed any eminent men, who do not rival one a-
" nother in paying these last presents to their prince. When
" the place is quite filled with a huge pile of spices and drugs,
" the whole order of Knights ride in a solemn procession
" round the structure, and imitate the motions of the Pyrr-
" hic dance. Chariots too, in a very regular and decent man-
" ner, are drove round the pile, having the coachmen cloath-
" ed in purple, and bearing the images of all the illustrious
" Romans, renowned either for their counsels and admini-
" stration at home, or their memorable atchievements in war.
" This pomp being finished, the successor to the empire, ta-
" king a torch in his hand, puts it to the frame, and at the
" same time the whole company assist in lighting it in several
" places; when, on a sudden, the chips and drugs catching
" fire, the whole pile is quickly consumed. At last, from the
" highest and smallest frame of wood, an eagle is let loose,
" which, ascending with the flames towards the sky, is suppo-
" sed to carry the Prince's soul to heaven."

CHAP.

CHAP. XI.

Of the ROMAN Entertainments.

THE peculiar customs of the Romans, in reference to eating and drinking, will easily fall under the three heads, of the time, the place, and the manner of their entertainments. As to the first, the Romans had no proper repast besides supper, for which the ordinary time was about the ninth hour, or our three o'clock. Thus Martial, reckoning up the business of every hour, iv. 8:

> *Imperat extructos frangere nona toros.*

But the more frugal made this meal a little before sunset, in the declension of the day; to which Virgil might possibly allude, though speaking of the customs of Carthage, and of its queen, when he says,

> *Nunc eadem labente die convivia quærit.* Æn. iv.

On the other side, the voluptuous and extravagant commonly began their feasts before the ordinary hour. Thus Horace, Book 1. Od. 1.

> *Nec partem solido demere de die*
> *Spernit.*

And Juvenal, Sat. 10.

> *Exul ab octava Marius bibit.*

Those, that could not hold out till supper, used to break their fast in some other part of the day, some at the second hour, some at the fourth, answering to our eight and ten; some at the sixth, or about noon; others at the eighth, or our two, as their stomachs required, or their employments gave them leave. At this time they seldom eat any thing but a bit of dry bread, or perhaps a few raisins or nuts, or a little honey. From the different hours of taking this breakfast, it is likely that the *jentaculum, prandium, merenda*, &c. had their original, being really the same repast made by several persons at several times (*a*).

The

(*a*) *Dacier on Horace,* Book 1. Od. 1.

The PLACE in which the Romans eat was anciently called *cœnaculum*. Seneca, Suetonius, and others, style it *cœnatio*. But the most common appellation, which they borrowed from the Græcians, was *triclinium*. Servius on the first of the Æneids, at that verse,

Aurea composuit sponda mediumque locavit.

takes an occasion to reprehend those grammarians who will have *triclinium* to signify a room to sup in, and not barely a table. Yet (to omit a tedious number of citations from other authors) Tully himself useth the word in that sense: For in one of his epistles he tells Atticus (a), that, when Cæsar came to Philippi, the town was so full of soldiers as to leave Cæsar scarce a *triclinium* to sup in.

Anciently the Romans used to sup sitting, as the Europeans at present, making use of a long table.

Perpetuis soliti patres consistere mensis. Virg. Æn. 8.

Afterwards the men took up a custom of lying down, but the women for some time after still kept sitting, as the most decent posture (b). The children too of princes and noblemen, for the same reason, used to sit at the backs of couches (c), whence, after a dish or two, they withdrew, without causing any disturbance. Yet, as to the women, it is evident that, in after times they used the same posture at the table as men. Thus Cicero, in an epistle to Pætus, telling him of one Clyteris, a gentlewoman that was lately at a treat with him, makes use of the word *accubuit*. And Ovid, in his fourth love-elegy of the first book, adviseth his mistress about her carriage at the table before her husband,

Cum premet ille torum, vultu comes ipsa modesto
Ibis, ut accumbas———

And Suetonius relates, that, at an entertainment of the Emperor Caligula, he placed all his sisters one by one below himself, *uxore supra cubante*, "his wife lying above him."

When they began thus to lye down, instead of sitting at meat, they contrived a sort of beds or couches of the same nature with those on which they slept, but distinguished from them by the

---

(a) Lib. 15. Epist. 50.   (b) Val. Max. lib. 2. cap. 1.   (c) Tacit. Ann. 13. Suetonius Claud. cap. 32.

the name of *lecti tricliniorum*, or *tricliniares*, the other being called *lecti cubicularii*.

They were made in several forms, but commonly four-square, sometimes to hold three or four, sometimes two persons, or only one. Yet, in the same entertaining-room, it was observed to have all the couches of the same shape and make. After the round citron tables grew in fashion, they changed the three beds (which denominated the *triclinium*) for the *stibadium*, one single large couch in the shape of a half-moon, or of the Græcian *sigma*, from which it sometimes borrowed its name, as in Martial.

> *Accipe lunata scriptum testudine sigma.*

The *stibadia* took their several names from the number of men that they had, as the *hexaclinon* for six, the *heptaclinon* for seven, and so on.

The higher the beds were, the more noble and stately, and the more decent too they were thought. Hence Virg. Æn. 2.

> *Inde toro pater Æneas sic orsus ab alto*

And again, Æn. 6.

> ———*Lucent genialibus altis*
> *Aurea fulcra toris*———

On the contrary, low couches were looked on as so extremely scandalous, that (Valerius Maximus tells the story) one Ælius Tubero, a man of great integrity, and of very noble progenitors, being a candidate for the Prætorship, lost the place, only for making use of a low sort of supping-beds, when he gave the people a public entertainment (*a*).

On the beds they laid a kind of ticks or quilts, stuffed with feathers, herbs, or tow, which they called *culcitræ*. Over these they threw in ancient times nothing but goat-skins; which they afterwards changed for the *stragula*, the coverlids or carpets: These we sometimes find under the name of *toralia*, on account of their belonging to the *torus*. Thus in Horace.

> ———*Ne turpe toral ne sordida mappa*
> *Corruget nares.*   1 Lib. 2. Epist. 5.

And

(*a*) *Val. Max.* lib. 7. cap. 5.

And again,

Et Tyriis dare circum illota toralia vestes. Lib. 2. Sat. 4.

On the carpets were laid *pulvini*, or pillows, for the guests to lean their backs on.

It will be endless to describe the variety and richness of the furniture with which they set off their tables. It will be enough to observe from Pliny, that, when Carthage was finally destroyed by Scipio Africanus, the whole mass of treasure found in that city, which had so long contended for riches, glory, and empire, with Rome itself, amounted to no more than what, in Pliny's time, was often laid out in the furniture of a table (*a*).

As to the manner of the entertainment, the guests in the first place bathed with the master of the feast, and then changed their ordinary clothes for the *vestis convivalis*, or *cœnatoria*, a light kind of frock; at the same time having their *soleæ* pulled off by their slaves, that they might not foul the fine carpets and furniture of the beds. And now taking their places, the first man lay at the head of the bed, resting the fore-part of his body on his left-elbow, and having a pillow or bolster to prop up his back. The next man lay with his head towards the feet of the first, from which he was defended by the bolster that supported his own back, commonly reaching over to the navel of the other man, and the rest after the same manner. Being settled on the beds, in the next place they washed their hands:

—————*Stratoque super discumbitur ostro;*
Dant manibus famuli lymphas.   Virg. Æn. 1.

After this they were served with garlands, or roses, and whatever other flowers were in season, which they did not wear only on their heads, but sometimes too about their necks and arms. This too was the time to present them with essences and perfumes.

The number of guests is by A. Gellius stated according to Varro, that they should not be fewer than three, or more than nine, to express the number of the Graces or the Muses.

The most honourable place was the middle bed, and the middle of that. Horace describes the whole order of sitting in his eighth Satyr of the second Book:

Summus ego, & prope me Viscus Sabinus, & Infra,
Si memini, Varius: cum Servilio Balatrone
                                                               Vibi-

(*a*) *Nat. Hist.* lib. 33. cap. 11.

Vibidius, quos Mæcenas adduxerat umbras,
Nomentanus erat super ipsum, Porcius infra.

So that *infra aliquem cubare* is the same as to lie in one's bosom, as St John is said to have done in our Saviour's; whence learned men have thought, that either the same custom was observed in almost all nations, or else that the Jews, having been lately conquered by Pompey, conformed themselves in this, as in many other respects, to the example of their masters.

At the beginning of the feast they lay on their bellies, their breasts being kept up with pillows, that they might have both their hands at liberty; but, towards the latter end, they either rested themselves on their elbows, as Horace says,

Languidus in cubitum jam se conviva reponet.   Sat. ii. 4. 38.

And in another place,

Et cubito remanete presso,   Carm. 1. Od. 27.

or if they had not a mind to talk, they lay all along; all which postures are to be seen in the old marbles which present the figure of an entertainment.

They seem to have brought in the several courses in tables, and not by single dishes; as Servius observes on that of Virgil, Æn. i. 220:

Postquam prima quies equites, mensæque remotæ.

But some will understand by *mensæ* in that place rather the dishes than the tables, because it follows presently after,

Dixit, & in mensa laticum libavit honorem.

unless we suppose, that, as soon as the table victuals was removed, another was set in its place with nothing but drink.

They wanted no manner of diversion while they were eating, having ordinarily music and antique dances, and in ancient times combats of Gladiators.

Plutarch tells us, that Julius Cæsar, once in a treat which he made for the people, had no less than twenty-two thousand *triclinia;* which is enough to give an idea of their public entertainments.

CHAP. XII.

Of the ROMAN *Names.*

THE Roman names, which many times grievously puzzle ordinary readers, may be divided into four sorts, the names of the *ingenui*, or free-born, the names of the freed men and slaves, the names of the women, and the names of adopted persons.

The *ingenui* had three several names, the *prænomen*, the *nomen*, and the *cognomen*. Hence Juvenal, Sat. v. 126.

———*Si quid tentaveris unquam
Hiscere, tanquam habeas tria nomina.*———

The *prænomen* answers to our Christian names, but was not imposed till the assuming the *manly gown*. The names of this sort most in use, together with the initial letters which ordinarily stand for them in writing, are as follows:

A. *Aulus,* C. *Caius,* D. *Decius,* K. *Cæso,* L. *Lucius,* M. *Manius* and *Marcus,* N. *Numerius,* P. *Publius,* Q. *Quinctus,* T. *Titus.*

AP. *Appius,* CN. *Cnæus,* SP. *Spurius,* TI. *Tiberius,* MAM. *Mamercus,* SER. *Servius,* SEX. *Sextius.*

The *nomen* immediately followed the *prænomen*, answering to the Græcian Patronymicks. For as among them the posterity of Æacus had the name *Æacidæ*, so the Julian family in Rome were so called from Iulus or Ascanius. But there were several other reasons which gave original to some of the *prænomens*, as living creatures, places, and accidents, which are obvious in reading.

The *cognomen* was added in the third place, on the account of distinguishing families, and was assumed from no certain cause, but usually from some particular occurrence. But this must be understood principally of the first original of the name, for afterwards it was hereditary, though frequently changed for a new one.

Grammarians usually add a fourth name, which they call *agnomen*, but this was rather an honourable title; as Cato was obliged with the constant epithet of the *Wise*, Crassus of the *Rich*: And hence came the Africani, the Asiatici, the Macedonici,

donici, &c. Tully frequently ufes *cognomen* to fignify thefe appellations, and therefore is no need of being fo fcrupulous, as to exprefs ourfelves in thefe cafes by the fourth word.

The flaves in ancient times had no name but what they borrowed from the *prænomen* of their mafters, as *lucipor, publipor, marcipor*; as much as to fay, *lucii puer, publii puer,* &c. (*a*). When this cuftom grew out of fafhion, the flaves were ufually called by fome proper name of their own, fometimes of Latin, fometimes of Græcian original; this was very often taken from their country, as *Davus, Syrus, Geta*, &c. Upon their manumiffion they took up the *prænomen* and the *nomen* of their mafters, but inftead of the *cognomen*, made ufe of their former name; as Marcus Tullius Tiro, the freed man of Cicero. After the fame manner it was cuftomary for any foreigner, who had been made a free denizen of Rome, to bear the *nomen* and the *prænomen* of the perfon on whofe account he obtained that privilege.

The women had anciently their *prænomens* as well as the men, fuch as *Caia, Cæcilia, Lucia*, &c. But afterwards they feldom ufed any other befides the proper name of their family, as *Julia, Marcia*, and the like. When there were two fifters in a houfe, the diftinguifhing term was *major* and *minor*; if a greater number, *prima, fecunda, tertia, quarta, quinta*, or by contraction, *fecundilla, quartilla*, and *quintilla*.

Adopted perfons affumed all three names of him who obliged them with this kindnefs, but, as a mark of their proper defcent, added at the end either their former *nomen* or *cognomen*; the firft exactly the fame as before, (as Q. Servilius Cepio Agalo Brutus, the name of M. Junius Brutus, when adopted by Q. Servilius Cepio Agalo;) the other with fome flight alteration, as C. Octavius, when adopted by Julius Cæfar, was called C. Julius Cæfar Octavianus.

Though the right and the ceremony of *adoption* be a fubject properly belonging to the notice of civil lawyers, yet it cannot be amifs to give fome little hints about the nature of that cuftom in general. Every one knows the meaning of the word, and that to *adopt* a perfon was to take him in the room of a fon, and to give him a right to all privileges which accompanied that title. Now the wifdom of the Roman conftitution made this matter a public concern. When a man had

---

(*a*) *Quinctil. Inftitut.* lib. 1. cap. 4. *Plin. N. H.* lib. 33. cap. 1.

a mind to *adopt* another into his family, he was obliged to draw up his reasons, and to offer them to the college of the pontifices for their approbation. If this was obtained, on the motion of the pontifices, the Consul, or some other prime magistrate, brought in a bill at the *Comitia Curiata*, to make the adoption valid. The private ceremony consisted in buying the person to be *adopted* of his parents for such a sum of money, formally given and taken; as Suetonius tells us Augustus purchased his grandsons Caius and Lucius of their father Agrippa.

Aulus Gellius makes a distinction between *adoptio* and *arrogatio*, as if the former only belonged to the care of the Prætor, and was granted to persons only under age; the latter to the cognizance of the people, and was the free act of persons grown up, and in their own power; but we learn from almost every part of history, that the Romans were not so nice in their practice as he is in his observation.

CHAP. XIII.

Of the ROMAN *Money.*

IN inquiring into the difference and value of the Roman coins, we may begin with the lowest sort, that of brass. The *as*, then, or most ancient money, was first stamped by Servius Tullius, whereas formerly it was distinguished only by weight, and not by any image. The first image was that of *pecus*, or small cattle, whence it took the name of *pecunia*. Afterwards it had on one side the beak of a ship, on the other a Janus; and such were the stamps of the *as*; for as for the *triens, quadrans*, and *sextans*, they had the impression of a boat upon them. A long time did the Romans use this and no other money, till after the war with Pyrrhus, *A. U. C.* 484, five years before the first Punic war, silver began to be coined. The stamps upon the silver *denarii* are for the most part waggons, with two or four beasts in them on the one side, and on the reverse the head of Rome, with a helmet. The *victoriati* have the image of Victory sitting, the *sestertii* usually Castor and Pollux on the one side, and both on the reverse the image of the city; so the custom continued during the commonwealth.

monwealth. Auguftus caufed Capricorn to be fet upon his coin, and the fucceeding Emperors ordinarily their own effigies; laft of all came up coin of gold, which was firft ftamped, fixty-two years after that of filver, in the confulfhip of M. Livius Salinator, with the fame ftamp and images. So much for the feveral kinds of money; we may now proceed to the feveral pieces under every kind.

The *as* was fo named *quafi æs*, or brafs, being of that metal, and at firft confifted of 1 lb. weight, till, in the firft Punic war, the poeple, being greatly impoverifhed, made 6 *affes* of the fame value out of one. In the fecond Punic war, Hannibal preffing very hardly upon them, and putting them to great fhifts, the *affes* were reduced to an ounce apiece; and in conclufion, by a law of Papirius, were brought down to half an ounce, and fo continued. The *as* contained the tenth part of the *denarius*, and was in value of our money about *ob. qua.* The *femiffus*, or *femi-as* half as much. The *triens* was the third part of the *as*, the *quadrans* the fourth, by fome called *triuncis* and *teruncius*, becaufe it contained 3 ounces, before the value was diminifhed. The *fextans*, or fixth part, was that which every head contributed to the funeral of Menenius Agrippa; but thefe were not fufficient for ufe, and therefore there were other pieces made, as the *unica*, or twelfth part of the pound, the *femuncia* of the weight of 4 drachms, and the *fextula*, or fixth part of an ounce. Varro fpeaks too of the *decuffis*, in value 10 *affes*, or of a *denarius;* the *viceffis* of two *denarii*, and fo upwards to the *centuffis*, the greateft brafs coin, in value 100 *affes*, 10 *denarii*, and of our money 6 *s*. 3 *d*.

For the filver money, the old *denarius* was fo named, becaufe it contained *denos æris* or *affes*, 10 *affes*, tho' its weight and value was not at all times alike; for the old Roman *denarius*, during the commonwealth, weighed the feventh part of an ounce, and was in value of our money 8 *d. ob. q.* with 1 *c;* but the *denarius*, which came up in the time of Claudius, or a little before, weighed exactly an Attic drachm; fo that the Greek writers, when they fpeak of it, for every *denarius* mention a *drachm*, which of our money was worth 7 *d. ob.* Computations are generally made with reference to this new fort of *denarius*; if refpect be had to the ancient times, then all reckonings are to be increafed one feventh part, for juft fo much the old one exceeded the new. When we meet with *bigatus* and *quadrigatus*, we muft underftand the fame coin as the *denarius*, fo called from the *bigæ* and *quadrigæ* ftamped

upon

upon it. There was another coin called *victoriatus*, from the image of Victory upon it, first stamped in Rome by an order of Claudius, in value half a *denarius*, and therefore named also *quinarius*, as containing the value of five *asses*; it was worth of our money 3*d*. *ob*. *q*. The next that follows, and which makes so much noise in authors, is the *sestertius*, so called *quasi sesquitertius*, because it contained two *asses* and a half, being half the *victoriatus*, and a fourth part of the *denarius*. It is often called absolutely *nummus*, because it was in most frequent use, as also *sestertius nummus*; it was worth of our money 1*d*. *ob*. *q*. The *obolus* was the sixth part of the *denarius*, equal to the Attic ὀϐολὸς, as much as 1*d*. *qu*. with us. The *libella* was the tenth part of the *denarius*, and equal in value to the *as*; so called as a little pound, being supposed equal to a pound of brass, worth of our money *ob*. *qu*. The *sembella*, as if written *semi libella*, was half this. And, lastly, the *teruncius* was the fortieth part of the *denarius*, so named, because it was worth three ounces of brass, being inconsiderable in value, and next to nothing.

To come at last to the golden coins; those most remarkable were the *aurei denarii*, so termed, either because they had the same stamp as the silver *denarii*, or because in bigness they much resembled them, the old *aureus* stamped, during the commonwealth, weighing two silver *denarii*; worth of our money 17*s*. 1*d*. *ob*. *qua*. The old *aureus*, stamped about the beginning of the empire, was lighter than the former by one seventh part, weighing two drachms, worth about 15*s*. of our money. Thus they continued *didrachmi* for the time of the first five Cæsars; and then lost much in their weight by the fraud and avarice of the succeeding princes. In Nero's time they wanted a few grains, under Galba a little more, under Nerva, Trajan, and Adrian, no fewer than eight; under Vespasian ten, and the like under Antoninus Pius, M. Aurelius Severus, and others. Domitian, indeed, had in his reign restored to the *aurei* their full weight of two drachms, and so did Aurelian afterwards, which was the last regulation of the matter, while Rome continued to be the seat of the empire.

The marks of the ordinary coins are as follow: The *as*, because at first it was a pound weight, is thus expressed, L. and the *sestertius*, because it contained in value two pounds of brass and a half, thus, H S. or L L S. The mark of the *quinarius*, or *victoriatus* was Λ. and of the *denarius* X or :!:

The

The sums in use among the Romans were chiefly three; the *sestertium*, the *libra*, and the *talent*. The *sestertium* contained a thousand *sestertii*, about 7 *l.* 16 *s.* and 3 *d.* of our money. We do not, indeed, find it in any ancient author in the singular number, as now it is used, but we very often meet with it in the plural, though with the same signification. In reckoning by *sesterces*, the Romans had an art, which may be understood by these three rules; the first is, if a numeral noun agree in case, gender, and number, with *sestertius*, then it denotes precisely so many *sestertii*, as *decem sestertii*, just so many; the second is this, if a numeral noun of another case be joined with the genitive plural of *sestertius*, it denotes so many thousands, as *decem sestertium* signifies ten thousand *sestertii*. Lastly, if the adverb numeral be joined, it denotes so many hundred thousand, as *decies sestertium* signifies ten hundred thousand *sestertii*; or if the numeral adverb be put by itself, the signification is the same: *decies*, or *vigesies*, stand for so many hundred thousand *sestertii*, or, as they say, so many hundred *sestertia*.

The *libra*, or pound, contained twelve ounces of silver, or ninety-six drachms, or later denarii, and was worth of our money 3 *l.*

The third sum was the *talent*, which contained twenty-four *sestertia*, and six thousand later *denarii*, being the same with the Attic talent; for the names of *talent*, *mina*, and *drachma*, the Romans took from the Greeks, as the Greeks borrowed from them the *libra* and the *unica*. The *talent* was worth of our present money 187 *l.* 10 *s.*

We meet too with a lesser sum, termed the *sportula*, being what the rich men gave to every one of their clients, after having waited upon them in public, and now and then at other times, as they pleased to appoint; it was in value about a hundred *quadrantes*, or 18 *d. ob. qua.* Formerly instead of this sum, they used to deal a dole to the clients without the door, who received the victuals in a little basket made of a kind of broom, called *sportum*.

INDEX.

INDEX.

A.

*A*BLECTI, a Sort of Soldiers Page	192
ACCA LAURENTIA	66
Accensi	123, 199
Accusatio	139
ACILIUS GLABRIO	112
Actionem intendere, vid. edere	136
Actiones Legis	149
Actium (the Fight there)	17
Actor	135
Actuarius	123
Ad bestias	147
Ad ludos	ib.
Ad metalla	ib.
Addictio	137
Adoptio	371
ADRIAN	22
Advocati	135
Ædes sacræ	88
Ædicula	ib.
Ædiles	116
Ædiles Cereales	117
Ædiles Curules	ib.
Ædiles Plebis	116
Ædilitii	194
ÆMILIAN	23
ÆMILIUS	12
Æneatores	208
Æqui	7, 8
Ærarium facere	113
Ære obruti	220
Æs	373
Æstimatio litis	141
Ætius	27
Agger	212
Agones	86
Agonalia	93

ALARIC King of the *Goths*	27
Albo-galerus	321
Alæ	192
ALEXANDER SEVERUS	23
Alicata Chlamys	3'0
Allocutio	210
Ambarvalia	66
Ambire magistratum	106
Ambitus	138
Ampliatio	140
AMULIUS	2, 3
Ἀναϰἀϰαι	277
ANCUS MARTIUS	4
Ancylia	74
Andabatæ (a Sort of Gladiators)	277
Animadversio	141
Animam in primo ore, or in primis labris tenere	338
ANNA PERENNA	94
Annus Bissextilis	88
Anquisitio	142
ANTHEMIUS	28
Antony 14. vid. *Marc.*	
ANTIOCHUS, King of Syria	12
ANTONINUS Caracalla	22
Vid. *Marcus* and *Lucius*.	
ANTONINUS Pius	22
ANTONINUS's Pillar	54
APER	25
Apex	321
Aphractum	243
Apparitores	122
APPIUS Claudius	7, 66
APPIUS the Decemvir	110
Aquæ & ignis interdictio	114
Aquæducts	57
Aquila (Standard of a Legion)	194

3 H *Aquæ*

INDEX.

Aquæ præesse	194
Arabia (made a Province)	21
Arbiter bibendi	249
Arbitri	135
Arches	52
Area of the Amphitheatre	44
Arena	ib.
Aries (the battering Ram)	238
Armatura	215
Armenia (made a Prov.)	21
Armillæ	221
Armorum concussio	209
Arms of the Romans	199
Arrogatio	372
Aruspices, vid. *Haruspices*.	
As	373, &c.
ASCANIUS	2
Assyria (made a Province)	21
Attellanæ (sort of Plays)	288
Athens (taken by Sylla)	13
Atrati	311
ATTALUS King of Pergamus)	13
ATTILA the Hun	27
Auctorati	272
Avens (River)	32
AVENTINUS an Alban King)	ib.
Augurale	205
Auguries	67, 68, 69
Augurs	ib.
AUGUSTULUS	28
AUGUSTUS, vid. *Octavius*.	
AVITUS	28
AULUS PLAUTIUS	18
Aurei Denarii	374
AURELIAN	24
Auspicia	191
Auspices	68
Auspiciis suis rem gerere	227
Auxilia	182

B.

Bagnios	56, 57

BALBINUS	23
Balista	238
Barritus	209
Basilicæ	48
Basilicus (a throw on the Dice)	249
Battalia of the Romans	203
Beds of Images carried in Procession at Funerals	346
Beneficiarii	189
Bestiarii	146, 268
Bidental	336
Bigatus	373
Bigæ	257, 373
Biremis	243
Bissextus dies	88
Blood-letting a punishment of the Roman Soldiers	220
Borrowing and Lending of Wives among the Romans, probably a mistake	332, &c.
Bridges of Rome	38
BRITAIN	17, 18, 22
BRUTUS	5, 6, 15, 16
Buccinatores	208
Buccinæ	ib.
Buccula	201
Bulla aurea	310
Burning of the Dead	335
Bustum	355

C.

Cæliolus, or minor *Cælius*	31
Cærites	232
Cæritum Tabulæ	113, 232
CÆSAR	14, 15
Calcei Lunati	323
Calcei mullei	374
Calculi	248
Caligoti	325
Caligæ	ib.
Caligæ Speculatoriæ	ib.
CALIGULA	17
CAMILLUS	7, 8
	Centuria

INDEX.

Camp (Form and Division of it)	210
Campagi	324
Campidoctores	215
Campus Martius	47
Campus Sceleratus	79
Candidatus	106
Candidatus Principis	115
Canicula (a throw on the Dice)	249
Cannæ (the Battle there)	11
Cantabria (subdued)	17
Capitol	39
Cappadocia (made a Prov.)	17
Caps and Hats ordinarily used by the Romans	308, 320
Capite censi	131
Caput porcinum	206
Carceres	46
CARINUS	25
Carmen Saliare	75
Carnifex	123
Carthage (destroyed)	12
CARUS	25
CASSIUS	15, 16
Castra æstiva	211
————hyberna	ib.
————stativa	ib.
Catapulta	239
Catastasis of the Drama	286
Catastrophe of the Drama	ib.
Catilinarian Conspiracy	14
CATTI	21
Cavea	44
Celeres	120
Celeustes	244
Cella of a Temple	41
Cenotaphia	359
Censors	112
Censorii	194
Census	112
Census put for a rich Man	170
Centesimutio	219
Centumviri litibus judicandis	122
Centumviri litibus judicandis	135
Centuria prærogativa	132
Centuries	130
Centuries, or *Ordines*, of Soldiers	190
Centurions	193
Centurionum primus	194
Cerealia	95
Cestus (the exercise described)	55
Chariot Races	ib.
Charista	93
Chirodota	314
Chlamys	312
vid. *alicata*.	
Chorus	290, &c.
CICERO	14
CIMBRI	13
Cincture of the Gown	307
Cinctus Gabinus	307, 308
Circensian Shows	252
Circos	46
Circus maximus	ib.
Circuitio Vigilum	214
Civilis quercus	221
Civitatis fœderatæ	233
Infra classem	131
Classes	130
Classici authores	ib.
Classicum	209
CLAUDIUS	18
CLAUDIUS the Second	24
Clavi	315, &c.
Clavum pangere	109
CLÆLIA	6, 7
CLEOPATRA	15, 17
Clients	97
Cloacæ	58
Closing of the eyes of departing Friends	339
Clusium	7, 8
COCLES	6
Coemptio	328
Cænaculum	366
	Cænatio

INDEX

Cænatio	366	Cornua (Parts of the Army)	192
Cognomen	371	Sub Corona venire	231
Cohors Prætoria	191	Corona Castrensis	222
Cohors prima	ib.	———— civica	221
COLLATINUS	5	———— muralis	222
Collis Dianæ	35	———— navalis	ib.
———— Hortulorum	33	———— obsidionalis	ib.
———— Pincius	ib.	———— rostrata	ib.
———— Quirinalis	31	———— triumphalis	ib.
Collocatio	342	———— vallaris	ib.
Colonies	231	Coronæ aureæ	ib.
Columna bellica	54	Corsica (subdued)	10
Columna rostrata	ib.	Corvus (Engine)	240
Columns or Pillars	53	Corybantes	81
Comitia	128, &c.	Cothurnus	288
———— Calata	129	Cottian Alps	18
———— Centuriata	ib.	CRASSUS	14
———— Curiata	130	Crepidæ	325
———— Tributa	129, 133	Cretata ambitio	307
Comitium	50	Crimen adulterii	138
COMMODUS	22	———— ambitus	ib.
Commons	97	———— falsi	ib.
Companies of Charioteers	255	———— inter sicarios	ib.
vid. Factio		———— majestatis	126, 138
———— the Golden	255	———— parricidii	138, 146
———— the Purple	ib.	———— peculatus	126, 138
———— the Silver	ib.	———— perduellionis	131
Conclamatio	342	———— plagii	138
Concussio armorum	209	———— repetundarum	126, 138
Confarreatio	328	———— veneficii	188
Congiaria	220	———— vis publica	ib.
Conquisitores	185	Crista	201
Consecration of Temples	40	Crupellarii	276
———— of Emperors	366	Cucullus	317
———— of Friends	ib.	Culcitræ	367
CONSTANTINE the Great	25	Culeus	146
Constantinople	ib.	Cultrarii	86
CONSTANTIUS	26	Cuneus	305
CONSTANT. CHLORUS	25	Curetes	31, 81
Consulares	194	Curia Hostilia	48
Consuls	107, &c.	Curia Pompeii	ib.
Consulares ordinarii	108	Curiæ	47, 48
Consules suffecti	ib.	Curio maximus	129
CORNELIUS SCIPIO	12	Curiones	ib.
Cornicines	208	Custos puerpera	311
Cornua (Music)	ib.	Cybele's Priest	81
			Daci

INDEX.

D.

Daci	21
Dacia (made a Province)	ib.
Δακτυλυς παιζειν	280
Dalmatia (subdued)	17
Damnum	143
Dapes saliares	75
Decemjugis	256
Decemviri	117
Decemviri litibus judicandis	122
Decemviri, Keepers of the Sybilline Oracles.	
DECII	198
Decimatio	219
DECIUS	23
Decuma	233
Decumani	ib.
Decuriæ	129, 192
Decuriones	195
Decursio, at Funerals	357
Decussis	366
Deductores	107
Defensio	139
Defuncti pro rostris laudatio	51, 351
Dejectio e rupe Tarpeia	145
Delatores	142
Delubrum	38
Denarius	373, &c.
Decennalia	360
Depontani	132
Deportati	144
Deportatio	ib.
Designatores	305
Devoting of the Generals	198
Diadem	322
DIADUMEN	23
Dibaphus	318
Dictator	109, &c.
DIDIUS JULIAN	22
Didrachmi	374
Dies atri	90
——*comitiales*	ib.
——*comperendini*	91
——*fasti*	ib.
——*festi*	89
Dies intercisi	89
——*præliares*	91
——*profesti*	89, 90
——*postriduani*	90
——*stati*	91
Diem dicere reo	141
Διηρης	242
Diffarreatio	328
Δικροτος	242
DIOCLETIAN	25
Diræ	68
Diribitores	132
Disceptatio causæ	ib.
Discus (the Exer. descr.)	254
Διαυπατος	110
Divorces	332, &c.
Do, dico, abdico	90
Dolabræ	237
DOMITIAN	21
Ductu suo rem gerere	197
Duumviri classis	244
Duumviri, Keepers of the Sibylline Oracles	78
Duumviri perduellionis, or capitales	122
Dux Legionis	194

E.

Edere actionem	136
Edicta (Bills for a show of Gladiators)	277
EGERIA	74
Εικοσοροι	243
Ἑκατονηρης	ib.
Ἑκκαιδεκηρης	ib.
Ἐλατηρ	252
Elatio	343
Elephants running in the Circus	256
Emeriti	189
Ensigns	207
Entertainments	365, &c.
Epitasis of the Drama	286
Epula, or Lectisternia	84
Epulæ	ib.
Epulones, or septemviri epulonum	ib.
Eques, Equestris Ordinis, & Equestri	

INDEX.

Equeſtri loco natus, the difference between them	98
Equeſtria	44
Equi redditio	187
Equitatus juſtus	192
Equites	185, 186
Equitum probatio	186
Equitum recenſio	ib.
Equitum tranſvectio	ib.
Equum adimere	113
Eſpouſals	326
Eſſedarii	277
Eſſedum	ib.
EVANDER	66
EUDOXIA	28
Evocatio deorum tutelarium	235
Evocati	189
Euphrates (the Bounds of the Empire)	22
Excubiæ	213
Exercitium ad palum	215
Exilium	144
Exire	278
Exodium	288
Exodium Atellanicum	ib.
Extiſpices	69
Extraordinarii	1, 2, 211, 314

F.

Fabius Maximus	11
Factio alba	255
——*praſina*	ib.
——*ruſſata*	ib.
——*veneta*	ib.
Vid. Companies of Charioteers.	
Fari tria verba	90
Faſces	108
Faſciæ	319
Faſcis	217
Favete linguis	85
FAUSTULUS	2, 3
Feaſts in honour of the Dead	361
Februaca	65
Feciales	76, 229
Femoralia	319
Feralia	93
Ferentarii	199
Feriæ conceptivæ	90
——*imperativæ*	ib.
——*ſtativæ*	89
Feſcennine Verſes	283, 331
Feſtivals in the Roman Kalendar	93, &c.
Filius familiæ	171

Flamen Dialis	73
——*Martialis*	ib.
——*Quirinalis*	ib.
Flaminica	ib.
Flaminia, or *Flammeum* (the Flamen's Cap)	72
Flammeum (the Bride's Veil)	329
Floralia	95
Fœderatæ civitates	233
Follis (a ſort of Ball)	251
Forfex (a way of drawing up an Army)	206
Form of Abſolution	40
——of Ampliation	ib.
——of Condemnation	ib.
Fortunate Names	184
Forums	48, &c.
Forum Auguſti	49
—— *Boarium*	50
Fora Civilia	49
Forum cupedinarium	50
——*Holitorium*	ib.
——*Julium*	49
——*Latium*	ib.
——*Nervæ*	ib.
——*Palladium*	50
——*Piſtorium*	ib.
——*Romanum*	49
——*Suarium*	50
——*Trajani*	ib.
——*tranſitorium*	49
Fora Venalia	ib.
Foſſa	212
Fratres Arvales	66
Freedom by Manumiſſion	100
Freedom by Teſtament	ib.
Frontis inuſtio	141
Frumentum æſtimatum	234
——*decumanum*	ib.
——*emptum*	ib.
——*honorarium*	ib.
——*imperatum*	ib.
Funditores	199
Funera	340
Funerals	334
Funeral Ceremonies before the Burial	340
——in the Act of Burial	343, &c.
——after the Burial	360, &c.
Funera acerba	338
Funera larvata	349

Funus

INDEX.

Funus indictivum	336
———— publicum	ib.
———— tacitum	337
———— translatitium	338
———— vulgare, or plebeium	337
Furca ignominiosa	145
Furca poenalis	ib.
Fustes	219

G.

GALBA	19
Galea	199, 201
Galericulum	321
GALERIUS	25
Galerus	321
Galli (Priests of Cybele)	81
GALLIENUS	23
GALLUS	ib.
Games	247
Gates of Rome	37
Gauls sack Rome	8
General	196
Genseric King of the Vandals	26
Gladiators	271
Gladiatores catervarii	274
———— fiscales	ib.
———— meridiani	ib.
———— ordinarii	ib.
———— postulatitii	ib.
Globus (Way of drawing up an Army)	206
Glycerius, vid. Liarius	28
GORDIAN	23
GRATIAN	27
Gregorian Style	88
Gubernator	244

H.

Habet, or hoc habet (a form of Speech used by Gladiators after giving a blow)	278
Habit of the Romans	306
HANNIBAL	11, 12
Harangues of the Generals	210
Harpastum	252
Haruspices	69, 70, 71
Hasta pura	220
Sub hasta vendi	122
Hastae	199
Hastati	190
HELIOGABALUS	23
Heptaclinon	367
Hepteres	242
Hercules, his Chapel near the Amphitheatres and Circos	281
Hexaclinon	367
Hexeres	242
Hippagines	ib.
HIRTIUS	16
Histriones	223, 287
Hoc age	84
Honorary Tombs	352
HONORIUS	27
Hoplomachi	277
Hostia	84

I.

Janiculum	33
Janus Imus	42
———— Medius	ib.
———— Summus	ib.
Idaei Dactyli	81
Ides	91
Jentaculum	365
Ignobiles	97
Ignominia	144
Ilicet	359
Illyricum (subdued)	17
Immolatio	85
Immunes	233
Imperator, vid. General.	
Imperatoris Contubernales	211
In crucem actio	145
In integrum restitutio	137
Infra aliquem cubare	369
Insula	85
Ingenui	99
Intercessio	104, 116
Interrex	120
JOVIAN	26
Ipsilae	75
Irrogatio	142
JUBA	15
Judex Quaestionis	138
Judgments	134, &c.
Judices selecti	138
Judicia Centumviralia	122
Judicium calumniae	137, 141
Judicium falsi	ib.
Judicium praevaricationis	136
Sub Jugum mitti	231
JUGURTHA	13
Jugurthine War	ib.
JULIAN	26

Julian

INDEX.

Julian Account	88	Agrarian of the Assemblies and	
Jupiter Feretrius	227	Meetings	154
Jure vocatæ (Centuries and Tribes)	132	———of Citizens	152
		———of Constitutions, Laws, and Privileges	160
Jus civile	149	———of Corn	165
Jus civitatis	130	———of Crimes	173
Jus dicere and *judicare* (the difference between them)	112	———of Expences	166
		———*Falsi*	175
Jus honorarium	149	———of Judges	171
Jus imaginis	99	———of Judgment	173
Jus Papirianum	148	———of Magistrates	157
Jus trium liberorum	181	———de *Majestate*	174
———*In jus reum vocare*	136	———of martial Affairs	168
———*In jus vocatus aut eat aut satisdet*	ib.	———Miscellaneous	180
Juramentum calumniæ	136	———of Money, Usury, &c.	170
JUSTINIAN	149	———de *parricidis*	175
		———de *pecuniis repetundis*	178
K.		———of Provinces and their Governors	161
Kalends	92	———of religion 150, &c.	
Καλάφρχιοι	242	———of the Senate	175
Καλασρώματα	ib.	———*Inter Sicarios*	ib.
Kissing of the dead Body	338	———de *Tutelis*	169
Knights	98	———de *Vi*	176
Knights Estates	ib.	———of Wills, Heirs, and Legacies	173
Κρηπίδις	325	Leagues (how made)	229
		Lecti tricliniorum, or *tricliniares*	367
L.		*Lecticæ*, or *Lecti* (Funeral Beds)	348
LABERIUS the Mimic	285		
Lacerna	217	Legati 127,	196
Lacernata amica	320	———*Consulares*	ib.
Laciniam trahere	307	———*prætoris*	ib.
Læna	318	*Legatio libera*	157
Lanistæ	272	*Leges* (how they differed from *Plebiscita*)	134
TITUS LARGIUS FLAVIUS, the first Dictator	109	Legions	191
		Lessus	346
LATINS	7	Levy of the Confederates	188
LATINUS	2	———of the Foot	183
Latio Sententiæ	140	———of the Horse	185
LATIUM	2	*Lex Acilia*	179
Latrones	249	———*Acilia Calpurnia*	177
Latrunculi	248	———*Ælia*	153
Laudatio (a Custom at Trials)	140	———*Æmylia*	167
LAVINIA	2	———*Ampia Labiena*	171
LAVINIUM	ib.	———*Antia*	167
LAURENTIA	ib.	*Antonia* 151, 159, 172,	174
LAURENTUM	ib.	*Apuleia*	174
Laws 148,	&c.	*Atia*	151
———de *adulterio & pudicitia*	175	———*Atilia*	169
Agrarian	263	———*Atinia*	159
———de *ambitu*	177	———*Aufidia*	

INDEX.

Atia Aufidia	177	Atia Maria Portia		168
——Aurelia	159, 172	——Marita		180
——Cæcilia Didia	160	——Memmia		173
——Cæcilia de jure Italiæ		——Muneralis		ib.
& tributis tollendis	180	——Ogulnia		150
——Cælia	155	——Oppia		167
——Calpurnia	178	——Orchia		166
——Campana	165	——Papia	151,	153
——Cassia	155, 156, 163	——Papia Poppæa		182
——Cincia	173	——Papiria	150,	155
——Claudia 155, 156, 171, 182		——Plautia	172,	176
——Clodia 151, 168, 152, 163,		——Pompeia	159, 171,	173,
165, 176, 182			176,	178
——Cornelia 150, 151, 153,		——Porcia		152
154, 157, 158, 159, 161, 167,		——Pupia		157
174, 175, 179		——Remmia		173
——Curia	155	——Roscia		152
——Didia	166	——Sacrata militaris		168
——Domitia	151	——Scatinia or Scantinia		175
——Fabia	177	——Sempronia 153, 155, 156,		
——Fannia	166	158, 161, 164, 165, 168, 171		
——Flaminia	164	——Sentia		156
——Flavia	165	——Servilia 153, 163, 171, 179		
——Furia	170	——Sextia Licinia	150,	158
——Fusia	154	——Silvani & Carbonis		153
——Gabinia 155, 156, 168,		——Sulpitia	154, 156,	168
171, 174		——Sulpitia Sempronia		150
——Gellia Cornelia	154	——Terentia Cassia		165
——Genutia	157	——Thoria		164
——Hieronica	166	——Titia	159,	163
——Hirtia	158	——Trebonia		163
——Hortensia	160	——Tullia	157,	177
——Julia 162, 163, 165, 167,		——de Vacatione		151
172, 174, 175, 178, 179		——Valeria	152, 159,	170
——Julia de Civitate	153	——Valeria Horatia		152
——Julia de maritandis or-		——Varia	153,	174
dinibus	180	——Vatinia		162
——Julia Papia	181	——Villia annalis		157
——Junia	153, 179	——Voconia		170
——Junia Licinia	160	LIARIUS or GLYCERIUS		28
——Junia Sacrata	159	Libanina prima		85
——Lætoria	169	Libatio		ib.
——Licinia 151, 152, 163, 166		Libella		374
——Licinia Albutia	160	Libelli (Bills for a Sword-		
——Licinia Matia	153	Play)		277
——Licinia de Sodalitiis	177	Liber censu, &c.		100
——Livia	171	Liberti		99
——Livia de Sociis	153	Libertini		ib.
——Mamilia	165	LIBITINA		340
——Manilia	165, 169	Libitinarii		ib.
——Manlia	151	Libra		375
——Marcia	158	Libri elephantini		41
——Maria	155	Liburnicæ		243

3 I   LICINIUS

INDEX.

LICINIUS	25	Magistrates	105
Lictores	122	———— when admitted	131
Litem intendere	136	———— when designed	ib.
Literæ laureatæ	223	*Magistratus curules*	105
Lituus	68, 208	*Magistratus extraordinarii*	ib.
LIVIUS ANDRONICUS	283	———— *majores*	ib.
Lorica	202	———— *minores*	ib.
Luci	43	———— *mixti*	ib.
LUCIUS ANTONINUS	283	———— *ordinarii*	ib.
LUCRETIA	5	———— *Patricii*	ib.
Luctus annuus	362	———— *Plebeii*	ib.
LUCULLUS	13	———— *Provinciales*	ib.
Ludi Actiaci	303	———— *Urbani*	ib.
———— *Apollinares*	297	*MAGNENTIUS*	26
———— *Augustales*	299	*MAJORIANUS*	28
———— *Capitolini*	298	*Mandatores*	142
———— *Cereales*	296	*Mandatum*	135
———— *Circenses*	252	*Manipulus*	190
———— *Compitalitii*	299	*MANLIUS*	8, 10
———— *Conjuales*	298	*Mappa*	257
———— *Decennales*	304	*MARK ANTONY*	16, 17
———— *Florales*	296	*MARCUS ANTONINUS*	22
———— *Funebres*	304	*MARIUS*	13
———— *Juvenales*	ib.	Marriages	326, &c.
———— *Juventutis*	ib.	Marriage by *Use*	318
———— *Magni*	302	Proper time for Marriage	327
———— *Martiales*	297	*Matronalia*	94
———— *Megalenses*	296	Μάχιμοι, Ships of War	243
———— *Miscelli*	304	*MAXENTIUS*	25
———— *Natalitii*	ib.	*MAXIMIAN*	ib.
———— *Palatini*	299	*MAXIMIN*	23
———— *Pontificales*	271	*MAXIMINIAN*	25
———— *Quinquennales*	303	*MAXIMUS*	28
———— *Romani*	298	*Megalesia*	296
———— *Sacerdotales*	271	*Mercidinus* or *Mercidonius*	88
———— *Sæculares*	299, &c.	*Merenda*	365
———— *Scenici*	282, &c.	Μισοπόρευρον	315
———— *Triumphales*	304	*Mesopotamia* (made a Province)	21
———— *Victoriæ*	303		
———— *Votivi*	302	*Meta* in the Circus	46
Ludii and *Histriones* at a Funeral	245	*Metallici*	147
		Miliarium aureum	55
LUPA	2	*Milites subitarii*	185
Lupercalia	64, 65	*Mimus*	284
Luperci	64	*Minerva*	94
Luperci Fabiani	65	*Missilia*	267
Luperci Quintiliani	ib.	*Missus* (the Matches in the Races)	256
Lustrum	113		
Lustrum condere	ib.	*Missus ærarius*	257
Lying on Couches at the Table	366, &c.	*MITHRIDATUS*, King of Pontus	13
M.		*Mitra*	321
Magister equitum	100, 110	*Mittere judices in consilium*	140
			Mola

INDEX.

Mola 85
Moneres 243
Of the Money 372, &c.
Mons Aventinus 32
———Augustus 31
———Caballus or Caballinus ib.
———Cælius ib.
———Capitolinus 30
———Esquilinus, exquilinus, or excubinus 32
———Murcius ib.
———Palatinus 30
———Querculanus, or quercetulanus 31
———Remonius 32
———Saturni 40
———Tarpeius ib.
———Vaticanus 33
———Viminalis 32
Montorius 33
Mors (Capital Punishment) 145
Mortuaria glossaria 346
Mourning 362
Mourning Habit 349
Municipia 232
Munus pronunciare, or proponere 277
Musculus 237
Music of the Army 208
MUTIUS 6, 7
Myrmillones 270

N.

Nænia 346
Of the Names 370
Natalis urbis 93, 94
Naval Affairs of the Romans 239, &c.
Naves apertæ 243
———constratæ ib.
———longæ 242
———onerariæ ib.
———rostratæ 243
———tectæ ib.
———turritæ ib.
Navis of a Temple 41
Naumachiæ (the Place) 46
———(the Sport) 269, &c.
NEPOS 28
NERO 18
NERVA 21
Nerva's Arch 50
Nobiles 99

Nomen 370
Nominis delatio 139
Nonæ Caprotinæ ib.
Nones 92
Notarius 123
Novennalia 360
Novi 99
Novissima verba 359
Novus homo 97
Nucibus relictis 330
NUMA 4
NUMERIAN 25
NUMITOR 2, 3
Nummus 374
Nundinæ 89
Nuts strewed at Marriage Feasts 330
Nymphæa 57

O.

Oath of the Soldiers 188
Obolus 374
Ocreæ 202
OCTAVIUS or AUGUSTUS 16, 17
Octeres 242
Odeum 46
ODOACER 27, 28
Officers in the Army 139, &c.
'Ολκάδις 243
OLYBRIUS 28
Omne tulit punctum 133
OPILIUS MACRINUS 23
'Οπλιταγωγοί 242
'Οπλομάχοι 277
Optimates 98
Optiones 194
Orchestra 44
Orcini 100
Ordines primi 193
ORESTES 28
ORMISDAS 50
Ornare Apparitoribus, Scribis, &c. 125
Ornari provincia ib.
Ossilegium 358
Ostia (the Port) 239
OSTORIUS SCAPULA 18
OTHO 19
Ovation 224
Ovilia 132

Pactum

INDEX.

P.

Pactum	136
Paganica (a sort of Ball)	251
Palantes	30
Palaria	215
Palatium	30
PALES	94
Palilia	95
Palla	319
Palladium	77
Palliatæ (Plays)	287
Palliatus	309
Palmyra	24
Paludamentum	197, 312
Palus Capreæ	95
Pannici terrores	209
Pannonia (subdued)	17
PANSA	16
Pantheon	39
Pantomimi	285
PAPIRIUS CURSOR	8
Paragaudæ	315
Par impar	251
Paria componere	278
Parma	199
Parricidium	94
Pater patratus	76
Patibulum	146
Patres conscripti	102
Patricians	97
Patrons	97, 135
Pay of the Soldiers	217
Pectorale	202
Pecunia	372
———— extraordinaria	234
———— ordinaria	ib.
PEDIUS	16
Πεντακόντλoρος	243
Pentathlum	253
Πεντεκαιδεκήρις	243
Πευθηρης	ib.
Penula	312, 317
Percussio securi	145
Περιῤῥυρον	309
Perones	323
PERSEUS	12
Persona	290
PERTINAX	22
Pescia	284
Petasus	321
Petere	279
Phaleræ	221
PHILIP	13
———— (of Macedon)	12
Philippi (the Battle there)	16
Φορτικοί	242
Phrygians (Priests of Cybele)	81
Picts	22
Pila trigonalis	251
Pilæ (the several Sorts)	ib.
Pilani	190
Pileo donari	100
Pileus	320, 321
———— (the reward of Gladiators)	280
Pilum	200
Pinarii	65, 66
Pinnirapi	276
PISO	19
Pitched Shirts	147
Place (which reckoned the most honourable at the Table)	368
Places for burning and burying the Dead)	353
Planipedes	284
Plebeians	97
Plebiscita	134, 149
Plutei	238
Pollicem premere	279
———— vertere	ib.
Pollinctores	340
Pomærium	29, 30
———— proferre	30
Pompa Circensis	296
POMPEY	13, 14, 15
De ponte dejici	252
Pontes	ib.
Pontifices	71, 72
———— majores	71

Pontifices

INDEX.

Pontifices minores	71	Prandium	365
Pontifex maximus	72	Prerogative Century	132
Pontificum cœna	75	Prerogative Tribe	ib.
PONTIUS PILATE	128	Priests	64, &c.
Popæ	86	Primipilarius	194
Poplifugium	95	Primipilus	193
Populares	98	Princeps juventutis	259
Popularia	44	———— senatus	101
PORSENNA	6, 7	Principalis constitutio	149
Porta Capena, or Appia	37	Principes	190
———— Carmentalis	ib.	———— Centurionum	ib.
———— Flaminia	ib.	———— ordinum	ib.
———— Flumentana	ib.	Principia	212
———— Nævia	ib.	PROBUS	24
———— Saliana	38	PROCAS	2
———— Triumphalis	ib.	Proconsuls	124, &c.
Porticos	51	Procuratores	135
Portitires	180	———— Caesaris	128
Portoria	ib.	Projectio in profluentem	145
Portorium	233	Proletarii	151
Posca	219	Proprætors	127
Postulatio actionis	136	Proquæstors	ib.
Potitii	65, 66	Proscensium	43
Præcingi	308	Proscripti	144
Præcipitatio de Robore	145	Proscriptio	ib.
Præcones	123	Protasis (of the Drama)	286
Præfecturæ	232	Provinces	233
Præfectus alæ	195	———— (Consular)	127
———— ærarii	121	———— (Prætorian)	ib.
———— classis	244	Provincial Magistrates	24
———— frumenti	121	Provocatores	276
———— legionis	193	Publius (the Mimic)	286
———— prætorii	121	PUBLIUS SCIPIO	12
———— vigilum	ib.	Pullarius	68
———— urbis	220	Pullata turba	312
Præfica	345	Pullatorum circulus	ib.
Prælusio	278	Pulvinarii	84
Prænomen	370	Pulvini	368
Prætexta, vid. Toga.		Punishments	143, &c.
Prætextatæ (plays)	287	Punishments of the Soldiers	219
Prætor Peregrinus	111	PUPIENUS	23
———— urbanus	ib.	Purpura Megalensis	296
Praetorium	211	Puteal Libonis	51
Prætors	112, &c.	———— Scribonium	ib.
Prætors of the Provinces	127	Puticulæ, or Puticuli	354

Pyra

INDEX

Stadia	46	*Testudo* 237
Stationes	213	Τεςεήρης 242
Status of a Play	286	*Teutones* 13
Stibadium	367	*Thalassius* 303
Stipendium	233	Theatre 53, &c.
Stola	319	———of Scaurus 44
Stragula	367	———of Pompey ib.
Strangulatio	145	*THEODORIC* the Goth 28
Στραγγαλίδις	242	*Thensa* 296
Subsula	75	*THEODOSIUS* 17
Succenturiones	194	Thracian Gladiators 276
Sudes	212	*Tiara* 322
SUEVI	17	*TIBERIUS* 27
Suggrandarium	335	*Tibiæ* 292
SULPICIUS	13	———*Dextræ* 293
Suovetaurilia	113	———*Impares* ib.
Supplicatio	123	———*Lydiæ* ib. 294
SYLLA	13	———*Pares* 293
T.		———*Phrygia* ib. 294
Tabella votiva	245	———*Sarranæ* 293
Tabellæ	130	———*Sinistræ* ib.
Tabernariæ (a sort of play)	287	*Tibialia* 319
Tablet marked with A	133, 140	*TIGRANES* 13, 14
———marked with C	140	*Tirones* 216
———marked with N L	ib.	*TITUS* (Emper.) 20
———marked with U R	133	*Toga* 306, &c.
TACITUS (Emper.)	24	———*alba* ib.
Talent	375	———*candida* ib.
Tali	249	———*libera* 311
Talio	143	———*palmata* 108, 312
Tarentine War	8	———*picta* ib.
TARQUINIUS PRISCUS	4	———*prætexta* 309
TARQUIN the Proud	4, 6	———*pulla* 311
Titus *TATIUS*	31	———*pura* ib.
Templum	38	———*purpurea* 312
Temple of Janus	41	———*sordida* 311
———of Saturn	ib.	———*virilis* ib.
Teruncius	373	*Togatæ* (Sort of Plays) 287
Terminalia	93	*Togatus* (opposed to *Pal-*
Τισσαραχόντυρες	243	*liatus*) 309
Tessera	210, 213	*Toralia* 367
Tesseræ, & tesserarum ludus	249	*Tornamenta* 263
Tesserarius	213	*Torques* 221
		Trabea

INDEX.

Trabea	313	Trochus	251
Trabeatæ (fort of Plays)	287	TROJA, or Ludus Trojæ 259, 269, &c.	
Tragedy	286		
TRAJAN	21	Trophies	55
Trajan's Pillar	53	Tuba	208
Transactio	136	Tubicines	ib.
Τριακόντορος	243	Tullianum	143
Triarii	190	TULLUS HOSTILIUS	4
Tribu movere	113	Tumuli inanes, or honorarii	359
Tribes of the City	34, 133	Tunica	313, 314, &c.
Tribunal	311	——— angusticlavia	315, 316
Tribunes (Junior)	183	——— laticlavia	ib.
——— (Senior)	ib.	——— palmata	314
——— of the People	115	Tunicæ talares	ib.
——— of the Soldiers	183, 194	Turmæ	192
		Turres mobiles	237
Tribuni angusticlavii	125	Turres (way of drawing up an Army)	206
——— comitiati	ib.		
——— ærarii	218	Tutulus	321
——— laticlavii	195		
——— militum, confulari potestate	119	V.	
		Vadari reum	139
——— rufuli	195	VALENTINIAN the First	26
Tribunus, or Præfectus Celerum	120	——— the Second	27
		——— the Third	ib.
Tribunitia potestate donati	116	VALERIAN	23
Tribus rustica	133	VALERIUS POPLICOLA	7
——— Urbanæ	ib.	Vallum	212
Tributa	234	Varronian Satire	284
Triclinium	360	VATICANUS, or VAGITANUS	33
Triens	372, 373		
Trierarchus	244	Vectigales	233
Τριήρης	242	VEII	7, 8
Tripudium	68	Velites	190
——— folistimum	ib.	Venatio direptioni	266
——— fonivium	ib.	Ventilatio	279
Triremis	242	Venus (throw on the dice)	249
Triumph	242, &c.	Verbera	143
Triumviri A. A. Æ. F. F.	121	Verfura	171
——— capitales	ib.	Vertere arma	278
——— monetales	ib.	VESPASIAN	18, 20
——— nocturni	ib.	Vespillones	340
Triuncis	373	Vestal Virgins	77, 78
			Vestis

3 K

INDEX.

Vestis convivalis, or *cœnatoria*	368	*Vitem poscere*	194
————— *forensis*	306	*Vites*	219
VETURIUS MAMURIUS	27	*Vittæ*	85, 319
Vexilla	221	Umbo of the Shield	200
Vexillarii	194	——— of the Gown	307
Via Appia	58	*Unica*	373
Viator	116	*Volsci*	7
Viatores	120	*Urbis natalis*	95
Vicesimatio	219	*Ustrina*	355
Victima	84		
Victimarii	86	**W.**	
Victoriatus	372	War (how declared)	229
Vigiliæ	112	Watch-word	209
Vigintiviratus	122	Ways	58
Vilis arca	348		
Villa publica	47	**X.**	
Vincula	143	XANTIPPUS	10
Vindicta	100	XERXES	
Vineæ	237		
VIRGINIA	110	**Y.**	
Visceratio	361	Of the Roman Year	86
VITELLIUS	19, 20	**Z.**	
Vitis	194	ZENOBIA	24
		Zysti	47

SCRIP-

SCRIPTORES

Qui in duodecim Tomis Thesauri Antiquitatum *Romanarum* a Magno GRÆVIO congesti inveniuntur.

TOM. I.

OCTAV. Ferrarius de Origine Romanorum.
Paulus Manutius de Civitate Romana.
Carolus Sigonius de antiquo jure civium Romanorum.
Onuphrius Panvinius de Civitate Romana.
――――――――――de Imperio Romano.
Paulus Manutius de Comitiis Romanorum.
Nicolaus Gruchius de Comitiis Romanorum.
――――――――Responsio ejusdem ad binas C. Sigonii Reprehensiones.
Caroli Sigonii posterior cum Nicolao Gruchio disputatio, de binis Comitiis & lege curiata.
Nicolai Gruchii ad posteriorem C. Sigonii disputationem refutatio.
Carolus Sigonius de Lege Curiata Magistratuum & Imperatorum, & eorum Jure.
Paulus Manutius de Senatu Romano.
Joannes Sarius Zamoschius de Senatu Romano.

TOM. II.

Paulus Manutius de Legibus Romanis.
Antoninus Augustinus de Legibus, cum Notis Fulvii Ursini.
Carolus Sigonius de antiquo Jure Italiæ.
――――――――de antiquo Jure Provinciarum.
――――――――de Judiciis.
Sibrandus Tetardus Siccamo de Judicio centumvirali.
Franciscus Hottomanus J. C. de Magistratibus Romanorum, eorumque Institutione.
――――――――de Senatu & Senatus-Consulto.
――――――――de Formulis antiquis.
Nicolai Rigalti, Ismaelis Bullialdi, & Henrici Galesii, Observationes de Populis Fundis.
Carolus Sigonius de Nominibus Romanorum.
Onuphrius Panvinius de antiquis Romanorum Nominibus.
Josephi Castalionis J. C. adversus Fœminarum Prænominum assertores disputatio.
――――――――De antiquis puerorum Prænominibus.

Thesaur. *Græv.* Catalog.
TOM. III.
Franciscus Robortellus de Provinciis Romanorum, & earum distributione atque administratione.
――――――――De Judiciis, & omni consuetudine causas agendi apud Romanos.
Junius Rabirius de Hastarum & Auctionum origine.
Franciscus Robortellus de Magistratibus Imperatorum.
――――De Gradibus Honorum & Magistratuum Romanorum.
Guido Pancirellus de Magistratibus Manicipalibus.
――――――――De Corporibus Artificum.
Sextus Rufus de Regionibus Urbis.
P. Victor de Regionibus Romæ.
Bartholomæi Marliani Urbis Romæ topographia, cum Notis ineditis Fulvii Ursini.
Onuphrii Panvinii antiquæ urbis imago.
G. Pancirolli Urbis Romæ Descriptio, Ejusdem de quatuor Urbis Regionibus Commentarius.
Alexandri Donati Roma vetus ac recens, utriusque ædificiis ad eruditam cognitionem expositis.

TOM. IV.
Famiani Nardini Roma Vetus lib. VIII. ex Italica in Latinam Linguam translati a Jacobo Tollio.
Octavii Falconeris, de Pyramide C. Cestii Epulonis, Dissertatio.
――――――――Ad Carolum Dacum V. Cl. Epistola de latere ex ædificii Veteris ruderibus eruto, quum paries ad instaurandum Panthei Porticum. A. 1661, dirueretur.
Isaaci Vossii de antiqua Urbis Romæ Magnitudine.
Olai Borrichii, de antiqua Urbis Romæ facie, Dissert. compend.
Sexti Julii Frontini, de Aquæductibus Urbis Romæ, Comment.
Raphaelis Fabretti, de Aquis & Aquæductibus Urbis Romæ, Dissertationes tres.
Johannis Chifletei Aqua Virgo, fons Romæ celeberrimus, & prisca Religione sacer; opus M. Agrippæ, in vetere annulari gemma.
Lucæ Holstenii Commentariolus in veterem picturam Nymphæum referentem.
Petri Ciaconii in Columnæ Rostratæ Inscriptionem, a se conjectura suppletam, Explicatio.
Antiquæ Inscriptionis qua L. Scipionis, F. Barbati, expressum est elogium, Explanatio, Auctore Jacobo Sirmondo.
Josephus Castalio de Templo Pacis; atque ex occasione, de Jani Gemini Templo, bellique Portis.

Josephus Castalio Ejusdem Explicatio ad inscriptionem Augusti, quæ in basi est Obelisci statuti per Sixtum V. Pont. ante Portam Flaminiam, alias Populi.

Petri Angeli Bargæi de privatorum publicorumque ædificiorum Urbis Romæ eversoribus Epistola
——————Commentarius de Obelisco.

Jos. Castalionis, de Columna Triumph Imp. Antonini Com.

Fragmenta Vestigii Veteris Romæ, ex Lapidibus Farnesianis nunc primum in lucem edita, cum Notis Jo. Bellonii.

Huic Tomo præmittitur Livini Cruylii Descriptio faciei variorum locorum Urbis Romæ, tam antiquæ quam novæ, in XV. Tabulis æri incisa.

TOM. V.

Jacobi Gutherii, de veteri jure Pont. Urbis Romæ, libri quat.

Jo. Andreæ Bosii, de Pontifice Maximo Romæ Veteris, Exercitatio Historica.

——————Ejusdem, de Pontificatu Maximo Imperatorum Romanorum Exercitatio Historica altera.

Mic. Angelus Causæus (de la Chausse) de insig. Pontificis Max. Flaminis Dialis, Auguris, & instrumento Sacrificantium.

Augustini Niphi, de Auguriis, libri duo.

Jul. Cæsar Bulengerus de Sortibus.

——————De Auguriis & Auspiciis.

——————De Ominibus.

——————De Prodigiis.

——————De Terræ Motu, & Fulminibus.

Joh. Bapt. Belli Diatriba de partibus Templi Auguralis.

Johannes Pierius Valerianus de Fulminum significationibus.

Justi Lipsii, de Vesta & Vestalibus, Syntagma.

Ezechielis Spanhemii de Nummo Smyrnæorum, seu de Vesta & Prytanibus Græcorum, Diatriba.

Antiquæ Tabulæ Marmoreæ, solis effigie symbolisque exsculptæ, explicatio, Auctore Hier. Alexandro Juniore. Accessit non absimilis argumenti expositio sigillorum Zonæ veterem statuam marmoream cingentis.

Michaelis Angeli Causæi Deorum Simulachra, Idola, aliæque Imagines æreæ.

Jo. Baptista Hansenii, de Jure-jurando Veterum, Liber.

Stephanus Trelierius de Jure-jurando.

Erycii Puteani de Jure-jurando Antiquorum Schediasma, in quo de Puteali Libonis.

Marci Zuerii Buxhornii, & aliorum, Quæstiones Romanæ.

TOM.

TOM. VI.

Franciscus Bernardus Ferrarius de Veterum Acclam. & Plausu.
Petrus Berthaldus de Ara.
Benedictus Bacchinus de Sistris, eorumque figuris, ac differentia.
Casparus Sagittarius de Januis Veterum.
Lazarus Bayfius de Re Vestiaria.
Octavius Ferrarius de Re Vestiaria.
Albertus Rubenius de Re Vestiaria Veterum, præcipue de Lato Clavo.
Octavii Ferrarii Analecta de Re Vestiaria.
Jo. Bapt. Donius de utraque Pænula.
Bartholus Bartholinus de Pænula.
Aldus Manutius de Toga Romanorum.
——————————de Tunica Romanorum.
——————————de Tibiis Veterum.
Theophilus Raynaudus de Pileo, cæterisque Capitis tegminibus, tam sacris quam profanis.

TOM. VII.

Richardus Streinnius de Gentibus & Familiis Romanorum.
Antonius Augustinus de Familiis Romanorum.
Familiæ Romanæ nobiliores, e Fulvii Ursini Commentariis.
Notitia Dignitatum utriusque Imperii, ultra Arcadii Honoriique tempora; & in eam G. Pancirolli J. U. D. celeberrimi, Commentarius.
Marmor Pesanum, de Honore Bissellii. Parergon inseritur de Veterum Sellis; cura Val. Chementelli J. C. Accedit Myodia, sive, de Muscis odoris Pisanis, Epistola.

TOM. VIII.

Vetus Kalendarium Romanorum, e marmore descriptum, in Ædibus Maffæorum ad Agrippinam.
Petri Ciaconii Toletani Notæ in vetus Roman. Kalendarium.
Fulvii Ursini Notæ ad Kalendarium rusticum Farnesiarum.
Kalendarii fragmentum, quod visitur in Ædibus Capranicorum.
Sibrandi Siccamæ Comment. in Fastos Kalendares Romanorum.
Aliud vetus Kalendarium, quod in libris antiquis præfigitur Fastis Ovidii.
Kalendarium Romanum sub Imp. Constantio Imp. Constantini magni Filio, circa Ann. Christi 354. compositum.
Lambecii Notæ in Kalendarium vetus.
Thomæ Dempsteri Kalendarium Romanum.
Dionysii Petavii Kalendarium vetus Romanum, cum Ortu Occasuque Stellarum.
Petri Gassendi Kalendarium Romanum compendiose expositum.

Petri Violæ Vicetini de veteri novaque Romanorum temporum ratione libellus.
Adrianus Junius de Annis & Menfibus.
────────ejufdem Faftorum liber.
Joannes Lalamantius de Anno Romano.
M. Jacobus Chriftimanus de Kalendario Romano.
Francifcus Robortellus Utinenfis de Menfium appellatione ex nominibus Impp.
Jofephus Scaliger de veteri Anno Romanorum.
Dionyfius Petavius de veteri Anno Romanorum.
Samuelis Petiti Eclogæ Chronologicæ de Anno & Periode veterum Romanorum.
Wilhelmus Langius de Veteri Anno Romanorum.
Erycii Puteani de Biffexto liber.
Petrus Taffinus de veterum Rom. Anno Sæculari, ejufque potiffimum per ludos Sæculares celebritate, eorumque Chronol.
Erycii Puteani de Nundinis Romanis liber.
E. Georgii Tholofani de Syntagmate Juris, Nundinis & Mercatibus.
Joannis Baptiftæ Belli Diatriba de Pharfalici Conflictus Menfe & Die.
Petri Morcftelli Philomufus, five de triplici Anno Romanorum, Menfibus eorumque partibus, deque Die civili, & diverfitate Dierum libri quinque.
────────Alypius, five de Prifcorum Rom. Feriis liber.
Julius Cæfar Bulengerus de Tributis ac Vectig. Populi Romani.
Vincentii Contareni, de Frument. Roman. Largitione, liber.
Joannis Shefferi Agrippa liberator, five Differt. de novis Tabulis.
Barnabas Briffonius de Ritu Nuptiarum, & Jure Connubiorum.
Antonii Hotmanni, J. C. de veteri Ritu Nupt. obfervatio.
──── ────, de Sponfalibus, de veteri Ritu Nuptiarum, & Jure Matrimoniorum, item de Spuriis & Legitimatione.
Joannes Meurfius de Luxu Romanorum.
Stanillai Kobyerzykii, de Luxu Romanorum, Commentarius.
Joachimi Joannis Muderi de Coronis, Nuptiarum præfertim, facris & profanis, libellus.

TOM. IX.

Onuphrius Panvinius Veronenfis de Ludis Circen. cum Notis.
Joannis Argoli J. U. D. & additamenta Nicolai Pinell J. C.
Julius Cæfar Bulengerus Juliodunenfis, Doctor Theologus, de Circo Romano, Ludifque Circenfibus, de Venatione Circi & Amphitheatir, ac de Theatro.
Onuphrius Panvinius Veronenfis, de Ludis Sæcularibus, liber.

Augefilai

Agesilai Marescotti de Personis & Larvis, earumque apud Veteres usu & origine, Syntagmation.
Marquardi Freheri Cecropistromachia, antiqua Duelli Gladiatorii Sculptura in Sardonyche exposita. Cum Notis Henrici Gunterii Thulemanii, J. U. Doct.
Justi Lipsii Saturnalium Sermonum libri duo, qui de Gladiator.
———ejusdem de Amphitheatro liber; in quo forma ipsa loci expresse & ratio spectandi: Ut &, de Amphith. quæ extra Romam sunt, libellus; in quo formæ eorum aliquot & typi.
Onuphrii Panvinii de Triumpho Commentarius, Notis & Figuris illustratus a Joachimo Joanne Mudero.

TOM. X.

Nicolai Bergierii, de publicis & militaribus Imperii Romani Juris, libri quinque, &c. ex Gallica in Latinam Linguam translati ab Henr. Chr. Henninio.
Henr. Chr. Henninii Notæ ad Bergierium.
Francisci Patricii Res Militaris Romana, ex Italica in Latinam Linguam versa a Ludolpho Neocoro.
Hygini Grammatici & Polybii Megalopolitani, de Castris Romanis, quæ extant, cum Notis & Animadversionibus Rathordi Hermanni Schelii.
Rat. Herm Schelii Dissertatio de Sacramentis.
——————————de Custodia Castrorum.
——————————de Stipendio Militari.
——————————de Stipendio Equestri.
——————————de Stipendio Ductorum.
——————————de Die Stipendii.
——————————de Frumento & Veste.
——————————de Tributo & Ærario.
——————————de Præda.
——————————de Victu Militum.
——————————de Itinere.
——————————de Agmine Polybiano.
——————————de Agmine Vespasiani.
——————————de Cohortibus Legionis antiquæ.
C. L. Salmasii, de re Militari Romanorum, liber. Opus Posthumum.
Jo. Henrici Boecleri Dissertatio de Legione Romana.
Franciscus Robortellus Utinensis. I. de Legionibus Romanorum ex Dione, lib. 4. II. de Commodis, Præmiis, & Donis Militaribus. III. de Pœnis militum, & Ignominiis.
Erycii Puteani, de Stipendio Militari apud Romanos, Syntagma; quo modus ejus, hactenus ignoratus, constituitur.

Vincentii

Vincentii Contareni, de Militari Roman. Stipendio, Comment.
Michael Angelus Caufæus, de Signis Militaribus.
Petri Rami, de Militia, Julii Cæfaris, liber.

TOM. XI.

Ezechielis Spanhemii Orbis Romanus, feu ad Conftitutionem Antonini Imperatoris, de qua Ulpianus leg. 17. Dig. de Statu Hominum, Exercitationes duæ.

Fafti Magiftratuum Romanorum ab Urbe condita ad tempora Divi Vefpafiani Augufti, a Stephano Vinando Pighio fuppletis Capitolinis Fragmentis reftituti.

Defcriptio Confulum, ex quo primi ordinati funt; five integri Fafti Confulares, quos Idatianos docti viri hactenus appellarunt, opera & ftudio Philippi Labbe.

Tironis Profperi, Aquitani, Chronicon integrum ab Adamo ad Romam captam a Genferico, Wand. Rege.

Fafti Confulares Anonymi, quos e codice MS. Bibliothecæ Cæfareæ deprompfit, & differt. illuftravit, F. Henricus Norris.

Anonymus de Præfectis Urbi ex temporibus Gallieni; ut & fragmentum Faftorum ab Anno Chrifti 205. ad 353. ex editione Ægidii Bucherii.

Epiftola Confularis in qua Collegia LXX. Confulum ab Anno Chriftianæ Ephochæ XXIX. Imperii Tiberii Augufti decimo quinto, ufque Annum CCXXIX. Imperii Alexandri Severi octavum, in vulgatis Faftis hactenus perperam defcripta, corriguntur, fupplentur, & illuftrantur, Auctore, F. Henrico Norris Veronenfi, Auguftiniano.

Sertorii Urfati, Equitis, de Notis Romanorum Commentarius.

Differtationes de Nummis Antiquis, divifæ in quatuor partes, Auctore Ludovico Savato. Ex Gallica in Latinum Linguam tranftulit L. Neocorus.

Alberti Rubenii Differt. de Gemma Tiberiana & Auguftæa.
——————————de Urbibus Neocoris Diatribe.

Marquardi Freheri, Confiliarii Palatini, de Re Monetaria veterum Romanorum, & hodierni apud Germanos Imperii.

Robertus Cenalis de vera Menfurarum Ponderumque Ratione.

Lucæ Peti Juris Confulti, de Menfuris & Ponderibus Romanis & Græcis, cum his quæ hodie Romæ funt, collatis, Libri quinque.

Prifciani Cæfarienfis, Rhemnii Fannii, Bedæ Angli, Volufii Metiani, Balbi ad Celfum, Libri de Nummis, Ponderibus, Menfuris, Numeris, eorumque Notis, & de vetere computandi per digitos Ratione, ab Elia Vincto Santone emendati, ut & a J. Frederico Gronovio.

Alexandri Serdi, Ferrariensis, de Nummis Liber, in quo prisca Græcorum & Romanorum Pecunia ad nostri æris rationem redigitur.

TOM. XII.

Vincentius Butius de calido, frigido, & temperato Antiquorum potu, & quo modo in Deliciis uterentur.

Julius Cæsar Bulengerus de Convivii; Libri quatuor.

Erycii Puteani reliq. Convivii prisci, tum Ritus alii, & Censuræ.

Andreæ Bacii, de Thermis veterum, Liber singularis.

Francisci Robortelli Laconici; seu Sudationis, quæ adhuc visitur in ruina Balnearum Pisanæ Urbis, explicatio.

Francisci Mariae Turrigii Notæ ad vetustissimam Ursi Togati, Ludi Pilæ vitreæ inventoris, inscriptionem.

Martini Lipenii Strenarium Historia, a prima Origine per diversas Regum, Consulum, & Imperatorum Romanorum, nec non Episcoporum ætates ad nostra usque tempora.

Marci Meibomii, de Fabrica Triremium, liber.

Constantini Opelii de Fabrica Triremium, Meibomiana Epistola per brevis ad amicum.

Isaaci Vossii de Trirem. & Liburnicarum construct. dissertatio.

Jacobi Philippi Thomasini, de Donariis ac Tabellis Votivis, liber singularis.

Vincentii Alsanii, de Invidia & Fascino Veterum, libellus.

Joannis Shefferi, de Antiquorum Torquibus, Syntagma.

Michaelis Angeli Causæi Dissertationes tres.

———I. De Vasis, Bullis, Armillis, Fibulis, Annullis, Clavibus, Tesseris, Stylis, Strigilibus, Guttis, Phialis Lacrymatoriis, & de Manibus æneis vota referentibus.

———II. De Mutini Simulacris.

———III. De Æneis Antiquorum Lucernis.

Octavii Ferrarii Dissertatio de Veterum Lucernis Sepulchralibus, Picturæ antiquæ Sepulchri Nasoniorum in Via Flaminia, delineatæ & æri incisæ, a Petro Sancto Bartolo; explicatæ vero & illustratæ a Joanne Petro Bellorio; ex Italica Lingua in Latinam vertit Ludolphus Neocorus.

Jacobi Gutherii de Jure Manium, seu de Ritu, More, & Legibus prisci Funeris, libri tres.

———Choartius major, vel de Orbitate toleranda ad Annum Robertum J. C. Præfatio.

Petri Morestelli Pompa Feralis, sive justa Funebria Veterum; Libri decem.

www.ingramcontent.com/pod-product-compliance
Lightning Source LLC
Chambersburg PA
CBHW022056300426
44117CB00007B/481